D1481858

Publications on the Near East
University of Washington
Number 6

Publications on the Near East
University of Washington

Poetry's Voice, Society's Song: Ottoman Lyric Poetry
Walter G. Andrews

The Remaking of Istanbul: Portrait of an Ottoman City in the Nineteenth Century
Zeynep Çelik

The Tragedy of Sohráb and Rostám from the Persian National Epic, the Shahname of Abol-Qasem Ferdowsi
Translated by Jerome W. Clinton

The Jews in Modern Egypt, 1914–1952
Gudrun Krämer

Izmir and the Levantine World, 1550–1650
Daniel Goffman

Medieval Agriculture and Islamic Science: The Almanac of a Yemeni Sultan
Daniel Martin Varisco

Medieval Agriculture and Islamic Science

The Almanac of a Yemeni Sultan

DANIEL MARTIN VARISCO

University of Washington Press

Seattle and London

Copyright © 1994 by the University of Washington Press
Printed in the United States of America

All rights reserved. No part of this publication may be reproduced or transmitted in any form or by any means, electronic or mechanical, including photocopy, recording, or any information storage or retrieval system, without permission in writing from the publisher.

Library of Congress Cataloging-in-Publication Data
Varisco, Daniel Martin.
Medieval agriculture and Islamic science : the almanac of a Yemeni sultan / Daniel Martin Varisco.
p. cm. — (Publications on the Near East, University of Washington ; no. 6)
Includes the Arabic text of Chapter 32 and English translation of al-Tabsira fi ʻilm al-nujūm by al-Malik al-Ashraf ʻUmar ibn Yūsuf.
Includes bibliographical references and indexes.
ISBN 0–295–97378–1 (alk. paper)
1. ʻUmar ibn Yūsuf, Sultan of Yemen, d. 1296. Tabṣira fi ʻilm al-nujūm. Chapter 32. 2. Agriculture—Yemen—Calendars. 3. Almanacs, Arab—Yemen. I. ʻUmar ibn Yūsuf, Sultan of Yemen, d. 1296. Tabṣira fi ʻilm al-nujūm. Chapter 32. English & Arabic. 1994 II. Title III. Series.
S414.U583V37 1994 94–13486
630'.9533'09022—dc20 CIP

The paper used in this publication meets the minimum requirements of American National Standard for Information Sciences—Permanence of Paper for Printed Library Materials, ANSI Z39.48–1984. ♾

Jacket and title page photograph: Mr. Ahmad Saʻd, village of al-Husn in the Yemeni highlands, September 1978. *Courtesy of Dr. Daniel Martin Varisco.*

FOR NAJWA,

who held my hand and held her breath until it was over

Contents

CONTENTS

Foreword

Of all Arab or Arabic-speaking countries, the Yemen has preserved the rich heritage of Arab and Islamic civilization least affected by the changes wrought by the external world in the nineteenth and twentieth centuries. It is consequently a most rewarding place for research, whether on its past or present. The present-day Republic of Yemen, or simply "Yemen," covers the areas that until recently went under the political titles of the Yemen Arab Republic and the People's Democratic Republic of Yemen. The latter comprises the mainly tribal districts of what was formerly known as the Western Aden Protectorate and Ḥaḍramawt, which is distinguished for its Islamic cultural tradition remounting to medieval times. The Yemen, with its high level of agriculture and well-organized medieval-type cities, preserves the most complex and sophisticated cultural tradition of the whole of southern Arabia. The political divisions are, of course, largely artificial and within the Yemen itself various areas have their own distinctive customs, as for instance the coastal strip of the Tihāma and the Zaydī highlands. Nevertheless, the veriest newcomer to Arabia cannot fail to see that all the areas of southern Arabia share in a culture linked with the broader tradition of the peninsula but at the same time contrasting with that of the Najd and the Gulf.

Southwest Arabia still preserves numerous vestiges of a civilization more ancient than that of medieval Islam. Some of the traditions of pre-Islamic Arabia still survive in everyday Yemeni life. The ancient customary law, locally called *ṭāghūt*, has effectively been rooted out by the Islamic *sharī'a* only in urban areas and still persists among the tribes. Strangely enough, the ritual chase connected with the pre-Islamic, indeed pre-Christian, gods Ilumqah and Ta'lab remains as a rainmaking rite that I saw flourishing in Ḥaḍramawt, though the gods themselves have long been forgotten.

The officer *coup d'état* of 1962 in the north propelled the Yemen beyond the slow adjustment that had commenced shortly before World War II to the twentieth century beyond its borders. In the aftermath many small towns and villages in the Zaydī north were destroyed, including medieval Mabyan, the learned center (*hijra*) of al-Kibs, much of the old mountain Zaydī capital of Shahāra, and various mosques, mansions, dams, and other structures. Regrettably, the inevitable destruction of buildings since the civil war and the bulldozing of archeological sites for building development, notably the

Rasulid sites outside Taʿizz, have destroyed much that should have been explored and recorded. Mocha's ruined buildings, perhaps three or four centuries old, have disappeared since my first visit there in 1969 because of quarrying in them for burned bricks. Nevertheless, when all is said and done, one cannot but appreciate the modern amenities of decent roads, piped water, and other services now to be found in the country.

The traditional learning and intellectual culture of the Yemen have also suffered unfortunate losses. Not all elements within the republic have been enamored with the historical tradition of scholarly learning. In the great center of medieval Islamic teaching that is Zabīd, for example, we found only one or two students (*muhājirūn*) in 1971. The widespread extension of general education has meant reliance on expatriate (primarily Egyptian and Sudanese) teachers. This is a break with tradition by the introduction of an un-Yemeni educational system of not very high quality, at least outside the main centers. On the other hand, the university education seems to have improved notably over the last decade, though still largely divorced from continuity with tradition. Of course, this has been the case in many another Islamic country. A keen interest by faculty and graduates at Ṣanʿāʾ University is taken in local studies, Yemen's history, and fieldwork within the country. Of course, the scholars and writers who received their education before the 1962 coup and who have often resided or studied in another Arab country have been very active. They have published much on the Yemen of permanent value, and will no doubt publish much more.

The Yemenis indeed are highly conscious of their "glorious past" and heritage. This most often takes the form of interest in history and literature rather than concern for the preservation of buildings and sites, although at present there is a project to preserve the architectural beauty of the old city of Ṣanʿāʾ. So outstanding is this city that UNESCO has designated it as one of three cities in the Arabic-speaking world to conserve, at least as far as is possible. Nor do Yemenis, a people endowed with lively intelligence, feel any sense of inferiority about their colloquial language, which after all is the Arabic of Arabia. As a result they do not feel that it should be replaced by standard classical Arabic, fine vehicle of expression though that is, but they accept both versions of the language as valid. Poets, for example, readily compose and publish verse in Yemeni dialect in the various media.

Learning appears always to have been valued in the Yemen. Under the rule of the Zaydī imams, officials were selected from those trained in the discipline of Islamic *ʿilm*, or scholarship, and the Shāfiʿī Rasulid sultans, whose capital was at Taʿizz in the "Lower Yemen," were individuals of no mean literary ability and learning. To take a case in point, a manuscript survives of mixed contents from the reign of al-Malik al-Afḍal al-ʿAbbās ibn ʿAlī that contains treatises on history, fiscal matters of the court, agriculture, astronomy, medicine, genealogy, and other subjects. This significant manuscript, certainly from the library of the sultan, is being prepared by Daniel Varisco and myself for publication in facsimile. Another important Yemeni text, the *Bughyat al-fallāḥīn* of al-Malik al-Afḍal, provides an excellent detailed survey of medieval Yemeni agriculture, as well as drawing on the Iraqi Ibn Waḥshīya and various authors from the Hellenistic world. This text also contains extensive quotes from Ibn Baṣṣāl of North Africa and Abū al-Khayr of Seville, copies of whose works must have reached the Yemen in the Rasulid era. This is a further indication of the intercommunication of scholars and texts in all parts of the Islamic world during the medieval period. It has been a pleasure to put my not-yet-complete edition of the *Bughyat al-fallāḥīn*, including my 1953 transcription of a copy found in Tarīm of Wādī Ḥaḍramawt, at Daniel Varisco's disposal.

The Rasulid almanacs first attracted my attention in connection with my work on the *Bughyat al-fallāḥīn* and the *Mulakhkhaṣ al-fitan*. I intend to publish the almanac in connection with the latter work. However, Daniel Varisco has made a thorough and detailed study of the Yemeni agricultural almanac tradition, drawing on a great wealth of additional information from a broad range of sources, including technical information on astronomy and meteorology going far beyond my own limited objectives. He has also utilized the research of Western scholars, to which he has made valuable contributions of his own.

Anthropologists Varisco and his wife, Najwa Adra, spent a year and a half in the pleasant valley of al-Ahjur, northwest of Ṣan'ā' in the former Yemen Arab Republic. This valley is part of the headwaters of Wādī Surdud, which has been the subject of a feasibility study for future agricultural development. While living among the tribesmen in the valley, he studied the agricultural practices and irrigation of the area throughout the seasons. Thus, he has gained the experience that has enabled him to act as an advisor and consultant on numerous agricultural development projects in the country and elsewhere. This combination of fieldwork, involving the use of colloquial Arabic and close acquaintance with the countryfolk, and study of relevant Arabic literature makes possible the extremely satisfying results in this present volume. Varisco's edition of al-Malik al-Ashraf's almanac from *al-Tabṣira fī 'ilm al-nujūm* is a comprehensive survey of medieval agriculture and Islamic science as practiced in medieval Yemen and a solid contribution to the history of agriculture in the Arabian Peninsula.

Robert Bertram Serjeant (1915–93)
Emeritus Professor of Arabic
Cambridge University

Acknowledgments

This translation was funded by a grant from the National Endowment for the Humanities (Washington, D.C.) in conjunction with a translation project shared with Herr Professor Dr. David A. King (Director, Institut für Geschichte der Naturwissenschaften, Universität Frankfurt). I wish to thank David King for first drawing my attention to this important almanac and his valuable suggestions and encouragement at all stages of the project. I am also indebted to Robert Bertram Serjeant, who was the first scholar to recognize the importance of the Rasulid agricultural corpus. I am grateful to Professor Serjeant for allowing me to look at the notes he had prepared for his edition of the *Bughyat al-fallāḥīn*. His death in April 1993 is a sad loss for all who work in Yemeni studies. Christian Robin graciously provided me with information on the South Arabic terms for the so-called Himyaritic month names noted in al-Ashraf's text.

In Yemen I received the assistance of many individuals and institutions. I wish to thank the Yemen Center for Research and Studies under the directorship of Dr. ʻAbd al-ʻAzīz al-Maqāliḥ, who has also been the rector of Ṣanʻāʼ University. Among the many scholars who assisted me in understanding the Rasulid texts and Yemeni dialects are Qāḍī Ismāʻīl ʻAlī al-Akwaʻ, former director of the Office for Antiquities and Libraries; Qāḍī ʻAlī Muḥammad al-Sharafī, of the Prime Minister's office and a scholarly practitioner of traditional astronomy and medicine; Qāḍī Muḥammad ʻAbd al-Raḥmān al-Ṭayr and Sayyid Aḥmad ʻAlī Zabāra of the Gharbīya library in the Great Mosque in Ṣanʻāʼ; the historian and bibliophile ʻAbd Allāh al-Ḥibshī; Muḥammad ʻAbd al-Raḥīm Jāzm, a contemporary historian and folklorist; Professor Muḥammad ʻAbd al-Malik al-Mutawwakil of Ṣanʻāʼ University; Muṣṭafā Sālim of Ṣanʻāʼ University; and Muḥammad al-Sharafī, the poet. I also acknowledge the assistance and companionship of friends and colleagues at the American Institute for Yemeni Studies in Ṣanʻāʼ.

During the course of this study I had the privilege of examining several important manuscripts in the Gharbīya library of the Great Mosque in Ṣanʻāʼ, as well as several Rasulid texts in private collections. Research was also conducted on manuscripts at the Egyptian National Library in Cairo, the Topkapi Saray and Suleymaniyeh libraries in Istanbul, and the National Library of Qatar. I am indebted to David King for providing me with access to copies of a number of important Yemeni manuscripts from various libraries around the world. I also consulted the excellent resources of the Oriental Collection in the New York Public Library. In Doha, Qatar, I was fortunate to have access to the superb private library of His Excellency Shaykh Ḥasan ibn Muḥammad ibn ʻAlī Āl Thānī, as well as the resources of the Arab Gulf States Folklore Centre, headed by ʻAbd al-Raḥmān al-Mannāʻī.

In addition to written sources, I have benefited from conversations with colleagues who have worked in Yemen. Preeminent among these is my wife, Dr. Najwa Adra, whose knowledge of Yemen, encouragement, and patience have contributed in no small way to the publication of this volume. I would be remiss in not thanking Pamela J. Bruton of the University of Washington Press for her careful and invaluable copyediting of this volume.

Finally, I wish to thank the people who first introduced me to the rich tradition of Yemeni agriculture. These are the men and women of the valley of al-Ahjur in the former Yemen Arab Republic. The people of this valley hosted Najwa and myself for eighteen months in 1978–79. I am especially grateful to ʻAbd Allāh ʻAbd al-Qādir and his family for their help and support. During this time I gradually learned how agriculture works in rural Yemen today. This experience was invaluable for my later analysis of medieval Yemeni agricultural texts. In a very real sense this volume could not have been written without the benefit of living among the farmers who continue the long-standing tradition so deftly described in the text translated here. This book is one way of saying thanks.

Conventions

TRANSLITERATION

The romanization of Arabic terms into English follows the system of the *International Journal of Middle East Studies*, except in cases of direct quotations or existing transliteration in published book titles. Words commonly cited in English (e.g., Aden, Dhofar, dinar, imam, Mecca, sheikh, wadi) are generally not transliterated.

TRANSLATION

All translation is that of the editor unless otherwise indicated. In rendering the almanac text every attempt has been made to maintain the original sense of the Arabic. In some cases, however, more suitable English idioms require a less literal translation. For example, in most cases in the almanac a crop or plant is referred to in the collective. Some translation options are straightforward, such as noting that cotton ripens. But, should one say that the peach ripens or peaches ripen? I have opted for the plural where the collective or singular does not play as well to my ear in English. There are also times when it is useful to add words not in the original text, since these can better explain the meaning. This has been kept to a minimum and is indicated by placing the added words in brackets. Similarly, in the translation I have provided the original Arabic in several cases where the translated equivalent may be vague or in need of further explanation. It is strongly recommended that Arabists consult the Arabic text as well rather than relying exclusively on the translation, which is of necessity tentative in a few places. A dash (–) indicates that nothing is recorded in the almanac for that date.

DATES

The details of each calendrical system mentioned in the almanac are discussed below in chapter 1. Most dates are given in the standard format of A.H./A.D., with the first date referring to the Islamic lunar calendar and the second to the Julian Christian reckoning. Since al-Malik al-Ashraf's almanac was compiled before the Gregorian reform of the Christian calendar, all Christian dates relating to the almanac are expressed as Julian. References to the Julian calendar are indicated by the standard numerical designation used today, where I is equivalent to January (i.e., *Kānūn al-Thānī*), etc. Thus, III:27 would be the twenty-seventh day of March (*Ādhār*).

REFERENCES

The Bibliography is separated into unpublished manuscript sources and published references. The referencing of published sources is according to the standard social science method of author and date. This creates a problem with some Arabic names, which do not conveniently sort out into a given name and a family name. I have tried to adopt the most commonly used form of a scholar's name, often his *nisba*, or else reference according to his proper name followed by that of his father. Some of the references in the Bibliography may not conform to previously published listings, which reflects the continuing lack of systematization for bibliographic references of Arabic sources overall. Sources for quotations from the major almanacs consulted are usually according to the relevant month and day rather than the page number of the manuscript or publication. References to manuscripts are according to an arbitrary abbreviation of the title or author's name, as indicated in the Bibliography. In addition, frequently cited lexicons are usually indicated by the title, for example, *Lisān al-'Arab* for Ibn Manẓūr, *al-Muḥīṭ* for al-Fīrūzābādī, *Shams al-'ulūm* for Nashwān ibn Sa'īd al-Ḥimyarī, and *Tāj al-'arūs* for al-Zabīdī.

Medieval Agriculture and Islamic Science
The Almanac of a Yemeni Sultan

Introduction

The image of Arabia is often that of a desert waste sparsely occupied by tribal nomads or oil-rich sheikhs. In fact an important agricultural tradition flourished in the southwestern corner of the Arabian Peninsula. During the Islamic period this fabled land of Arabia Felix came to be known as the Verdant Yemen (*al-Yaman al-khaḍrā'*) and not without reason. A Yemeni savant of the tenth century A.D., Abū Muḥammad al-Ḥasan al-Hamdānī (1983:317), characterized the rain-fed agricultural system as one of the marvels of the Arabian Peninsula. An adequate supply of rainfall in much of the country, supplemented by highland springs and hand-dug wells, fostered cultivation on even the most inaccessible and rugged mountain slopes. Over many centuries, the seemingly endless energy of resourceful Yemeni farmers transformed these slopes into terraced plots. In the coastal region, where rainfall was minimal, the regular seasonal floods each spring and late summer descended along the major wadis and permitted extensive cultivation of grains, fruits, and vegetables. Although in the past most of the production provided only for subsistence needs, virtually every food crop known in the Arab world was grown to some extent in medieval Yemen.

It is arguable that the zenith of agricultural diversity in Islamic Yemen occurred during the Rasulid dynasty during the thirteenth, fourteenth, and fifteenth centuries A.D.[1] The richest corpus of agricultural texts for any medieval Arab society stems from this dynasty (Varisco 1989c). The Rasulid sultans were enthusiastic patrons of the sciences, especially agriculture. Several agricultural treatises from this period combine observations of farming practices in various parts of Yemen with the scientific heritage of previous scholarship. At least eight Rasulid almanacs provide an overview of the agricultural cycle with valuable information on local terminology. The earliest extant Rasulid almanac was compiled by the third sultan, al-Malik al-Ashraf 'Umar ibn Yūsuf, around the year 670/1271. The single known copy, which almost certainly dates close to the time of the author, is also the most detailed and error-free of the surviving almanacs from Yemen. The text of this unique almanac, an English translation, and a commentary on the scientific information and folklore contained in the almanac are presented in this volume.

The Verdant Yemen is also *terra incognita*, a land long isolated from the

West and to a great extent from other Arab countries.[2] This isolation resulted in no small part from the geography of the country, which is quite diverse. A narrow coastal strip, called the Tihāma, extends inland about fifty kilometers from the Red Sea. The climate here is very hot and humid, although rainfall is quite limited. Until the arrival of hydraulic pumps at midcentury, most agricultural production in the Tihāma was based on irrigation from seasonal floods, with only marginal rain-fed crops. The most important town in this region during the medieval period was Zabīd, a center of Islamic education famous even beyond the borders of Yemen.

The flat coastal region grades quickly into a series of tropical foothills rising in elevation to the major north-south mountain chain, known as the Sarāt.[3] The highest peak on the Arabian Peninsula, Jabal al-Nabī Shu'ayb, is located here. Access through these rugged mountains, which reach well over 3,000 meters in elevation, is limited to a few major roads along wadi courses. Rainfall is generally sufficient for cultivation, especially since slope runoff is often directed to rain-fed plots. This rain is dropped by the rising eastward-bearing clouds, with more rainfall to the south than to the north. In addition to rain-fed terraced plots, local flood flow is exploited where appropriate and irrigation systems are also found around major springs. East of the Sarāt chain is a series of broad, level basins crosscut by several small ranges of hills. Life in the northern highland plateau centers on Ṣan'ā', which was usually the seat of the Zaydī imamate. In the southern highland region the town of Ta'izz dominated in the Rasulid era. Below Ta'izz on the southern coast lies the important port of Aden, from which there has historically been a brisk trade east and west. The eastern plateau of Yemen has long been sparsely populated and defied major exploitation during the Islamic period. However, there were several important city-states here during the pre-Islamic era, when the massive agricultural system associated with the renowned Ma'rib dam was created. Ranging eastward into the pure emptiness of the desert only a few pastoral nomads were to be found. Indeed, this was the part of Yemen closest in lifestyle and economy to the pastoral nomadism for which the peninsula is justly famed but did not exclusively sustain.

Yemen received the message of Islam during the lifetime of Muḥammad and legend states that his son-in-law 'Alī ibn Abī Ṭālib visited Yemen (al-Ahdal 1986:41–44). However, Islam did not really take hold in the country as a whole until the Zaydī imamate was established in the north at the end of the ninth century A.D. (Smith 1990). This imamate survived the vicissitudes of history, although it was by no means the only theocratic power in Yemen, until the Republican revolution in 1962, creating the modern Yemen Arab Republic. After 1839 the British controlled the southern port of Aden, an important coal-fueling station for their fleet, until the establishment of the

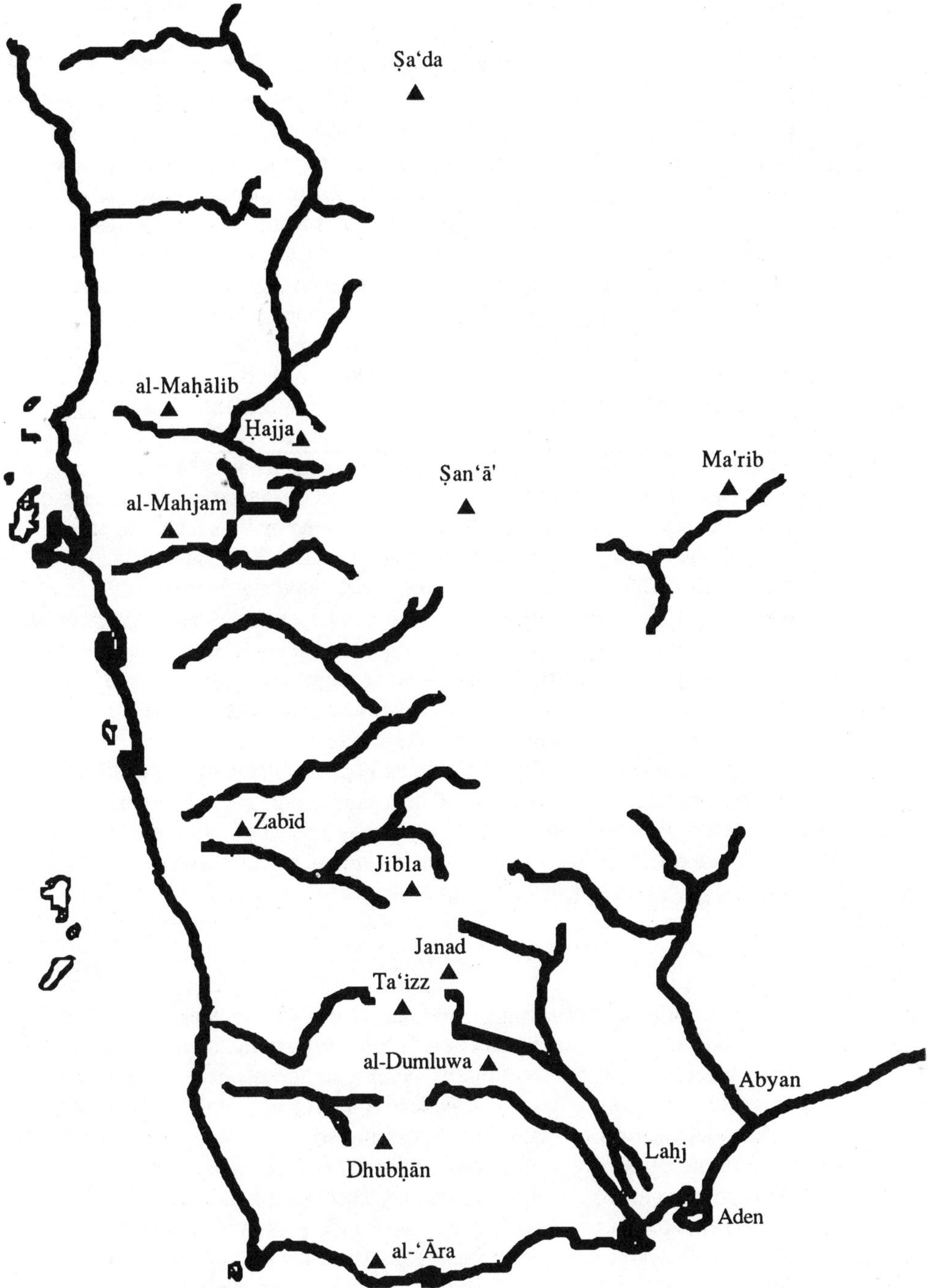

MAP 1. Medieval Yemen

People's Democratic Republic of Yemen in 1967. No Western power, however, ever dominated the highlands; even the Ottoman Turks held sway in Yemen by an uneasy balance of power with the Zaydī imams of Ṣan'ā'. In May 1990, the two Yemens finally united to become the present Republic of Yemen.

The people of Yemen are primarily farmers; only in parts of the coastal region and the eastern plateau do pastoralists range. The population has always been overwhelmingly rural, with no large cities to rival medieval Baghdad, Cairo, or Damascus. The history of the northern part of Yemen has been dominated by the major tribal confederations of Bakīl and Ḥāshid.[4] No dynasty in the country ever managed to overcome tribal influence; even the modern nation-state has a distinctively tribal character. In the southern highlands, however, tribal organization was weaker, and more of a peasant-landlord relationship evolved. Traditionally, three major social groupings were recognized in Yemen. In much of the country, the highest status was credited to the *Sāda*, descendants of the Prophet Muḥammad, who formed the government of the Zaydī imamate. The bulk of the population consisted of free men, most of whom claimed local tribal descent, in clearly demarcated tribal boundaries. The tribes in Yemen are descended from Qaḥṭān (the biblical Joktan), legendary ancestor of the so-called Southern Arabs. The lowest status was ascribed to several service groups, including many people engaged in commerce. The Jews, a significant community in medieval Yemen, were generally protected and well treated, but they were regarded as having a low status.[5] In the last two decades, social consciousness has developed dramatically in Yemen, with an emergent nationalism helping to diminish past social inequalities.

THE ALMANAC TRADITION

Historians, unlike ethnographers, are unable to immerse themselves in the daily context of history or history being made. While texts do often provide a fairly detailed description of places, people, and events, whether accurate or not, the information is always fragmented and frozen in time. The danger is that, lacking means of independent confirmation, a text may be viewed as an accurate accounting of the reality being described. This problem also arises in the study of the almanac as a text, since it purports to be a practical guide rather than a philosophical dialogue or fancy of the imagination. To what extent can the almanac be trusted as a scientific document, as a source which records the scientific tradition of the day and at the same time accurately refers to events and activities? A major concern of the present study is to go beyond the edition and translation of the text to a fuller understanding of the context being described.

An almanac, simply put, is a documentation of the seasonal reckoning of changes in nature and human activities. Many almanacs focus on agriculture, although a range of observations on people and nature will generally be found. Thus, as a text the almanac contains references to a broad range of information gleaned from the experience of the compiler and from previous texts and the existing scientific tradition. Such an almanac contains a great deal of practical information derived from the application of the compiler's scientific background and training to defining a relevant calendar of events and activities. It is, in fact, as much a portrait of how the world and cosmos are perceived as a straightforward calendar to mark events. This makes it a difficult text to understand fully, because it was never meant to be a text which stands on its own. At the same time the almanac can provide valuable insight into the often ignored process of applying science to real life.

The almanac as a literary and scientific genre in Arab tradition has virtually been ignored by Arab and Western scholars.[6] Hundreds of manuscripts exist, perhaps well over a thousand, but few have been published and there is still no bibliography of the genre. The limited attention paid to the almanac by Western scholars has been devoted to its liturgical function, because most Arab almanacs are arranged according to the solar Christian calendar and contain numerous references to Christian feasts and saints. For example, one of the most famous almanacs is the *Calendar of Cordova* compiled in Islamic Spain during the tenth century A.D. Interest in this calendar was stimulated in the West because it was available in Latin translation at a very early date. Although it is primarily focused on Spain, this almanac draws on a range of earlier folklore from the Arabian Peninsula. Similarly, the published examples of Egyptian almanacs according to the Coptic months contain a large amount of information on Coptic holidays. One of the earliest known almanacs in Arabic, a compilation by the Iraqi physician Ibn Māsawayh in the ninth century A.D, contains elaborate details on Christian feasts and saints. This is one of the few non-Egyptian almanacs to have been both edited and translated from Arabic.

A major problem in establishing the genre of the Arab almanac is that no single term or format characterizes it in Arabic.[7] The term most often used in the sources is *taqwīm*, which literally refers to a table or chart in tabular form. The almanac information on agriculture and related seasonal information is usually called *tawqī'āt* (literally, "events") in the Rasulid almanacs. The Arab almanac as a seasonal reckoning system, primarily according to the months of the solar or lunar year, did not exist as an entirely separate genre. Extant almanacs can be found as distinct texts, especially more recent examples, but they also occur in treatises on astronomy, astrology, agriculture, medicine, language, and general encyclopaedic works. Most almanacs within other texts are not referenced separately in literary collections, due to the lack of previous study, but even the distinct texts are rarely catalogued properly. Some almanacs are presented in narrative form, and others provide quite detailed astronomical and astrological information in a chart format. This present volume represents a first step in the study of the almanac as a scientific genre in Arab tradition.

The almanac as a text presents a number of problems for study, especially in the isolated context of a library. Given the lack of previous research, the criteria for judging the importance and accuracy of almanac information have not been determined. Often the language is cursory and written down quickly with a likely potential for error. The information itself is usually cryptic, at times not clearly understood by the compiler or copyist. In some almanacs local dialect terms and place names are difficult to identify from available texts and lexicons. Later copies of early almanacs frequently contain errors that are not readily apparent without an extensive study of the genre. The few published texts of Arab almanacs are to a great extent in need of revision. Finally, but certainly not least, the study of almanac information necessarily draws one across the arbitrary boundaries of disciplines into the full array of medieval science and esoterica. One must gain a sense of the knowledge available to the compiler in order to understand what the almanac lore means and why it is important enough to be recorded.

As a written document the almanac throughout the Islamic period was aimed at a scholarly audience. Unlike the modern almanac tradition in the West and much of the contemporary Arab world, almanac information was meant for other scholars rather than as a practical guide to put in the hands of a farmer or the average person. A casual glance at almost any almanac indicates that much of the information is of such a general nature as to be of little value to someone who has to make a living. No Yemeni farmer, for example, would have needed the Rasulid almanacs, because his own local knowledge was far more useful and detailed. Fortunately, however, some almanacs record enough details to allow one to form a general picture of agricultural practices and related activities. The essential point is that the almanac was not intended as a faithful documentation of the oral tradition and it should not be treated as such.[8] This is not to deny the importance of the almanac as a source but to caution against reading too much into the fragmentary information available.

There is practically no information known today as to how and why almanacs were compiled in Arabic during the medieval period. A core body of almanac lore is found in texts across the Islamic world, much of it relating back to the classical scientific tradition and events in Hellenistic Egypt.

While some compilers were in fact astronomers or competent scientists, others blindly copied from earlier texts. This is especially apparent for astronomical calculations, which of necessity vary over time according to the Julian reckoning used in the medieval period. This complicates the translation of almanacs, because the reconstruction of the text, to the extent this is possible, must go hand in hand with critical analysis of the data.

Study of an almanac is enhanced if the research is part of a more comprehensive approach to the tradition. It is obviously important to examine a number of almanac texts rather than to rely on any particular text as definitive. It would be wrong to assume that there was one basic almanac text, despite the seeming similarity of much of the information, and that eventually this text will come to light, if it is not assumed to be already known. No single almanac speaks for the tradition, because different compilers invariably add and subtract information. An event omitted or barely mentioned in one text may be elaborated in another. In some cases a compiler may cite the source for the information, although this is dropped from another text. To fully understand the almanacs, which document a wide range of scientific ideas, it is usually necessary to go beyond the almanac text and find other scholarly references from the relevant time period and place. This makes study of an almanac a rather burdensome task and is no doubt one reason why so little research has been done on almanac lore.

The almanac as a text is closely related to oral folklore, especially that regarding agriculture, astronomy, and the seasons in a region. While it is not meant to be an ethnographic record of the agricultural cycle, for example, it is obvious that some of the information is based on observation of actual practices and knowledge of the folklore. One of the rewarding aspects of studying the Yemeni almanacs is that many of the agricultural activities mentioned can still be observed and documented. It is virtually impossible to understand some of the almanac terminology without fieldwork in Yemen on dialects. Certain terms, such as local plant names, are not found in any published source or may not denote what is mentioned in a medieval lexicon. Study of the continuing tradition also allows one to fill in some of the gaps as to why information is important enough to be recorded. For example, a number of almanacs mention the arrival of the hoopoe bird (*hudhud*) in Yemen in the spring. Today in Yemen some farmers associate the arrival of this bird with the onset of the spring rains and use this as a marker for the start of ploughing. Ethnographic study of traditional agriculture and folk science, despite the changes over time, can help to flesh out the bones of old, written almanacs. Even if there is no direct historical continuity for a tradition, the context allows for a better understanding of how a custom or idea can function in the society.

INTRODUCTION

THE ALMANAC TRADITION IN YEMEN

The earliest agricultural almanacs in Arabic are not from Yemen. Overall, there are more almanacs surviving from Egypt than from any other part of the Arab world, although the earliest surviving Arab almanacs are not in fact from Egypt.[9] However, the agricultural regime of the Nile, documented in considerable detail in the Coptic almanacs, has changed dramatically in this century due to the construction of the Aswan dam and introduction of modern methods and technology. It is no longer possible to take an almanac in hand and go out to the field to see if the things described for medieval Egypt are still happening the same way. Fortunately, it is still possible to check some of the traditional practices described for Yemen, despite the recent economic change in the country. The study of a medieval almanac as part of a living tradition can be accomplished in Yemen better than perhaps anywhere else in the Arab world. The older generation still retains much of the accumulated agricultural and environmental lore from scores of previous generations. No doubt hundreds of almanacs and small treatises exist on the subject of agriculture in Islamic Yemen, yet only a handful of these have thus far come under study.

Before the Rasulid period there are no known almanacs describing the agricultural context in Yemen, although there is no reason to doubt that they were compiled. There are several poems, mostly *arājīz*, written for the solar months. The earliest is attributed to al-Baḥr al-Naʿāmī, who flourished in Yemen around the end of the fifth/eleventh century.[10] This poem correlates the solar months in the Syriac rendering with the so-called Himyaritic months of pre-Islamic South Arabia. The emphasis in the poem is on diet and health, a standard feature in the almanac tradition, but no specific information on Yemeni agriculture is given. Indeed, the poem could have been written almost anywhere were it not for the references to the Himyaritic months. The famed Yemeni scholar Nashwān ibn Saʿīd al-Ḥimyarī (died 573/1177) wrote a famous poem on the health regimes for each month, but again there is no information on Yemeni agriculture.[11] The third important poem was written by ʿAbd Allāh ibn Asʿad al-Yāfiʿī (died 768/1367), but it also focuses on health.[12]

The earliest extant almanac in prose about Yemen was included by al-Malik al-Ashraf ʿUmar in his astronomical collection entitled *Kitāb al-Tabṣira fī ʿilm al-nujūm.* This almanac was probably compiled around the year 670/1271. The next major Rasulid almanac is ascribed to a scholar (*qāḍī*) named Abū al-ʿUqūl Muḥammad ibn Aḥmad al-Ṭabarī.[13] Abū al-ʿUqūl is mentioned as the first teacher appointed by al-Malik al-Muʾayyad Dāwūd, the brother and successor of al-Ashraf, to the Muʾayyadīya school in Taʿizz, for which this scholar was given an annual salary of thirty dinars (I. al-Akwaʻ 1980:155). There is probably an almanac in the agricultural treatise of al-Malik al-Mujāhid ʻAlī, but this treatise has not yet been found. Two Rasulid almanacs are also included in a mixed manuscript belonging to al-Malik al-Afḍal al-ʻAbbās. One of these examples is a unique perpetual almanac according to the degrees of the zodiacal constellations entitled *Kitāb Salwat al-mahmūm fī ʻilm al-nujūm.*[14] The other example is an anonymous almanac called *Fuṣūl majmūʻa fī al-anwāʼ wa-al-zurūʻ wa-al-ḥiṣād.* This was said to be drawn from several previous almanacs and is very similar to that of al-Malik al-Ashraf ʻUmar. An almanac also exists in the tax treatise of al-Ḥasan ibn ʻAlī (Cahen and Serjeant 1957). Finally, there are three anonymous Rasulid almanacs currently in the Egyptian National Library in Cairo. One is a very general description of each month for 727/1326–27 and is similar to another short text probably from the fifteenth century. There is also a complete almanac arranged primarily for the Islamic months for 808/1405–6 (Varisco 1985a, forthcoming). A partial almanac can also be found in the *Bughyat al-fallāḥīn* of al-Malik al-Afḍal al-ʻAbbās.

Later almanac compilers in Yemen sometimes copied from Rasulid texts, usually introducing errors due to misunderstanding of the original sources. Several copies exist of an almanac attributed to a certain Ibn Jaḥḥāf (fl. seventeenth century A.D.), but the text is virtually identical to the almanac of Muḥammad ibn ʻAbd al-Laṭīf al-Thābitī for the year 1047/1636–37. An anonymous almanac obviously derived from the same source as these two examples can be found in a manuscript obtained by R. B. Serjeant in Yemen. This text also contains agricultural poems by Shihāb al-Dīn Aḥmad al-Zumaylī (Serjeant and al-ʻAmrī 1981) and Ḥasan ibn Jābir al-ʻAffārī (Varisco 1989b). The first known printed almanac in Yemen was penned by Muḥammad al-Ḥaydara of Taʻizz for many years both before and after the revolution that created the Yemen Arab Republic. Al-Ḥaydara's almanac for the year 1365/1946 has been translated by Serjeant (1954), but there were annual changes. A unique almanac chart according to the Yemeni agricultural marker stars (*maʻālim al-zirāʻa*) was drawn up by Muḥammad Ṣāliḥ al-Sirājī in the year 1379/1959–60. In fact local almanacs are still being written in Yemen today.

A survey of the entire Yemeni tradition of almanacs is beyond the scope of the present study, although relevant information from the available texts has been used for understanding the Rasulid tradition. Three main points should be made regarding the history of the Yemeni almanac. First, while the major Rasulid compilers were clearly scientists aware of the intricacies of astronomical and calendrical correlations, most later Yemeni compilers did not have such sophistication. For example, the Rasulid scholars were aware of the concept of precession of the equinoxes, but later compilers sometimes copied an earlier date for the rising of a zodiacal constellation even though several centuries had elapsed since the date quoted would apply. The Rasulid compilers were also well versed in the earlier scientific traditions of both East and West, but the sources available to them during the zenith of the Rasulid court were not available to later Yemeni writers.

A second major point is that later compilers often misunderstood earlier information, even though this is not readily apparent from the later text. For example, al-Malik al-Ashraf ʻUmar mentioned a variety of wheat named *quṣaybī*, named in fact for the obscure village of al-Quṣayba near Ta'izz. The Rasulid sultans owned land here, but it was not a place name commonly recognized after the Rasulid period. In later almanacs the term *quṣaybī* was invariably glossed as *qayḍī*, which literally means "summer cropping," even though there is no evidence for a *qayḍī* sowing as such. The reason for the error is that the two words have a roughly similar form in written Arabic. Similarly, al-Thābitī in his almanac misreads a difficult local term for sorghum (*kharajī*) as *jirjīr* (watercress). In the compiler's defense, the term in the surviving original Rasulid manuscripts is not consistently provided with diacriticals; indeed my own reading may still be taken as tentative. There is also evidence for copying from more than one source. Thus, one anonymous almanac (*Tawqīʻāt*) places a parching (*jahīsh*) of *sābiʻī* sorghum at Zabīd on XII:3 but also a parching (*farīk*) of the same variety at the same place on XII:7. The Arabic terms are interchangeable, and they do not refer to two separate parchings in Zabīd.

Third, the written almanacs do not cover the entire range of agricultural activities and seasonal knowledge in Yemeni folklore. The emphasis in the Rasulid texts is on the Tihāma and southern highlands, where the Rasulids had a power base. Later almanacs repeat much of this information but rarely provide details for other regions. A notable exception is the almanac chart of al-Sirājī, which contains details on agriculture north of Ṣanʻāʼ as far as Ṣaʻda, near the border with contemporary Saudi Arabia. It is also obvious that some compilers recorded information about areas they may not have visited. For all of these reasons it is very important to examine each almanac critically and determine which information appears to be from the compiler's own experience and which is simply copied or miscopied from an older text.

THE AUTHOR

Al-Malik al-Ashraf Mumahhid al-Dīn ʻUmar ibn Yūsuf ibn ʻAlī ibn Rasūl ibn Hārūn ibn Abī Fattāḥ al-Ghassānī al-Turkumānī was the third of the Rasulid sultans in Yemen.[15] The Rasulid sultans descended from emirs accompanying the Ayyubid Tūrānshāh (brother of the famed Saladin), who conquered the Yemeni lowlands in 569/1173. Although the Rasulids claimed descent from the ancient Yemeni tribe of al-Azd, they were in fact of Turkoman extraction. The Ayyubids gained control of the coastal region and much of the southern highlands in a relatively short amount of time. By the time that the first Rasulid sultan, Nūr al-Dīn 'Umar, succeeded the last of the Ayyubids, the holdings of the newly formed dynasty were well consolidated.

The life and reign of Nūr al-Dīn's grandson, al-Malik al-Ashraf 'Umar, were overshadowed by the long (about forty-six years) and prosperous rule of the latter's father, al-Malik al-Muẓaffar Yūsuf (Varisco 1993c). The famed Venetian traveler Marco Polo (1958:309) remarked that al-Muẓaffar was one of the richest men in the world, his wealth derived in large part from customs duties at the bustling medieval port of Aden. Al-Malik al-Muẓaffar was in fact the preeminent Rasulid patron of major religious schools and mosques in Yemen; he even contributed to the enhancement of the *ka'ba* in Mecca.[16] As a scholar and author himself, it is not surprising that his eldest son, al-Malik al-Ashraf 'Umar, gained a reputation in the sciences. The Rasulid sultans brought a variety of foreign scholars and scientists to their court and elevated the level of scholarship in Yemen to the highest level it had ever seen and ever would achieve.

None of the historical sources mention when 'Umar was born; indeed the details on his life are quite fragmentary. As the eldest son of al-Malik al-Muẓaffar, whose birth is recorded for 619/1222, it is likely that 'Umar was born sometime after 640/1242–43. His younger brother, Dāwūd, was born in 662/1264. By the year 665/1266–67 'Umar was old enough to command a military mission for his father to the northern town of Ḥajja. His father later appointed him governor of al-Mahjam along Wādī Surdud in the coastal region and at one point he was given charge of Ṣan'ā', a city the Rasulids did not always hold. In the month of *Jumādā al-Ulā*, 694/1295, the aging al-Muẓaffar made 'Umar co-regent and then retired to his royal residence at al-Tha'bāt near Ta'izz in the southern highlands. Four months later, when his father died, 'Umar foiled a potential political move by his younger brother, Dāwūd, and became sultan in his own right.[17]

The reign of al-Malik al-Ashraf was short-lived and without major historic significance. Coinage bearing his name was minted even before his father's death, a strong symbolic act for the transfer of authority. During 695/1295 the new sultan visited his treasure city of al-Dumluwa and later the coastal town of Zabīd, where he joined in celebration of the date harvest in the annual *sabt al-subūt* festivities. During his reign the sultan had to deal with years of unchecked corruption by officials in the date palm groves of Zabīd, where owning palms had become a financial liability. The historical sources note that a cold rainstorm descended on Yemen in A.H. 695, so that many sheep were killed. Coupled with the woes of bad weather there was a major locust infestation that severely damaged crops to the point that taxes were eased by the sultan. Coinciding with his reign was that of the Zaydī imam Muṭahhar ibn Yaḥyā al-Murtaḍā, who died in A.H. 697 at the ripe age of eighty-three.

After only twenty-one months in office, al-Malik al-Ashraf died on a Tuesday night, 23 *Muḥarram* 696/22 November 1296. He was buried in the Ashrafīya school he had founded in Ta'izz.[18] Most of the historical sources are silent on the cause of the sultan's death. Waṭyūṭ (fol. 43r) records a note of treachery. A slave-girl of al-Malik al-Mu'ayyad Dāwūd is said to have passed by al-Ashraf with a dish that gave off an aroma no one could resist. Al-Ashraf asked her, "My pretty one, what's that dish?" She replied that it was the supper of her master, his brother. Al-Ashraf demanded the dish for himself, but it turned out to be poisoned; he died within an hour of eating it. Whether or not this story is true, it points to an undercurrent of rivalry at the Rasulid court.

Little is known about the personal life of the author. He sired at least six sons who survived to maturity ('Umar ibn Yūsuf 1949:91): al-Malik al-Nāsir Jalāl al-Dīn Muḥammad, Ḥasan, 'Īsā, al-Malik al-'Ādil Ṣalāḥ al-Dīn Abū Bakr, Aḥmad, and Asad al-Dīn Dāwūd. There were at least two daughters, who married sons of his brother, Dāwūd (Tāj al-Dīn 1985:102). None of al-Malik al-Ashraf's sons were destined to sit on the throne, since his brother succeeded him. History has recorded the names of eighteen horses owned by the sultan, two of the most famous being Mawj (Meadow) and Ra'd (Thunder) (*Aqwāl*, fol. 106r).

Al-Malik al-Ashraf was a prolific scholar, perhaps in part because the greater part of his life was spent under his father's rule. The Rasulid sultans pursued education to a high degree, particularly in nonreligious sciences. Scholars and teachers were brought in from other lands and schools were founded by each sultan. Among the author's teachers was a certain Sa'īd ibn As'ad al-Ḥarārī (al-Khazrajī 1913:4:216). At least a dozen titles are attributed to the pen of al-Ashraf, although not all of these texts have survived. His known works include:

1. *al-Asṭurlāb*. This is a treatise on the use of the astrolabe, including an illustration of one of the sultan's astrolabes which is now in the Metropolitan Museum of Art in New York (King 1985). The two extant copies of this text are ms. Cairo Taymūr *riyāḍīyāt* 105, copied ca. 690/1291, and ms. Tehran Majlis al-Umma al-Irānī from 888/1483–84 (King 1983a:28–29). It should be noted that the published texts of Ibn al-Dayba' (1977:2:51) and al-Khazrajī (1981:276) give the title as *al-Iṣtibāh* (!).

2. *al-Dalā'il fī ma'rifat al-awqāt wa-al-manāzil.* This is a text on time-keeping and the sundial, but no known copies exist. It was mentioned in the biographies recorded by Ibn al-Dayba' (1977:2:51) and al-Khazrajī (1981:276).

3. *al-Ibdāl limā 'alama fī al-ḥāl fī al-adwīya wa-al-'aqāqīr.* This is a medical text said to be located in the Āl al-Kāf library in Tarīm of the Ḥaḍramawt (al-Ḥibshī 1977:556). The title is given as *al-Ibdāl limā 'adama fī al-ḥāl* by I. al-Akwa' (1980:141), but this is probably a printing error.

4. *al-Ishāra fī al-'ibāra fī 'ilm ta'bīr al-ru'yā.* This is a text of dream interpretation mentioned by Ibn al-Dayba' (1977:2:51), but no known copy exists.

5. *al-Jāmi' fī al-ṭibb.* This is a medicinal work apparently written before 667/1268–69, when the author was quite young (Zettersteen in 'Umar ibn Yūsuf 1949:36). This title is mentioned in the bibliographic listing of al-Ḥibshī (1977:556) and by I. al-Akwa' (1980:142).

6. *Jawāhir al-tījān fī al-ansāb.* This genealogical work is noted in the listings of al-Ḥibshī (1977:556) and Sayyid (1974:131).

7. *Milḥ al-malāḥa fī ma'rifat al-filāḥa.* This very important agricultural treatise exists in at least two copies. The best copy is in the Glaser Collection in Vienna, although it is not complete. Another incomplete copy exists in a private library in the Yemen. The latter text was edited by the contemporary Yemeni historian Muḥammad 'Abd al-Raḥīm Jāzm and published in the Yemeni journal *al-Iklīl* ('Umar ibn Yūsuf 1985a), although there are numerous printing errors. After this an inaccurate version of the same text was edited by 'Abd Allāh al-Mujāhid in book form ('Umar ibn Yūsuf 1987), but this edition is without scholarly merit (Varisco 1989c:151). Substantial portions of al-Malik al-Ashraf's text appear in the later agricultural treatise of the *Bughyat al-fallāḥīn*. *Milḥ* is apparently the same work as that called *al-Tufāḥa fī ma'rifat al-filāḥa*, as noted in the texts of Ibn al-Dayba' (1977:2:51) and al-Khazrajī (1981:276). The Yemeni historian Muḥammad ibn 'Alī al-Akwa' (in Ibn al-Dayba' 1977:2:51, note 1) claims to have a copy of this manuscript.

8. *al-Mughnī fī al-bayṭara.* This is a medical treatise on horses and camels. Several copies exist (Brockelmann 1937:1:901), including one in the Egyptian National Library in Cairo as ms. Taymūr *ṭibb* 377, and others in Berlin, Milan, Rome, and Ṣan'ā'.

9. *Shifā' al-'alīl fī al-ṭibb.* This is a medical treatise mentioned by I. al-Akwa' (1980:142).

10. *al-Tabṣira fī 'ilm al-nujūm.* This major work is a collection of astronomy, astrology, and time-keeping. The single known copy is ms. Huntington 233 (Uri 905) in the Bodleian Library of Oxford (King 1983a: 28). The almanac edited and translated here comes from chapter 32 of the text.

11. *Tuḥfat al-adab fī al-tawārīkh wa-al-ansāb.* This is a genealogical text referred to by I. al-Akwa' (1980:141), al-Ḥibshī (1977:556), and Sayyid (1974:132). Perhaps it is a variation of the manuscript described below (#12).

12. *Turfat al-ashāb fī ma'rifat al-ansāb.* This genealogical work was edited by K.V. Zettersteen in 1949. A second edition, which is basically a reprint of the original, was published in Yemen in 1985. Valuable information on the author and text was provided by Zettersteen in the introduction to the text.

13 (?). The well-known medical herbal entitled *al-Mu'tamad fī al-adwiya al-mufrada* has been attributed to al-Malik al-Ashraf by the modern Yemeni bibliophile 'Abd Allāh al-Ḥibshī (1980:60). This text is usually assigned to the author's father, al-Malik al-Muẓaffar. It was first published in Cairo in 1327/1909, with later editions in 1370/1951 in Cairo and 1402/1982 in Beirut. Despite the claim of al-Ḥibshī, there is no evidence that this important and widely circulated herbal should not be attributed to al-Malik al-Muẓaffar. It is in fact largely derivative from previous Arabic herbals and offers little information specific to Yemen.

THE TEXT

The almanac edited and translated here is one of fifty chapters in al-Malik al-Ashraf's astronomical treatise *al-Tabṣira fī 'ilm al-nujūm.* Thus far only one copy of this text is known to exist, although it has been claimed that there are copies still in Yemen. The Bodleian manuscript does not have a colophon, but it appears to have been copied about A.D. 1400. The script and general form of the text indicate that it is definitely Rasulid in origin. In that this is the oldest and most detailed Rasulid almanac, it is the most important almanac source for the period.

The text of *Tabṣira* is in essence an introduction to the medieval science of astronomy, including basic zodiacal and planetary astrology, as well as a range of information on time-keeping systems. The subjects covered in the text include the zodiac, course of the sun, course of the moon, planets, fixed stars, eclipses, astrolabe, lunar stations, calendar systems, determination of the *qibla* (direction toward Mecca), weather, medicinal regimes for each season, the agricultural calendar, and systems of numbers. The author draws on a wide variety of earlier texts, including several no longer extant *zīj* tables.[19] In general, however, his precise references are not mentioned in the textual discussion of subjects.

Al-Malik al-Ashraf's almanac is arranged in tabular form with each page containing data by day for half of the solar Christian month. The almanac begins with the month of *Tishrīn al-Awwal* (October), the beginning of the Christian year according to the Byzantine reckoning. The Syriac month name is highlighted in red ink, as are the numbers indicating the day of each month and references for the entry of the sun into each zodiacal constellation. The corresponding Himyaritic month name and the bulk of the text, as well as the chart outline per se, are marked in black. Along the left-hand margin of each page are calculations of the hours of daylight and darkness for the beginning and middle of the month respectively. On the right-hand margin the shadow lengths for the noon and midafternoon prayers, as well as the end of the afternoon, are indicated for the beginning and midpoint of each month. In a few places the copyist has continued the text outside the lined margins or made a small addition. There are several lines written by a different, and presumably later, hand (for example, at XII:24).

The basic text of the almanac is written in short phrases and sentences, at times almost like shorthand. As is common in medieval Yemeni texts, the letter *dāl* is indicated by one dot underneath, while no dot signifies the *dhāl*. In numerous cases diacritical marks are omitted, especially for the initial letter of an imperfect verb. The final *ḥamza* is generally dropped, or replaced by *yā'* or *wāw*. For example, the word *bad'* (beginning) takes the written form *badw* at X:8. The copyist sometimes replaces an *alif* with an *alif maqṣūra* as in the case of *janā* (harvest) at XII:1. The *shadda*, which indicates doubling of a letter, is usually dropped. There are also a number of standard medieval variants such as *thalath* for *thalāth* (three). In several places words or even phrases have been left out, as in the case of the lunar station *sa'd bula'*, which is rendered simply as *bula'*.

In translating the text there remain a few difficulties with local dialect terms, although most of these could be deciphered through comparison with variations in existing Yemeni dialects. One of the more unusual features of some Yemeni dialects is a shift from *lām* to *nūn*, which can occur in Tihāma speech. This appears in the term *matlam* (cultivation or ploughing), which is rendered *matnam* in the almanac and most of the Rasulid texts (Serjeant 1974a:71, note 170). The Tihāma dialect can also soften the *'ayn* to a *ḥamza* as in the case of classical *'ilb* (*Zizyphus spina-christi*), which is written *ilb* in the text. The term used for "quail" is *simmān*, a colloquial variant of the classical *sumāna*. This is probably an influence of Egyptian dialect, since the Rasulids arrived in Yemen from Egypt as retainers of the Ayyubids. There are a number of terms which are only found in Yemeni Arabic and which fortunately survive in modern usage. One of the major examples is *ṣirāb* or *ṣurāb* (harvest), which is derived from South Arabic. Another example is *naṣīd* (harvest or cutting), which survives in the dialect of Ḥaḍramawt (Landberg 1901:1:311) and Laḥj (Maktari 1971:173). An interesting variant, which has not yet been documented in contemporary Yemeni dialects, is the use of *qushār* for *'ushar* (*Calotropis procera*) at IX:16. Two local plant names, occurring at XI:15 and I:27, have not been identified, although an equivalent term for the second plant name is given in the text.

The information in the almanac is derived both from the general almanac tradition, which extended well beyond the borders of Yemen, and from knowledge of local practices and folklore. In the majority of cases the sources of specific information are not provided, an exception being the reference to a caution from Hippocrates on drinking purgatives, for example, at VI:27 and VIII:10. The author also mentioned the important source of Ibn Qutayba in his treatise and this is undoubtedly the text he consulted for the information recorded on the *anwā'* system at I:28–31. It is unclear which Egyptian sources were consulted by al-Malik al-Ashraf, but there is substantial discussion of the Nile and agriculture in Egypt.

The chief value of the almanac is the wide variety of information relative to medieval Yemen. The details of the agricultural cycle, primarily for the coastal region and the southern highlands, are extremely valuable and supplement the discussions in the extant Rasulid agricultural treatises. Local details on the weather, especially rain and wind periods, are provided, including reference to the winter mist (*kharf*) at Dhofar. The timing of the sailing seasons in and out of the port of Aden is of exceptional importance because this is the earliest source to document the range of sailing periods. It was written about two centuries before the major navigational treatise of Ibn Mājid. Later Yemeni almanacs often copy information on sailing seasons, but they generally introduce errors in the process and are thus not reliable.

One of the more interesting puzzles regarding the almanac is the date for which it was compiled. Since there is no reference to the Islamic lunar calendar, it is not immediately obvious when the author composed the almanac. For most of the information the exact year of the almanac is unimportant. Some of the calendrical data, however, must be linked to a specific year, assuming they are accurate. Al-Malik al-Ashraf provided information on the date of Easter and of the Persian New Year (*nayrūz*), and there are several examples of a date with the corresponding day of the week. This allows for the determination of the probable time for which the almanac was written.

From the internal evidence the best fit of this almanac is for the year A.D. 1271, which corresponds with A.H. 670–71, the Persian Yazdagird year 640, the Coptic 987–88 and the Alexandrian 1582–83. This date was arrived at from the following clues within the text. First, the Persian New Year is cited as occurring on I:8, which would be accurate for A.D. 1269–72. Al-Malik al-Ashraf also referred to the *nayrūz* of India at I:10. Neither of these *nayrūz* dates correlates exactly with the numerous references to the sailing seasons vis-à-vis the *nayrūz* dates, but this is no doubt due to the general confusion between the change of the timing of the actual Persian New Year every four years and the more general navigational *nayrūz* calendar used by sailors for a number of centuries. The second line of evidence is the fixing of V:2 as a Saturday, because it was the time for the Saturday outing known as *sabt al-subūt* in Zabīd. If this date is accurate, it establishes the first day of the year as a Thursday, assuming it is not a leap year, which fits the year A.D. 1271. Third, Easter Sunday is given as IV:4, although this date does not in fact correspond with the timing indicated for Palm Sunday (III:21) or for the beginning of Lent (II:4 or 13)! If an error of one day is assumed, so that Easter should be placed on IV:5, the almanac would be accurate for A.D. 1271. It should be noted that the author places Christmas on XII:24, one day before the actual holiday. It is doubtful that al-Malik al-Ashraf was ignorant of the exact date; perhaps he took an Islamic view in beginning the holiday on the "night" before. A final clue that helps confirm the evidence above is the mention of A.H. 671, which correlates with A.D. 1271, as an example when discussing calendrical calculations in another part of the treatise.

Part One

TEXT

English Translation

Chapter Thirty-two: Discussion of the Twelve Christian (Rūmī) Months and Account of the Lunar Stations (*Anwā'*) and Seasons

Tishrīn al-Awwal (October), or *Dhū Ṣirāb*

1 Byzantine New Year. First sowing of *quṣaybī* wheat. First sowing of *ṣawmī* [sorghum].

2 The Nile recedes and Egyptians plant.

3 As dawn breaks, the third star of *haq'a* is at midheaven.

4 The east wind erupts. Availability of hyacinth bean (*kishd*) at Jabal Ṣabir.

5 Last of the time for cutting wood.

6 Dawn rising of *simāk* and setting of *baṭn al-ḥūt*, the *naw'* of which is four nights for rain. Last of the *lawāqih* days [that harm the face?].

7 First planting of *'ishwī* [sorghum].

8 Beginning of the decline in water sources.

9 There are fewer fleas. Arrival of the crane and wagtail to Egypt.

10 Select days for sowing *quṣaybī* wheat until the twenty-fifth [of the month].

11 As dawn breaks, the fifth and last star of *han'a* and Sirius are at midheaven.

12 Planting of clover in Egypt. Availability of parched grain from *shabb* [sorghum].

13 At the break of dawn Spica is visible on the eastern horizon. This is the day of the arrival of the Mogadishu ships in Aden at 280 [days] after the *nayrūz*.

14 Evening rising of the Pleiades. The southern *azyab* wind blows. Planting of the narcissus bulb.

15 Entry of the sun into Scorpius. Autumn is established and its regime strengthens. Last sowing of *ṣawmī* [sorghum].

16 The first *mihrajān* [festival of the Persians]. Departure of the Indian *dīmānī* ships for Aden at the First of the Season (*awwal al-zamān*). Sailing of the Egyptian *ṣā'iḥ* [ships] from Aden.

17 Season for harvesting sorghum in the mountains. Availability of young *ṣirbīya* camels [for eating]. First of the harvest in Wādī 'Udayna of al-Sha'bānīya.

18 Start of the first Forty Days (*arba'īnīyāt*). Chicken eggs are more plentiful because of the chickens' expansion into pasture areas, the increase of grain, and the strengthening of the sun due to the decrease in rainfall, with the opposite being true.

19 Beginning of the decline of the Nile in Egypt.

20 Dawn rising of *ghafr* and setting of *sharaṭān*, the *naw'* of which is three nights. Last of the [autumn] *ṣafarīya* days.

21 The [southern] *azyab* wind strengthens. The *mirām* (?) [wind] rises. Sailing of the Ziyāli' [ships] from Aden. Their sailing is not restrained, nor is their arrival broken off, as they sail from Aden to Zayla' on the *azyab* wind. They reach al-'Āra from al-Barbara and return from al-'Āra to Zayla'. They arrive in Aden on the north wind.

22 Foliage falls.

23 The ground is ploughed. Picking of pomegranates in Ṣan'ā' and the coastal region.

24 As dawn breaks, α β Canis Minoris (*al-dhirā' al-yamānīya*) are at midheaven. Presence of the honeycomb from the Dead Sea apple (*qushār*) and collection of this honey in the mountains.

25 Evening rising of Aldebaran. Last of the select [days] for sowing *quṣaybī* wheat.

26 –

27 –

28 First of the Mixed Nights (*al-layālī al-bulq*).

29 First inflorescence of early-variety (*miqdām*) date palms.

30 Season for harvesting *ṣirbī* wheat in Qā' al-Ajnād.

31 –

Tishrīn al-Thānī (November), or *Dhū Muhla*

1 First of the Yemeni *rabī'* rain, which is the *wasmī* rain in Syria. This falls occasionally in Yemen. Beginning of planting wheat in Egypt. Arrival of the Indian [ships] called *dīmānī* to Aden during the First of the Season. This is at 300 [days] after the *nayrūz*.

2 Dawn rising of *zubānān* and setting of *buṭayn*, the *naw'* of which is three nights. It is said that this is the last departure of the *badrī* [hawk]. Arrival of the ships of Dhofar.

3 Water cools. This is the first of the cold weather. First harvesting

(*naṣīd*) of *shabb* [sorghum].

4 Entering of ants underground. The time passes for manna and quails.

5 As dawn breaks, the luminous star of *nathra* is inclined slightly from midheaven.

6 Olives are picked in Egypt. The south wind strengthens. First arrival of the Indian and Qaysī ships to Aden.

7 End of the days for Indian bananas in the area of al-Dumluwa.

8 End of the days for pomegranates in the coastal region.

9 First of the two [cold] months of *jumaydā*. Season for harvesting the poppy.

10 Last harvesting of *shabb* [sorghum] and first carrying of this to storage chambers.

11 Departure of the assayers for recording the *shabb* [sorghum harvest] and assessing the tax on this. Availability of *halbā* wheat in Ba'dān and al-Mikhlāf (Mikhlāf Ja'far).

12 Cane and raisins are taken from the threshing floor to the granary, although opinions vary on this. They are then sold everywhere.

13 Infectious diseases are lifted from people. Evening rising of Orion (*jawzā'*).

14 Entry of the sun into Sagittarius. First of the third autumn month. Spreading of cold mist (*jānifa*?), known as *fṣy'a* (?), on the ground.

15 As dawn breaks, the bright star of *ṭarf* is at midheaven. Dawn rising of *iklīl* and setting of the Pleiades (*thurayyā*), the *naw'* of which is one night. Presence of *mtsha* (?) honey in the mountains of Surdud. This is white, excellent-tasting, sticky, viscous honey which does not harden. It is brought from al-Madāra.

16 Availability of sugarcane. First occurrence of frost (*ḍarīb*). Cultivation of *nasrī* [sorghum], which is called *kharajī* in the coastal region.

17 Last of the first Mixed Nights.

18 As dawn breaks, the southern star of *jabha* is at midheaven. Last sowing of *quṣaybī* wheat.

19 The sea is locked up and no ship sails on it.

20 Arrival of the Dhofar boats at Aden.

21 End of the sailing of Egyptian Kārim [merchant ships] as the *ṣā'iḥ* [sailing] from Aden. This is 320 [days] after the *nayrūz*.

22 Sailing of the Mogadishu [ships] from Aden at 320 days after the *nayrūz*.

23 Cultivation (*matnam*) of red [sorghum], which follows the *kharajī* [sorghum], in the coastal region. Availability of hyacinth bean in the

coastal foothills.

24 As dawn breaks, the star which follows the southern [star] of *jabha* is at midheaven.

25 Availability of asparagus in al-Janad. Presence of quail and sand grouse in the coastal region.

26 Last of the first Forty Days and start of the second, which is the well-known one. Rutting of camels.

27 Availability of rushnut (*du'bub*).

28 Dawn rising of *qalb* and setting of Aldebaran, the *naw'* of which is one night.

29 First of the *walī* rain, which may fall occasionally. Last presence of the heads of screwpine (*kādhī*).

30 Mixing of autumn with winter. Season in which the *quṭrub* [spirit] goes about in Egypt. [This is] a type of ghoul which is active in certain places.

Kānūn al-Awwal (December), or *Dhū al-Āl*

1 Season for harvesting cotton in Abyan. Harvest of *bukr* [sorghum] in Abyan.

2 Greatest availability of young *ṣirbīya* camels. These are excellent tasting and fatter than the *ṣayfīya* variety.

3 As dawn breaks, *zubra* is at midheaven. First parching of *rub'ī* [sorghum] in Dathīna.

4 Vapors come out of mouths; these may also come out in the days of heavy rain clouds at the time of the autumn (*rabī'*) rain.

5 Last availability of clarified butter in al-Mikhlāf (Mikhlāf Ja'far).

6 –

7 –

8 Season for the presence of parched grain from *sābi'ī* [sorghum]. Disappearance of Canopus [from the night sky].

9 Cultivation of *jaḥrī* [sorghum] in the coastal region.

10 Snakes go blind.

11 Dawn rising of *shawla* and setting of *haq'a*, the *naw'* of which is one night. As dawn breaks, *ṣarfa* is at midheaven. Arrival of the Qaysī, Hurmuzī, and Qalhātī [ships] to Aden at 340 [days] after the *nayrūz*.

12 Last of the time for frost. Extreme limit of the sun's declination to the south.

13 Season for planting black cumin in Yemen.

14 Entry of the sun into Capricornus. During this time are the shortest day and longest night, intense cold, and entering of winter. The

daytime begins to increase and the night to decrease.

15 Trees are bare of leaves. Evening rising of Sirius, which the farmers call *'alib.*

16 First crushing of sugarcane. Availability of the honeycomb from christ's-thorn (*ḍāl*) and collection of this honey in the mountains. The humor of phlegm is active. Sailing of the Mogadishu [ships] from Aden.

17 Planting of *qiyāḍ* [wheat and barley] in the mountains.

18 First inflorescence of date palms.

19 Season for harvesting *sābi'ī* [sorghum] in the coastal region. Assessing of the tax on *ṣirbīya* cotton. Cotton is most available and at its lowest price.

20 Water freezes.

21 End of the last arrival of Indian *dīmānī* [ships] as First of the Season at 350 days after the *nayrūz.*

22 End of the days of hyacinth beans in al-Mahjam.

23 –

24 Dawn rising of *na'ā'im* and setting of *han'a,* the *naw'* of which is one night. (The 24th day [and] the 25th are Christmas.)

25 Second *mihrajān* [festival of the Persians].

26 Last of the Black Nights.

27 Pasturing of horses for two months in Egypt. First of the second Mixed Nights.

28 Availability of *ḥumar,* which is tamarind, in the coastal region.

29 Harvest of *rub'ī* [sorghum] in Dathīna.

30 As dawn breaks, the second star of *'awwā* is at midheaven.

31 –

Kānūn al-Thānī (January), or *Dhū Da'w*

1 Sap flows in wood.

2 Evening rising of Canopus.

3 Hunting with sparrow hawks and the merlin, which are in the coastal foothills (Ḥawāzz). This is better than for the sea fowl which are hunted when the *badrī* [falcon] departs, because those [earlier] days are weaker.

4 Noxious vermin disappear from view.

5 Last of the second Forty Days and start of the third Forty Days. Cultivation of *baynī* [sorghum] in Wādī Mawr.

6 Dawn rising of *bula'* and setting of *dhirā',* the *naw'* of which is one night. Epiphany in the Byzantine rite.

7 Most intense cold, [after which] it begins to be moderate.

8 [Dawn] rising of Vega. Availability of [mixed] honey of *Euphorbia* and of christ's-thorn tree in the mountains of Surdud. The Persian New Year (*nayrūz*), which the Indian [sailors] use.

9 Availability of lebbek (*labakh*?) in the coastal region. Major arrival of the boats from Qalhāt. Availability of the *farḍ* date in Aden.

10 Season for planting tree seedlings. First day of the Indian New Year (*nayrūz*).

11 The Pollenating Winds, which pollenate trees, blow. Domestic animals (*bahā'im*) lose weight.

12 Entry of the sun into Aquarius. Season of winter, the regime of which strengthens. There are fewer illnesses. The underground warms.

13 As dawn breaks, the middle star of *'awwā* is at midheaven.

14 Trees bud and blossoms shimmer. As dawn breaks, Arcturus is at midheaven.

15 Last of the second Mixed Nights. Season for assessing the tax on crop produce (*ghalla*), which is estimated, in the mountains.

16 Departure of the hoopoe. Cultivation of melon in the coastal region. Dispersal of cold mist (*jānifa*?) from the ground surface.

17 Canopus is seen in the Maghreb.

18 End of availability of young *ṣayfīya* camels.

19 Dawn rising of *dhābiḥ* and setting of *nathra*, the *naw'* of which is one night. At evening the Pleiades are positioned at midheaven.

20 The Nile's water clears.

21 [Dawn] rising of Altair in Yemen. First pollenation of date palms.

22 Clover is ready in Egypt.

23 –

24 –

25 Last cultivation of *baynī* [sorghum].

26 Presence of parched grain from *quṣaybī* wheat.

27 End of the availability of young *ṣirbīya* camels in al-Sha'bānīya and other areas. Availability of the honeycomb from the acacia (*ẓubba*) called *ḥmja* (?) and collection of this honey, which is the best variety, in the mountains.

28–31 The *anwā'* are markers by which the Arabs designate rain periods by their dawn risings according to what is said at the rising. This means [the rising] at dawn except for what is [equal to] the setting, such as the evening rising of the Pleiades. The general meaning of the dawn [rising] is the basis for all the *anwā'*. God knows best.

ENGLISH TRANSLATION

Shubāṭ (February), or *Dhū Ḥulal*

1 Dawn rising of *bulaʻ* and setting of *ṭarf*, the *naw'* of which is one night. Sap seeps from wood. Cultivation of *tamrī* [sorghum] in the coastal region.

2 As dawn breaks, the northern star of *zubānān* is at midheaven.

3 Season for pruning grapevines in the mountains.

4 The silkworm stirs. The Great Fast (*al-ṣawm al-kabīr*) of the Christians.

5 First harvest of *quṣaybī* wheat. Harvest of *ṣawmī* [sorghum].

6 Fast of the Sabians. This is the time most trees are in leaf and blossoms shimmer.

7 Falling of the First Coal (*jamra*). As dawn breaks, the northern star outside Scorpius is at midheaven.

8 Presence of parched grain from the second cropping (*ʻaqb*) of *sābiʻī* [sorghum].

9 Setting of the first [two stars] of *ṣawāb* (square of Pegasus).

10 First of the *rabīʻ* rain, which is the Yemeni *wasmī*, or the first rain occurring in the year. Occurrence of heavy mists (*ghamām*) even if no rain comes. The heavy mists may come before or after this time and up until the Nights of the Old Woman. It is said that these heavy mists are cold (*ḥulal*), hence the Himyaritic designation of *Shubāṭ* as (*Dhū Ḥulal*. When there is a slight rainy mist, it is called *dīma*, but the Indians call it *kharf*.)

11 Entry of the sun into Pisces. First of the third winter month.

12 Ants come out of their hives.

13 Christian Lent, which comes between 2 *Shubāṭ* and 7 *Ādhār*. This is on a Monday.

14 Dawn rising of *suʻūd* and setting of *jabha*, the *naw'* of which is one night. Falling of the Second Coal.

15 Setting of the last [two stars] of *ṣawāb*.

16 The Pollenating Winds strengthen. Noxious vermin emerge from the ground.

17 –

18 Slackening of the cold. Availability of the honeycomb from acacia (*ẓubba*) and the collection of this honey in the mountains.

19 As dawn breaks, the faint star of *qalb* is at midheaven.

20 End of the planting of tree seedlings.

21 Falling of the Third Coal.

22 Every plant with permanent roots bears.

23 Sexual arousal of wild animals. The north wind blows.

24 Last of the Pollenating Winds.
25 Harvest of the second cropping of *sābi'ī* [sorghum].
26 First of the Nights of the Old Woman (for seven nights and eight days). Last pollenating of date palms.
27 Dawn rising of *sa'd al-akhbiya* and setting of *zubra*, the *naw'* of which is one night. Mixing of winter with spring.
28 Season for planting *dithā'* [wheat] in the mountains. Last arrival of the boats from Qalhāt.

Ādhār (March), or *Dhū Ma'ūn*

1 First opening of the rose.
2 Planting of gourds.
3 Harvest of millet in al-Mahjam.
4 Last of the Nights of the Old Woman.
5 Season for flowering of the sweet pomegranate.
6 As dawn breaks, the bright star of [text illegible] is at midheaven.
7 –
8 Snakes regain sight. Last sailing of the Indian [ships] from India to Aden at the Last of the Season (*ākhir al-zamān*).
9 Last presence of quail and sand grouse in the coastal region.
10 Setting of α Centauri (*al-sā'iq al-awwal*). (The silkworm bears.)
11 Trees are dressed with leaves. End of the decline in water sources. The east wind blows gently.
12 Dawn rising of *muqaddam* and setting of *ṣarfa*, the *naw'* of which is four nights for rain. (The star from the brow [*jabha*] of the stars of Leonis is at midheaven.)
13 Entry of the sun into Aries. Night and day are equal in length. The heat and cold become temperate. The daytime increases. The season of spring is entered.
14 Time for drinking medicines. The humor of blood is active.
15 Appearance of blue flies and noxious vermin of the ground.
16 First planting of sorghum. Harvest of *qiyāḍ* [wheat and barley] in the mountains. End of the sailing of Indian [ships] from India [to Aden]. No one ventures out after this day.
17 The cold passes away and the heat advances.
18 –
19 Availability of parched grain from *baynī* [sorghum].
20 Pestilential diseases are common.
21 The north wind blows. Palm Sunday.
22 First sailing of the *dīmānī* [boats from Aden].

23 Sailing to Dhofar by whoever wants to put in there for a spell before the wind, which allows the Dhofar boats to return to Aden, changes direction.
24 The first *bakhnīṭas*. Last harvest of *quṣaybī* wheat.
25 Dawn rising of *mu'akhkhar* and setting of *'awwā*, the *naw'* of which is one night for rain.
26 Setting of β Centauri (*al-sā'iq al-thānī*). Beginning of the *dīmānī* sailing of Indian [ships] from Aden at the First of the Season. This is 80 [days] after the *nayrūz*.
27 Date palms are ascended [with ropes].
28 Harvest of *baynī* [sorghum] in Wādī Mawr.
29 Cultivation of *zi'ir* [sorghum] in Surdud and Mawr.
30 Balsam oil is pressed.
31 The second *bakhnīṭas*. End of the days for broad beans (*fūl*).

Nīsān (April), or *Dhū Thāba*

1 Beginning of the increase in water sources. First availability of apricots, apples, and plums.
2 As dawn breaks, the star called the "eye" of *na'ā'im* is at midheaven.
3 The small *Sha'ānīn* [holiday of the Christians]. Start of the *naw'* of the Pleiades.
4 First availability of melons in the coastal region. Christian festival of Easter. Presence of parched grain from *baynī* [sorghum] in Surdud.
5 Presence of fumitory in al-Janad.
6 Disappearance of the Pleiades for forty days.
7 The third *bakhnīṭas*.
8 Hatching of birds. As dawn breaks, the middle star of the second part of *na'ā'im* is at midheaven.
9 Dawn rising of *baṭn al-ḥūt* and setting of *simāk*, the *naw'* of which is one night. Roses are plentiful.
10 Head colds and eyes diseases are common.
11 First bearing of young *ṣayfīya* camels in al-Sha'bānīya and the southern part of the Ta'izz region.
12 –
13 The fourth *bakhnīṭas*.
14 Entry of the sun into Taurus. The spring season is established [and its regime strengthens]. Appearance of truffles.
15 The Jewish Passover, which is [really] at the middle of their *Nīsān*. This is not the Byzantine *Nīsān* but is rather connected with the Arab

(i.e., lunar) months. There is a method for deriving this. The Feast of Tabernacles is in the middle of their *Tishrī* at the full moon in the Arab reckoning. First arrival of the Indian [ships] in Aden during the Last of the Season at 100 days after the *nayrūz*. This is the *tīrmāh*, or Great Season (*al-mawsim al-kabīr*). Also at this time is the beginning of the first arrival of Egyptian [ships] to Aden. God knows best.

16 As dawn breaks, the second star of *qilāda* (part of Sagittarius) is at midheaven.

17 Last of the *lāḥiq* sailing to Egypt. Last of the *dīmānī* sailing from Aden [to India].

18 Season for blossoming of *Carissa edulis* (*'arm*).

19 First planting of *ṣayf* [sorghum] in the coastal region. First of the *khamsīn* winds.

20 Dawn rising of *sharaṭān* and setting of *ghafr*, the *naw'* of which is three nights and favorable. First of the *thawr* (Taurus) rain.

21 The fifth *bakhnīṭas*.

22 Positioning of the sun directly overhead at . . . in Yemen at midday. The sun inclines to the north and the shadow thus returns to the southern direction.

23 Season for picking flax in Egypt.

24 The Euphrates reaches maximum flood stage (and sailing begins on it).

25 First availability of Indian bananas in the area of al-Dumluwa.

26 First of the ten select [days for sowing sorghum].

27 The east wind blows.

28 The sixth *bakhnīṭas*.

29 Season for sailing in the western Mediterranean Sea.

30 Melons are good to eat.

Ayyār (May), or *Dhū Mabkar*

1 First intense heat. First planting of sesame in the mountains. Cultivation of *thawrī* [sorghum] in Mawr.

2 First of the *subūt* [holiday], which is the first Saturday in *Ayyār*.

3 Dawn rising of *buṭayn* and setting of *zubānān*, the *naw'* of which is three nights.

4 First planting of *'ishwī* [sorghum] in the coastal region. Evening rising of *qalb*.

5 Last of the ten select [days for sowing sorghum]. The seventh *bakhnīṭas*.

6 As dawn breaks, the bright star of Vega is at midheaven. End of the *dīmānī* sailing from Aden [to India] at 120 [days] after the *nayrūz*. Also at this time is the beginning of the (*lāḥiq* sailing of Egyptian [ships] to Aden. This is the last of the *azyab* wind at 120 days after the *nayrūz*. Last arrival of the first Egyptian [ships] to Aden.)

7 Greatest availability of young *ṣayfīya* camels, which make excellent eating in al-Sha'bānīya.

8 Disappearance of Canopus from [view in] Yemen. It is not seen until it arrives again at the place of its appearance on 25 *Tammūz*. At this rising the rain is plentiful, as has been said, "When Canopus rose, it announced flood after flood." Its evening rising is the opposite of this.

9 Festival of the Rose in Egypt.

10 End of the days for melons in the coastal region. First opening of the [heads of] screwpine (*kādhī*).

11 End of the availability of rushnut (*du'bub*?). First assessment of the tithe tax (*'ushr*) in al-Mahjam.

12 [First of the actual *subūt* festival of] the date palms, but it may be two days either way of the last Saturday according to the agreement of the date palm growers [about this] Saturday.

13 Apricots and plums are good to eat.

14 Entry of the sun into Gemini. First of the third month of spring. Rising of Capella (*'ayyūq*). Availability of the *ṣihla* figs. Dates redden and yellow. Fresh ripe dates (*ruṭab*) change color.

15 First planting of *jawzī* [sorghum] in the coastal region. Hatching of birds.

16 Dawn rising of the Pleiades and setting of *iklīl*, the *naw'* of which is five nights. Beginning of the sailing of Qaysī, Hurmuzī, and Qalhātī [ships] from Aden at 130 [days] after the *nayrūz* (as First of the Season. End of the *lāḥiq* sailing of Egyptian [ships] at 130 [days] after the *nayrūz*.)

17 First availability of grapes, figs, and fresh ripe dates. First of the [hot] *bawāriḥ* winds.

18 First planting of *muqādim* [barley] in the mountains and sorghum in the Ṣan'ā' region.

19 First of the *thawr* rain. Planting of the poppy. Opening of the Mediterranean Sea (al-Baḥr al-Māliḥ).

20 Season for harvesting rice in Egypt. The select time for cultivating *ṣayf* [sorghum or millet] in the coastal region.

21 Last of the roses.

22 As dawn breaks, *sa'd bula'* is at midheaven.

23 Season for the availability of mulberries in the districts of Jibla. First availability of grapes.
24 Last sailing to Qays.
25 Last of the [hot] *bawāriḥ* winds.
26 Last crushing of sugarcane. First sailing of Qalhātī [ships] from Aden. Last of the *lāḥiq* sailing from Aden [to Egypt].
27 Presence of the jasmine blossom.
28 Last planting of sorghum in the mountains.
29 Dawn rising of *dabarān* and setting of *qalb*, the *naw'* of which is three nights. The [hot] *samūm* wind blows. Season for assessing the tax on future *ṣayfīya* cotton in al-Mahjam.
30 First of the *ḥamīm* rain.
31 Mixing of spring with summer. (Sailing on the Euphrates ceases.)

Ḥazīrān (June), or *Dhū Qayḍ*

1 Season for availability of peaches. First availability of fresh ripe dates. First availability of the ben seed.
2 First of the [hot] *samā'im* [winds]. Intense *bawāriḥ* [winds].
3 As dawn breaks, the faint southern star of *sa'd al-su'ūd* is at midheaven.
4 Sailing of the Mogadishu [ships] from Aden.
5 End of the arrival of the *tīrmāh* [sailing] of Indian [ships] to Aden as Last of the Season at 150 [days] after the *nayrūz*. End of the sailing by Qaysī, Hurmuzī, and Qalhātī [ships] from Aden. First sailing of the Mogadishu [ships] from Aden.
6 First sailing of the Mogadishu [ships] from Aden.
7 Sexual activity is stimulated.
8 The Nile of Egypt becomes full of sediments. Last of the *khamsīn* winds.
9 –
10 The intense heat of summer is ignited. Blowing of violent (*'awāṣif*) winds.
11 Dawn rising of *haq'a* and setting of *shawla*, the *naw'* of which is three nights. This is [the start of] the *mu'taḍadī* New Year.
12 Arrival of the sun at its northern declination. Availability of grapes and peaches in al-Jannāt.
13 As dawn breaks, the two stars of *sa'd al-akhbiya* are at midheaven.
14 Entry of the sun into Cancer. The longest day and shortest night. Intense heat. Rising of the shoulder of Orion (*mankib al-jawzā'*).
15 The humor of black bile is active.

16 Figs are good to eat. The thick mist (*kharf*) is present at Dhofar.
17 –
18 First availability of walnuts.
19 First of the [hot] days of *bāḥūr*.
20 As dawn breaks, the middle star of *akhbiya* is at midheaven.
21 The *thi‘l* variety of date is good to eat.
22 Availability of grapes and peaches in al-Jannāt.
23 Flooding of the Nile. As dawn breaks, the third star of *sa‘d al-akhbiya* is at midheaven.
24 Dawn rising of *han‘a* and setting of *na‘ā’im*, the *naw’* of which is three nights.
25 First of the *ramaḍī* rain.
26 Last of the [hot] days of *bāḥūr*.
27 Start of Hippocrates’ prohibition of [drinking] medicines.
28 –
29 The mulberry ripens.
30 Departure of Egyptian Kārim (merchant ships) from Egypt to Aden.

Tammūz (July), or *Dhū Madhrā*

1 Season for availability of quince and pomegranates. As dawn breaks, the two faint stars of *muqaddam* are at midheaven.
2 –
3 Grapes ripen. Figs are good to eat. Season for the availability of grapes in al-Jannāt.
4 –
5 The *ṣihla* figs are no longer available. The grapes of al-Jannāt are good to eat.
6 –
7 Dawn rising of *dhirā‘* and setting of *balda*, the *naw’* of which is three nights for rain.
8 Pestilential diseases go away.
9 Most intense heat. [Dawn] rising of Sirius.
10 Water in springs decreases. First planting of *bājisī* [sorghum] in the coastal region.
11 Eye diseases are common.
12 As dawn breaks, the northern star of *mu’akhkhar* is directly overhead and the southern one is in front.
13 Availability of the honeycomb from acacia (*‘asaqī*) and the collection of this honey in the mountains.
14 Season for assessing the *mustaftaḥ* tax in the mountains.

15 Entry of the sun into Leo. The summer season is established and its regime strengthens. First arrival of Egyptian [ships]. The underground cools.

16 The underground cools. Season for picking walnuts.

17 Last planting of wheat in the mountains.

18 Peaches ripen and are good to eat.

19 Harvesting days of date palms.

20 Dawn rising of *nathra* and setting of *sa'd al-dhābiḥ*, the *naw'* of which is three nights for rain.

21 Fleas are active.

22 End of the rising of the Euphrates in Iraq.

23 Sowing of *nusūl* and *wasnī* [varieties] of wheat in al-Dhanbatayn, al-'Amākir, and 'Arār (?) in Qā' al-Ajnād, [which is] known for *ṣawmī* [sorghum].

24 End of the days for figs. Lowering of the Tigris and Euphrates.

25 Morning rising of Canopus at dawn. The small *mihrajān* [festival of the Persians]. As dawn breaks, the star called the "navel of the fish" (*surrat al-ḥūt*) [is at midheaven]. Beginning of the last arrival of Egyptian [ships] at 200 [days] after the *nayrūz*.

26 Last availability of young *ṣayfīya* camels in al-Sha'bānīya.

27 Greatest availability and abundance of jasmine.

28 Season for assessing the cotton tax.

29–30 End of abundant rainfall in the mountain areas from the first of [*Āb*?]. Sometimes a rain may occur at the rising of *simāk* as the last of [*ḥamīm*?] . . . The beginning of the rainfall, i.e., the first of the *wasmī* in Yemen, is from *Shubāṭ*. Some years the rain comes later, as in the case of a rain outside a known season. For example, the *rabī'* rain [sometimes] appears during the harvest days. Every rain occurring after the *naw'* of *simāk* is [called] *rabī'*. The *shitā'* (winter) rain may also occur at this *naw'*, because some years the *anwā'* may be later or earlier and the *rabī'* rain only occurs occasionally. This is the most harmful rain for farmers, because of the damage to crop produce in the storage chambers when the rainwater reaches it. God knows best.

31 Cultivation of *thālithī* [sorghum] in the coastal region. The mulberry is no longer available.

Āb (August), or *Dhū Kharāf*

1 [Dawn] rising of the first star of Ursa Major. Grapes are good to eat. First cutting of cane in Najrān. Collection of acacia (*'asaqī*) honey

in al-Ma'āfir, Dhubḥān, and throughout the mountains.

2 Dawn rising of *ṭarf* and setting of *sa'd bula'*, the *naw'* of which is three nights for rain. Availability of broad beans in the mountains. First planting of *bukr* [sorghum] in Laḥj.

3 As dawn breaks, the two faint stars of *sharaṭān* are at midheaven.

4 First planting of *khāmisī* [sorghum] in the coastal region.

5 –

6 The sun is positioned directly overhead [at Ṣan'ā'?] in Yemen at noon. It changes course to the south and [thus] the shadow returns to the north.

7 As dawn breaks, the third star of *sharaṭān* is at midheaven.

8 Rising of the second star of Ursa Major. Canopus rises and disappears. This is also the day of its rising in Iraq. The time between the rising and the disappearance is fourteen days, when it is visible and seen by most people. It will rise before dawn and go to the place of its disappearance, this course being its *i'tirāḍ*. Sometimes the verb *a'ruḍa* is used for this. The hours [between] its rising in the east and setting in the west are nine and seven-tenths hours [i.e., nine plus a half plus a fifth]. The hours between its disappearance and its rising in the east are fourteen and three-tenths [i.e., fourteen plus a fifth plus a tenth]. This is for every day and night over the passage of time.

9 [Dawn] rising of Canopus in the Hejaz and its disappearance from [view in] Yemen. The sun is positioned directly overhead at Ta'izz.

10 Last of Hippocrates' prohibition of drinking medicines. The select time for cultivating *shabb* [sorghum], which is called *khāmisī*, in Surdud and Mawr.

11 –

12 End of the days for peaches and dates.

13 The night cools and the heat of the day increases. Dew falls. [Dawn] rising of Canopus in Syria.

14 The date tax revenues are transported to Zabīd. The taste of fresh ripe dates changes. End of the arrival of the last Egyptian [ships] to Aden at 220 days after the *nayrūz*. First of the *mu'tadilāt* (i.e., temperate weather) for forty days.

15 Dawn rising of *jabha* and setting of *su'ūd*, the *naw'* of which is three nights for rain.

16 Entry of the sun into Virgo. First of the third summer month.

17 Domestic animals gain weight. Chicks increase.

18 Last of the *samūm* [wind].

19 As dawn breaks, the bright star of *buṭayn* is at midheaven. Last

vestiges of cane in Najrān and first transport of this to the districts. Picking of grapes in 'Abadān and areas east (*mashāriq*) of Ṣan'ā'.

20 [Dawn] rising of Canopus in Egypt. Sailing of the Ceylonese and Coromandel (Ṣūliyān) [ships] from Aden.

21 Rising of the third star of Ursa Major. This time is the *tīrmāh* sailing from Aden to India at the Last of the Season, or the Great Season. Vega disappears from view.

22 Availability of parched grain from sorghum in the mountains. First presence of *Carissa edulis* (*'arm*), which is *barbārīs*. This is first present along with the parching in the mountains. It ripens in *Aylūl* and some of it remains until the days of the wheat harvest and the beginning of the sorghum [harvest].

23 This is the most suitable day for the *tīrmāh* sailing of Indian [ships] during the Last of the Season, or the Great Season. This begins at 230 [days] after the *nayrūz*.

24 The taste of fruit changes. Sailing of Dhofari [ships] from Aden by those who want to return to Aden in a short time.

25 The manna and quails fall in certain places.

26 Final ripening of fruit.

27 –

28 Dawn rising of *zubra* and setting of *akhbiya*, the *naw'* of which is four nights for rain.

29 First of the *kharīf* rain. First of the nights of *majar* (?). The Coptic New Year.

30 Rising of the fourth star of Ursa Major. As dawn breaks, the faint star after the Pleiades is at midheaven.

31 Mixing of summer with autumn.

Aylūl (September), or *Dhū 'Allān*

1 First of the time for cutting wood. Availability of apricots in al-Mikhlāf (Milkhlāf Ja'far). As dawn breaks, the bright star of Aldebaran is at midheaven.

2 The select time for planting *khāmisī* [sorghum] in Wādī Zabīd.

3 Falling of dew. Sailing of the Qaysī, Hurmuzī, and Qalhātī [ships] from Aden during the Last of the Season at 240 [days] after the *nayrūz*.

4 Last of the nights of *majar* (?). The thick mist is lifted from Dhofar.

5 Availability of pomegranates in the coastal region.

6 Last sailing of Indian [ships] from Aden and their first sailing from Dhofar.

7 Availability of green peas and green cowpeas at [Jabal] Ṣabir.

8 Season for the *ṣayf* [cropping of sorghum and millet] tax. Last standing of cane on the threshing floors.

9 Arrival of infectious diseases on people. First blowing of the *azyab* wind, which is the southern.

10 Dawn rising of *ṣarfa* and setting of *muqaddam*, the *naw'* of which is three nights for rain. First opening of the narcissus flower. First harvest of [grapes for] raisins in al-'Udayn, al-Ẓāhir, and the Ṣan'ā' region.

11 The heat is over, which is related to the [lunar] station [*ṣarfa*]. As dawn breaks, the star called the "eye" of the Pleiades is at midheaven.

12 First harvest of *muqādim* [barley].

13 First planting of *sābi'ī* [sorghum] in the coastal region. End of the last sailing of Indian [ships] from Aden during the Great Season, or the Last of the Season, at 250 [days] after the *nayrūz*. The usual sailing of the Nbṭī (?) and Barbarī [ships] from Aden. Picking of grapes in the Ṣan'ā' region.

14 Rising of the fifth star of Ursa Major. First departure of the *badrī* [hawk]. Hunting with birds of prey. Departure of sea fowl. This first [departure] is also said to be at the rising of the fourth star [of Ursa Major].

15 Entry of the sun into Libra. Night and day are equal in length.

16 The humor of black bile is active. First collection of honey from the Dead Sea apple in the mountains.

17 First of the wheat and barley harvest in the mountains.

18 As dawn breaks, the head of Orion, or *haq'a*, is at midheaven. Cultivation of *sābi'ī* [sorghum] in Wādī Sihām and at al-Maḥālib in Mawr.

19 The select time for planting *sābi'ī* [sorghum] in the coastal region.

20 The harvest of [grapes for] raisins ceases until the rising of the seventh star [of Ursa Major], because grapes picked during the sixth star will have weak raisins of little value.

21 Rising of the sixth star [of Ursa Major]. Foliage turns yellow.

22 Last of the *mu'tadilāt* [temperate weather of forty days].

23 Dawn rising of *'awwā* and setting of *mu'akhkhar*, the *naw'* of which is three nights for rain. First of the [autumn] *ṣafarīya* days.

24 Passing of the heat and advance of the cold.

25 Season for production of young *ṣayfīya* camels, which are called *ṣirbīya* in al-Sha'bānīya and areas south of Ta'izz.

26 Dates redden in the Hejaz and the coastal region.

27 First of the *lawāqiḥ* days and intense midday sun, which is harmful

to faces.

28 Arrival of the boats from al-Shiḥr in Aden.

29 Last picking of grapes at Ṣan‘ā’. First cutting of sesame in the mountains.

30 Rising of the seventh star of Ursa Major. Last cultivation of *sābi‘ī* [sorghum] in the coastal region. Beginning of the second picking of [grapes for] raisins until the end of them. These are placed on the threshing floors [to dry] for a month or, more often, for two months.

Arabic Text

الباب الثاني والثلثون في القول
على الشهور الإثنى (!) عشر الرومية وذكر الأنواء والمواقيت

تشرين الأوّل – ذو صراب

١ نيروز الروم وأوّل ذري البرّ القصيبي وأوّل ذري الصومي .

٢ ينصرف النيل ويزرع أهل مصر .

٣ يطلع الفجر والثالث من الهقعة وسط السماء .

٤ تنفجر ريح الصبا ووجود الكشد في جبل صبر .

٥ آخر وقت قطع الأخشاب .

٦ الفجر بالسماك وغروب بطن الحوت نوءه أربعة ليال مطراً ، آخر أيّام اللواقح .

٧ أوّل زراعة العشوي .

٨ بدء نقص المياه .

٩ تقلّ البراغيث ، مجيء الكركي وأبو فصادة الى مصر .

١٠ المختار من أيّام ذري البرّ القصيبي الى الخامس والعشرين .

١١ يطلع الفجر والخامس من نجوم الهنعة وهو آخرها والشعري العبور وهي اليمانية في وسط السماء .

١٢ زراعة القرط بمصر وفيه وجود فريك الشبّ .

١٣ يرى السماك الأعزل في أفق المشرق مع طلوع الفجر وفي هذا اليوم وصول المقدشي إلى عدن على مائتين وثمانين من النيروز .

١٤ طلوع الثريّا عشاءً ، تهبّ ريح الجنوب الأزيب وفيه قلع بصل النرجس .

١٥ حلول الشمس العقرب ، يثبت الخريف ويقوي حكمه ، آخر ذري الصومي .

١٦ فيه المهرجان الأوّل وخروج الهندي الديماني إلى عدن أوّل الزمان وفيه سفر المصري من عدن صائح .
١٧ أوان حصاد الذرة بالجبال ووجود الفصلان الصربيّة وأوّل صراب وادي عدينة في الشعبانيّة .
١٨ أوّل الأربعينيّات الأولى ويكثر بيض الدجاج لإنفساحها في المراعي وكثرة الطعام وقوة الشمس لقلّة الأمطار وبالضدّ .
١٩ بدء نقصان النيل بمصر .
٢٠ الفجر بالغفر وغروب الشرطين نوءه ثلث ليال وآخر الأيّام الصفريّة .
٢١ تقوى ريح الأزيب وينقطع خروج الجوارح من البحر ويرفع المرام (المرماك!) وفيه سفر الزيالع من عدن وسفرهم لا ينضبط ووصولهم لا ينقطع يسافرون من عدن بالريح الأزيب إلى زيلع ويصلون على بربرة إلى العارة ويرجعون من العارة إلى زيلع ويصلون بالشمال إلى عدن .
٢٢ يتساقط ورق الشجر .
٢٣ تتشقّ الأرض ، قطع الرمان بصنعاء والتهائم .
٢٤ يطلع الفجر والنجم الذي من الذراع اليماني والنجم الثاني في وسط السماء وفيه وجود شبك القشار وقطع عسله في الجبال .
٢٥ طلوع الدبران عشاء وهو آخر المختار من ذري البرّ القصيبي .
٢٦ —
٢٧ —
٢٨ أوّل الليالي البلق .
٢٩ أوّل طلع النخل المقدام .
٣٠ أوان حصاد البرّ الصربي في قاع الأجناد .
٣١ —

تشرين الثاني – نو مهلة

١ أوّل مطر الربيع باليمن وهو وسمي الشام ويقع أحياناً باليمن وفيه إبتداء زراعة الحنطة بمصر وفيه وصول الهندي إلى عدن ويسمّى

الديماني وهو أوّل الزمان بدائته على ثلثمائة من النيروز .
٢ الفجر بالزبانان وغروب البطين نوءه ثلث ليال ، قيل فيه آخر خروج البدري ووصول مراكب ظفار .
٣ تبرد المياه وهو أوّل وقت البرد وأوّل نصيد الشبّ .
٤ دخول النمل جوف الأرض ، يذهب زمان المنّ والسلوى .
٥ يطلع الفجر واللمعة من النثرة قد مالت عن وسط السماء قليلاً .
٦ يلقط الزيتون بمصر ، تقوى ريح الجنوب وأوّل وصول الهندي والقيسي (قيسي!) إلى عدن.
٧ إنقضاء أيّام الموز الهندي في بلاد الدملوة .
٨ إنقضاء أيّام الرمّان في التهائم .
٩ أوّل شهري جميدى وأوان حصاد الخشخاش .
١٠ آخر نصيد الشبّ وأوّل حمل عليه إلى الأهراء .
١١ خروج المسّاح لقلم الشبّ وإستخراج ماله ووجود البرّ الهليا في بعدان والمخلاف .
١٢ يرفع القصب (العشب!) والزبيب من المجران إلى المخزان ويقع الإختلاف به والبيع إلى كلّ مكان .
١٣ إرتفاع الوباء عن الناس ، طلوع الجوزاء عشاء .
١٤ حلول الشمس القوس أوّل الشهر الثالث من الخريف ، تشبيكة الجانفة على وجه الأرض وتسمّى الفصيعة (؟) .
١٥ يطلع الفجر والنجم النيّر من الطرف وسط السماء ، الفجر بالأكليل وغروب الثريّا نوءه ليلة واحدة وفيه وجود عسل المتشة (؟) في جبال
سردد وهو عسل أبيض طيّب رزين ثخين غليظ لا يجمد [و] يجلب من المدارة (؟) .
١٦ وجود قصب السكّر ، أوّل حدوث الضريب ، متنم النسري في التهائم وهو الخرجي .
١٧ آخر الليالي البلق الأولى .
١٨ يطلع الفجر والنجم الجنوبي من الجبهة في وسط السماء وفيه آخر ذري البرّ القصيبي .

١٩ ينغلق البحر ولا تمشي فيه سفينة .
٢٠ وصول مراكب ظفار إلى عدن .
٢١ فيه نهاية سفر الكارم المصري من عدن في الصائح وهو على ثلثمائة وعشرين من النيروز .
٢٢ سفر المقدشي من عدن على ثلثمائة وعشرين يوماً من النيروز .
٢٣ متنم الحمراء التي تكون بعد الخرجي في التهائم ووجود الكشد في جبال التهائم .
٢٤ يطلع الفجر والنجم الذي يلي الجنوبي من الجبهة في وسط السماء .
٢٥ وجود الهليون في الجند ووجود السمّان والقطا في التهائم .
٢٦ آخر الأربعينيّات الأولى وأوّل الثانيّة وهي المشهورة ، هيجان الإبل .
٢٧ وجود الدعبب .
٢٨ الفجر بالقلب وغروب الدبران نوءه ليلة واحدة .
٢٩ أوّل مطر الولي قد يقع أحياناً وآخر وجود سبول الكاذي .
٣٠ إمتزاج الخريف بالشتاء ، أوان خروج القطرب في مصر ، جنس الغول يهيج بالجهات .

كانون الأوّل – ذو الال

١ أوان جنى القطن في أبين وصراب البكر بابين .
٢ معظم وجود الفصلان الصربيّة وطيّب أكلها وهي أسمن من الصيفيّة .
٣ يطلع الفجر والزبرة في وسط السماء وأوّل جهيش ربعي دثينة .
٤ يخرج البخار من الأفواه وقد يخرج أيضاً في أيّام الغيم في وقت مطر الربيع .
٥ آخر وجود السمن في المخلاف .
٦ —
٧ —
٨ أوان وجود فريك السابعي ، مغيب سهيل مع الفجر .
٩ متنم الجحري في التهائم .

١٠ تعمى الحيّات .

١١ الفجر بالشولة وغروب الهقعة نوءه ليلة واحدة ، يطلع الفجر والصرفة في وسط السماء وفيه وصول القيسي والهرمزي والقلهاتي على ثلثمائة وأربعين من النيروز إلى عدن .

١٢ آخر وقت الضريب ونهاية ميل الشمس في الجهة الجنوبيّة .

١٣ أوان زراعة الكمّون الحبشي باليمن .

١٤ حلول الشمس الجدي وفيه قصر النهار وطول الليل وشدّة البرد ودخول الشتاء ويأخذ النهار بالزيادة والليل بالنقص .

١٥ يتعرى الشجر عن الورق ، فيه طلوع الشعري اليمانيّة عشاء يسمّونها (!) الزرّاعون العلب .

١٦ أوّل كسر قصب السكّر ووجود شبك الضال وقطع عسله في الجبال ، يهيج الخلط البلغمي وسفر المقدشي من عدن .

١٧ زراعة القياض بالجبال .

١٨ أوّل طلع النخل .

١٩ أوان حصاد السابعي في التهائم وإستخراج شجير العطب ويسمّى الصربيّة وهو معظم وجود العطب ورخصه .

٢٠ تجمد المياه .

٢١ نهاية آخر وصول الهندي الديماني إلى عدن الذي يكون في أوّل الزمان على ثلثمائة وخمسين يوماً من النيروز .

٢٢ إنقضاء أيّام الكشد في المهجم .

٢٣ —

٢٤ الفجر بالنعائم وغروب الهنعة نوءه ليلة واحدة (يوم رابع وعشرين ليلة خامس [وعشرين] الميلاد) .

٢٥ المهرجان الثاني .

٢٦ آخر الليالي السود .

٢٧ ربيع الخيل شهرين بمصر ، أوّل الليالي البلق الثانيّة .

٢٨ وجود الحمر وهو التمر هندي في التهائم .

٢٩ صراب ربعي دثينة .

٣٠ يطلع الفجر والنجم الثاني من العوّا وسط السماء .
٣١ —

كانون الثاني – نو داو

١ يجري الماء في العود .
٢ طلوع سهيل عشاء .
٣ صيد البواشق واليؤيؤة التي تكون في الحوازّ وهي أجود من البحريّة التي تصاد في خروج البدري لأنها تكون تلك الأيّام معتلة .
٤ تختفي الهوامّ .
٥ آخر الأربعينيّات الثانية وأوّل الأربعينيّات الثالثة ومتنم البيني في وادي مور.
٦ الفجر ببلع وغروب الذراع نوءه ليلة واحدة ، عيد الغطاس للروم .
٧ أقصى شدّة البرد ويأخذ إلى الإعتدال .
٨ طلوع النسر الواقع وفيه وجود العسل الصيّاب وهو الألب في جبال سردد ، نيروز الفرس وهو يستعمله الهند .
٩ وجود اللبخ (؟) في التهائم ومعظم وصول مراكب قلهات ووجود التمر الفرض في عدن .
١٠ أوان غرس الأشجار وهو أوّل يوم من نيروز الهند .
١١ تهبّ الرياح اللواقح وهي التي تلقح الأشجار وتهزل البهائم .
١٢ حلول الشمس الدلو فصل الشتاء ويقوى حكمه ، فيه تقلّ الأمراض ويسخن باطن الأرض .
١٣ يطلع الفجر والنجم الأوسط من العوّا في وسط السماء .
١٤ تورّق الأشجار وتلألأ الأزهار ، يطلع الفجر والسماك الرامح وسط السماء.
١٥ آخر الليالي البلق الثانيّة وأوان إستخراج مال الغلّة بالجبال وهو المثمّن .
١٦ خروج الهدهد ومتنم البطّيخ في التهائم وإنقشاع الجانفة عن الأرض .

١٧ يرى سهيل بأرض المغرب .
١٨ إنقضاء وجود الفصلان الصيفيّة .
١٩ الفجر بالذابح وغروب النثرة نوءه ليلة واحدة ، تتوسّط الثريّا السماء عشاء .
٢٠ يصفو ماء النيل .
٢١ طلوع النسر الطائر باليمن ، أوّل تلقيح النخل .
٢٢ فيه يدرك القرط بمصر .
٢٣ —
٢٤ —
٢٥ آخر متنم البيني .
٢٦ وجود فريك البرّ القصيبي .
٢٧ إنقضاء وجود الفصلان الصربيّة في الشعبانيّة وغيرها وفيه وجود شبك الحمجة (؟) وقطع عسله وهو الظبّة في جبال سردد وهو أطيب الأنواع .
٢٨-٣٠ الأنواء علامات العرب يتعاهدون فيه الأمطار عند طلوعها مع الفجر بكلّ ما يقال عند طلوعه فهو يعني مع الفجر إلا ما كان مغيباً مثل طلوع الثريّا عشاء وما كان مطلقاً فهو يعني مع الفجر أصل في الأنواء كلّها والله أعلم .

شبـــاط – نو حلل

١ الفجر ببلع وغروب الطرف نوءه ليلة واحدة ، يخرج الماء من العود ومتنم التمري بالتهائم .
٢ يطلع الفجر والنجم الشمالي من الزبانان في وسط السماء .
٣ أوان تقليم الكرم في الجبال .
٤ يتحرّك دود القزّ ، الصوم الكبير للنصارى .
٥ أوّل حصاد البرّ القصيبي وحصاد الصومي .
٦ صوم الصابئين وهو وقت معظم يورّق الشجر تلألأ الأزهار .

٧ سقوط الجمرة الأولى ، يطلع الفجر والنجم الشمالي من غير العقرب في وسط السماء .

٨ وجود فريك عقب السابعي .

٩ سقوط أوّل الصواب .

١٠ أوّل مطر الربيع وهو وسمي اليمن أوّل مطر يقع في السنة وحدوث الغمام إذا لم يكن مطر وقد يتقدّم حدوث الغمام عن هذا الوقت ويتأخر إلى ليالي العجوز والغيم المذكور يقال له الحلل ومن ذلك سمّى شباطاً بالحميريّة (ذو حلل فإن كان به طشّ هين قيل ديمة ويسمّونها (!) أهل الهند الخرف) .

١١ حلول الشمس الحوت أوّل الشهر الثالث من الشتاء .

١٢ يخرج النمل من الأجحرة .

١٣ صوم النصارى قد يتقدّم ويتأخر ما بين ب من شباط إلى ز من آذار ويكون يوم الأثنين .

١٤ الفجر بالسعود وغروب الجبهة نوءه ليلة واحدة ، سقوط الجمرة الثانيّة .

١٥ سقوط آخر الصواب .

١٦ تقوى الريّاح اللواقح وتخرج الهوامّ من الأرض .

١٧ —

١٨ فتور البرد ووجود شبك الظبّة وقطع عسله في الجبال .

١٩ يطلع الفجر والنجم الخفي من القلب في وسط السماء .

٢٠ إنقضاء غرس الأشجار .

٢١ سقوط الجمرة الثالثة .

٢٢ تحمل كلّ شجرة ذات عرق .

٢٣ هيجان الوحوش وفيه تهّب ريح الشمال .

٢٤ آخر الريّاح اللواقح .

٢٥ نصيد عقب السابعي .

٢٦ أوّل ليالي العجوز (سبع ليال وثمان ايّام) ، آخر تلقيح النخل .

٢٧ الفجر بسعد الأخبية وغروب الزبرة نوءة ليلة واحدة ، إمتزاج الشتاء

بالربيع .
٢٨ أوان زراعة الدثاء بالجبال ، آخر وصول مراكب قلهات .

آذار – نو معــون

١ أوّل فتح الورد .
٢ زرع اليقطين .
٣ نصيد الدخن بالمهجم .
٤ آخر ليالي العجوز .
٥ أوان زهر الرمّان الحلو .
٦ يطلع الفجر والنجم النيّر . . . في وسط السماء .
٧ —
٨ تفتح الحيّات أعينها ، فيه آخر سفر الهندي من الهند إلى عدن يسمّى آخر الزمان .
٩ آخر وجود السمّان والقطا في التهائم .
١٠ سقوط السائق الأوّل (يحمل دود القزّ) .
١١ يكتسى الشجر بالورق ، نهاية نقص المياه ، تتنفّس ريح الصبا .
١٢ الفجر بالمقدّم وغروب الصرفة أربع ليال مطراً والنجم الذي في الجبهة من نجوم الأسد في وسط السماء .
١٣ حلول الشمس الحمل ويستوي الليل والنهار بالطول ويعتدل الحر والبرد ويأخذ النهار بالزيادة ويدخل فصل الربيع .
١٤ أوان شرب الأدوية ويهيج الخلط الدموي (البلغمي!).
١٥ ظهور الذباب الأزرق وهوامّ الأرض .
١٦ أوّل زراعة الذرة وحصاد القياض بالجبال ، نهاية سفر الهندي من الهند ولا بقي يسافر بعد هذا اليوم .
١٧ يولّي البرد ويقبل الحرّ .
١٨ —
١٩ وجود فريك البيني .

٢٠ تهيج الطواعين .
٢١ تهبّ ريح الشمال ، الشعانين الكبير .
٢٢ أول سفر الديماني .
٢٣ فيه السفر إلى ظفار لمن أراد الإقامة بها مدّة حتى تدور الريح التي تصل بها مراكب ظفار إلى عدن .
٢٤ البخنيطس الأوّل ، آخر حصاد البرّ القصيبي .
٢٥ الفجر بالمؤخّر وغروب العوّا نوءه ليلة واحدة مطراً .
٢٦ سقوط السائق الثاني وفيه بداية سفر الهندي من عدن الديماني أوّل الزمان وهو على ثمانين من النيروز .
٢٧ يرقى النخل .
٢٨ حصاد البيني في وادي مور .
٢٩ متنم الزعر بسردد ومور .
٣٠ يعصر دهن البلسان .
٣١ البخنيطس الثاني ، إنقضاء أيّام الفول .

نيسان – ذو ثابـــه

١ بدء زيادة المياه ، أوّل وجود المشمش والتفّاح والأجّاص .
٢ يطلع الفجر والنجم الذي يسمّى عين النعائم في وسط السماء .
٣ الشعانين الصغير وأوّل نوء الثريّا .
٤ أوّل وجود البطّيخ في التهائم وفيه عيد الفصح للنصارى وفيه وجود فريك البيني في سردد .
٥ وجود الشاهترّج في الجند .
٦ إستتار الثريّا أربعين يوماً .
٧ البخنيطس الثالث .
٨ تفريخ الطير ، يطلع الفجر والنجم الأوسط من نجوم النعائم الثانيّة في وسط السماء .
٩ الفجر ببطن الحوت وغروب السماك نوءه ليلة واحدة ، يكثر الورد .

١٠ هيجان الزكام وأوجاع العين .
١١ أوّل ولادة الفصلان الصيفيّة في الشعبانيّة والجنوب من أعمال تعزّ .
١٢ —
١٣ البخنيطس الرابع .
١٤ حلول الشمس الثور يثبت فصل الربيع [ويقوى حكمه] ، فيه ظهور الكمأة .
١٥ عيد الفطير لليهود وهو في نصف نيسان عندهم ليس هو نيسان الروم وهو مرتبط بشهور العرب وله عمل يستخرج فيه وعيد المظلّة في نصف تشريهم مع الإستقبال العربي وفيه بداية وصول الهندي إلى عدن آخر الزمان على مائة يوم من النيروز وهو تيرماه الموسم الكبير وفيه أيضاً بداية وصول المصري إلى عدن الأوّل والله أعلم .
١٦ يطلع الفجر والنجم الثاني من القلادة في وسط السماء .
١٧ آخر سفر اللاحق إلى مصر ، آخر سفر الديماني من عدن .
١٨ فيه أوان فتح زهر العرم .
١٩ أوّل زراعة الصيف في التهائم ، أوّل ريّاح الخمسين .
٢٠ الفجر بالشرطين وغروب الغفر نوءه ثلث ليال محموداً وأوّل مطر الثور .
٢١ البخنيطس الخامس .
٢٢ تسامت الشمس الرأس ويرى بـ ... نصف النهار باليمن وتسير إلى الشمال ويرجع الظلّ إلى ناحية الجنوب .
٢٣ أوان قلع الكتّان بمصر .
٢٤ فيه مدّ الفرات مدّه الأعظم (ويبدأ السفر فيها) .
٢٥ أوّل وجود الموز الهندي في بلاد الدملوة .
٢٦ أوّل العشر المختارة .
٢٧ فيه تهبّ الريح الشرقيّة .
٢٨ البخنيطس السادس .
٢٩ أوان ركوب بحر المغرب .
٣٠ يطيب البطّيخ

أيّــار – نو مبكر

١ أوّل شدّة الحرّ وأوّل زراعة السمسم في الجبال ومتتم الثوري في مور.

٢ أول السبوت ، هو أوّل سبت من آيّار .

٣ الفجر بالبطين وغروب الزبانان نوءه ثلث ليال .

٤ أوّل زراعة العشوي بالتهائم ، طلوع القلب عشاء .

٥ آخر العشر المختارة ، البخنيطس السابع .

٦ يطلع الفجر والنيّر من النسر الواقع وسط السماء وفيه نهاية سفر الديماني من عدن على مائة وعشرين من النيروز وفيه أيضاً بداية سفر المصري في (اللاحق وهو آخر ريح الأزيب على مائة وعشرين من النيروز وفيه نهاية وصول المصري الأوّل إلى عدن) .

٧ معظم وجود الفصلان الصيفيّة وطيّب أكلها في الشعبانيّة .

٨ أوّل إستتار سهيل باليمن فلا يرى حتى يعود إلى موضع ظهوره في الخامس والعشرين من تموّز وعند طلوعه تغزر الأمطار كما قيل إذا طلع سهيل فأبشر بسيل بعد سيل وطلوعه عشاء ضدّ ذلك .

٩ عيد الورد بمصر .

١٠ إنقضاء أيّام البطّيخ في التهائم وأوّل فتح الكاذي .

١١ إنقضاء وجود الدعبب (؟) وأوّل إستخراج مال العشر في المهجم .

١٢ [أوّل سبوت] النخل الحقيقي لكن قد يتقدّم بيومين أو يتأخر كذلك لآخر يوم السبت لإصلاح أهل النخل يوم السبت .

١٣ يطيب المشمش والأجّاص .

١٤ حلول الشمس الجوزاء أوّل الشهر الثالث من شهور الربيع ، طلوع العيّوق ووجود بلس صهلة ويزهى النخل ويتلوّن الرطب .

١٥ أوّل زراعة الجوزي بالتهائم ، حضان الطير .

١٦ الفجر بالثريّا وغروب الأكليل نوءه خمسة ليال ، بداية سفر القيسي والهرمزي والقلهاتي من عدن على مائة وثلثين من النيروز (أوّل الزمان وفيه نهاية سفر المصري في اللاحق على مائة وثلثين منه) .

١٧ آوان وجود الكرم والتين والرطب ، أوّل الريّاح البوارح .

١٨ أوّل زراعة المقادم بالجبال والذرة بالأعمال الصنعانيّة .
١٩ أوّل مطر الثور وزراعة الخشخاش ، إنفتاح البحر المالح .
٢٠ آوان حصاد الأرزّ بمصر وهو الوقت المختار لمتنم الصيف في التهائم.
٢١ إنقضاء الورد .
٢٢ فيه يطلع الفجر وسعد بلع في وسط السماء .
٢٣ آوان وجود التوت في نواحي جبلة وأوّل وجود العنب .
٢٤ آخر السفر إلى قيس .
٢٥ فيه آخر البوارح .
٢٦ آخر كسر قصب السكّر وأوّل سفر القلهاتي من عدن وآخر سفر اللاحق من عدن .
٢٧ وجود زهر الياسمين .
٢٨ آخر زراعة الذرة بالجبال .
٢٩ الفجر بالدبران وغروب القلب نوءه ثلث ليال ، تهبّ ريح السموم وآوان إستخراج العطب بالمهجم مقبلاً ويسمّى الصيفيّة .
٣٠ أوّل مطر الحميم .
٣١ إمتزاج الربيع بالصيف (ويبطل سفر الفرات) .

حزيران – نو قيــض

١ آوان وجود الخوخ وأوّل وجود الرطب وأوّل وجود حبّ البان .
٢ أوّل السمائم وشدّة البوارح .
٣ يطلع الفجر والنجم الجنوبي الخفي من سعد السعود في وسط السماء.
٤ فيه سفر المقدشي من عدن .
٥ نهاية وصول الهندي في تيرماه إلى عدن آخر الزمان على مائة وخمسين من النيروز ونهاية سفر القيسي والهرمزي والقلهاتي من عدن.
٦ أوّل سفر المقدشي من عدن .
٧ فيه تتحرّك الباه .

٨ توخم النيل بمصر ، آخر ريّاح الخمسين .
٩ تلهب (!) .
١٠ تلهب حمارّة القيض ، هبوب الريّاح العواصف .
١١ الفجر بالهقعة وغروب الشولة نوءه ثلث ليال ، فيه النيروز المعتضدي .
١٢ حلول الشمس في الجهة الشماليّة ووجود العنب والخوخ في الجنّات .
١٣ فيه يطلع الفجر ونجما سعد الأخبية في وسط السماء .
١٤ حلول الشمس السرطان طول النهار وقصر الليل وشدّة الحرّ وطلوع منكب الجوزاء .
١٥ يهيج الخلط الصفراوي .
١٦ يطيب التين ووقوع الخرف بظفار .
١٧ —
١٨ أوّل وجود الجوز .
١٩ فيه أوّل أيّام الباحور .
٢٠ فيه يطلع الفجر والنجم الأوسط من الأخبية في وسط السماء .
٢١ يطيب الرطب الثعل .
٢٢ وجود العنب والخوخ في الجنّات .
٢٣ إندفاع النيل ، فيه يطلع الفجر والثالث من نجوم سعد الأخبية بوسط السماء .
٢٤ الفجر بالهنعة وغروب النعائم نوءه ثلث ليال .
٢٥ أوّل مطر الرمضي .
٢٦ فيه آخر أيّام الباحور .
٢٧ أوّل نهي بقراط عن الدواء .
٢٨ —
٢٩ يطيب التوت .
٣٠ خروج الكارم المصري من مصر إلى عدن .

تمّــوز – نو مـــذرا

١ آوان وجود السفرجل والرمّان ، يطلع الفجر والنجمان الخفيان من المقدّم في وسط السماء .

٢ —

٣ تستوي الأعناب ويطيب التين وآوان وجود عنب الجنّات .

٤ —

٥ ينقضي بلس صهلة ويطيب عنب الجنّات .

٦ —

٧ الفجر يالذراع وغروب البلدة ونوءه ثلث ليال مطراً .

٨ تذهب الطواعين .

٩ أقصى شدّة الحرّ ، طلوع الشعري اليمانيّة .

١٠ تغور عيون المياه ، أوّل زراعة الباجسي في التهائم .

١١ تهيج أوجاع العين .

١٢ يطلع الفجر والنجم الشمالي من المؤخرّ على الرأس والجنوبي قبال الوجه .

١٣ وجود شبك العسقي وقطع عسله في الجبال .

١٤ آوان إستخراج مال المستفتح في الجبال .

١٥ حلول الشمس الأسد يثبت فصل الصيف ويقوى حكمه وفيه أوّل وصول المصري ويبرد باطن الأرض .

١٦ يبرد باطن الأرض ، آوان لقط الجوز .

١٧ آخر زراعة البرّ بالجبال .

١٨ يستوي الخوخ ويطيب .

١٩ إنصرام (!) أيّام النخل .

٢٠ الفجر بالنثرة وغروب سعد الذابح ونوءه ثلث ليال مطراً .

٢١ تتحرّك البراغيث .

٢٢ نهاية مدّ الفرات بالعراق .

٢٣ ذري البرّ النسول والوسنى بالذنبتين والعماكر وعرار بقاع الأجناد

المعروف بالصومي .

٢٤ إنقضاء أيّام التين ، فيه نقصان دجلة والفرات .

٢٥ طلوع سهيل صبحاً وقت الفجر وفيه المهرجان الصغير وفيه يطلع الفجر والنجم الذي يقال له سرّة الحوت [في وسط السماء] وفيه بداية وصول المصري الآخر على مائتين من النيروز .

٢٦ آخر وجود الفصلان الصيفيّة في الشعبانيّة .

٢٧ معظم وجود الياسمين وكثرته .

٢٨ آوان إستخراج مال العطب .

٢٩-٣٠ نهاية غزر الأمطار في الأعمال الجبليّة من أوّله ... وقد يقع مع طلوع السماك المطر أحياناً وهو آخر أمطار [الحميم] ... وأما إبتداؤها فمن شباط وهو أوّل الوسمي باليمن وقد يتأخر الأمطار في بعض السنين كما قد يأتي المطر أيضاً في غير وقته كمطر الربيع الذي يظهر أيّام الحصاد لأنّ كلّ مطر يقع بعد نوء السماك فهو منأمطار الربيع وقد يتفّق مع نوءه مطر الشتاء لأنّ الأنواء قد تتأخر في بعض السنين وقد تتقدّم ومطر الربيع يأتي في بعض سنين دون بعض وهو أعظم مضرّة على الزرّاعين لأضراره في الغلة في المخازين فيبلغها المطر والله أعلم.

٣١ متنم الثالثي في التهائم وفيه ينقضي التوت (الفول!) .

آب – ذو خـراف

١ طلوع أوّل بنات نعش ، تطيب الأعناب وهو أوّل قطع القصب (العشب!) بنجران وقطع العسل العسقي في المعافر وذبحان والجبال كلّها .

٢ الفجر بالطرف وغروب سعد بلع نوءه ثلث ليال مطراً ، وجود الفول بالجبال وأوّل زرع البكر بلحج .

٣ يطلع الفجر والنجمان الخفيان من الشرطين في وسط السماء .

٤ أوّل زراعة الخامسي بالتهائم .

٥ —

٦ تسامت الشمس الرأس ويرى بـ ... نصف النهار باليمن وتسير إلى الجنوب ويرجع الظلّ إلى الشمال .

٧ يطلع الفجر والنجم الثالث من الشرطين في وسط (اوسط!) السماء .

٨ طلوع ثاني بنات نعش ، يعرض سهيل وفي هذا اليوم أيضاً يكون طلوعه بالعراق فإذا أعرض سهيل يكون [بين] طلوعه وإعتراضه أربعة عشر يوماً وفي هذه الأيّام التي بين طلوعه وإعتراضه يتبين ويراه الجمهور من الناس ويكون يطلع قبل الفجر ويسير إلى موضع مغيبه وسيره هذا هو إعتراضه فيقال حينئذٍ إعترض سهيل وأما الساعات بين طلوعه من مشرقه وبين مغربه فتسع ساعات ونصف وخمس والساعات بين مغيبه وطلوعه من مشرقه أربعة (!) عشر ساعة وخمس عشر وذلك في كلّ يوم وليلة على مرور الزمان .

٩ طلوع سهيل بالحجاز وإستتاره باليمن وتسامت الشمس الرأس بتعزّ .

١٠ آخر نهي بقراط عن شرب الدواء وهو الوقت المختار لمتنم الشبّ المسمّى الخامسي بسردد ومور .

١١ —

١٢ إنقضاء أيّام الخوخ والنخل .

١٣ يبرد الليل وينقص حرّ النهار ويسقط الطلّ ، طلوع سهيل بالشأم .

١٤ يرتفع رسم النخل بزبيد ويتغيّر الرطب وفيه نهاية وصول المصري الآخر إلى عدن على مائتين وعشرين يوماً من النيروز وأوّل المعتدلات وهي أربعون يوماً .

١٥ الفجر بالجبهة وغروب السعود نوءه ثلث ليال مطراً .

١٦ حلول الشمس السنبلة أوّل الشهر الثالث من شهور الصيف .

١٧ تسمن البهائم وتكثر الفراريج .

١٨ آخر السموم .

١٩ يطلع الفجر والنجم المضيء من البطين في وسط السماء ، إنتهاء قلّة القصب (العشب!) بنجران وأوّل حمله إلى المخاليف وقطع العنب بعبدان ومشارق صنعاء.

٢٠ طلوع سهيل بمصر ، سفر السيلان والصوليان من عدن .

٢١ طلوع ثالث بنات نعش وفيه سفر التيرماه من عدن إلى الهند ويسمّى آخر الزمان وهو الموسم الكبير وفيه يغيب النسر الواقع .

٢٢ وجود فريك الذرة بالجبال وأوّل وجود العرم وهو البرباريس فأوّل وجوده مع وجود الفريك في الجبال ويستوي في أيلول ويقيم شيء بعد شيء إلى أيّام حصاد البرّ وأوّل الذرة .

٢٣ في هذا اليوم سفر الهندي تيرماه وهو الأصحّ آخر الزمان وهو الموسم الكبير بدايته على مائتين وثلثين من النيروز .

٢٤ يتغيّر طعم الفاكهة وفيه سفر الظفاري من عدن لمن أراد يرجع إلى عدن قريباً .

٢٥ يسقط المنّ والسلوى في مواضعه .

٢٦ إستكمال الثمار .

٢٧ —

٢٨ الفجر بالزبرة وغروب الأخبية نوءه أربع ليال مطراً .

٢٩ أوّل مطر الخريف ، أوّل ليالي مجر وفيه نيروز القبط .

٣٠ طلوع رابع بنات نعش ، يطلع الفجر والنجم الخفي الذي بعد الثريّا في وسط السماء .

٣١ إمتزاج الصيف بالخريف .

أيلول – ذو علاّن

١ أوّل وقت قطع الأخشاب ووجود المشمش في المخلاف ، يطلع الفجر والنجم النيّر من الدبران في وسط السماء .

٢ هو الوقت المختار لزراعة الخامسي بوادي زبيد .

٣ سقوط الطلّ وفيه سفر القيسي والهرمزي والقلهاتي من عدن آخر الزمان على مائتين وأربعين من النيروز .

٤ آخر ليالي مجر ، يرتفع الخرف من ظفار .

٥ وجود الرمّان في التهائم .

٦ آخر سفر الهندي من عدن وأوّل سفرهم من ظفار .

٧ وجود العتر الأخضر بصبر واللوبياء الخضراء .
٨ أوان إستخراج مال الصيف وآخر إقامة القصب (العشب!) في المجارين .
٩ حلول الوباء بالناس ، أوّل هبوب الأزيب وهو الجنوب .
١٠ الفجر بالصرفة وغروب المقدّم نوءه ثلث ليال مطراً وأوّل فتح النرجس وإبتداء قطف الزبيب في العدين والظاهر وبلاد صنعاء .
١١ ينصرف الحرّ وإليه نسبت المنزلة ، يطلع الفجر والنجم الذي يقال له عين الثريّا في وسط السماء .
١٢ أوّل حصاد المقادم .
١٣ أوّل زراعة السابعي في التهائم وفيه نهاية آخر سفر الهندي من عدن في الموسم الكبير الذي هو آخر الزمان على مائتين وخمسين من النيروز وفيه سفر النبطي (؟) والبربري على الأغلب من عدن وفيه قطف الأعناب بالأعمال الصنعانيّة .
١٤ طلوع خامس بنات نعش وهو أوّل خروج البدري وصيد جوارح الصيد وخروج الطيور البحريّة وقد قيل يكون أوّلها في طلوع الرابع .
١٥ حلول الشمس الميزان يستوي الليل والنهار بالطول .
١٦ يهيج الخلط السوداوي وأوّل قطع عسل القشار في الجبال .
١٧ أوّل حصاد البرّ والشعير في الجبال .
١٨ يطلع الفجر ورأس الجوزاء وهو الهقعة في وسط السماء ومتنم السابعي بوادي سهام ومور بالمحالب .
١٩ هو الوقت المختار لزراعة السابعي بالتهائم .
٢٠ يتوقّف قطيف الزبيب إلى طلوع السابع لأنّ العنب إذا قطف في السادس جاء زبيبه خفيفاً هيّناً .
٢١ طلوع سادس بنات نعش ، يصفر ورق الشجر .
٢٢ آخر المعتدلات .
٢٣ الفجر بالعوّا وغروب المؤخّر ونوءه ثلث ليال مطراً وأوّل أيّام الصفريّة .
٢٤ يولّي الحرّ وإقبال البرد .
٢٥ أوان نتاج الفصلان الصيفيّة وتسمّى الصربيّة في الشعبانيّة والجنوب

التعزّيّة .

٢٦ يحمّر النخل بالحجاز وتهامة .

٢٧ أوّل أيّام اللواقح وشدّة الهواجر ، تلقح الشمس الوجوه .

٢٨ وصول مراكب الشحر إلى عدن .

٢٩ آخر قطيف الأعناب بصنعاء وأوّل قلع السمسم في الجبال .

٣٠ طلوع سابع بنات نعش ، آخر متتم السابعي في التهائم ، إبتداء القطيف الثاني للزبيب إلى إنتهائه ويقيم في المجارين شهراً ومعظمه شهرين .

Part Two

CONTEXT

Chapter 1

Calendars

The almanac is essentially an annotated calendar, so it is first and foremost a documentation of medieval time-keeping. A number of calendars were available in the Islamic world. The lunar calendar, which was the basis for the religious year, could only be used for a seasonal almanac if it was correlated to the solar or stellar time-keeping systems, which defined the annual round of seasons. Al-Malik al-Ashraf followed the standard almanac tradition in Arabic by orienting his information according to the Julian reckoning of the Syriac months. However, he also provided correlations to the local Himyaritic months, the Coptic months, the Persian calendar, and various star calendars. This chapter discusses the types of calendar referred to in the text, with details on basic festivals and commemorations of past religious events. The star calendars are described in chapter 2.

JULIAN RECKONING

The almanac is arranged in chart form, with each folio comprising a month in the Julian reckoning of solar months. The month names are from the Syriac (Suryānīya) calendar, which was adopted into Arabic, and begin with *Tishrīn al-Awwal*, the equivalent of October. The Syriac month names are in many cases cognates of older names found in the Hebrew and Babylonian calendars. In Yemen the Syriac months are referred to as Rūmī, a reference to the Byzantine Christian culture in this context.[1] Use of these month names survives to the present in Arabic and they were the basis for medieval Arab almanacs compiled east of Egypt. The month names used in the Christian West, including Islamic Spain, are not cited in al-Ashraf's almanac; however, the author refers to them directly in another part of his astronomical treatise. These are the terms which serve as the basis of the modern Western calendar (i.e., January, etc.).

The Julian reckoning, as the name indicates, stems from the era of Julius Caesar, who instituted a solar year of 365 1/4 days in 45 B.C. It is interesting to note that in the medieval Islamic period this reckoning system was attributed to the famed Dhū al-Qarnayn, who is usually identified with Alexander the Great.[2] This system became the dominant calendar in the early Christian church, although different names were used for the specific months according to the rite. The Julian calendar included a leap year every four years, but there was still a loss vis-à-vis the sidereal year of eleven minutes and fourteen seconds per year. This amounted to about one day about every 128 years due to lack of a precise fit with the seasonal round.[3] By A.D. 1582 the cumulative error of the Julian calendar had reached thirteen days and was wreaking havoc with the determination of Church festivals and liturgical time-keeping. At this time Pope Gregory sponsored a reform of the calendar to the present system, although it was not immediately adopted in Christendom. It is still not a perfect fit, but the loss now is only one day every 3,300 years.

Because the almanac was compiled about the year A.D. 1271, well before the reform of Pope Gregory, the dates expressed are about eight days earlier than they should be. This error factor is not relevant for most seasonal and agricultural activities, but it must be taken into account for the analysis of star risings and settings. The dates discussed in this study are not correlated to the modern system, since the important point is the comparison of these dates with those in other medieval and earlier classical texts. As a practical guide, however, the correlation can readily be made by adding eight days to any date mentioned in the almanac.

The Syriac month names in the almanac are *Tishrīn al-Awwal* (October), *Tishrīn al-Thānī* (November), *Kānūn al-Awwal* (December), *Kānūn al-Thānī* (January), *Shubāṭ* (February), *Ādhār* (March), *Nīsān* (April), *Ayyār* (May), *Ḥazīrān* (June), *Tammūz* (July), *Āb* (August), *Aylūl* (September).

HIMYARITIC MONTH NAMES

For each month of the solar calendar al-Malik al-Ashraf provided the equivalent Himyaritic term, as preserved in the medieval Yemeni dialects of Arabic. A number of the terms, as noted below, survive as names of seasons or agricultural periods in the Yemeni countryside today. Several Yemeni texts include the Himyaritic month names, although there is a fair amount of variation in the Arabic renderings.[4] It should be noted that there was more than one listing of months in pre-Islamic South Arabia, although medieval Yemeni writers standardized a list of so-called Himyaritic months in Arabic. Unfortunately, the author of the almanac did not provide a description of how the Himyaritic system worked, nor did he discuss it anywhere else in his astronomical treatise. It appears that the original calendar was poorly understood by the medieval Yemeni scholars who have preserved the month names. While the Arabic renderings provide a useful source for comparison with the South Arabic inscriptions, they must be used with caution. There is no independent evidence that the Himyaritic names originally corresponded exactly to the Julian reckoning as implied in the text. The general meanings of the names and their sequence fit known periods in the agricultural cycle. This was a common tradition for naming months in earlier Semitic contexts, for example, at Mari (Greengus 1987:221).

Each of the Himyaritic month names mentioned by the author is discussed below in the order arranged in the almanac. The prefix *dhū* appears in each name and its use is related to the well-known function of the term as an *ism ishāra*, which was quite common in Yemeni place names (e.g., Dhū Jibla) and proper names (e.g., Dhū Nuwās). This usage also survives in the two Islamic month names of *Dhū al-Qa'da* and *Dhū al-Ḥijja.*

Dhū Ṣirāb (October, or *Tishrīn al-Awwal*)

This important term is derived from the South Arabic month name *ḏṣrbn*. In South Arabic the term refers to the harvest or a harvest season (Beeston et al. 1982:144). There is no voweling indicated for this term in the almanac, but *ṣirāb* (voweled the same as *kitāb*) is the form documented in *al-Muḥīṭ* and *Tāj al-'arūs*. Ismā'īl al-Akwa' (1984:2:864, 965) also reads this as *ṣirāb* in his discussion of a Yemeni proverb. In contemporary dialects the word often sounds more like *ṣurāb* (Rossi 1940:310; Serjeant 1974a:64, note 67; Varisco 1985a:84). In the later *Bughya* the name *Dhū al-Ṣirāb al-Awwal* is used for October. In *Shams al-'ulūm*, however, *Dhū al-Ṣirāb* is equated with September (*Aylūl*), which is indicative of the lack of precise fit with the Julian months.

The term *ṣirāb/ṣurāb* is used throughout Yemen for the autumn harvest (I. al-Akwa' 1968:409, 1984:2:722; al-'Ansī 1980; al-'Awdī 1980:147; Dostal 1983:280; Glaser 1885:89; Grohmann 1934:2:18; 'Inān 1980:72; Messick 1978:440; Mitchell et al. 1978:58; Rossi 1939:151, 1940:310; Serjeant 1974a:57; Varisco 1982a:113). The author of the almanac equates *ṣirāb* with *ḥiṣād*, the common Arabic term for "harvest." The Yemeni usage is recorded in *al-Muḥīṭ* as what is sown and then reaches its full extent in autumn (*mā yuzra'u ba'dmā yurfa'u fī al-kharīf*). According to the *Bughya*, the *ṣirāb* harvest occurs in October for *sha'īr* (barley), *zabīb* (raisins), *tīn* (figs), *'atar* (sweet peas), and *ḥilba* (fenugreek). The almanac also mentions a variety of wheat called *ṣirbī,* which is harvested in October. In his almanac chart the contemporary al-'Ansī (1980) defines *ṣirāb* as a cropping of wheat, barley, and legumes planted in July and harvested in October. Serjeant (1974a:64, note 67) equates this term with *ḥaṣīl al-ṣayf*, a harvest in late August and September. The sense of an autumn season is also found outside the Yemeni highlands among the al-Qarā (Dostal 1975:36; Thomas 1932:18) and in Dhofar (Johnstone 1981:24). The almanac uses the term *ṣirbīya* for young camels born in the autumn; this usage is said by the author to come from al-Sha'bānīya near the southern highland town of Ta'izz.

The verbal form *ṣaraba* is equivalent in many instances to *ṣarama* or *qaṭa'a*, as noted in *al-Muḥīṭ*, *Shams al-'ulūm*, *Tāj al-'arūs*, and al-Hamdānī (1884:1:199). This sense of cutting or harvesting has been widely recorded in contemporary Yemeni dialects (al-Adīmī 1989:233; I. al-Akwa' 1984:2: 800, 1177; Johnstone 1981:241; Landberg 1901:1:311; Rossi 1940:310; Varisco 1985a:66).

Dhū Muhla (November, or *Tishrīn al-Thānī*)

This term is derived from the South Arabic *ḏmhltn*, which is apparently related to the Arabic root *mhl*. No voweling is indicated in the text or in the other sources. The form *muhla* is found in the major lexicons, but none record the usage as a month name or specific time period. Beeston (1956:17) suggests that the basic meaning of the term is a delaying or slackening, based on the Arabic usage, and thus may refer to a time when there is less agricultural activity. In fact this is a busy month for farmers, so the idea of a slackening in agricultural activity is not viable. Muḥammad al-Akwa' (1981:13), on the other hand, thinks the term derives from the desire of the farmers to delay the march of time so as to complete the harvest. It is interesting to note that the *Bughya* refers to this month as *Dhū al-Ṣirāb al-Ākhir*, and al-Baḥr al-Na'āmī apparently recorded *al-Ṣirāb al-Thānī*. This would refer to a second or last part of the harvest.

The original meaning of the term is not readily apparent from later Arabic usage. *Lisān al-'Arab* notes the expression *dhū muhal/muhla* as referring to someone who is advanced in something such as knowledge or goodness. Perhaps the term refers to the advanced stage of the harvest, although such speculation implies a close link between the Himyaritic system and the application of the Julian calendar to the Yemeni agricultural cycle. The related term *mahl* can refer to a period without rain; the autumn rains usually end by November in Yemen. Whatever the original intent, firm evidence for the origin of the term must await future research on the growing corpus of South Arabic texts.

Dhū al-Āl (December, or *Kānūn al-Awwal*)

The meaning of this month name is also unclear from the available evidence. The related South Arabic month name is *ḏ'aln*. The South Arabic root, *'wl*, signifies "obtain, bring back, get back" (Beeston et al. 1982:10). The term *āl* in Arabic has a variety of meanings; it can refer to a family or tribal group, as in the popular designation Āl Fulān. The same term can also denote the best variety of camel. The lexicon *al-Muḥīṭ* records a usage of *āla* with the meaning of "intensity" (*shidda*) or "quick death." Could this be a reference to the intensity of the cold in December, a phenomenon mentioned in the almanacs? It should be noted that Muḥammad al-Akwaʿ (1981:13) cites *Dhū al-Awwal* (!) in his flawed edition of the almanac poem of al-Baḥr al-Naʿāmī.

Dhū Daʾw (January, or *Kānūn al-Thānī*)

There is considerable confusion about this term in the available almanacs and related Yemeni texts. The almanac records *daʾw*, while the *Bughya* has *dwā* (!), al-Baḥr al-Naʿāmī apparently reads *dbāw* (!),[5] Ibn Raḥīq has *rbāda* (!), al-Rāzī al-Ṣanʿānī (1974:241) recorded *Dhū al-Dibā* (!), and Jaʿfar al-Ṣādiq has *dithā* (!). Although a certain number of copyist errors are to be expected, this term appears to have given Yemeni copyists particular trouble. Beeston (1974) assumes that this term should be read as the South Arabic *ḏdṯʾn* in reference to a month term found in some texts, but Robin (1981:44) argues that the latter was only found among the Banī Sumʿay, a pre-Islamic tribe located north of Ṣanʿāʾ. The precise term and its origin are still uncertain, pending the discovery of further inscriptions.

"Spring harvest" is the basic meaning of the South Arabic term *dithāʾ* (Beeston et al. 1982:36). Pliny called the spring incense crop in Arabia Felix *dathiathum*, which is obviously taken from the South Arabic. In contemporary usage in Yemen *dithāʾ* and its variants can refer to a spring harvest (Glaser 1885:89; Rossi 1939:151, 1940:302), spring planting (M. al-Akwaʿ 1971:62; Dostal 1983:280; Dresch 1989:297; Serjeant 1974a:40), or spring rain (Glaser in Grohmann 1934:2:19 for Dhamār). A Hebrew cognate of *dithāʾ* was used in the 1st-century A.D. calendar of the Qumran sect in Palestine, where the term referred to spring or the season of tender shoots (de Vaux 1965:184). The term is also found in Akkadian in the sense of spring grass or pasture and the season itself (Talmon 1986:105).

The sense of a spring rain is found among the pre-Islamic Arabian Bedouins (Varisco 1987:255–56). *Dathaʾī*, or *dafaʾī*, is a rain that falls when the heat begins to intensify. Ibn Kunāsa added that this was a rain at the time of heat following the cold of winter, a fact which implies a connection with the spring season. The authors of the early *anwāʾ* texts (see chapter 2) place the *dathaʾī* or *dafaʾī* rain under the setting stations of *jabha*, *zubra*, and *ṣarfa*, that is, commencing around II:10 and lasting until about III:20. This rain is usually said to follow the winter (*shatawī*) rain and precede the spring (*ṣayyif* or *rabī'*) rain.

Dhū Ḥulal (February, or *Shubāṭ*)

The South Arabic term for this month is *ḏḥltn*, and in the other almanac sources the feminine form is sometimes used. Al-Malik al-Ashraf provided a discussion of the term, including the voweling as *ḥulal*. He described it as a Himyaritic term for coldness at the appearance of heavy rain clouds in February (*dhū al-ḥulal li-kathrat al-ghaym ka-al-ḥilla*).[6] This definition of coldness is echoed by al-Rāzī in *Mukhtār al-ṣiḥāḥ*. In the *Mu'allaqāt* poems Imru' al-Qays cited the related term *muḥallal* in reference to the start of the cold season (al-Zawzanī 1978:16). A contemporary Yemeni proverb may reflect a related usage of the term, according to Muḥammad al-Akwa' (1981:14). This proverb reads "When the month of Seven has arrived, the earth will be adorned" (*ḥīn mā ḥallat al-sab' ḥalliyat*).[7] The reference here is to a tribal reckoning of months according to the conjunction of the moon and the Pleiades (Varisco 1989b). The number "seven" in this context refers to the occurrence of the conjunction between the moon and the Pleiades at this time of year about seven nights after the first new moon of the lunar month. Muḥammad al-Akwa' believes that the use of this verb implies the coming of the spring rains. In Kuwait the Bedouins use the term *ḥilāl* to mean going out to pasture in the spring, when plants appear from the rains (al-Muṭayrī 1984:14, 20).

Dhū Ma'ūn (March, or *Ādhār*)

The meaning of this term is not clear from Arabic usage, although *mā'ūn* can refer to water according to the lexicons. The South Arabic month name is *ḏm'nn*, with Rossi (1940:307) defining *ma'ūn* as the beginning of spring. This is the major time for the spring rains in Yemen, so it is likely that the original meaning relates to this important seasonal event.

Dhū Thāba (April, or *Nīsān*)

The South Arabic name for this month is *ḏṯbtn*, which has the general meaning of "permanence" or "enduring" based on the Arabic. The South Arabic term *ṯbt* is apparently used for a cistern or tank of water (Beeston et al. 1982:149). The origin of the month name is not explained in any of the texts. Robin (1981) argues that this was the first month in the Himyaritic calendar. One possibility for the meaning of the term is that at this time there is permanent pasture established by the earlier spring rains. The verbal form *tathbatu* was used in a later Rasulid almanac (Taymūr at I:30) to indicate that pasture was available, although this may be a coincidence. This name is cited as *Dhū al-Thāna* (!) in Ja'far al-Ṣādiq and *Dhū Nāba* (!) in the edition of al-Baḥr al-Na'āmī's almanac poem. Both of these are no doubt copyist errors.

Dhū Mabkar (May, or *Ayyār*)

The South Arabic month name *ḏmbkrn* survives in contemporary Yemeni dialects as a synonym of *Ayyār*, or May (Messick 1978:440; Serjeant 1954:441; Serjeant and al-'Amrī 1981:425, notes 130, 131). Beeston (1974:4) argues that it is so called because it is the first month in the calendar, although this is disputed by Robin (1981). The term literally refers to the first of something. Thus *bakūr* in classical Arabic refers to the first fruits of dates or crops (Ibn Sīda 1965:9:8), as does a Hebrew cognate. The date crop first starts to ripen in Yemen in May. In al-Ḥujarīya *bikr al-ṣayf* refers to the start of the spring rains (Nāmī 1948:7). The almanac records a variety of sorghum at Laḥj called *bukr*, which was harvested in August.

Dhū Qayḍ (June, or *Ḥazīrān*)

The term *qayḍ* is a variant of *qayẓ*, a general term in Arabic for the heat of summer. The South Arabic month name *ḏqyẓn* relates to the sense of summer or a summer harvest. There is also a Hebrew cognate for the summer season (de Vaux 1965:184). It is not uncommon to find *qayẓ* cited in medieval texts for summer rather than *ṣayf*, which in most of the Arabian Peninsula, including Yemen, refers to the spring season. The rain falling in *qayẓ* was important for the farmers in Yemen, as noted long ago by Ibn Qutayba (1956:114), although it was not necessarily welcomed by pastoralists, who would see the resulting grass quickly dry up in the heat. The pre-Islamic terms for rain falling during *qayẓ* include *ḥamīm, ṣayyif, ramaḍī*, and *shamsī*; all of these share the sense in Arabic of a warm rain. To the contemporary Bedouins of the Arabian Peninsula the summer season of *qayẓ* is when the heat is most intense, plants dry up, and they must return to their water sources (al-Muṭayrī 1984:13). The *Bughya*, Ja'far al-Ṣādiq, and the published text of al-Baḥr al-Na'āmī all render the Himyaritic term as *qiyāḍ* (!). This is no doubt due to confusion with the well-known Yemeni term *qiyāḍ*, but the latter refers to a winter cropping and is unrelated to classical usage.

Dhū Madhrā (July, or *Tammūz*)

The South Arabic month name *ḏmḏr'n* is related to the sense of sowing, the usage in classical Arabic. The author explains that this month was so named because it was the main time for sowing grains such as wheat and barley in the mountains of Yemen.[8] As noted in the almanac, several varieties of sorghum are also planted in the coastal region during this month. The common dialect term for "sowing" in Yemen today is *dharī* [9] and a sowing time is often called *waqt al-madhārī* (I. al-Akwa' 1984:2:858; Serjeant 1974a:37; Serjeant and al-'Amrī 1981:426, note 194; Varisco 1985a:62). The *Bughya* reads the month name as *Dhū Madhrān* (!), and the texts of al-Baḥr al-Na'āmī, Ibn al-Raḥīq, and Ja'far al-Ṣādiq all cite *Dhū Amdhrān* (!).

Dhū Kharāf (August, or *Āb*)

The South Arabic month name *ḏkhrfn* is clearly related to the Arabic usage of *kharīf* for "autumn" or "autumn rain." The author said that the term is derived from the harvesting (*ikhtirāf*) at this time.[10] This Arabic usage relates primarily to the date harvest on the Arabian Peninsula. Even the man guarding the date palms at harvest time is called a *khārif*, as noted in *Shams al-'ulūm*. The original meaning of "date harvest" gave rise to the designation of rain falling at this time as *kharīf*, according to Ibn Kunāsa (in A. al-Marzūqī 1914:1:201). Thus, the *kharīf* rain follows the period of *qayẓ* in the seasonal reckoning of the Arabian Bedouins. This rain is placed at the end of *Āb* in the Rasulid almanacs.

Dhū 'Allān (September, or *Aylūl*)

The South Arabic term *ḏ'lnn* survives in contemporary Yemeni dialects as the season of early autumn. The *shadda* in the term is noted in the text and survives in contemporary usage.[11] The origin of the term is unclear from the South Arabic inscriptions. Muḥammad al-Akwa' (1979:124) makes the rather fanciful suggestion that the term means that autumn (*kharīf*) gave notice (*a'lana*) of the coming of winter (*shitā'*). It should also be noted that the term *'allān* means "ignorant" (*jāhil*) in classical Arabic. In the Yemeni highlands *'allān* refers to a period at the beginning of the sorghum harvest (I. al-Akwa' 1984:2:965; al-'Awdī 1980:191; Glaser in Grohmann 1934:2:17; Rossi 1939:151, 1953:360; Serjeant 1954:437, 1974a:62, note 25; Varisco 1985a:65) or an autumn rain (Glaser in Hann 1911:1861; Rossi 1953:360). The term *'allānī* refers to a variety of wheat or barley in Kuḥlān of the highlands (Serjeant 1974a:30). In parts of the Yemeni highlands the rainbow is called *qaws 'allān* (literally, "the bow of *'allān*") instead of the standard Arabic *qaws quzaḥa*. This may result from the occurrence of rain in autumn under the stars known as the fifth, sixth, and seventh of *'allān*. In this context *'allān* refers to the stars of Ursa Major (*banāt na'sh*), which rise at dawn in the early autumn (Varisco 1989b:12). This localized terminology for the stars of Ursa Major is derived probably from the fact that these stars rise at this time and is not an original name for these stars. It should be noted that September is equated with *Dhū al-Ṣirāb* in *Shams al-'ulūm.*

ISLAMIC LUNAR CALENDAR

There is no mention of the Islamic calendar in the almanac, apart from a note in conjunction with the determination of the major Jewish feasts. Of the extant Rasulid almanacs only Taymūr is arranged according to a specific lunar year with the necessary correlations to the solar Julian reckoning. The almanac of Abū al-'Uqūl, however, mentions the birth date of Muḥammad on IV:20 and the murder of 'Uthmān on I:29; these are events transposed from the Islamic lunar calendar. A lunar calendar is impractical as an agricultural or seasonal guide, because it is some eleven days shorter than the solar year and the seasonal round. Every thirty-two and one-half years the months make a complete regression through the seasons. Thus, it would have been necessary to recorrelate the almanac lore for each year in order for the almanac to have practical value as a seasonal calendar, a process which was in fact widely practiced by scholars in later periods.

Within his astronomical text the author has an extended discussion of methods for correlating the Islamic lunar dates to the various solar calendars in use.[12] Assuming the almanac was intended for the calendar year A.D. 1271, the Islamic year would have started on VIII:20 of A.D. 1270. The starting date of X:1, A.D. 1270, would have equaled 12 *Ṣafar*, A.H. 669. The corresponding Julian dates for the beginning of each lunar month of 669 are provided below:

1 *al-Muḥarram*	VIII:20, 1270
1 *Ṣafar*	IX:19
1 *Rabī' al-Awwal*	X:18
1 *Rabī' al-Thānī*	XI:17
1 *Jumādā al-Ūlā*	XII:16
1 *Jumādā al-Ākhira*	I:15, 1271
1 *Rajab*	II:13
1 *Sha'bān*	III:15
1 *Ramaḍān*	IV:13
1 *Shawwāl*	V:13
1 *Dhū al-Qa'da*	VI:11
1 *Dhū al-Ḥijja*	VII:10

CALENDARS

COPTIC CALENDAR

Al-Malik al-Ashraf's almanac does not provide the names of the Coptic months, but it does refer to the start of the Egyptian Coptic calendar, a date fixed at VIII:29. In addition there is mention of several Coptic holidays and periods recognized in Egypt. In another part of his treatise the author does describe the Coptic months and their correlation with the Syriac months and the Islamic calendar.[13] The Rasulid authors were well acquainted with Egyptian sources and include much valuable information on Egyptian agriculture and the seasons and stages of the Nile.

The Coptic month names are derived from ancient Egyptian terms and represent the seasonal round as perceived along the Nile. The Muslims in Egypt adopted the Christian Coptic terms for the months as the standard solar calendar. In medieval Islamic science this mode of reckoning was attributed to the Era of the Martyrs in the second year of the Roman emperor Diocletian, that is, A.D. 284. By the time of the Islamic conquest these months had been fixed to the Julian reckoning used by the Church. The Coptic year began with the month of *Tūt*, named for the ancient Egyptian god Thoth. The first of *Tūt* occurred on VIII:29 in the Julian calendar. Each of the twelve months had thirty days, followed by an intercalation (*nasi'*) of five days or six days during a leap year.

Much of the information on Egypt, especially regarding the stages of the Nile, must have been transposed from the Coptic system to the Syriac system. Similarly, Coptic almanacs contain information clearly derived from the Syriac reckoning. In this process mistakes were easy to make, especially for the timing of religious festivals. The almanac contains no information on Coptic saints' days, although several Coptic holidays were shared with other branches of the Church.

The correlation between the Coptic and Syriac months is shown below:

1 *Tūt*	VIII:29
1 *Bābih*	IX:28
1 *Hatūr*[14]	X:28
1 *Kiyahk*	XI:27
1 *Ṭūba*	XII:27
1 *Amshīr*	I:26
1 *Baramhāt*	II:25
1 *Barmūda*	III:27
1 *Bashans*	IV:26
1 *Ba'ūna*	V:26
1 *Abīb*	VI:25
1 *Misrā*	VII:25
1 *nasi'*	VIII:24

CALENDARS

PERSIAN AND NAVIGATIONAL *NAYRŪZ* CALENDAR

The term *nayrūz* (variants, *nawrūz* and *nīrūz*) is derived from the Persian for the first day of the year. In the Arabic almanacs the first day of the year in any calendar system was often called its *nayrūz*, since this Persian term was widely applied in the medieval Arab world. The Persian calendar in use at the time of the author was the old Zoroastrian solar calendar as adopted by the Sasanian monarchs.[15] The form was similar to the Coptic system in that each month comprised thirty days, with an intercalation of five days. The standard reckoning had been established by Yazdagird, last of the Sasanian rulers, and began on 22 *Rabī' al-Awwal*, A.H. 11/VI:16, A.D. 632. In the almanac each Persian month name ends with *māh* (literally, "moon" and by extension "month"). The month names are *Afarwardīn, Ardibhisht, Khurdādh/d, Tīr, Murdādh/d, Shahrīwar, Mihr, Ābān, Ādhar/Ādhūr, Day, Bahman, and Isfandārmādh/Isfandār*. It should be noted that the rendering of the Persian terms into Arabic is not always consistent.

The major problem with the Persian calendar was that it did not contain a leap year and thus one day was lost every four years vis-à-vis the Julian reckoning of the time. This became a critical problem for the caliphs in that taxes were assessed by this calendar and it soon varied from the actual seasons of harvest. The caliph al-Mu'taḍad bi-Allāh Abū al-'Abbās Aḥmad ibn Ṭalḥa reformed the Persian calendar in 281/825 by transferring the beginning of the year (i.e., 1 *Afarwardīn*) to VI:11. This date, marking the collection of the *kharāj* tax, became known as *al-nayrūz al-mu'taḍadī*. In 471/1079 the Seljuk sultan Jalāl al-Dīn once again reformed the calendar and placed the *nayrūz* at III:15 to coincide with the vernal equinox. This is referred to as *al-nayrūz al-sulṭānī* and was fixed to the Julian reckoning by the addition of a leap day. However, the common people continued to use the old system and the days continued to regress accordingly.

The almanac of al-Malik al-Ashraf places the Persian New Year at I:8. This would be accurate for the years A.D. 1269–72 or for the span 638–41 in the Yazdagird reckoning. At I:10, only two days later, the author mentioned the Indian New Year. Throughout the text references to the sailing times to and from the important Yemeni port of Aden are correlated with the number of days elapsed from the beginning of the Persian New Year, or *nayrūz*. This *nayrūz* reckoning system was the common calendar of sailors using the Indian Ocean.[16] The later navigational texts of Ibn Mājid (1971; Tibbetts 1971) and Sulaymān al-Mahrī (1925) provide a detailed description of the use of this calendar for ports as far away as China. The origin of the navigational *nayrūz* calendar has not yet been documented, although it was clearly used before the Rasulid era by sailors in the region. The details provided by the author in the almanac are in fact the earliest recorded for actual use of the calendar, coming some two hundred years earlier than the time of Ibn Mājid. A similar navigational calendar, in part based on units of ten days each, is still known in the Persian Gulf, although this refers to the days elapsed from the summer rising of Canopus (Varisco 1990).

The navigational *nayrūz* calendar was obviously an approximate system, since the times are expressed in units of ten rather than specific days. Since it was the common Persian calendar that was used, one day was lost every four years so that every forty years a unit of ten days in fact shifted. This created a problem for sailors, who had to shift the numbers in succeeding generations. By the time of Ibn Mājid in A.D. 1488 the actual *nayrūz* had regressed to XI:14 without calculation of a leap year. In the time of the later author Sulaymān al-Mahrī another five days had been lost, and in the time of the Turkish author Sīdī Çelebī the *nayrūz* was in October. Thus, it is not advisable to compare navigational *nayrūz* dates between sources before determining the approximate date of each source. As Tibbetts (1971:362) has noted, it is curious that Ibn Mājid did not comment on this shift, although he must have been aware of it.[17]

The *nayrūz* dates provided in the almanac are not entirely consistent with the starting point indicated at I:8, a further indication that the system was meant to be an approximate reckoning rather than a specific day-by-day calendar. By the year 738/1337–38 the Indian *nayrūz* is said to correlate with XII:20 (*Bughya*, fol. 92v). The correlations noted in al-Ashraf's text are provided below:

Julian Date	Days from *Nayrūz*
I:8	Persian *nayrūz*
I:10	Indian *nayrūz*
III:26	80
IV:15	100
V:6	120
V:16	130
VI:5	150
VII:25	200
VIII:14	220
VIII:23	230
IX:3	240
IX:13	250
X:13	280
XI:1	300
XI:21,22	320
XII:11	340
XII:21	350

CALENDARS

RELIGIOUS HOLIDAYS

Virtually all the Arab almanacs compiled by Muslims mention the major Christian festivals, and there are occasional references to major Jewish and Persian holidays. The interest in biblical events by Muslim scholars is not surprising, given the coverage of many of them in the Quran. The timing of festivals and holidays is not always consistent, even in the same local almanac tradition, which in part reflects differences in celebration times between various Christian sects (al-Bīrūnī 1879:282). However, authors in Yemen had the disadvantage of not having a local Christian population to observe or question. Marco Polo (1958:296) claimed that Christians were bitterly hated at Aden in the Rasulid period. He said that in A.D. 1288 a Christian priest was forcibly circumcised in Aden, an event which allegedly prompted an invasion by the Abyssinians. Interest in several Persian festivals is probably due to the presence of Persian scholars at the royal court. Although this almanac does not refer to the commemoration of any events in the Islamic calendar, such references can be found in other Rasulid almanacs.

Christian Holidays

Since the almanac is organized according to the Christian solar calendar, the mention of major Christian holidays is only to be expected.[18] This almanac is unique in that it provides dates for the moveable feasts of the beginning of Lent, Palm Sunday, and Easter; the other Rasulid texts only mention the fixed feasts. The advantage of this is that it allows us to date the time for which the almanac was written, assuming the timing of the feasts is accurate or nearly so. Most of the references are to the Coptic tradition. The other major rites at this time were the Jacobites, with the patriarch in Mosul, and the Nestorians, based in Baghdad. Marco Polo (1958:296) claimed there were Nestorians on the island of Socotra during the early Rasulid period. The holidays are discussed in the order of their appearance in the almanac.

Arba'īnīyāt. This term literally refers to a period of forty days, a common motif in Semitic cosmology and Christian thinking. Among the many biblical examples there come to mind the duration of Noah's flood, the wandering of the children of Israel in the desert, and Jesus' seclusion in the wilderness. In Sufi writings the number 40 symbolized trial and patience (Schimmel 1980:lx), no doubt drawing on the biblical examples. The number 40 is also popular in Arabic literature, as in the well-known story of Ali Baba and the forty thieves.

Al-Malik al-Ashraf mentioned three periods of *arba'īnīyāt* in the almanac.

The first of these is said to begin on X:18 according to the almanac and *Fuṣūl*, although Abū al-'Uqūl noted this at X:16. There is no mention of the forty-day fast before Christmas (al-Bīrūnī 1879:286), which was not celebrated by the Copts. The second period noted by the author and the other Rasulid almanac compilers begins on XI:26 and is said to be the most famous of the *arba'īnīyāt* of the Copts. It is the common Coptic forty-day period which begins on the first day of *Kiyahk* and ends at Epiphany. Al-Malik al-Ashraf was one day early in the almanac, as is also the case for his dating of Christmas and Easter. This second period is equivalent to the so-called Mixed (*bulq*) Nights[19] and thus a time of intense cold, ice, and snow. The third forty-day period begins on I:5 or 6, the first day of the holiday of Epiphany. This period is said to mark the end of the intense cold and the first planting of trees. It probably refers to the Feast of Forty Martyrs, which al-Shayzarī noted at I:7 for Armenia; this commemorated the children killed in Bethlehem by Herod the Great. The Syrian *arba'īnīyāt*, which is generally recorded as beginning about XII:12–14, is not mentioned in al-Ashraf's almanac.

The term *arba'īnīyāt* can also refer to a weather period without any religious significance. It is the term used for a cold period by the Sinai Bedouin (Bailey 1974:585) and is related to the term *mirba'ānīya* for the cold season in the Gulf (Varisco 1990) and Saudi Arabia (al-Quway'ī 1984:327). The designation of forty days is also used for the period in which the Pleiades disappear from local view in spring.

Al-Mann wa-al-salwā. The reference to manna and quails (*salwā*) at VIII:25 stems from the biblical account of the wandering of the children of Israel in the wilderness, where they were miraculously fed manna and quails from heaven.[20] This event is also recorded in the Quran in surahs 2:57, 7:160, and 20:80. There is considerable discussion within Islamic tradition about the meaning of the term "manna." There are various interpretations: honey, something from the ginger plant, or something falling from the leaves of certain trees (Ibn Kathīr 1973:1:66–67 for surah 2:57). The Coptic almanac of *Nubdha* defines manna as a type of dew resembling honey that fell from the sky on V:13 (18 *Bashans*). Another interpretation links it to a type of dew (*ṭall*) that occurs on plants and rocks (Yūsuf ibn 'Umar 1982:507–8). Ibn al-Mujāwir (1954:277–78) remarked that in his day manna still settled on olive trees in the mountains of the Byzantine Empire (Rūm), and al-Nuwayrī (1935:11:329) mentioned the falling of manna near Damascus in Syria.

The term *salwā* is invariably used to refer to quail in this context, although the terms *sumāna* and *simmān* refer to quail in everyday usage. In the biblical story the Israelites were prohibited from storing the quail meat from one day to the next. When they disobeyed this rule, the meat turned putrid except for that saved on Friday for the following Sabbath day. The Prophet Muḥammad is reported to have said that the quail flesh would not have spoiled if they had not disobeyed God (al-Damīrī 1908:2:61).

The Rasulid almanacs place the falling of manna and quails as an event between VIII:25 and XI:4. These are essentially the same dates used in the non-Yemeni almanacs. Abū Ḥanīfa al-Dīnawarī (1914) said they fell in Syria and Palestine under the *naw'* of *akhbiya* and signaled the end of the hot summer (*qayẓ*) season.

Mīlād. The reference in the almanac to Christmas (*mīlād*) appears to have been rewritten in a different hand, although there is no reason to doubt that al-Ashraf made the original reference. The date mentioned here and in Abū al-'Uqūl is XII:24, which *Fuṣūl* notes as the fast (*ṣawm*) as distinct from the celebration on the following day. The difference here is probably due to confusion over the celebration on the eve and on the day itself. Al-Bīrūnī (1879:287) argued that Christmas should really be on XII:26, according to a legend that Christ was born on a Thursday night.

Ghiṭās al-Rūm. The holiday of Epiphany (*ghiṭās*) occurs on I:6, the day of celebration of Christmas (*al-mīlād al-akbar*) for some sects. The almanac marks I:5 as the beginning of the last forty-day period. Abū Ḥanīfa al-Dīnawarī (1914) described I:6 as a windy day and the coldest part of winter. This holiday celebrates the baptism of Christ by John the Baptist in the Jordan river.[21] Al-Malik al-Ashraf commented that this was a popular day for baptism, even though the water was still cold (see al-Bīrūnī 1879:288). In later years Lane (1973:540) recorded that Copts in Egypt would jump in the Nile on Epiphany. The timing of this holiday may in fact be derived from the ancient Egyptian celebration of the winter solstice (Weiser 1958:141).

Al-Ṣawm al-kabīr. The so-called Great Fast (*al-ṣawm al-kabīr*) is no doubt meant to designate the season of Lent in the Christian church; it is commonly referred to this way in Coptic almanacs. However, there is some confusion between the citing of this term at II:4 and another apparent reference to Lent as *ṣawm al-naṣāra* for II:13. At the latter reference al-Malik al-Ashraf said that Lent begins on a Monday between II:2 and III:7 (see al-Bīrūnī 1879:299, 302). In fact neither day would be correct for the date of Easter provided in the almanac. Assuming that Easter fell on IV:5, the beginning of Lent should be II:9 for the Byzantine rite and II:8 for the Coptic rite. It appears that the author was simply copying the date from another source, although the calculation should have been readily known from available sources. It is relevant to note that al-Malik al-Ashraf had very little, if any, contact with

Christian scholars.

Al-Sha'ānīn al-kabīr. Palm Sunday, generally designated as *al-sha'ānīn al-kabīr*, is the last Sunday in Lent and occurs exactly one week before Easter Sunday. This important holiday commemorating Christ's entry on a donkey into Jerusalem is also known as *tasbīḥ* (al-Qalqashandī 1913:2:425) and the Festival of the Olive Branches, or *zaytūna* (al-Nuwayrī 1923:1:191). This Coptic festival celebrates the entry of Christ on a donkey called Ya'fūr into Jerusalem. Although in another part of the treatise the author noted that this day is a week before Easter, the placement at III:21 is in fact two weeks before his date for Easter. This was probably a simple copyist error.

Al-Sha'ānīn al-ṣaghīr. This festival is known as the lesser celebration of *sha'ānīn* and is a rather uncommon reference in the almanacs. Al-Bīrūnī (1879:304) said it falls on a Friday after Easter. Here the date is IV:3. The anonymous Saray almanac for 1009/1600 records this festival at IV:17 and the earlier Palm Sunday at III:29.

'Īd al-fiṣḥ. Easter Sunday (*'īd al-fiṣḥ*) is the key moveable feast in the Christian liturgy, so an exact date for it provides a clue for the date of the almanac. In the medieval period the date for Easter was calculated using the so-called golden numbers and dominical letters. First it was necessary to date the full moon occurring after March 20 and then determine the next Sunday with this method of calculation. The date for Easter Sunday had to fall between III:22 and IV:25 (al-Bīrūnī 1879:299–303). Al-Malik al-Ashraf recorded a date of IV:4 for Easter, but this cannot be a Sunday, given that V:2 is defined as a Saturday. If it is assumed that the date should be IV:5, a variation of only one day, this fits the other internal data in the almanac and establishes the year for which the almanac is intended as A.D. 1271.[22] This shift of one day can be justified because the author was one day early for Christmas and for the second *arba'īnīyāt*, as noted above.

'Īd al-ward. The Festival of the Rose (*'īd al-ward*) was an important Christian holiday for a number of sects, including the Copts. It celebrates the time Mary brought roses to Elizabeth after the birth of John the Baptist. The Rasulid almanacs place it at V:9, which does not correlate with any of the non-Yemeni almanacs. A distinction is usually made in the almanac genre between the old and new dates for celebration. Thus *Nubdha* mentions the old holiday at IV:23 (28 *Barmūda*) and the new holiday at V:15. Al-Bīrūnī (1879:292, 295) said the Jacobites in Khuwārizm celebrated the old on V:3 and the new on V:15. In Syria this holiday fell on V:25, according to al-

Qazwīnī (1859).

Persian Holidays

The first day of the Persian New Year, *nayrūz* or *nīrūz*, was a major holiday in Iran and Iraq.[23] This Arabic term is derived from the Persian *nawrūz*, the first day of the Persian solar year, coinciding with the spring equinox. It is interesting to note that al-Bīrūnī (1879:201) argued that the date must have been originally the summer solstice because this was easier to observe. The first person to incorporate the *nayrūz* celebration into Islam was al-Ḥajjāj ibn Yūsuf al-Thaqafī (al-Alūsī 1882:1:350). It was a time for giving gifts, especially sweets. In Abbasid Iraq people lit fires in the streets and celebrated for six days. At the time of *al-nayrūz al-mu'taḍadī* (i.e., VI:11) the people of Baghdad would "splash in the water, strew about in dust, and play other games, as is well-known" (al-Bīrūnī 1879:258). Al-Qazwīnī referred to this time as *nayrūz al-khalīfa.* There were also *nayrūz* celebrations in India (al-Bīrūnī 1879:249) and along the African coast (J. M. Gray 1955).

Al-Malik al-Ashraf provided a number of references to the first day (*nayrūz*) of the year in several calendars, but the Persian calendar was said to begin on I:8 in the almanac. At XII:18 Abū al-'Uqūl cited the magical notion that if there is thunder on this day, it will be a fertile year.

The term *mihrajān*, also denoting a Persian celebration, is mentioned three times in the almanac. The first celebration is said to occur in the middle of the Persian month *Miḥr,* and is noted in the almanac at X:16. The author appears to have simply transposed the date in the Persian month to the Syriac month, a shortcut not uncommon in the almanac tradition. The later author al-Waṭwāṭ (fol. 122r) noted that this *mihrajān* was on 16 *Mihr,* or X:26. It was originally a six-day festival to celebrate the autumnal equinox (al-Maqrīzī in Griveau 1914:335). Al-Mas'ūdī (1861:3:404) said that this festival occurred 169 days after the *nayrūz* and marked the first day of winter in Iraq and Syria. During this time gifts were exchanged and the king was allowed a day off and problems were not brought before him. The later Yemeni almanac poem of al-'Affārī notes that the *mihrajān* on XI:28 was the start of the *qiyāḍ* (winter) sowing of wheat. The second *mihrajān* falls on XII:23 and is said to mark the marriage day of the caliph al-Ma'mūn. Ibn Raḥīq recorded this event on the same day and remarks that it was the start of agricultural activity and for many the head of the year. The last or lesser (*ṣaghīr*) *mihrajān* is cited for VII:25 but is not explained.

The almanac also includes an obscure reference to a Sabian fast (*ṣawm*) at II:6. The Sabians were a pagan group living in Iraq. There is no mention of this fast in the other almanacs. Al-Bīrūnī (1879:316) and Ibn al-Nadīm

(Dodge 1970:2:755–65) do not record a fast for the Sabians at this date.

Jewish Holidays

References are made in the almanac to Passover (*'īd al-faṭīr*) and the Feast of Tabernacles (*'īd al-miẓalla*).[24] These are not correlated to the Julian calendar. However, in the discussion at IV:15 the author noted that the Jewish Passover occurred in the middle of their month of *Nīsān*, which was lunar and not tied to a given date in the solar calendar. During this seven-day period the Jews celebrated their deliverance from Egyptian bondage by eating unleavened bread (*faṭīr*), hence the Arabic name. The Arabic cognate of Passover, which is *fiṣḥ*, was also used in some Rasulid texts (for example, *Mumtaḥan*, fol. 10v), but this term could also refer to Easter in the Christian tradition. In the same discussion the author mentioned that the Feast of Tabernacles occurred in the middle of the Hebrew month of *Tishrī*, in the autumn, as a celebration of the harvest. Other Rasulid almanacs mention several events from the biblical history of Israel, including the birth of Moses (II:27 or VI:30); Moses receiving the law (IV:3); sun standing still for Joshua (VI:21 or 24); destruction of Jerusalem (VI:30); offering of Ishmael for sacrifice (X:6); Devil's rebellion against God (XI:9).

Chapter 2

Astronomy

A rich tradition of mathematical astronomy developed in Yemen under the patronage of the Rasulid sultans, some of whom appear to have been accomplished astronomers in their own right.[1] In the reign of al-Malik al-Muẓaffar, the scholar Abū 'Abd Allāh Muḥammad al-Fārisī compiled a handbook of astronomical tables for Yemen drawing on no fewer than twenty-eight earlier sources, including the no longer extant *zīj*[2] text of Abū al-Ḥasan al-Fahhād. The Rasulid astronomical texts reflect a thorough knowledge of the earlier tradition, including basic works from the classical Greek sciences. In his astronomical text al-Malik al-Ashraf discussed the range of subjects within medieval Islamic astronomy and astrology, particularly zodiacal and planetary data. In addition to his interest in writing, the author also sponsored the production of at least four astrolabes, one of which is now located in the Metropolitan Museum of Art in New York (King 1977, 1983a: plates 5 and 6, 1985).

Within the medieval Islamic world there was great interest in astronomy for practical religious reasons. Accurate time-keeping was of primary concern for determining the prayer times and, to a lesser extent, fixing the start of the fasting month of *Ramaḍān*. These times differed throughout the year as the amount of daylight changed due to the position of the sun along the ecliptic. During the day it was possible to measure time by the length of the shadow cast by a gnomon; the almanac published here provides the basic figures for the beginning and midpoint of each month. Later Yemeni almanacs give the shadow lengths for each day in the Islamic year. For the timing of the dawn prayer the position of a star is sometimes noted by al-Ashraf. In addition to knowing the time of day, the Muslim also needed a way to find the true direction of the *qibla* from any place Islam had spread to. Although the use of stars as a coordinate system was widely practiced in pre-Islamic Arabia, as well as in formal astronomical science, this type of information was not relevant to the almanac genre.

It is important to recognize the distinction between the formal science, as it has been preserved in astronomical texts and tables, and the local knowledge of the heavens, or folk astronomy, in Yemen. Contemporary ethnographic study shows that farmers use the risings and settings of certain stars to mark seasonal activities in the agricultural calendar, particularly the likely occurrence of rain. The nightly progression of stars also provides a local star clock for determining periods of time at night, as, for example, in the case of measuring the time of an irrigation share. Throughout Yemen people also developed shadow calendars fixed to a specific locale. These could be used to mark out the seasons locally or to estimate the time of day for prayer or measuring irrigation shares. The author of the *Bughyat al-fallāḥīn* (fol.19r) said that farmers in Yemen derived their knowledge of the heavens from the Himyarites before Islam. The same author observed that the farmers had their own seasonal reckoning and did not use the formal systems of the astronomers.[3] Indeed, there was considerable variation in the folk astronomy of the country, even between neighboring valleys (Serjeant 1974a:29).

The Rasulid corpus of agricultural and astronomical texts is especially valuable for the information provided on Yemeni folk astronomy in the medieval period. A number of local star names are mentioned and correlated with the classical system of constellations derived from the Ptolemaic writings. The times for risings and settings of important stars for Yemen are also documented. A number of cropping periods and crops are named for the stars recognized at that time of year. However, there is no overall description of the local star calendars. Such a description must be pieced together from the clues in the texts and comparative data on folk astronomy in Yemen today.

Yemeni farmers observed the risings and settings of many of the same stars known throughout the region, although the timing in various parts of Yemen would necessarily differ from areas to the north in the Arabian Peninsula. The stars chosen tended to be the obvious candidates because of their brilliance, as in the case of Sirius and Canopus, or their importance as zodiacal stars, such as the Pleiades. In Yemen today there are two main star calendars recognized throughout the country. One of these is an ancient calendar based on the conjunction of the moon and the Pleiades, and the other is a system of twenty-eight agricultural marker stars (*ma'ālim al-zirā'a*) linked to the astronomical model of the lunar stations (Varisco 1993a). No reference is made to the first system in the Rasulid texts, although it was undoubtedly in use at the time. This is probably because the Pleiades calendar has affinities with the Bedouin system of the Arabian Peninsula and thus was more common in the northern areas of Yemen not controlled by the Rasulids. The second system is not described in its present form, but several of the local star names can be found in the almanac.

Al-Malik al-Ashraf was aware that Yemeni farmers had their own system of using the stars as markers. In discussing the dawn rising of the station *dhirā'* at VII:7, he noted that the Yemenis marked the presence of abundant rain at this time by the dawn rising of Sirius.[4] This is remarkably close to the current dating of Sirius as a marker star in Yemen. The almanac also mentions the sowing of a sorghum crop called *thawrī* at V:1. The name refers to a star (or stars) in Taurus (*thawr*). The later almanac poem of al-'Affārī places this marker at V:1 in the reckoning of the farmers (Varisco 1989b:11). The almanac also mentions the stars of *ṣawāb*, a reference to the square of Pegasus. The first part of *ṣawāb* is said to set at II:9 and the second at II:15. In the modern system of agricultural markers three stars in *ṣawāb* are generally recognized and their risings cover the month of February. This particular star cluster is mentioned as early as the tenth century A.D. by al-Hamdānī (1884:1:191) as a sign of rain during the zodiacal period of Pisces (*ḥūt*). Other examples from the contemporary marker stars include the stars of the Pleiades, Ursa Major (*banāt na'sh*), Canopus (*suhayl*), the shoulder of Orion (*ṣulm*), and α β Centauri (*ẓāfirān*). An alternative listing of the marker stars is provided in the existing copies of Abū al-'Uqūl's almanac, some of which may date from the Rasulid period.[5]

ZODIAC AND SEASONS

Arab scholars adopted the classical model of four seasons derived from Greek science. This model divided the year into spring (*rabī'*), summer (*ṣayf*), autumn (*kharīf*), and winter (*shitā'*) according to the entry of the sun into the first zodiacal constellation of each season. Thus, the year for the astronomers began when the sun was said to enter the zodiacal space of Aries (*ḥamal*) at the spring equinox. According to Ptolemy (1976:21) spring is the beginning of the year because it was a wet time, not unlike human birth, and a time of rebirth of animal and plant life after the cold of winter. The Arab authors (e.g., al-Mas'ūdī 1899:16) followed the Greek tradition (e.g., Pseudo-Aristotle 1983:44–48) in relating this sequence of seasons to the stages of human life. Spring represented infancy (*ṭufūlīya*), childhood (*ṣabā'*), or youth (*shāba* or *jārīya*), summer evolved into youth (*shabāb*) or one ready to be married (*'arūs*), autumn stood for maturity (*kuhūla*), and winter advanced into old age (*shaykhūkha* or *'ajūz*).

The Arabs of the peninsula developed a number of different concepts of the seasons, but they do not appear to have used a four-season model before contact with the classical Greek concept. The pre-Islamic Bedouins divided the year into seasons based primarily on climatic change, especially the possible occurrence of rain, the lifeblood of both pastoralism and cultivation.

Much of this folklore survives in fragmented form in the *anwā'* genre and early lexical sources. Unlike the Greek concept, however, the year for the Bedouins began with the autumn rains, when it was once again possible to go into the desert in search of pasture. Thus, the youth (*shabāb*) of the seasons was the autumn, designated as *rabī'* (al-Tha'ālibī n.d.:257).

As al-Malik al-Mujāhid was quoted in the *Bughya* (fol. 18v), the ordinary farmers of Yemen looked to the state of vegetation and the weather to define their seasons rather than to the arbitrary astronomical mode of reckoning by the sun's course through the zodiac. To the farmer spring was not an arbitrary unit but signaled the appearance of animals that had been hibernating or had gone away and the renewal of plant life, as well as the time for important spring rains. There would have been no useful purpose for the formal four-season model, even if the farmer knew about it. Thus, it is doubtful that the common farmer in medieval Yemen had any concept of the zodiacal system which informed Islamic astronomical science.

The Rasulid authors have preserved some of the folk astronomy and local knowledge of the seasons that farmers did use. However, their purpose was not to document this in an ethnographic sense as a scholar might do today. The role of these scholars was one of interpreting what people actually did by harmonizing this with the formal systems, to the extent this was possible. The very idea of a written almanac according to the Syriac month names was an academic exercise at the time. The Rasulid interest in using this calendar was no doubt to coordinate the tax system in a more systematic way. As a result the Rasulid texts represent a translation of the folklore into the scientific genre of the time. Scholars' use of the four-season model and zodiacal astronomy presented a certain problem in terminology. The seasons arrived earlier in Yemen and other southern climes than in the area where the system had developed. Medieval geographers dealt with this by a rather ingenious terminological shift. Thus, the usage of *ṣayf* for summer was applied to the earlier season of spring, and each other term was shifted back one season as well (Abū al-'Uqūl; *Bughya,* fol. 19r; al-Hamdānī 1983:308). In the case of *ṣayf* this shift reflected the origin of the term, which refers to the beginning of the heat as opposed to the intense heat of *qayẓ* (summer). Such a practice was little more than an intellectual exercise, however, since the common people had little need to adapt their terms to a formal scientific model derived from another culture.

The Rasulid almanacs usually provide the beginning dates for each season according to the entry of the sun into the relevant zodiacal space. The beginning of the zodiacal year with Aries (*ḥamal*) was called *al-nayrūz al-sulṭānī*, which *Fuṣūl* notes was a Buddhist festival. The minor variations in the dates assigned are probably due to simple copyist errors. These dates are listed below:

Source	Spring	Summer	Autumn	Winter
Tabṣira	III:13	VI:14	IX:15	XII:14
Abū al-'Uqūl	III:1	VI:14	IX:15	XII:14
Fuṣūl	III:13	VI:14	IX:15	XII:14
Isharāra	III:12	VI:13	IX:12	XII:14
Milḥ	III:12	VI:14	IX:14	XII:13

The Rasulid astronomers were well aware of precession of the equinoxes, a standard part of the classical heritage they were influenced by. The principle of precession was first articulated ca. 150 B.C. by Hipparchus of Rhodes, who determined that the equinoxes migrated westward at a rate of about 1° degree every 100 years. Islamic astronomers at the court of al-Ma'mūn calculated an improved rate of 1° every 66 1/2 years (Kunitzsch 1993:98). Thus the beginning of spring could not be calculated by the actual entry of the sun into the constellation of Aries. For calculation's sake an arbitrary zodiac was adopted in medieval astronomy. In *Mumtaḥan* (fol. 26v) the noted court astronomer al-Fārisī quoted the legendary sage Hermes on the measurement of precession. According to Hermes, it was said, the spring equinox originally occurred in the Pleiades in the zodiacal constellation of Taurus some 3,000 years before the time of Alexander the Great. Calculation of precession was not difficult for Rasulid astronomers; the date of III:13 is accurate for the time of the almanac. Later almanac compilers often were not aware of precession and simply copied earlier dates for the beginning of each zodiacal month. Thus, al-Zumaylī (Serjeant and al-'Amrī 1981:421) in his agricultural poem quoted III:15 for the spring equinox, although the correct date in his time would have been about III:10. Al-Zumaylī appears to have copied the date from the agricultural work of Cassianus Bassus (Qusṭūs), a date also mentioned in the *Bughya*.

The twelve zodiacal constellations were known as the *burūj* (*burj*, singular). In addition to the study of astronomical data on the stars within these constellations and use of the zodiacal grid as a coordinate system, Islamic scholars also delved into a wide range of astrological lore related to each zodiacal sign and the planets. Astrology was a standard part of many astronomical treatises from the time period, although it was generally frowned upon by religious scholars (Ibn al-Jawzī 1980:275–76). A well-known Islamic tradition notes that three things destroy a man's intellectual capacity: looking too long at a woman, too much laughter, and looking to the stars (al-Ibshīhī 1981:497). A distinction must be made, however, between the astrology viewed as outside God's purpose and the astrology within the principles set in motion by God as the creator. It was wrong to trust the movement of stars rather than God, a point made on several occasions by the Prophet Muḥammad.[6] Yet within the medieval Islamic worldview the cosmos was intricately linked and the stars and planets were essential parts of this link. Everything seemed to be related to everything else, whether material or spiritual, by an almost infinite series of cosmological permutations. Many Islamic scholars believed that God used the stars in this sense to communicate to his creation.

The Rasulid texts, including the astronomical compilation of al-Ashraf, treat zodiacal and planetary astrology at great length. The almanacs of *Salwa* and Taymūr record astrological data for each degree and day, respectively, of the year. Almost all of this information is derived from the textual and scholarly tradition, with few confirmable examples from magical beliefs about the stars in the folklore. Such a tradition of folklore undoubtedly existed as evidenced by the numerous rites in South Arabia (Serjeant 1976), despite the Islamicization of the country for several centuries before the time of the Rasulids. Zodiacal astrology was used before Islam, at least for dedication of important buildings (Ryckmans 1975–76:527), but the scholarly presentation was no doubt of little or no practical significance for most of the population, who would not have been able to read the texts. The later entry of zodiacal lore into popular culture was no doubt stimulated by local scholars who read of the link between the signs and planets and healing rites. The mixed Rasulid manuscript of al-Malik al-Afḍal contains several charts full of details on medical astrology.

In the scientific tradition each zodiacal sign, as well as each planet, had fundamental associations with the elements and humors.[7] In the fifth chapter of *Tabṣira* al-Malik al-Ashraf enumerated some of the basic characteristics of each zodiacal sign. This information was the basis for dates of almanac references to the humors and certain medical practices. A summary of the basic associations mentioned by the author is provided below:

Aries (*ḥamal*): male, day, fire, yellow bile, planet Mars
Taurus (*thawr*): female, night, earth, black bile, planet Venus
Gemini (*jawzā'*): male, day, air, blood, planet Mercury
Cancer (*saraṭān*): water, [night], [water], phlegm, moon
Leo (*asad*): male, day, fire, yellow bile, sun
Virgo (*sunbula*): female, night, earth, black bile, planet Mercury
Libra (*mīzān*): male, day, air, blood, [planet Venus]
Scorpius (*'aqrab*): female, night, water, phlegm, planet Mars
Sagittarius (*qaws*): male, day, fire, yellow bile, planet Jupiter
Capricornus (*jady*): [female], [night], earth, [black bile], planet Saturn
Aquarius (*dalw*): male, day, air, blood, planet Saturn
Pisces (*ḥūt*): female, night, water, phlegm, planet Jupiter

SUN: ZENITH AND SHADOW LENGTHS

Since the almanac follows a solar reckoning it is not surprising to find references to the effect of the sun's apparent movement. Even if medieval Arab astronomers had been aware that it was the earth that actually moved around the sun, the calculations of the sun's zenith and seasonal shadow lengths would not have differed. From the viewpoint of an observer on earth the position of the sun changes from north to south throughout the year, as defined by the solstices, although this varies according to the latitude of the observer. Data on the zenith of the sun for particular localities, hours of daylight, and shadow lengths are often provided in medieval astronomical tables, including the major *zīj* texts from Rasulid Yemen.[8]

The almanac notes the sun's zenith (*samt al-ra's*) for three specific days of the year. The primary observation point was Ta'izz, for which most of the Rasulid tables were compiled. Al-Malik al-Ashraf noted the sun's zenith at noon over Ta'izz on VIII:9, a date also copied in *Fuṣūl*, where it is linked to 24° Leo. The zenith also occurred earlier for Ta'izz, although this is not mentioned in the almanac. Abū al-'Uqūl mentioned this other zenith for Ta'izz at IV:20, while *Fuṣūl* provides a date of IV:19 (7° Taurus) and *Salwa* has IV:18 (6° Taurus). In Taymūr the date is IV:18 as well. The later Yemeni almanac of al-Thābitī notes the zenith at IV:15, an indication that as an astronomer he was aware of precession. Two dates are also given by al-Malik al-Ashraf for a zenith for an unspecified place in Yemen: these are IV:22 and VIII:6. The relation of these to the dates for Ta'izz shows that the reference must be for an area north of this southern highland town. Abū al-'Uqūl mentioned the same dates but does not specify where. However, *Salwa* clarifies the zenith of VIII:6 (or 21° Leo) as being for Ṣan'ā'. Taymūr notes the zenith for Ṣan'ā' at VIII:5. The reference could also be for Zabīd, since al-Thābitī noted in his later almanac that the zenith is the same for both these cities; he records a date of IV:18 for his time. The later almanac *Tawqī'āt* notes IV:20 and VIII:6 for Ṣan'ā', but the latter date is probably a copy of the earlier Rasulid material. The later almanac of al-Thābitī also gives dates for the zenith in his time for Dhamār (IV:16), Ma'rib (IV:21), Ṣa'da (IV:23, VIII:1), and Najrān (IV:26, VII:28).

Information is also provided in the almanac for the amount of daylight and corresponding nighttime for the beginning and midpoint of each solar month. This is a standard feature of many almanacs, which often provide very detailed calculations for various times of the year. *Salwa* includes these lengths in chart form for each degree of the zodiacal signs. In al-Malik al-Ashraf's almanac the data are placed along the left side of each page of the almanac. The lengths are listed on the next page:

Month	Daytime	Nighttime
I	11 1/5	12 4/5
	11 2/5	12 3/5
II	11 1/2	12 1/2
	11 2/3	12 1/3
III	11 5/6	12 1/6
	12 3/10	11 7/10
IV	12 1/3	11 2/3
	12 1/2	11 1/2
V	12 2/3	11 1/3
	12 3/4	11 1/4
VI	12 5/6	11 1/6
	12 5/6	11 1/6
VII	12 5/6	11 1/6
	12 3/4	11 1/4
VIII	12 7/12	11 5/12
	12 2/5	11 3/5
IX	12 1/6	11 5/6
	12	12
X	11 3/4	12 1/4
	11 7/12	12 5/12
XI	11 2/5	12 3/5
	11 1/5	12 4/5
XII	11 1/6	12 5/6
	11 9/10	12 1/10

On the right margin of each almanac page the shadow lengths are recorded for midday (*ẓuhr*), midafternoon (*'aṣr*), and the end of the afternoon. These are calculated for the beginning and midpoint of each month. The units are given in terms of a foot (*qadam*). Generally a man measured his own shadow length with his own foot, although in important mosques a gnomon might be set up and an official appointed to calculate the prayer times. A gnomon survives to this day in the mosque at al-Janad (King 1990: plate 1a). The shadow lengths are noted on the next page, according to a reconstruction of the text by David A. King (1990:153). There are several errors, including an error or miscopying of 6 1/4 (!) for the start of *'aṣr* in X and 3 2/3 1/4 (!) for the start of *'aṣr* in III. In the chart all the fractions are additive unless otherwise noted. A single asterisk denotes an approximation and two asterisks indicate an error in the original calculation of either of the entries for *'aṣr*.

Month	*Zuhr*	*'Asr* (start)	*'Asr* (end)
I	5	11 2/3	18 2/3
	4 1/2	11 1/6	18 1/6
II	3 1/2 1/4	10 1/4 1/6	17 1/4 1/6
	3	9 2/3	16 2/3
III	2 1/4	8 2/3 1/4	16 2/3 1/4 **
	1 1/2	8	15 1/5 **
IV	1/2 1/4	7 1/3 1/10	14 1/3 x 1/10 **
	1/4	6 2/3 1/4	13 2/3 1/4
V	1/3	7	14
	1/2	7 1/4 1/6	14 1/4 1/6 **
VI	1 1/2 x 1/10	7 2/3	14 2/3 *
	1 1/10	7 1/2 1/4	14 1/2 1/4 *
VII	1	7 2/3	14 2/3
	1/2 1/4	7 1/3	14 1/3 **
VIII	1/5	6 1/2 1/3	13 1/2 1/3 *
	1	7	14 **
IX	1 1/2 x 1/10	7	14 2/3 **
	1 1/2 1/4	8 2/5	15 2/5 **
X	2 1/3 1/4	9 1/4	16 1/4 **
	3 1/3	10	17
XI	4 1/6	10 1/2	17 1/2 1/3 **
	4 1/2 1/4	11 1/4 1/6	18 1/4 1/6
XII	5 1/6	11 1/2 1/3	18 1/2 1/3
	5 1/4	11 2/3 1/4	18 2/3 1/4

LUNAR STATIONS: *ANWĀ'* AND *MANĀZIL AL-QAMAR*

One of the primary reckoning systems in Islamic astronomy was the so-called lunar stations (*manāzil al-qamar*), which were equated by scholars with the solar *anwā'* of pre-Islamic Arabia.[9] The formal system consisted of twenty-eight asterisms along the zodiacal belt. Both the sun and the moon were said to station themselves in these asterisms along their respective courses. As indicated by the Arabic name, the idea of the lunar stations originated from the general observation of the moon occupying a different set of stars each night during its orbit of some twenty-seven and one-half days around the earth. This concept of a lunar zodiac did not originate with the Arabs but was borrowed from India, perhaps through Sasanian influence. It is a thoroughly Eastern concept, found in a variant form in China, with no parallel in classical Greek science or the Ptolemaic tradition. As a grid for the daily positioning of the moon, the main value of the system was for astrology. In his treatise Al-Malik al-Ashraf records information on what would be suitable or not when the moon was in each station, but this information is not provided in the almanac. Such data do appear in the later Rasulid almanac of Taymūr.

The almanac records the standard system of lunar stations as noted in the chart below. The system traditionally begins with *sharaṭān* as the start of Aries and thus the spring equinox. It should be noted that the zodiacal position, as recorded by the author in his treatise, is simply an arbitrary division of each zodiacal space into two and one-third stations. Thus, it represents the arbitrary space of each station rather than the location of the actual stars identified. The primary identification of the stations is based on the work of al-Ṣūfī (1954) in transcribing the Ptolemaic catalogue of forty-eight major constellations, although there were variations in actual usage.[10]

No.[11]	Arabic Name	Identification	Zodiacal Location
1	*sharaṭān*	β γ Arietis	1° Aries
2	*buṭayn*	ε δ ρ Arietis	12° 51' Aries
3	*thurayyā*	Pleiades	25° 42' Aries
4	*dabarān*	α Tauri	8° 34' Taurus
5	*haq'a*	λ φ^1 φ^2 Orionis	21° 25' Taurus
6	*han'a*	γ ξ Geminorum	4° 17' Gemini
7	*dhirā'*	α β Geminorum	17° 8' Gemini
8	*nathra*	ε γ δ Cancri	1° Cancer
9	*ṭarf*	κ Cancri, λ Leonis	12° 15' Cancer
10	*jabha*	ζ γ η α Leonis	25° 42' Cancer
11	*zubra*	δ θ Leonis	8° 34' Leo
12	*ṣarfa*	β Leonis	21° 25' Leo
13	*'awwā'*	β η γ δ ε Virginis	4° 17' Virgo
14	*simāk*	α Virginis	17° 8' Virgo
15	*ghafr*	ι κ λ Virginis	1° Libra
16	*zubānān*[12]	α β Librae	12° 51' Libra
17	*iklīl*	β δ π Scorpii	25° 42' Libra
18	*qalb*	α Scorpii	8° 34' Scorpius
19	*shawla*	λ υ Scorpii	21° 25' Scorpius
20	*na'ā'im*	σ φ τ ζ γ δ ε η Sagittarii	4° 17' Sagittarius
21	*balda*	vacant space	17° 8' Sagittarius
22	*sa'd al-dhābiḥ*	α β Capricorni	1° Capricornus
23	*sa'd bula'*	μ ε Aquarii	12° 51' Capricornus
24	*sa'd al-su'ūd*	c^1 Capricorni, β ξ Aquarii	25° 42' Capricornus
25	*sa'd al-akhbiya*	γ π ζ η Aquarii	8° 34' Aquarius
26	*al-fargh al-muqaddam*	α β Pegasi	21° 25' Aquarius
27	*al-fargh al-mu'akhkhar*	δ γ Pegasi	4° 17' Pisces
28	*baṭn al-ḥūt*	β Andromedae	17° 8' Pisces

As can be seen from the chart the system of lunar stations is in a sense an expanded version of the solar zodiac. This system could then be used as a coordinate system for fixing the location of the sun along the ecliptic. Thus it was often included on the astrolabe and was important as well in Arab nautical astronomy (Ibn Mājid in Tibbetts 1971:77ff.). Another function of this grid was as a night-sky clock, to be read in much the same way that a clock face might be read. Since by definition half of the stations would rise in a twelve-hour period, it is relatively easy to calculate the approximate amount of time it takes for one station to rise, which is another way of saying the amount of time that the sky appears to shift by about thirteen degrees. For example, if the Pleiades is the rising station at the beginning of the evening, it will be at midheaven in six hours. This approximate sky clock was described in the Rasulid texts, and variants survive in local usage up to the present.

Although originally developed as a lunar zodiac, which achieved great importance in India, these same asterisms could be plotted along the course of the sun since there is only about a five-degree difference between the planes of the two orbits. According to Arab scholars this was the rationale for the system of twenty-eight *anwā'*, a system attributed to the pre-Islamic Bedouins of the Arabian Peninsula, that provided a sort of expanded zodiac in which each period defined by the rising or setting of a station was equal to about thirteen days. By transposing the 360° of the ecliptic onto the 365 days of the solar year, the result was twenty-seven stations with thirteen days each, plus one with fourteen days. Never at a loss for explanation, some scholars went so far as to claim that the extra day for the one station, usually *jabha*, was the day in which the sun stood still for Joshua in the days of the Israelite conquest of Canaan.

The *anwā'* genre documents the folk astronomy and meteorological lore associated with these periods. The earliest almanacs, such as those of Ibn Māsawayh and the famous *Calendar of Cordova*, all draw on this earlier Arabian folklore and place it in the context of the Julian reckoning. In fact a great deal of the information in all Arab almanacs has been derived from this *anwā'* tradition. Some almanacs, such as the important text of Ibn al-Ajdābī written shortly before the time of al-Malik al-Ashraf, include quotes from the poetry and sayings recorded in the *anwā'* literature. The pre-Islamic terminology developed on the Arabian Peninsula is applied to seasonal phenomena as far away as Islamic Spain.

One of the major texts consulted by the author was the *Kitāb al-Anwā'* of the ninth-century scholar Ibn Qutayba (1956). Although not the earliest text in the *anwā'* genre, it was one of the most often quoted in later periods and it survives in numerous manuscripts. The almanac contains certain information probably taken from this text, although there is no reference to it in the almanac per se. In another part of the treatise the author quoted Ibn Qutayba and provides his own commentary on the subject of the *anwā'*. This reads as follows:

> The *anwā'* are times for rain. The singular is *naw'*, which means a rising (*nuhūḍ*) of one of the lunar stations. Specifically, it is the rising (*ṭulū'*) of an asterism in the east or its descending (*inḥidār*) in the west. The Arabs say: "We were rained upon by the *naw'* of a certain star." They associate the rising as a marker of days of rain. There are also those who observe the setting (*suqūṭ*) and call it the *bāriḥ*, but in Yemen it is known only by the term *naw'*. The *anwā'* mentioned are those with fixed nights attributed to them, because the timing differs in different latitudes [literally, "climes," or *aqālīm*]. For example, the *anwā'* which signify the most plentiful rain in Yemen are *anwā'* of little rain in Syria, as has been mentioned.
>
> The markers of abundant rain [in Yemen] include the rising of Sirius, which the mountain farmers call *'ilb* [or *'alib*] and the coastal farmers call *bājis*. They plant at the time of its [summer] rising and the associated rains, which are equivalent to the *anwā'* and rains associated with the constellation Leonis. This is because Sirius rises at the same time as the station *dhirā'*, which is the first of the *anwā'* of Leo. Similarly, the rain of the seventh star of Ursa Major (*sābi' banāt na'sh*) is connected with the rain of *simāk*, the last of the *anwā'* of Leo. At such time there is less rain, and water sources begin to decline in Yemen.
>
> Ibn Qutayba said that "the meaning of *naw'* is the setting (*suqūṭ*) of an asterism from the lunar stations at dawn in the west as the one opposite rises at the same time in the east."[13] It is called a *naw'* because when the setting star sets, the rising star rises as a *naw'*, which means a rising (*nuhūḍ*). Some place the *naw'* with the setting star as though the opposite was the case. Every one of these asterisms takes thirteen days to set. The twenty-eight stations complete a cycle once a year, when the order returns to the first asterism. They say that when one of these stars sets and the opposite rises, there will be rain, wind, cold, or heat, which are all attributed to the setting star until the one after it sets. If one of these sets and there is no rain, it is said that the star *khawā* or *akhwā*. God knows best.[14]

The Rasulid almanacs record a variety of information on the lunar stations. The most common reference is to the dawn rising (*ṭulū'*) of a station; this corresponds with the dawn setting (*ghurūb*) of its opposite in the sky. Thus, if *sharaṭān* (#1) is rising, the station of *ghafr* (#15) is setting. The dates recorded in the major Rasulid almanacs for the dawn setting of each station are provided in the chart below. The date of the dawn rising can be found by simply adding 14 to the number of the station and finding the dawn setting for that station. For example, the dawn rising of *sharaṭān* (#1) is the same as the dawn setting of *ghafr* (#15). The dates below were calculated for the time of the Rasulids and thus differ from the dates found in Arab almanacs from other centuries. It should be noted that these are approximate dates and not based on actual observation of each asterism.

No.	Arabic Name	*Tabṣira*	*Fuṣūl*	Abū al-'Uqūl	Taymūr
1	*sharaṭān*	X:20	X:18	X:18	X:17
2	*buṭayn*	XI:2	X:31	X:31	X:31
3	*thurayyā*	XI:15	XI:13	XI:13	XI:13
4	*dabarān*	XI:28	XI:26	XI:26	XI:25
5	*haq'a*	XII:11	XII:9	XII:9	—
6	*han'a*	XII:24	XII:22	XII:22	XII:22
7	*dhirā'*	I:6	I:3	I:4	I:3
8	*nathra*	I:19	I:17	I:17	I:16
9	*ṭarf*	[II:1]	I:30	I:30	I:29
10	*jabha*	II:14	II:12	II:12	II:10
11	*zubra*	II:27	II:25	II:25	II:22
12	*ṣarfa*	III:12	III:10	III:10	III:7
13	*'awwā'*	III:25	III:23	III:23	III:22
14	*simāk*	IV:9	IV:5	IV:5	IV:5
15	*ghafr*	IV:20	IV:18	IV:18	IV:16
16	*zubānā*	V:3	V:1	V:1	IV:29
17	*iklīl*	V:16	V:14	V:14	V:11
18	*qalb*	V:29	V:27	—	V:27
19	*shawla*	VI:11	VI:9	VI:9	VI:8
20	*na'ā'im*	VI:24	VI:22	VI:22	—
21	*balda*	VII:7	VII:5	VII:5	VII:2
22	*sa'd al-dhābiḥ*	VII:20	VII:18	VII:18	VII:17
23	*sa'd bula'*	VIII:2	VII:31	VII:31	VII:29
24	*sa'd al-su'ūd*	VIII:15	VIII:13	VIII:13	—
25	*sa'd al-akhbiya*	VIII:28	VIII:27	VIII:26	VIII:25
26	*al-fargh al-muqaddam*	IX:10	IX:9	IX:9	IX:7
27	*al-fargh al-mu'akhkhar*	IX:23	IX:22	IX:22	IX:20
28	*baṭn al-hūṭ*	X:6	X:5	X:5	X:4

Another way of looking at the stations is according to the times when the observable stars for each station actually rise and set. Since the stars are not evenly spaced, as the arbitrary system of equal intervals might lead one to believe, the amount of time between each station varies considerably. The dates for the true rising of each station for Ta'izz are provided in *Salwa* and Taymūr, as noted below:

No.	Arabic Name	*Salwa*	Taymūr
1	*sharaṭān*	XI:1 (16° Scorpius)	XI:2
2	*buṭayn*	XI:17 (3° Sag.)	XI:17
3	*thurayyā*	XI:26 (13° Sag.)	XI:26
4	*dabarān*	XII:4 (21° Sag.)	XII:4
5	*haq'a*	XII:16 (3° Capr.)	XII:16
6	*han'a*	I:2 (20° Capr.)	I:2
7	*dhirā'*	I:18 (7° Aquarius)	I:18
8	*nathra*	II:4 (23° Aquarius)	II:4
9	*ṭarf*	II:20 (10° Pisces)	II:20
10	*jabha*	II:26 (17° Pisces)	II:26
11	*zubra*	III:21 (9° Aries)	III:21
12	*ṣarfa*	III:31 (19° Aries)	III:31
13	*'awwā'*	IV:12 (30° Aries)	IV:12
14	*simāk*	IV:22 (10° Taurus)	IV:24
15	*ghafr*	V:14 (2° Gemini)	V:14
17	*iklīl*	V:22 (9° Gemini)	V:22
18	*qalb*	VI:6 (24° Gemini	VI:6
19	*shawla*	VI:19 (6° Cancer)	—
20	*na'ā'im*	VI:30 (16° Cancer)	VI:30
21	*balda*	VII:18 (3° Leo)	VII:18
22	*sa'd al-dhābiḥ*	VIII:2 (18° Leo)	VIII:2
23	*sa'd bula'*	VIII:10 (25° Leo)	VIII:10
24	*sa'd al-su'ūd*	VIII:22 (7° Virgo)	VIII:27
25	*sa'd al-akhbiya*	IX:5 (21° Virgo)	IX:5
26	*al-fargh al-muqaddam*	IX:22 (7° Libra)	IX:22
27	*al-fargh al-mu'akhkhar*	X:8 (23° Libra)	—
28	*baṭn al-ḥūt*	X:24 (9° Scorpius)	X:24

The almanac of al-Malik al-Ashraf includes the times for the positioning of almost every station at midheaven during the course of the year. These are calculated for dawn and presumably would have been useful for determining the dawn prayer. The only other Rasulid almanac to provide similar dates is *Salwa*, although these timings differ in at least two cases. The chart on the next page shows the dates as recorded in the almanac:

No.	Arabic Name	*Tabsira*
1	*sharaṭān*[15]	VIII:3 (two faint stars)
		VIII:7 (third star)
2	*buṭayn*	VIII:19
3	*thurayyā*	IX:11 (*'ayn al-thurayyā*)
4	*dabarān*	IX:1
5	*haq'a*	IX:18
		X:3 (third star)
6	*han'a*	X:11 (fifth and last star)
7	*dhirā'*	X:24 (second and southern stars)
8	*nathra*	XI:5 (bright star near middle)
9	*ṭarf*	XI:15 (bright star)
10	*jabha*	XI:18 (southern star)
		XI:24 (star after the southern one)
11	*zubra*	XII:3
12	*ṣarfa*	XII:11
13	*'awwā'*	XII:30 (second star)
		I:13 (middle star)
14	*simāk*	—
15	*ghafr*[16]	—
16	*zubānā*[17]	II:2 (northern star)
17	*iklīl*	—
18	*qalb*	II:19 (faint star)
19	*shawla*	—
20	*na'ā'im*	IV:2 (*'ayn al-na'ā'im*)
		IV:8 (middle star of second group)
21	*balda*	—
22	*sa'd al-dhābiḥ*	—
23	*sa'd bula'*	V:22
24	*sa'd al-su'ūd*	VI:3 (faint southern star)
25	*sa'd al-akhbiya*[18]	VI:13 (two stars)
		VI:20 (middle star)
		VI:23 (third star)
26	*al-fargh al-muqaddam*	VII:1 (two faint stars)
27	*al-fargh al-mu'akhkhar*	VII:12 (northern star)
28	*baṭn al-ḥūt*	VII:25 (*surrat al-ḥūt*)

In the *anwā'* texts each station is assigned a number of days or nights as its *naw'*. Although there is no clear description of what this number means, it probably represents the time during which the star is said to have influence. The almanac provides the number of "nights" for each station, as noted in the chart below. These numbers are sometimes indicated in the other Rasulid almanacs, although the Rasulid reckoning is unique and does not relate to the earlier *anwā'* tradition as recorded by Abū Ḥanīfa al-Dīnawarī, Abū Isḥāq al-Zajjāj, Ibn Qutayba, and Ibn al-Ajdābī. The time periods enumerated by Ibn Qutayba are shown for comparative purposes.

No.	Arabic Name	*Tabṣira*	Ibn Qutayba
1	*sharaṭān*	3	3
2	*buṭayn*	3	3
3	*thurayyā*	1	5 or 7
4	*dabarān*	1	3
5	*haq'a*	1	6
6	*han'a*	1	3
7	*dhirā'*	1	5
8	*nathra*	1	7
9	*ṭarf*	1	6
10	*jabha*	1	7
11	*zubra*	1	4
12	*ṣarfa*	4	3
13	*'awwā'*	1	1
14	*simāk*	1	4
15	*ghafr*	3	1 or 3
16	*zubānā*	3	3
17	*iklīl*	5	4
18	*qalb*	3	1
19	*shawla*	3	3
20	*na'ā'im*	3	1
21	*balda*	3	3
22	*sa'd al-dhābiḥ*	3	1
23	*sa'd bula'*	3	1
24	*sa'd al-su'ūd*	3	1
25	*sa'd al-akhbiya*	4	1
26	*al-fargh al-muqaddam*	3	3
27	*al-fargh al-mu'akhkhar*	3	4
28	*baṭn al-ḥūt*	4	1

The most famous of the stations is the Pleiades (*thurayyā*), a group of closely spaced stars referred to in several traditions of the Prophet Muḥammad. In the *anwā'* tradition and in ancient Greece (Theophrastus 1916:2:395) the rising and setting of the Pleiades divided the year in half. It is also an asterism of great importance to the farmers of Yemen, who still know it as *kāma*, a cognate of the Hebrew *kīma*. (One of the most important dates in the agricultural cycle was the evening rising (*'ishā'*) of the Pleiades, recorded in the almanac for X:14. The coastal sowing of sorghum at this time was called *'ishwī* after the evening rising.) The evening rising of the Pleiades is also recognized in Yemen as the start of an ancient reckoning system based on the conjunction (*qirān*) of the Pleiades and the moon.[19] Although this reckoning system is not mentioned in the Rasulid sources, it has considerable antiquity on the Arabian Peninsula. It is based on the number of days elapsed between the new moon (the beginning of the lunar month) and the conjunction of the moon with the Pleiades. The moon and the Pleiades approach each other in the sky once each sidereal rotation of the moon in twenty-seven and a half days. However, people observed that the interval of days between the new moon and the conjunction was fairly consistent every year. The first month was called "nineteen" or "seventeen," depending on the tradition, and every succeeding month dropped two days in the interval until a night was reached called *layla wa-lā shay'* (the night when there was nothing). This refers to the disappearance from view of the Pleiades from the night sky in the first part of April.

Al-Malik al-Ashraf noted that the disappearance (*istitār*) of the Pleiades occurred on IV:6. He appears to be copying the date from the tradition recorded by Abū Ḥanīfa al-Dīnawarī rather than providing an observation for Yemen. In another part of the treatise the author said that at this time the Pleiades disappear from view beneath the rays of the morning sun for about forty days. During this period there were said to be harmful winds and head colds (*nazalāt* and *zukām*). This linkage of the disappearance of the Pleiades and illness is also found in the tradition of the Prophet's medicine (e.g., Ibn Qayyim al-Jawzīya 1957:32–33 and al-Suyūṭī 1986:144–45), as well as in the important almanac of al-Bīrūnī. The last source also noted that this disappearance marked the start of a market fair at Dayr Ayyūb in Syria. The positioning of the Pleiades at dawn in midheaven is given as the evening of I:9 in al-Ashraf's almanac.

STARS AND CONSTELLATIONS

In addition to the zodiacal constellations and lunar stations there are references in the almanac to the risings and settings of several important stars (*nujūm*) and constellations (*ṣuwar*). The author followed the *Almagest* of Ptolemy (Kunitzsch 1974) in defining the names and positions of the stars. As the author noted,[20] there were 1,022 visible stars: 346 in the zodiacal constellations, 360 in the northern celestial hemisphere, and 316 in the southern celestial hemisphere. Each star was ordered according to its magnitude (*qadr*), from the brightest first-magnitude star, Sirius, to the faintest sixth-magnitude star. In the Ptolemaic system described by the author, the number of stars in each magnitude was as follows: first, 15 stars; second, 45 stars; third, 208 stars; fourth, 474 stars; fifth, 217 stars; and sixth, 63 stars. One of the most valuable parts of his discussion is the identification of local

Yemeni names for the stars with the names in Islamic astronomy.

The fixed stars, other than the stations and zodiacal signs, mentioned by the author in his almanac are examined below in alphabetical order by the Arabic name.

Banāt na'sh al-kubrā. One of the most important constellations for Yemeni farmers was Ursa Major, called *al-dubb al-akbar* in the direct scientific translation from Greek. For Ptolemy this consisted of thirty-five stars, the hind part known as *banāt na'sh al-kubrā* (daughters of the bier) in Arab folk astronomy. This well-known grouping is known in the West as the Big Dipper or the Plough, and it is one of the easiest groups of stars to recognize in the sky. In Arab folklore this constellation consists of seven stars. The four in the shape of a square (*murabba'*) represent the bier or litter (*na'sh*) on which a dead man is being carried. The three stars in front are the daughters (*banāt*), who are crying for their murdered father.[21] Ibn Mājid (Tibbetts 1971:69) claimed that some people saw Noah's ark (*safīnat* Nūḥ) in this constellation, but this only contains five of the stars (Kunitzsch 1967:65). Some of the individual stars are given separate names by the author, as derived from the formal astronomical tradition, but in the almanac they are referred to simply by number, as noted below:

No.	Individual Name		Identification
1	*awwal*	(*na'sh*) [1–4]	α Ursae Majoris
2	*thānī*		β Ursae Majoris
3	*thālith*		γ Ursae Majoris
4	*rābi'*		δ Ursae Majoris
5	*khāmis*	(*jawn*[22])	ε Ursae Majoris
6	*sādis*	(*'anaq*)	ζ Ursae Majoris
7	*sābi'*	(*qā'id*)	η Ursae Majoris

The almanac indicates the rising time at dawn for six of the stars of Ursa Major in the autumn, as follows:

No.	*Tabṣira*	Abū al-'Uqūl	*Fuṣūl*	*Salwa*	Taymūr
1	—	VIII:2	VIII:1	VIII:9 24° Leo	VIII:9
2	VIII:8	VIII:9	VIII:8	VIII:12 26° Leo	VIII:12
3	VIII:21	VIII:20	VIII:21	VIII:21 6° Virgo	VIII:21
4	VIII:30	VIII:29	VIII:30	VIII:28 13° Virgo	VIII:28
5	IX:14	IX:14	IX:14	IX:14	IX:13

				29° Virgo	
6	IX:21	IX:20	IX:20	IX:21 6° Libra	—
7	IX:30	IX:30	IX:30	IX:30 15° Libra	IX:30

The dating of the evening rising and the positioning of each star in midheaven at dawn are given in *Salwa*:

No.	Evening Rising	Midheaven
1	XII:30 17° Capricornus	XII:6 22° Sagittarius
2	I:6 24° Capricornus	XII:11 23° Sagittarius
3	I:21 9° Aquarius	XII:19 5° Capricornus
4	I:22 10° Aquarius	XII:24 10° Capricornus
5	II:3 22° Aquarius	I:3 21° Capricornus
6	II:13 2° Pisces	I:11 29° Capricornus
7	—	I:16 4° Aquarius

A number of important events in the agricultural cycle are associated with the risings of the stars of Ursa Major. In his *Tabṣira*, al-Malik al-Ashraf noted that the summer rains ended with the rising of the fourth star at VIII:30. According to the almanac, grapes picked for raisins during the rising of the sixth star will be weak; they should not be picked until the rising of the seventh star. Several varieties of sorghum were named for sowings at the fifth, sixth, and seventh stars. In the central and northern highlands of Yemen the term *banāt na'sh* has been replaced today with *'allān*, a term stemming back to the Himyaritic calendar. This time period is one of the most important in the agricultural cycle.

Al-Dhirā' al-yamānīya. This is a reference to the southern foreleg of Leo, also known as the "outstretched foreleg" (*al-dhirā' al-mabsūṭa*). This should not be confused with the lunar station called the "contracted foreleg" (*al-dhirā' al-maqbūḍa*). The southern foreleg consists of α β Canis Minoris, the first of which is Procyon (*al-shi'rā al-ghumayṣā'*) and the second of which is called *mirzam*. The almanac notes that these two stars are in midheaven at dawn on X:24.

Mankib al-jawzā'. This star name signifies the shoulder of Orion, or α Orionis; sometimes it includes γ Orionis as well. In Arab astronomy the term *yad al-jawzā'* may also be used for α Orionis. *Fuṣūl* records the variant term *mankib al-jabbār*, but in fact both *jawzā'* and *jabbār* were used for Orion. Both the almanac and *Fuṣūl* mention the rising of this star at VI:14, while Abū al-'Uqūl located it at VI:11. According to Abū al-'Uqūl the local name of this star in Yemen is *ṣulm*, marking a week-long sowing period of *sarb* beginning on VI:2. This term survives in the contemporary system of agricultural marker stars (Varisco 1993a). The contemporary Yemeni scholar Ismā'īl al-Akwa' (1984:2:1239) dates the marker of *ṣulm* at VI:11, clearly copying from the Rasulid tradition. This Yemeni term is sometimes confused in the literature with a star called *ẓulm* or *al-ẓulm al-awwal* (al-Iryānī 1980:61). The term *ṣulm* is mentioned in al-Fārisī's *Mumtaḥan* (fol. 65r) as a star located near the zodiacal constellation of Aries.

Al-Nasr al-ṭā'ir. This important star of the second magnitude is Altair (α Aquilae), a name derived from an Arabic word for "eagle." Altair is separated from Vega, the other eagle (*al-nasr al-wāqi'*), by the Milky Way. The Arabs sometimes referred to these two asterisms as *nasrān*. The almanac and *Fuṣūl* note the dawn rising of Altair at I:21, but Abū al-'Uqūl places it at 1:10, and *Salwa* records it even earlier, at I:5 (23° Capricornus). According to Ibn Qutayba (1956:151), Altair rose at the time of the dawn setting of *dhirā'* (#7) and set with the dawn rising of *nathra* (#8). *Salwa* also includes the evening rising at VI:2 (19° Gemini) and the positioning in midheaven at dawn on V:1 (19° Taurus). Altair was a marker for east in the star compass of the Indian Ocean.

Al-Nasr al-wāqi'. The other eagle for the Arab astronomers was Vega (α Lyrae), a modern star name also adopted from the Arabic. The almanac places its rising at dawn on I:8, although Abū al-'Uqūl noted this at XII:16 and *Salwa* at XII:8 (24° Sagittarius). The almanac also records the positioning in midheaven at dawn on V:6 and the dawn setting on VIII:21. Ibn Qutayba (1956:151) said that Vega rose at the same time as Antares (*qalb*) on XII:2 during the cold of winter. Their joint rising was called *harrārān* because of the intense cold at the time. *Salwa* also notes the evening rising of Vega on V:9 (27° Taurus). A variety of sorghum sown at the rising in December was called *nasrī*. Ibn Mājid (Tibbetts 1971:137) observed that Capella (*'ayyūq*) rose when Vega set in late August.

Qilāda. This term refers to a "necklace" of six stars (ξ^2 ο π d ρ υ

Sagittarii). Al-Ṣūfī (1954:220) equates this name with *qalā'iṣ*, which refers to "she-camels" that Aldebaran drove before him in demanding marriage with the Pleiades (*Tāj al-'Arūs, q-l-ṣ*), but these are several stars near Albebaran and the Pleiades. Ibn Qutayba (1956:76) reported that the moon sometimes stationed in these stars rather than in the station of *balda* (#21). The almanac notes that the second star of this group is in midheaven at dawn on IV:16.

Sā'iqān. The almanac mentions a first and second *sā'iq*, "driver." The first is said to set on III:10 and the second on III:26. This term has not been reported in contemporary Yemen, but fortunately al-Malik al-Ashraf equated it in *Tabṣira* (fol. 52r) with the two stars of α β Centauri, which are equated with *muḥlifān*, or *haḍāri* and *wazn*. The term *muḥlifān* refers to the fact that these first-magnitude stars are sometimes mistaken for Canopus when they rise together (al-Ṣūfī 1954:220). Sailors called these two stars *ḥimārān* (the two donkeys).[23] Al-Malik al-Ashraf added that another local term for the two was the first and second *ẓāfir*, a terminology which survives in the contemporary system of agricultural marker stars. The dates for these two recorded by the Yemeni poet Ḥasan al-'Affārī (Varisco 1989b:11) are virtually identical with those of al-Ashraf.

Ṣawāb. This star was not identified by al-Ashraf, although he said (*Tabṣira*, fol. 109v) it consists of four stars in a square rising in the path of Canopus and opposite the position of Ursa Major. The same name is mentioned by the Yemeni historian al-Hamdānī (1884:1:191) as being associated with the zodiacal sign of Pisces. This description and timing would fit an identification with the square of Pegasus, consisting of the two lunar stations *al-fargh al-muqaddam* (#26) and *al-fargh al-mu'akhkhar* (#27). According to the almanac, *Fuṣūl*, and Abū al-'Uqūl, the first *ṣawāb* set at II:9 and the second *ṣawāb* set at II:15. Al-Malik al-Ashraf said that this setting signaled the start of the spring *wasmī* rains in Yemen. The term *ṣawāb* survives in the contemporary system of marker stars, although today there are three divisions instead of two (Varisco 1993a:136). The timing of *ṣawāb* in contemporary Yemeni almanacs is a few weeks before the dawn rising of the square of Pegasus as two of the lunar stations in late winter. Thus, the reference in the almanac is to an evening setting, as is usually the case with later use of the marker stars in Yemen.

Al-Shi'rā al-'abūr. The Arabic terms *al-shi'rā al-'abūr* and *al-shi'rā al-yamānīya* refer to Sirius, the brightest star in the sky and an obvious marker throughout the region. The word *'abūr* refers to the fact that Sirius has crossed over (*'abara*) the Milky Way. This was a star worshipped in pre-Islamic

Arabia, as noted in a Quranic reference (surah 53:50). In ancient Egypt Sirius, as the god Sothis, marked the annual flooding of the Nile at its dawn rising and thus served as the herald of the New Year. The Egyptian term for Sirius was literally "dog" (*kalb*), as noted by Ptolemy and quoted in the *Bughya* (fol. 21v). It was an important star for navigation on the Indian Ocean, where it marked the direction of east-southeast (Ibn Mājid in Tibbetts 1971:146). A number of non-Yemeni almanacs refer to a magical rite associating the summer rising of Sirius and a way of knowing which crops will grow in the coming year (e.g., al-Bīrūnī at VII:18). A variety of astrological uses of Sirius are described in the *Bughya* (fol. 21v), which also notes the Egyptian variant of the crop prognostication rite of Sirius.

The time of the dawn rising of Sirius in Ta'izz in Yemen is VII:9 (24° Cancer) in the Rasulid almanacs. The evening rising of Sirius is placed at XII:15, and *Salwa* adds the positioning in midheaven at dawn on X:10 (25° Libra). *Salwa* and Taymūr note the dawn rising in Mecca at VII:13 (24° Cancer) and in Egypt at VII:20 (5° Leo).

The author noted that the local name for Sirius in the mountains was *'ilb*[24] (which is generally pronounced in the Yemeni highlands today as *'alib*), while the name in the coastal region was *bājis*.[25] The term *bājis* is apparently derived from the sense that it "makes the water flow" (*Tāj al-'arūs, b-j-s*). A variety of sorghum called *bājisī* was associated with its summer rising, the almanac noting this at VII:10. Abū al-'Uqūl mentioned a sowing period of *'alibīya* at VI:16. According to his almanac this star was also known as *mijdaḥ* in Ṣan'ā', but this is a term usually identifying Aldebaran (Ibn Qutayba 1956:37; al-Ṣūfī 1954:154). Abū al-'Uqūl went on to say that its summer rising signaled the time for ploughing and the time highland Yemenis came down to work in the date harvest at Zabīd. Al-Malik al-Ashraf identified Sirius as one of the markers (*'alāmāt*) of abundant rain in Yemen, a usage still found in parts of Yemen (al-Baraddūnī 1985:38). As an agricultural marker, however, Sirius is associated today with the end of the hot and dry season of *jaḥr* in May and June (I. al-Akwa' 1984:1:366; al-Baraddūnī 1985:56). This parallels the ancient Bedouin association of the dawn rising of Sirius with a period of heat called *waghra* (Ibn al-Ajdābī 1964:170).

Al-Simāk al-rāmiḥ. This star is Arcturus (α Boötis), a bright red star of the first magnitude. In Arabic nomenclature a distinction is made between *al-simāk al-rāmiḥ*, which means "the one with a lance," and *al-simāk al-a'zal*, "the one without a weapon." The latter, Spica, is the fourteenth lunar station. Among Bedouins the two together are sometimes referred to as *simākān*. Another name for Arcturus common in the Persian Gulf and among sailors is *uḥaymir*, in reference to the redness of the star. Arcturus marks east-northeast in the star compass of navigators in the Indian Ocean (Ibn Mājid in Tibbetts 1971:146).

According to the almanac this star is in midheaven at dawn on I:14, although *Salwa* places this at I:24 (12° Sagittarius). *Salwa* records the dawn rising (X:12, 27° Libra), evening rising (III:13, 1° Aries), and evening position in midheaven at dawn (VI:11, 28° Gemini).

Suhayl. The important star *suhayl* is Canopus (α Carinae), the second brightest star in the sky. Sailors sometimes refer to it as a green (*akhḍar*) star (Serjeant 1982:122). This star is always near the horizon in the south and served as the most important star for measuring latitudes among sailors in the Persian Gulf and Indian Ocean (Ibn Mājid in Tibbetts 1971:132). Because it is visible so far to the south, for which it has long served as a marker on the Arabian Peninsula, it is not visible in areas too far north, such as Spain or Khūrasān (Ibn Qutayba 1956:11).

The Rasulid almanacs place the dawn rising of Canopus in Yemen at VII:25. Virtually the same date is recorded in the later Egyptian almanac of Ibn Mammātī. The Yemeni astronomer al-Aṣbaḥī (fol. 50r) claimed that in Zabīd[26] Canopus rose at the same time as *ṭarf* (at VIII:7), and set with Aldebaran (i.e., XII:2), whereas in Ta'izz Canopus rose with *nathra* (at VII:25) and set with *han'a* (at XII:28). Thus, even within Yemen there was recognition of an appreciable variation in the times when Canopus could be seen. *Fuṣūl* records the sighting of Canopus in Mecca at VIII:7, a date that agrees with the tradition in the *anwā'* genre (e.g., Ibn al-Ajdābī at VIII:6). On the other hand, *Salwa* mentions the rising at Mecca on VII:27 (12° Leo), which is far too early. For the rising in Egypt, *Fuṣūl* has VIII:20, the same as in the *anwā'* genre. *Salwa*, however, records the rising in Egypt at VIII:15 (30° Leo). Abū al-'Uqūl said that the rising in the Maghrib was on IX:6, a date which agrees with the almanac of the North African Ibn al-Ajdābī. This date was also included in the earlier almanac of al-Shayzarī. It was claimed by some that ten days stood between the dawn rising of Canopus in the Hejaz and in Iraq (A. al-Marzūqī 1968:2:392).

The dawn rising of Canopus in late summer was probably the most important astronomical event on the Arabian Peninsula. There is a Yemeni proverb which says there is no other star like Canopus (*mā fī al-nujūm illā suhayl*, Agaryshev 1968:33, 1986:74; I. al-Akwa' 1984:2:1056; al-Baraddūnī 1985:55). For the pre-Islamic Bedouins this rising signaled the beginning of the pastoral cycle after the blistering heat of summer (Ibn al-Ajdābī 1964:158). This tradition survives among the Bedouins of the Arabian Peninsula today (Musil 1928:8). In Yemen the rising of Canopus meant the beginning of the important late summer rains. This is reflected in the proverb quoted in the almanac at V:8: "When Canopus rose, it announced flood after flood" (*Idhā ṭala' suhayl fa-abshara bi-sayl ba'd sayl*). The same proverb is recorded by Abū al-'Uqul and in *Fuṣūl*. Variations of this proverb still exist in Yemen.[27]

Al-Malik al-Ashraf observed that two weeks after its rising in Yemen Canopus was obscured from view by the rays of the sun. This is referred to as its *i'tirāḍ* or *istitār*.[28] The Rasulid almanacs place this event at VIII:8. The reference in Taymūr to VII:7 is clearly a copyist error. The almanac and *Fuṣūl* have the evening rising of Canopus at I:2, although *Salwa* places it at XII:18 (4° Capricornus), perhaps not in reference to Yemen but for an area to the south. Abū al-'Uqūl gives the time of the evening rising in the Maghrib as I:23, which is in virtual agreement with the date in the North African almanac of Ibn al-Ajdābī.

Surrat al-ḥūt. The "navel of the fish" (*surrat al-ḥūt*) refers to a star or several stars in Pisces, usually β Andromedae (Kunitzsch 1983:79). The almanac notes that it is at midheaven at dawn on VII:25. The almanac of Ibn Mammātī, at III:31, identifies it as equivalent to the star known as the "throat of the camel" (*naḥr al-nāqa*). The stars of the Arabic constellation designated the "camel" (*nāqa*) are generally located in Cassiopeia.

Chapter 3

Meteorology

Knowledge of the weather was of the utmost importance to the Yemeni farmer, since the bulk of agriculture in the region was dependent on the rains. The almanac reflects an intimate experience with the climate of Yemen, as well as some of the special weather periods known in Yemeni folklore. Yet there are also references to several weather periods from the *anwā'* literature that were probably not known in the same terms to farmers in Yemen. While it is not always possible to determine the local usage from information copied from earlier almanacs, ethnographic data from Yemen supplement the rich corpus of Rasulid agricultural texts.

The climate varies considerably within the relatively small area of Yemen due to the great geographical diversity and its location in the path of the summer monsoon system flowing east out of Africa.[1] As a result of the monsoon between May and September much of the southern part of the country is exposed to rainfall. There is relatively little rain in the hot and humid coastal region called the Tihāma, but there can be heavy precipitation on the westward-facing slopes above about 1,500 meters elevation in the Sarāt chain. The area around Ta'izz and Ibb, where the Rasulids were firmly in control, receives the most rain in Yemen. Thus the Rasulid texts describe the agriculture in the optimum environment of the country. Temperatures during the winter can reach freezing in the mountains, but the central plains are often protected from the more extreme temperatures. During the summer the coastal region can feel like an inferno, while the highland towns have a pleasant temperate climate. During the winter months of October through February the air masses of the Central Asia anticyclone predominate and provide clear, rainless skies over the country. In the spring the year is renewed and the rains begin again in many parts of Yemen.

In addition to the rainfall, Yemeni agriculture is greatly facilitated by the presence of late summer dew (*ṭall*).[2] The almanac places the major time for dew between VIII:13 and IX:3, while Abū al-'Uqūl mentioned dew from VIII:12. References to late summer dew are common in the almanacs, which often caution the reader about sleeping under an open sky at this time. As the traveler Madden (1829:389) observed, the "heavy dews of the summer nights are to be avoided as much as possible by the traveller; for to them dysentery and opthalmia are in most instances to be referred." The later Yemeni almanacs of al-Thābitī and Ibn Jaḥḥāf record the presence of dew on crops from as early as V:13.

During the winter there are late afternoon winter mists and thick clouds, generally referred to as *ghamām* or *ghaym* in the Rasulid texts. *Ghaym* almost always refers to these winter mists, although it literally means "clouds" in classical Arabic. Al-Malik al-Ashraf placed the appearance of these mists from the time of the autumn rains. *Salwa* and Taymūr mention these mists from XI:8 (25° Scorpius), while Abū al-'Uqūl noted them at XI:22. The clouds begin to thicken at X:27, according to Abū al-'Uqūl. Al-Malik al-Ashraf observed that if rain had not already fallen in early February, there would be thick clouds through the Nights of the Old Woman at the end of the month. By III:26, according to Abū al-'Uqūl, the thick clouds and late afternoon mists would have thinned out over Yemen. These wet winter mists are an important source of moisture for crops over the rainless stretch of the cold period (Bury 1915:108).

RAIN PERIODS

There are two main rain periods in Yemen: a minor one in early spring and a major one in late summer. This fact was widely noted in the early Arabic texts (e.g., al-Hamdānī 1983:308; Ibn Khurradādhbih 1889:156; Ibn Rusta 1892:109; al-Rāzī al-Ṣan'ānī 1974:96). The thirteenth-century traveler Ibn Baṭṭūṭa (1980:251) remarked that the rain in Ethiopia, Yemen, and India fell in summer, an obvious reference to the summer monsoon so important to travel in the Indian Ocean.

Al-Malik al-Ashraf described the periods of rain in Yemen at length in his treatise (*Tabṣira*, fols. 115v–116r), as quoted below:

> As for the rain periods, the first time for the occurrence of rain is at the *naw'* of *ṣawāb* (square of Pegasus) setting at dawn during the middle ten days of *Shubāṭ* (February). This is the *rabī'* rain [of Syria] or Yemeni *wasmī* rain. Every rain occurring after the *wasmī* is called *walī*. The last period of known rainfall is at the dawn rising of the last three stars of Ursa Major (*banāt na'sh al-kubrā*) because these are positioned in the sky opposite the stars of *ṣawāb*. Thus, the first of the rain periods is at the dawn setting of *ṣawāb*, while at the dawn rising of *ṣawāb* Ursa Major rises.
>
> The limits of abundant rainfall are between the dawn rising of

> Canopus (*suhayl*) on 25 *Tammūz* (July) and the dawn rising of the fourth (*rabi'*) star of Ursa Major on 30 *Āb* (August). The Arabs say: "When Canopus rose, it announced flood after flood."[3] This is due to the influence of very plentiful rainfall between it and the rising of the fourth star of Ursa Major. The Arabs also say: "When the four [stars of Ursa Major] were distinguishable, the stalk (literally, *zarī'*) was tied to whatever was near it."[4] The poet is referring to the square [of four stars] as being distinguishable when all four stars are visible at dawn, which is close to the time for the rising of the fifth (*khāmis*) star [of Ursa Major]. Sometimes the rains are minimal, but then an abundant rainfall occurs at the rising of the fifth star. The rain connected with the rising of the four stars does not last long, but goes along quickly, as God wills. The Arabs say: "At the rain of the fifth star, the autumn returns to greenery."[5] When the Arabs say "tie the crop to whatever is near it," this means they fear for it because of the intensity of the abundant rainfall. During this rainy season the cold occurs along with intensely violent winds (*'awāṣif*). The wind roars over the ground, lacerating, breaking, and weakening the heads of grain to a great extent. Since this is the time when heads appear, that which has already appeared falls from the intensity of the blowing and violent winds in this rain period. After the rising of the fifth star, the only rain is that which is light, temporary, or minimal, like the rains at the beginning of the year, as we mentioned for *Shubāṭ* at the rising of *sa'd al-su'ūd* (c^1 Capricorni, β ξ Aquarii). The Arabs called this *sa'd al-su'ūd* because of the rain associated with its rising.[6]

In the almanac al-Malik al-Ashraf noted that plentiful rainfall ended in the mountain areas around VII:29, which differs by a month from the discussion quoted above. At this point in the almanac he added some comments on occasional rainfall after this time, such as the autumn *rabī'* rain noted at XI:1 and the *shitā'* rain, which the author seems to equate with the *rabī'* rain. *Salwa* notes the end of plentiful rainfall at VII:27 (12° Leo).

Despite the fact that the farmer and the pastoralist welcomed the opening of the heavens, there were times when rain was deemed inappropriate. As discussed in the almanac, the rain occurring at the time of the late autumn harvest was harmful, because it could destroy the crop drying on the threshing floor or already stored away. Al-Malik al-Ashraf specifically drew attention to the danger of water reaching crops stored in storage chambers (*makhāzīn*), which is better understood when one realizes that in the mountains most grain is stored in underground chambers. In the coastal region and foothills stalks are often stored in bundles up in trees. The farmer was mainly concerned about the intensity of the rain, as noted in the proverb quoted in the passage above. The historical sources often mention when a rain was so intense it destroyed crops.[7] On the other hand, the late summer rain of *ḥamīm* was beneficial in Yemen, but not for the Bedouins of the peninsula. Ibn Qutayba (1956:11) explained that in the desert this rain would produce plants that were dangerous for camels to graze on. A plentiful rain during the heat of summer is still considered destructive by the Bedouins (Musil 1928:9).

In the *Bughya* (fol. 24v) advice is given on how to predict rain. Some of this is common knowledge to societies around the globe, such as observance of red or a dark color in the moon. Another clue is the rapid chatter of birds, such as the chicken, swift (*khuṭṭāf*), and crane (*kurkī*). Dogs are also said to dig holes in the ground before a rain. This is lore taken primarily from earlier almanacs and magical texts, although some might also have been independently arrived at by Yemeni farmers.

Most of the names of rain periods cited in the almanac are from the *anwā'* literature and stem back to pre-Islamic usage (Varisco 1987). There are at least three names (*kharf, Tammūz, thawr*) which are not mentioned outside of Yemen. The rain periods mentioned in al-Ashraf's almanac are discussed in alphabetical order:

Ḥamīm. This term refers to a well-known rain period of the Arabian Bedouins. It is usually identified as the rain falling in the hot summer season of *qayẓ* (Ibn Qutayba 1956:114; *Kifāya*, fol. 93r; al-Marzūqī 1914:1:200). Quṭrub (1985:98) claimed this term was the equivalent in the Tamīm dialect to the *kharīf* rain in the Hejaz dialect. He added that it referred to a period between ten and fifteen days from the dawn rising of Aldebaran in late May. The almanac in fact places this rain at V:30, as does Abū al-'Uqūl. *Fuṣūl* marks the *ḥamīm* rain at V:29, with *Salwa* and Taymūr giving a date of VI:2 (18° Gemini). In the Dathīna dialect of southern Yemen this term refers to a summer rain (Landberg 1920:1:478), while in Dhofar it is said to be an autumn rain (Rhodokanakis 1911:2:13). There is no doubt some confusion from the Yemeni usage of *kharīf* for "late summer" rather than "autumn" in the classical sense of the four-season model. Serjeant (1954:438) observed that at Daw'ān in the south of Yemen the term *ḥamīm* could refer to any period of rain and not just one falling at a particular time.

Kharf. Al-Malik al-Ashraf defined *kharf* as an Indian term for light precipitation (*ṭashsh* or *dīma*) or mist which occurs at Dhofar on the coast of southwestern Yemen. This term survives in the Mahrī dialect of today in reference to the summer monsoon.[8] The term is apparently derived from *kharīf*, with the Arabic usage being documented for India (Spate 1963:731). The author said in *Tabṣira* (fol. 111r) that this was a mist rather than a rain with drops and that this mist could block out the sun. *Dīma* refers to a steady rain without thunder (al-Tīfāshī 1980:270). In the almanac this mist is said to occur at Dhofar between VI:16 and IX:4, clearly a reference to the monsoon season.

Kharīf. The term *kharīf* is classical Arabic usage for "autumn" in the four-season model, although in Yemen it refers to summer, particularly the late summer rains (al-Hamdānī 1977:120; Varisco 1982a:112). In the Himyaritic calendar *Dhū Kharāf* was the equivalent of August. Al-Malik al-Ashraf placed this rain at VIII:2 and Abū al-'Uqūl added that it ended at IX:12. In the *anwā'* system the *kharīf* rain was associated with the setting of *na'ā'im* (at VI:23) through *al-fargh al-muqaddam* (until IX:22), although Quṭrub (1985) associated this rain with the dawn setting of *nasrān* (Altair and Vega) in August. This name derives from the fact that the rain fell at the time of the autumn date harvest (Abū Zayd in Ibn Sīda 1965:9:78; *Kifāya*, fol. 97r). Quṭrub claimed that *kharīf* in the Hejaz dialect was the same as *ḥamīm* in the speech of Tamīm. The Rwala Bedouins refer to the rain falling at the rising of Canopus in midsummer as *kharfī* (Musil 1928:8).

Qayḍ/qayẓ. The term *qayḍ* or *qayẓ* was equivalent to the month of June in the Himyaritic calendar. The basic meaning is the heat of summer. As described in *Tabṣira* (fol. 111v), this rain falls during *Ḥazīrān* (June) and could be dangerous to standing crops (al-Tīfāshī 1980:232). Ibn Kunāsa (in Ibn Sīda 1965:9:87) defined *qayẓ* as the name of a rain period in Yemen. The Yemeni savant al-Hamdānī (1977:116, 120) referred to the rain during *Tammūz* (July) and *Āb* (August) as *muqīḍ*, which he equated with the *kharīf* rain.

Rabī'. In the four-season model of Islamic astronomy *rabī'* meant "spring." However among the Bedouins and farmers of the peninsula this term had a variety of meanings. Abū Ḥanīfa al-Dīnawarī (quoted in *Lisān al-'Arab*, *r-b-'*), one of the early writers of the *anwā'* genre, said that the six cold months of winter could be divided into a *rabī'* of water and a following *rabī'* of plants. In another tradition the first *rabī'* is a time of pasture and truffles, while the second refers to the ripening of crops in the autumn. In yet another system there is a *rabī'* in early autumn and another in the spring. Ibn Qutayba (1956:118) claimed that this term could be used for any rain period. Among the Bedouins *rabī'* often refers to the pasture following the rain rather than the rain itself (al-Jawālīqī n.d.:140; Musil 1928:13). Given the scholarly shift of seasons for Yemen, *rabī'* should technically cover the period of winter, a pedantic shift in meaning it never had in local dialects.

The almanac places the *rabī'* rain at XI:1 and indicates this was the Yemeni equivalent of the autumn *wasmī* rain that falls in Syria (in reference to areas north of Yemen). Similarly the Syrian *rabī'* was said to be called the *wasmī* rain in Yemen during *Shubāṭ* (February). Al-Malik al-Ashraf observed that a rain at this time was rare in Yemen, although it could fall from time to time. In *Salwa* the *rabī'* rain is placed at IV:8 (27° Aries). The confused references in the Rasulid texts appear to represent a scholarly inport rather than local usage, since it was difficult to ignore this important name for a rain period in other parts of the Arabian Peninsula.

Ramaḍī. This rain was defined by the author as one falling during the intense heat and thus harmful to pasture at the time. The term *ramaḍ* signifies the intensity of heat and survives in the Islamic month name of *Ramaḍān*, which was originally a hot summer month in the Arab lunar-solar calendar before Islam. Ibn Qutayba (1956:114) called this a rain of *qayẓ* and equated it with *ṣayyif* and *shamsī*. The almanac mentions the *ramaḍī* rain at VI:25, while *Fuṣūl* and *Salwa* record VI:24 (10° Cancer). Ibn al-Bannā', in his North African almanac, referred to this rain as falling at V:28 and VII:19 and the *Calendar of Cordova* places it during the *naw'* of *balda* after VII:6. There is no evidence that this term was used by Yemeni farmers.

Shitā'. This is the rain of winter, usually referred to as *shatawī* in adjectival form. The term *shitā'* refers to winter in the four-season model, although this would technically be "autumn" in the artificial scholarly reconstruction for Yemen. Abū al-'Uqūl in fact mentioned the first of this rain at X:30 along with the intensification of the southern *azyab* wind. In the almanac al-Malik al-Ashraf noted that this rain could sometimes occur in Yemen after the setting of *simāk*. In the *anwā'* system this rain was said to fall between the settings of *han'a* and *ṭarf* (from XII:20 until II:9). The Rwala Bedouins use this term for a rain period of about forty nights in January and February (Musil 1928:8). The Bedouins of Kuwait, however, refer to *shitā'* as a cold dry season between the autumn *wasm* rain and the spring rain (Dickson 1951:256).

Tammūz. Al-Malik al-Ashraf said in his treatise (*Tabṣira*, fol. 111v) that the rain falling in the month of *Tammūz* (July) could also be called by this month name. He noted that when there was plentiful rain in June, the rain falling in July would not be beneficial because of the intense heat at the time. This is apparently in reference to rain in a pastoral setting, rather than for Yemen's agriculture. It is doubtful that this was a local term for rain.

Thawr. The term *thawr* refers to the evening rising of Taurus, although the specific stars intended are not indicated in the text. This is a term of local usage for a rain period and has not been documented in non-Yemeni almanacs. The Rasulid almanacs place this rain at V:19.[9] The agricultural marker stars listed by al-Hattār include *thawr* as a seven-day period starting on V:20, while in the contemporary system of agricultural marker stars there is both a rising and setting of *thawr* (Varisco 1993a).

Walī. The almanac mentions the *walī* rain at XI:29, although *Fuṣūl* clarifies this as occurring in Syria rather than Yemen. Taymūr adds that this rain rarely fell in Yemen. This term literally refers to a rain following a rain, usually for the rains that follow the autumn *wasmī* rain (al-Ḥimyarī 1980:226; Ibn Qutayba 1956:116). While this was a well-known rain period among the Arabian Bedouins (Musil 1928:8-9), the term was probably not used locally in Yemen by farmers. It is important to note that the Rasulid text of *Salwa* misreads *walī* as *wabā* (!), literally, "infectious disease." This error is repeated in a number of later Yemeni almanacs.

Wasmī. This is the most famous of the pre-Islamic rain periods, and the name survives in contemporary usage across the Arabian Peninsula (Dickson 1951:250; Musil 1928:8; al-Muṭayrī 1984:14) and Sinai (Bailey 1974:588). The lexicographers stated that it was so named because it marks (*yasimu*) the ground with plants. Thus it usually refers to the first rains of the year after the hot summer drought. These are the rains that bring pasture and truffles in the desert. Al-Tha'ālibī (n.d.:24) compared the *wasmī* to other rains as the *subḥ* (dawn) to the rest of the day (*nahār*). In the classical *anwā'* system the *wasmī* rain started with the setting of *al-fargh al-mu'akhkhar* at IX:23 and ended at the conclusion of the setting of the Pleiades at XI:23. The *wasmī* or *wasm* rain is commonly associated with the dawn setting or evening rising of the Pleiades in the folk astronomy of the peninsula (Varisco 1990:15–16). Al-Malik al-Ashraf (*Tabṣira*, fol. 115v) said the *wasmī* rain in Syria fell in the autumn at XI:1, but that in Yemen this term referred to the early spring rain during *Shubāṭ* at the dawn setting of the stars of *ṣawāb*, a reference in fact to the same stars as were recognized in the lunar station of *al-fargh al-mu'akhkhar*.

WINDS

In his treatise al-Malik al-Ashraf described the winds according to the scientific perspective of his day.[10] The four cardinal directions, which define the winds, are called *ṣabā* (east), *dabūr* (west), *jirbiyā'*[11] (north), and *yaman* (south) in the text. These are classical terms, but the latter two are somewhat academic, since north is generally *shamāl* and south is *janūb*. The early names of the cardinal winds suggest a cosmological portrait of the sacred shrine of the *ka'ba* at Mecca, a tradition described in detail by David A. King (1982, forthcoming). Simply put, the cardinal directions appear to have been defined from the perspective of someone at the *ka'ba* facing the sunrise. The wind coming from the cast is sometimes called *qabūl* because it is in front (*min qubul*). The opposite wind blowing from the west is thus styled *dabūr* because it is from the back (*dubur*) of the *ka'ba*. Blowing from north would be the *shamāl*, which has the literal meaning of "left" in Arabic usage. Then to the right would be the south (*yaman*), from which the *janūb* wind comes.

There is a wealth of folklore in Arab tradition regarding the winds, especially those from the four cardinal directions. Ibn Mājid (in Tibbetts 1971:143) claimed that the north wind divides clouds, the east wind gathers clouds together, the south wind draws out the rain, and the north wind scatters the clouds. These winds are sometimes defined according to astronomical coordinates as well. For example, the direction from which the south wind blows is often defined by the location of Canopus (*suhayl*).

Al-Malik al-Ashraf included a diagram of twelve winds defining the basic compass points. This is not an indigenous Arab concept, but one derived from classical tradition (Aristotle 1978:187; Pseudo-Apollonios 1979:137; and Qusṭūs, fol. 7b) and commonly cited by Islamic scholars (e.g., al-Hamdānī 1983:268), including the later Rasulid text of the *Bughya* (fol. 24). In the classical system each wind is assigned a sign of the zodiac, for astrological purposes rather than defining the direction. These winds are defined by al-Ashraf as follows:

Term	Direction
janūb	south
ṣarṣar[12]	south by southwest
ṣirr[13]	southwest by west
dabūr	west
'āṣif	west by northwest
'aqīm[14]	northwest by north
shamāl	north
ṣabā	north by northeast
'āṣif	northeast by east
qabūl or *ṣabā*	east
samūm	east by southeast
nakbā'[15]	southeast by south

The twelve winds mentioned by the author make up a scholarly system that would not have been used by Yemeni farmers, apart from the commonly known wind names. The distinctions created by the scholar are somewhat arbitrary and not necessarily related to usage in dialects of Yemen and the rest of the Arabian Peninsula.

In the almanac a number of winds are mentioned, including the major summer monsoon on which the *dīmānī* or *tīrmāh* sailings to India occurred. During January and February Yemeni farmers anticipated the annual *lawāqiḥ* winds, which assisted in pollenation of the date palms. In the coastal region, however, the hot winds of summer, called *bawāriḥ, khamsīniyāt,* or *samā' im*, were dreaded. Each of the winds referenced in the almanac is discussed below:

'Awāṣif. The term *'awāṣif* is the plural of *'āṣif* and indicates a violent or intense blowing for a period of time. It has the force of a gale wind in English usage. This is a commonly cited term in the almanac tradition and in Yemeni dialect. The variant terms *mu'ṣif* and *mu'ṣifa* are also recorded in the lexicons. The author referred to it as similar to the wind called *za'āzī'*, which al-Tha'ālibī (n.d.:176) defined as a violent wind capable of swaying branches and uprooting plants. It has been identified as a wind that God sends for punishment on the sea (al-Tha'ālibī n.d.:250).

Al-Malik al-Ashraf reported that the *'awāṣif* winds came from the northeast or northwest at VI:10, while *Salwa* and Taymūr place them at VI:9 (26° Cancer). Waṭyūṭ (fol. 77v) wrote that in August of A.D. 1286 (*Rabī' Akhir*, A.H. 685) a violent wind came to Yemen from the north. The sky grew dark and great rains fell on Yemen at the rising of Vega. This storm destroyed so many houses, crops, and animals that the tax burden was lifted for an entire year.

The modern almanac of al-Ḥaydara (Serjeant 1954:451) places the blowing of the west wind at VI:9. The reference is clearly to the hot and dry winds of summer, also referred to as *khamsīn* and *samūm* by the author. As such this usage of *'awāṣif* probably reflects usage by farmers. *Fuṣūl* cites these winds at XI:23, when the sea became so rough that it was closed for shipping. This reference to the sea is common in the non-Yemeni almanacs (e.g., Ibn Mammātī at XI:19 or 23 *Hatūr*).

Azyab. Along the Yemeni coast *azyab* refers to a wind from the south (Ibn al-Mujāwir 1954:265; *Kifāya*, fol. 92r; Rossi 1939:244; Serjeant 1954:447, note 45) or the southeast (Landberg 1920:1:76; Sulaymān al-Mahrī 1925:38v). Ibn Sīda (1965:9:85) claimed the term originated in the Hudhayl dialect. In *Tāj al-'arūs* the term refers to south in general, but any violent wind may be called *dhāt azyab*, where *azyab* can refer to a type of spirit or devil. In the almanac it is equated with the south (*janūb*) wind. Both the author and *Fuṣūl* equate this wind with *mirām/marām* in local dialect. Al-Malik al-Ashraf said in *Milḥ* that the *lawāqiḥ* winds are from the south, that is, the same as the *azyab*.

The almanac notes the blowing of the *azyab* wind at IX:9 and X:14, with a strengthening at X:21 and the end at V:6. *Fuṣūl* records the blowing of the *azyab* at X:17. Abū al-ʻUqūl indicated the starting date at X:14, but also mentions a blowing earlier at IX:9, similar to al-Malik al-Ashraf. Abū al-ʻUqūl placed the strengthening at X:30 and Taymūr puts this at X:22. Abū al-ʻUqūl also noted the end of this wind at V:13. During this wind period the ships of India and China came west to Aden and ships went up the Red Sea to Egypt. Ibn Mājid (Tibbetts 1971:372) said that there was a break in this wind for Yemen and the Hejaz at the end of February, when the sea was closed there to most shipping due to the calm.

Bawāriḥ. This term is the plural of *bāriḥ*, which refers to a hot summer wind in the *anwā'* genre. Ibn Sīda (1965:9:85) claimed it could also mean a wind that stirs up dust or an intensely cold wind. According to Ibn Qutayba (1956:88) the term is derived from the fact that it came (*tabraḥu*) from the north of the *kaʻba*, a reference to the cosmology of the sacred shrine at Mecca. Serjeant (1954:450, note 57) records the use of *baraḥ* in the dialect of the Ḥaḍramawt for a breeze in general.

The author equated these hot summer winds with the *samūm*, which comes from the north between the dawn risings of the Pleiades at V:16 and *jabha* at VIII:15. However, in the almanac the dates for the *bawāriḥ* are indicated as V:17–25, with a return at increased strength after VI:2. In the anwā' tradition these winds were said to blow from the dawn setting of *zubānā* after IV:29 (Ibn al-Ajdābī 1964:159).

Dīmānī. The almanac refers to *dīmānī* as a major sailing season associated with the monsoon winds. Arab navigators used this term or the variant *damānī* to mean part of the southwest *kaws* or *tīrmāh* winds (Ferrand 1914:2:487; Khūrī 1981:217; Shihāb 1982:220). Ibn Mājid (Tibbetts 1971:132) said this wind blew from mid-August; at this time travel on the sea was difficult (Grosset-Grange 1972:77). Along the African coast it blows from September through November (Serjeant 1974c:217). There is some confusion over the origin of the usage in Arabic. The term is derived from the Persian, where it refers to the main sheet of a ship (Steinglass 1930:494; Tibbetts 1971:367, 524). Serjeant (1982:126) records a usage in the Arabian Gulf for the starboard side of a ship. The term *damān* in Persian can also refer to traveling or migrating (Johnson 1852:553).

Janūb. This is the common term for the south wind in Arabic, sometimes referred to as *azyab* by sailors and known as *marīsī*[16] in Egypt. The almanac notes this wind at IX:9 and X:14 with an intensification after XI:6. Al-Malik al-Ashraf is referring to the southwest *azyab* wind, which took ships east to India or north to Egypt. In the *Bughya* (fol. 240) it is noted that this could become quite a violent wind in winter. During winter it is a dry wind for the Yemeni farmer (al-Baraddūnī 1985:312), but in spring it brings the rain (Ibn Qutayba 1956:167). The contemporary Yemeni almanac of al-Ḥaydara (1974) mentions a blowing of the wind at V:5, probably in reference to the end of it.

Khamsīn. This commonly used term throughout the Arab world literally refers to a period of fifty days. The plural *khamsīniyāt* is also cited by the author (*Tabṣira*, fol. 109v), who described this as a period of fifty days with violent winds (*'awāṣif*), twisting gusts, and troublesome storms (*zawābi'*). The almanac and *Salwa* place these winds at IV:19 (7° Taurus). *Fuṣūl* notes these winds at IV:20, where they are defined as a hot southern wind (*hayf*). Abū al-'Uqūl said that the wind at IV:19 is called *raqīb al-thurayyā*.[17] At this time the dates begin to yellow and reach the *busr* stage. Al-Malik al-Ashraf said that the *quṭrub* spirit is active at the blowing of these winds. In Egypt these winds are generally known as *khamāsīn* (Amīn 1953:195), which are said to begin the day after Easter and last until Whitsunday of Pentecost (Lane 1973:488). The first day of this period is called *shamm al-nasīm*, a popular time in Egypt for outings before the blistering heat of the summer winds.

Lawāqiḥ. The *lawāqiḥ*, or Pollenating Winds, are so named because they impregnate clouds with rain (*Lisān al-'Arab*, *l-q-ḥ*), and they are also the winds which pollenate the date palms and fruit at the end of winter. The popularity of the term is enhanced in no small part by a reference to these winds in surah 15:22 of the Quran. Al-Malik al-Ashraf defined them as the *azyab* or south wind, a common identification in the scholarly tradition (al-Hamdānī 1977:113; Ibn Qutayba 1956:163). The Yemeni scholar al-Shawkānī (n.d.:220) argued that variable winds were more important than a single blowing for successful pollenation at this time.

The exact dating of these winds is not consistent in the Rasulid almanacs. Al-Malik al-Ashraf said they blow from I:11 until II:24, but Abū al-'Uqūl gave the range as I:14 to II:23 and *Fuṣūl* as I:13 to II:14, with a strengthening of the wind at II:15. *Salwa* notes these winds from 1:5 (23° Capricornus) and from II:7 (27° Aquarius). The latter date is apparently copied from the earlier almanac tradition, such as the text of Abū Ḥanīfa al-Dīnawarī (1914).

Mirām/marām. Both the author (*Tabṣira*, fol. 116r) and *Fuṣūl* record this name as a Yemeni variant for the south *azyab* wind which blows from mid-

October. Al-Malik al-Ashraf included a proverb which reads, "When the south wind made a noise, the sorghum dried up" (*Idhā harrat mirām/marām zakā al-ṭa'ām*). The term *mirām/marām* is not explained in the Rasulid texts and the meaning is not readily apparent from the Arabic lexicons. The use of *ṭa'ām* refers literally to grain, but sorghum is clearly intended. In *Fuṣūl*'s citation of the proverb *zakā* is replaced with *yabisu*, which also means "to dry up." This wind can also be defined as a cold wind blowing from the northwest at X:15 (*Bughya*, fol. 23r).

Ṣabā. This is the most common Arabic term for the east wind in the almanac genre. It is equivalent to *qabūl* and *sharqīya*. The lexicons derive the usage from the fact that it is "desired" because it is a pleasant wind. The Yemeni physician al-Azraq (1978:31) described this as the best wind for health. Al-Marzūqī (1914:1:218) claimed that the Arabs of the desert opened their tents to receive this wind. Lane (1984:1640), however, sees a connection with the religious sect of the ancient Sabians. The almanac mentions a blowing at X:4, while Abū al-'Uqūl and *Fuṣūl* record this at X:3. According to al-Malik al-Afḍal (*Bughya*, fol. 18v), this wind signals the start of autumn. The contemporary almanac of al-Ḥaydara (1974) notes the east wind at X:11. Reference to the east wind around this time is common in the non-Yemeni almanacs (e.g., Ibn Mammātī at IX:28). Al-Malik al-Ashraf, *Fuṣūl*, and *Salwa* mention an additional blowing of this wind at III:11 (1° Aries), with Taymūr giving III:13. The latter reference is apparently taken from the classical tradition, where the east wind was seen as a sign of spring (Qusṭūs, fol. 7r).

Samūm/samā'im. The simoon, or sirocco, is the hot summer wind similar to *bawāriḥ* and *khamsīn*. The author called it a southwest wind, but the later Yemeni astronomer al-Thābitī referred to it as a south wind. A distinction is made in the almanac between the wind of *samūm* and the period of *samā'im*; the former blows at V:29 and the latter begins at VI:2 with the intensification of the *bawāriḥ* winds. Abū Ḥanīfa al-Dīnawarī (1914) equated the blowing of the *samā'im* winds with the dawn rising of the Pleiades at V:16. Ibn Mammātī (1943), however, said this wind began with the midsummer rising of Sirius at VII:6 (12 *Abīb*). This association with Sirius, the so-called Dog Star, is noted by Ibn al-'Awwām (1802:2:443) as a forty-day period in Islamic Spain and it survives in the French term *canicule* ("dog days"). Lane (1973:2) claims that the *samūm* in Egypt is even more oppressive than the hot *khamsīn* period. According to al-Maqrīzī (in Rabie 1981:77), a sandstorm around A.D. 1294 destroyed crops of rice, sugarcane, sesame, and *Colocasia* in Lower Egypt, leading to widespread famine. Dickson (1951:252) describes these hot summer winds "as though driven out of a great furnace by some gigantic bellows." At the medieval port of Hormuz, Marco Polo (1958:67) called this "a wind so overpoweringly hot that it would be deadly if it did not happen that, as soon as men are aware of its approach, they plunge neck-deep into the water and so escape the heat." A century later Ibn Baṭṭūṭa (1980:278) described the graves near Hormuz as the resting places of victims of this hot blast.

Shamāl. The term *shamāl*, often pronounced *shimāl*, refers to the north in classical Arabic. The author equated it with the more academic *jirbiyā'*, while Ibn Qutayba (1956:159) noted the usage among the Bedouins as *sha'mīya* in reference to the northern location of Syria (al-Sha'm). According to al-Malik al-Afḍal (*Bughya*, fol. 24r), this wind blows in spring and late summer and is beneficial for plants and animals. The almanac places the blowing of the north wind between II:23 and III:21, with *Fuṣūl* noting this was the last of the *lawāqiḥ* winds. Abū al-'Uqūl placed this north wind between II:27 and III:21, adding that it blows at night. *Salwa* places the end of the north wind as III:21 (8° Aries). According to *Fuṣūl* the north wind at VIII:26 takes the Indian ships from Aden. The north wind blows at the end of *qayẓ* during the *naw'* of *sa'd al-akhbiya* from VIII:28, according to Abū Ḥanīfa al-Dīnawarī (1914).

Sharqīya. This is a common name for the east wind, also called *ṣabā* in the almanac. Al-Malik al-Ashraf said this east wind blows from IV:27, although *Fuṣūl* records this at IV:28. As the modern Yemeni poet al-Baraddūnī (1985:31) has observed, this is a spring wind carrying rain. Perhaps this is the same as the wind of *raqīb al-thurayyā* mentioned at IV:19 by Abū al-'Uqūl.

Tīrmāh. *Tīrmāh* is a Persian month name, originally designating the hot summer period in June-July. In Persian *tīr* means "Sirius," in this case its summer rising. For sailors in the Indian Ocean, *tīrmāh* denotes the southwest monsoon, which comes in late summer. According to the almanac the *tīrmāh* sailing began from Aden at VIII:21. In the medieval navigational texts the *tīrmāh* was essentially the same as the *kaws* or *dabūr* winds from the west. According to Ibn Mājid (Tibbetts 1971:144) the *kaws* wind is also associated with the setting of Sirius for the period of one hundred days after the start of January. Similarly, the noted historian al-Mas'ūdī (1861:1:327) recorded the term *tīrmāh* as a wind blowing in January.

TEMPERATURE AND SPECIAL WEATHER PERIODS

Variations in temperature between the extremes of hot and cold were of great concern for Yemeni farmers. This was especially the case in the mountains, where the possibility of winter frost created a danger for most crops. The almanac includes information on several hot and cold periods commonly known in Arab tradition, although it is not clear if all of the cited terms were actually used in Yemeni dialect. As a scholarly document, there is also mention of the changes in temperature based on the classical model of four seasons and earlier weather lore in the *anwā'* literature.

The transition from summer heat to the cool temperatures of autumn was an important event throughout the Arabian Peninsula. The almanac uses a formulaic reference to the "passing of the heat and advance of the cold" at IX:24. This timing is not derived from Yemeni folklore but from the *anwā'* tradition as reported by Abū Zayd al-Anṣārī, who linked it to the start of an autumn period known as *ṣafarīya* (Ibn 'Āṣim 1985:40). Reference is also made at VIII:14 to a temperate period called *mu'tadilāt* after the summer rising of Canopus. Both of these seasons are based on early Arabic usage and are not related to the formal autumnal equinox at IX:15 in the reckoning of the almanac.

By XII:4 it is cold enough that one's breath leaves vapors in the air, a common reference in the almanacs. The coldest weather is said to occur with the rising of *dhirā'* on XII:16 (*Bughya*, fol. 19v). Water freezes on XII:20, according to the almanac, Abū al-'Uqūl, and *Fuṣūl*, but on III:18 in Taymūr. By the winter solstice the cold reaches its greatest intensity. Several distinct cold periods, some of which overlap, are mentioned in the almanac: the Scorpions of Winter (*'aqārib al-shitā'*), the two cold months of *jumaydā,* the Mixed Nights (*al-layālī al-bulq*), and the Black Nights (*al-layālī al-sūd*). *Fuṣūl* notes that the cold abates after the Christian holiday of Epiphany. The almanac marks the moderation of the cold weather at 1:7, with a further slackening at II:18. The latter date is clearly derived from the *anwā'* tradition, where the cold breaks at the setting of *jabha* on II:18, according to Ibn al-Ajdābī (1964).

The cold passes and the heat advances at III:17, according to the almanac. Before this the cold weather has a last hurrah, because in medieval Islamic science it was thought that the last of the season saw the most intense weather (al-Bīrūnī 1879 at VIII:26). The month of February is characterized by the falling of three Coals (*jamār*) and by the well-known Nights of the Old Woman (*layālī al-'ajūz*) for seven days shared between the end of February and beginning of March. The heat of summer appears with the blowing of hot, dry winds known as *bawāriḥ*, *samūm* or *samā'im*, and *khamsīniyāt*. On VI:10, according to the almanac, the intense heat of summer (*ḥamārrat al-qayẓ*) is ignited. *Fuṣūl* records intense heat between VI:14 and VII:15, while Abū al-'Uqūl said heat reaches its greatest intensity at VII:7. In the *anwā'* tradition the heat is said to be most intense at the summer rising of Sirius (Ibn al-Ajdābī 1964 at VII:19). *Salwa* adds that sometimes the weather turns cool briefly at VII:2 (17° Cancer), but it is unclear if this is in reference to Yemen. The last hurrah for the summer heat is a period of seven days known as *majar* (?) from VIII:29. This is said to end the summer in much the same way that the Nights of the Old Woman conclude winter.

The specific weather periods mentioned in the almanac are discussed below in alphabetical order:

'Aqārib al-shitā'. The name of this season, the Scorpions of Winter, plays on the fact that the stations of Scorpius are rising at this time and the sting of winter can be felt. According to Ibn Qutayba (1956:119), this refers to the three stations of *iklīl, qalb,* and *shawla* (all stars in Scorpius), which rise during the coldest part of winter. Ibn Mājid (Tibbetts 1971:108) noted that winter is strongest at the rising of *shawla*. The related sense of *'aqārib al-bard* (Scorpions of the Cold), used by Arabian Bedouins, stands in opposition to the hot *waghra* periods of summer (Ibn Qutayba 1956:119). Al-Malik al-Ashraf followed an older tradition, recorded in the *Calendar of Cordova* and by Ibn 'Āṣim (1985), that the scorpion periods do not correspond to the rising of the stations but rather a system that links the solar and lunar calendars. The first *'aqrab*, or scorpion, occurs with the new moon in the month of November, the second with the new moon in December, and the third with the new moon in January. The start of this reckoning occurs about the time of the rising of *iklīl*, but it extends for three lunar months and thus far beyond the stations of Scorpius. In the almanac of al-Shayzarī, for example, the setting of *nathra* at I:17 is still called an *'aqrab*. This system appears to have survived in the Hejaz (al-Bilādī 1982:325; al-Suwaydā' 1983:217) and has parallels to the Yemeni Pleiades calendar based on the conjunction of the new moon and the Pleiades (Varisco 1993a).

The Scorpions of Winter represent a time of cold weather, similar to the two cold months of *jumaydā* from the *anwā'* tradition. Al-Malik al-Ashraf said that in some years frost (*ḍarīb*) occurs. If there are winter mists or heavy clouds at this time, it will prolong the harmful cold. At times a winter rain may fall and damage the crops. If, however, the harvest has already been completed, the farmers are pleased to see the rain and plant a winter sowing known as *qiyāḍ* or *'aqar*. The former term is noted by the author as a distinct sowing period, while the latter is a Yemeni term for any planting on rain-fed land rather than irrigated fields (Varisco 1982a:443).

Ayyām al-bāḥūr. The term *bāḥūr* (*bawāḥīr*, plural) refers to a week during the heat of the summer, which the author placed between VI:19 and VI:26. Al-Malik al-Ashraf recorded this a month early in his timing, an indication that it was not local usage in Yemen. Abū al-'Uqūl said that people in the coastal region called this time *kwya'* (?), a reading which is unclear in all the extant copies of his almanac. The modern almanac of al-Ḥaydara (1974) cites a week called *kry'a* (?) at Zabīd around this time. Al-Bīrūnī (1879) began these days at VII:18 and associated them with the dog days at the rising of Sirius. It is interesting to note that al-Bīrūnī said some people start these days on VII:19, which may be the date that al-Malik al-Ashraf miscopied. There is some variation in the timing from the almanac sources; for example, al-Qazwīnī (1859) cited them from VII:12. The contemporary Yemeni almanac of al-Ḥaydara places these days from VII:31.

In his discussion of this period, al-Bīrūnī (1879:259–62) offered several theories about its origin. One possibility is that the term is derived from *baḥr* (sea), since this is a critical time for determining the course of an illness and the state of a sick person is similar to the ebb and flow of the sea. This is surely an academic play with Arabic etymology and hardly seems appropriate. Another option is that the term is derived from a Greek or Syriac word (*bāḥūr* or *buḥrān*),[18] which al-Bīrūnī defined as meaning "the decision of the rulers." It should be noted that *bāḥūr* is an Arabic term for the moon (al-Nuwayrī 1923:1:51). The almanac of al-Khalījī notes that this is a time when it is not appropriate to have sex or to wash clothes, two things that may or may not be connected. A number of non-Yemeni almanacs, such as the texts of al-Bīrūnī (1879) and al-Qazwīnī (1859), describe a practice of weather prediction, which was probably derived from Syriac sources. This was the common medieval system of association days (Trachtenberg 1982:253–54). In this case the first day of the week of *bāḥūr* was associated with the first month (i.e., October) of the year so that the weather on this day prefigured the weather in the associated month and so on. It is obvious that such a practice did not develop on the Arabian Peninsula but rather in a climate where rain or cool weather might occur throughout the year. These days may also be linked to the Sirius agricultural rite in which the plants sprouting under the light of Sirius prefigured the success or failure of crops in the coming agricultural harvest.

Ayyām al-lawāqiḥ. At IX:27 in the almanac the author mentioned a period of ten days known as *lawāqiḥ*, a term which usually refers to pollenation as in the Pollenating Winds, which blow in January and February. *Fuṣūl* starts these days at IX:26, a day earlier. This is not a time for pollenation in Yemen, however, and a different meaning is obviously intended. The references in the Rasulid almanacs are not clear, especially in the copies of the text of Abū al-'Uqūl. There is no mention of this term in the non-Yemeni almanacs or the *anwā'* references. Given that this is said to be a ten-day period, it may be the author's interpretation of a period from the Greek tradition.

The interpretation which has been adopted in the translation here is that this is a plural for the term *laqwa*, which literally refers to a disease of the face (*dā' fī al-wajh*), according to Aḥmad ibn Fāris (1984:2:811). This refers to a disease that can distort the face (al-Suyūṭī 1986:284, note 1). In describing the term, al-Malik al-Ashraf (*Tabṣira*, fol. 110v) said that at this time of year the midday heat (*hawājir*) is very intense. This heat is described as *takhḍaru al-wujūh;* relating to the darkening of the skin from the intense heat of the sun at this time. Both al-Ashraf and *Fuṣūl* add that Yemeni farmers call this time *lawāhif*, a term which has the sense of being distressed. Al-Ashraf also remarked that this time is the start of the wheat and barley harvest.

Ayyām al-ṣafarīya. In Arab meteorological lore this is the transitional period between the heat of summer and autumn. The term is derived from the fact that at this time the leaves of trees begin to turn yellow (*ṣafrā'*), as noted in *Fuṣūl*. This is also the etymology of the pre-Islamic month name of *Ṣafar* (al-A'rābī in al-Marzūqī 1914:1:168 and al-Jawālīqī n.d.:140). As is true with much of the etymological gamesmanship of the lexicographers, however, there are numerous arguments among lexical scholars over the origin of the month name of *Ṣafar*. Al-Mas'ūdī (1982:2:504) thought it came from a marketplace in Yemen, where a major fair was held in the pre-Islamic era. Al-Bīrūnī (1879:321), who can be particularly clever in his linguistic arguments, noted that at this time people generally become sick and their faces turn yellow. Lane (1984:1698) records yet another meaning that this was the time when granaries were empty (*ṣifr*). The more common reference to the yellowing of the autumn leaves seems the most reasonable and practical choice. *Fuṣūl* adds that this period was known as *dhahābiyāt* in Egypt, where yellow appears to have turned into gold (*dhahab*). Ibn Sīda (1965:10:204–5) said that at this time a plant known as *rabl* springs up on land hardened by lack of rain.

In the Rasulid almanacs the timing of these days of temperate weather is from IX:23 to X:20, following the period designated as *mu'tadilāt*. Abū al-'Uqūl said it was the true start of *shitā'*, no doubt meaning autumn in the general sense, in Yemen. This dating is in fact derived from the *anwā'* tradition of Abū Zayd al-Anṣārī, who said that *ṣafarīya* consists of thirty days from the setting of *al-fargh al-mu'akhkhar* (i.e., from ca. IX:23). This rendering differs from Quṭrub (1985), who began these days from the summer rising of Canopus, a usage still found among Bedouins of the Arabian Peninsula (Cole 1975:39; Dickson 1951:247; al-Muṭayrī 1984:13–14; Musil 1928:8; Philby 1928:60; Varisco 1990:15). In *Tāj al-'arūs* (*ṣ-f-r*) these are the last twenty days of summer.

Ḍarīb. The frost or crop-killing cold is called *ḍarīb* in the Yemeni highlands, where it can occur often in the winter. The origin of the term stems from the fact that this cold literally "hits" because of its freezing action. This term is still widely used in the Yemeni highlands, as well as *ḍarba* in the Ḥaḍramawt (Serjeant 1954:439). The term *ḍarīb* is equated in the lexicons with *jalīd, saqī,'* and *bard* (al-Ḥimyarī 1980:224; Ibn Sīda 1965:9:120; al-Jawālīqī n.d.:134; al-Marzūqī 1914:2:90).[19] In *Tabṣira* (fol.110r) the author stated that if this frost occurred before the grain was formed, it would destroy the yield. This observation is echoed in a contemporary Yemeni proverb: "The results of the intense cold are weak yields" (*'awāqib al-bard al-akhlāf*).[20]

The timing for frost ranges between XI:16 and XII:12, according to the almanac, although *Fuṣūl, Salwa,* and Taymūr begin it at XI:15. This date is taken from the *anwā'* tradition in which Abū Ḥanīfa al-Dīnawarī (1914) placed the frost (*jalīd*) from XI:15 at the setting of the Pleiades. *Fuṣūl* adds that the frost can occur in the two cold months of *jumaydā*. The later Yemeni almanac of al-Thābitī mentioned the frost occurring as early as X:20 in the mountains.

Ḥamārrat al-qayẓ. This is a common reference to the fact that the summer heat ignites (*talhabu*)[21] in the hottest part of the year (Ibn al-Ajdābī 1964:166; Ibn Sīda 1965:9:74; al-Jawālīqī n.d.:141; al-Tha'ālibī n.d.:20). During the lunar-solar calendar of pre-Islamic Arabia this occurred during the month of *Ramaḍān*. Later Arabic almanacs usually miscopy *ḥamārra* as *jamra* (coal), a term which would seem at first glance to fit equally well but is clearly a misreading. There is no evidence in the *anwā'* literature that the Arabs referred to a *jamra* in summer as distinct from the *jamār* of February. The pre-Islamic usage survives in Kuwait, where there is a hot period known as *ḥamārrat al-qā'ila*, in which the local people do not go out under the midday sun (al-Sa'īdān 1981:1:440). Al-Malik al-Ashraf (*Tabṣira*, fol. 111v) explained that the hot *samūm* wind blows at this time and the sand it raises can look like a column of smoke. Abū al-'Uqūl said that it is so hot at this time that a person becomes thirsty returning from the well to the house. This is in fact a reference to the *anwā'* tradition, in which thirst is said to come again between the cistern (*ḥawḍ*) and the well, as noted by al-Shayzarī at VI:11.

The Rasulid almanacs place the *ḥamārra* at VI:10, which apparently is derived from the rising of *haq'a* in the *anwā'* tradition (e.g., at VI:9 according to Ibn al-Ajdābī 1964). The almanac attributed to Ja'far al-Ṣādiq, however, equates this period with the rising of *han'a* at VI:24, while in the *Calendar of Cordova* the date is VII:17. In the Arabic translation of the agricultural treatise of Qusṭūs the expression *ḥamārrat al-qayẓ* is used to refer to the forty days after the rising of Sirius, an important period in Greek meteorology.

Jamra. The *jamra* (*jamār* or *jamrāt*, plurals) refers to a live coal or ember from a fire. Most Arab almanacs mention the falling (*suqūṭ*) of three Coals in the month of February. Al-Malik al-Ashraf cited the common placing of the First Coal at II:7, the Second at II:14, and the Third at II:21. The almanac of Abū al-'Uqūl notes that the Second Coal is known locally as *qarāqir*[22] or *ṣarāṣir*,[23] two terms which refer to cold weather, while the Third Coal was the first day of *ẓāfir*, the Yemeni marker for α β Centauri. The falling of these three Coals signals the end of the wintry cold. According to the *Bughya* (fol. 93r), pollenation of date palms lasts forty days from XII:10 until the falling of the First Coal (*jamra*).

Arab scholars provided a number of alternatives for the origin of this concept. Al-Malik al-Ashraf (*Tabṣira*, fols. 109r–109v) gave a unique interpretation that the *jamra* refers to an extremely hot pebble kicked up from the ground and pricking the hooves of a mount.[24] While this may very well be a suitable explanation for one meaning of the term *jamra* it is not relevant to a period of February nor to the meaning of cold associated with the Coal. One of the more common origin myths for this term is described in the almanac of al-Qazwīnī (1859). Here it is argued that the Coal refers to the embers of Bedouin campfires at the end of winter. The Bedouins made camp during the winter in three circles around the tents. The inner circle was reserved for the larger animals, such as camels, horses, and cattle, since they were most sensitive to the cold. Sheep and goats were kept in the second circle, and the Bedouins resided in the third. When a fire was lit, the coals or embers would be taken to the hearth in each circle. When it was II:7, the story goes, the large mounts were able to go out to pasture since the cold had passed, while sheep and goats moved to the inner circle and the Bedouins moved to where the sheep and goats had been. At this time the coals of the third circle were allowed to go out without being renewed. By II:14 it was warm enough to take the smaller animals to pasture and the Bedouins moved inside the innermost circle, as another hearth fire was allowed to die. Finally, when there was no longer a need for a hearth fire by II:21, the last of the coals was extinguished. Regardless of the accuracy of the details of this story, it fits well with the Bedouin context.

Several authors associated the Coals with the settings of certain stations. Abū Ḥanīfa al-Dīnawarī, Ibn Māsawayh, and al-Mas'ūdī equated the first *jamra* with the setting of *jabha*, which occurs in early February although not on II:7 exactly. The second is associated with the setting of *zubra* and the third with the setting of *ṣarfa*. This is necessarily an arbitrary fit, because each station is said to set for thirteen days rather than the weeklong period for each

Coal. It does have the merit of ending with the setting of *ṣarfa*, a station known for the transition to warmer weather. A variant tradition is cited in the more recent text of Sheikh al-Alūsī (1882:3:245). Here the First Coal is the setting of a star in Draconis (*ra's al-ḥayya*) during the *naw'* of *ṭarf*, at which time the air starts to warm. The Second refers to α β Geminorum (*al-dhirā' al-sha'mīya*), when water starts to warm. The Third is for the star α Leonis (*qalb al-asad*), when the soil starts to warm.

The idea of a staged warming of the elements is basic to the discussion of these Coals in many almanacs. Al-Bīrūnī (1879:243–44), apparently drawing on a Greek tradition, said the Coals symbolize the spreading of heat from the interior of the earth to the surface. Thus, the First Coal refers to vapors warming the earth, the Second to vapors warming water, and the Third to vapors warming plants. There are, however, numerous variations on this theme. The *Calendar of Cordova* notes that heat exits from the ground at the First, it increases at the Second, and it breaks the cold of winter at the Third. The Coptic almanac of al-Maqrīzī mentions the First Coal as being cold, the Second lukewarm, and the Third hot. Most relatively recent almanacs from Egypt (al-Falakī and Būz Bāshā 1893–94:68; Mitchell 1900:86–88; Muñoz 1977:75) link the First Coal with the warming of air, the Second with the warming of water, and the Third with warming of the earth itself. However, this appears to be a recent concept, as was noted by al-Alūsī (1882:3:245).

Jumaydā. This reference is to the two cold months of *Jumādā al-Ūlā* and *Jumāda al-Akhīra* in the lunar-solar calendar of pre-Islamic Arabia. The name is derived from the fact that at this time water froze (*jamada*).[25] According to al-Malik al-Ashraf this cold period starts at the setting of the Pleiades on XI:9. The Rasulid almanac of *Fuṣūl* places this period from XI:15 at the time when frost can occur. The author (*Tabṣira*, fol. 111r) said that the first of these two months was also known as *shaybān* and the second as *milḥān*. Both of these terms refer to snow and frost, with *shaybān* and *milḥān* being used for the last two Nights of the Old Woman, according to al-Bīrūnī (1879:245). Ibn Qutayba (1956:105) explained that the pre-Islamic Arabs also referred to this time as the two cold months of *qimāḥ*,[26] when camels raise their heads while drinking due to the cold. This cold period is contrasted by al-Malik al-Ashraf with the hot period of *nājir*[27] in the summer, derived from the fact that camels cannot slake their thirst at this time (al-Hamdānī 1977:119).

Layālī al-'ajūz. One of the most frequently cited weather periods in the almanacs is that of the Nights (*layālī*) or Days (*ayyām*) of the Old Woman (*'ajūz*), which are generally fixed as the last three days of February and the first four days of March (i.e., II:26–III:4).[28] Sometimes the numbers are simply transposed in the Coptic calendar to 26 *Amshīr* (II:20) to 4 *Baramhāt* (II:27), as in the case of the almanac of Ibn Mammātī (1943). There are, in fact, numerous legends regarding this expression and it is clearly one of the most authentic cases of indigenous Arab folk meteorology cited in the almanac genre.[29] According to Ibn Kunāsa (in Ibn Qutayba 1956:119, 1982:95) this week occurs during the setting of *ṣarfa* in February. These days stand for the last of winter's cold, which may be the most intense cold (al-Bīrūnī 1879:245). According to the author, these nights stand in opposition to the nights of *majar* (?) at the end of the summer.

In the standard interpretation of the Days of the Old Woman each day has a special name, each of which appears to relate to the cold. Although these names are not mentioned by al-Malik al-Ashraf, they are listed in several medieval almanacs. Al-Mas'ūdī (1982) and al-Qazwīnī (1859) identified the days as follows: one, *ṣinn*; two, *ṣinnabr*; three, *wabr*; four, *amir*; five, *mu'tamir*; six, *mu'allil*; seven, *muṭfi' al-jamr*. In some sources only five days are mentioned (e.g., al-Ḥimyarī 1980:224; Ibn Qutayba 1956:119), and in others there are only three (al-Marzūqī 1968:1:274). The translated treatise of the Byzantine Qusṭūs (fol. 9v) indicates a ten-day cold period from II:24.

The etymology of the expression is widely debated in the sources. Al-Malik al-Ashraf (*Tabṣira*, fol. 110r) mentioned a unique story in which the old woman is the mother of Caesar. The story goes that after Caesar was killed, his mother and her entire army were destroyed by a violent cold. This particular account is not known from the other sources. The most common legend is that this expression refers to an old woman or sorceress in the days before Islam. According to the account of al-Qazwīnī, she was an old Bedouin woman who warned her people that a violent cold was coming at the end of winter that would kill their flocks. She was ignored and the sheep were sheared; the next day a violent cold destroyed the sheep.

A similar story is recorded by al-Jawālīqī (n.d.:134), based on an anecdote from al-Sharqī ibn al-Quṭāmī. In this version an old Bedouin woman was afraid to shear her sheep lest the cold of winter not really be over. Everyone laughed at her and made preparations for spring, but the cold came again and killed their shorn beasts. In yet another version of the origin legend, the old woman is linked to the pre-Islamic tribe of 'Ād, whom God destroyed with a violent wind (al-Bīrūnī 1879:295; Dalman 1928:1:184; Lane 1984:1961). This wind blew for seven days, after which the old woman is either the last survivor or dies on the eighth day. This is clearly derived from surahs 41:16 and 69:7 of the Quran, which explains why the term *ḥuṣūm*[30] is sometimes used for this period. In Yemen today some people say the reference to the old woman is simply because at this time an old woman can feel the cold in her bones (Serjeant 1954:447, note 48). The lexicologist Ibn Durayd (as quoted in al-Jawālīqī n.d.:134) argued that the expression *ayyām al-'ajūz* was not used in the pre-Islamic period. Abū 'Alī al-Fārisī, quoted by al-Jawālīqī, said that the reference was originally to the tail end or *pars postica* (*'ajuz*) of winter.

Al-layālī al-bulq and *al-layālī al-sūd.* Two cold periods frequently mentioned in the Arab almanacs are the so-called Mixed (*bulq*) Nights and Black (*sūd*) Nights. The former is in reference to a mixing of black and white in the sky as the weather turns very cold, according to al-Malik al-Ashraf. *Bulq* is the plural of *ablāq*, which is used to denote piebalding in a horse. In North Africa these periods are simply referred to as *layālī* (e.g., Westermarck 1926:1:260). The Black Nights are considered the most intense part of winter, in this sense the *samā'im* (Ibn al-'Awwām 1802:2:434) or *kalib*[31] (*Calendar of Cordova*) of winter.

The timing of these two periods varies in the almanacs. Al-Malik al-Ashraf (*Tabṣira*, fols. 109v–110r) began the first period of Mixed Nights at X:28, lasting for twenty nights, followed by the Black Nights at XI:18 for forty nights, and finally the second twenty-night period of Mixed Nights from XII:27. For Egypt, however, the author noted a different reckoning of these eighty nights. There the first period of Mixed Nights began on 1 *Hatūr* (X:38) and lasted forty nights, followed by the forty Black Nights from 10 *Kiyahk* (XII:6). This is the time period recorded by al-Maqrīzī and al-Khalījī in their Coptic almanacs, but different dates were noted by al-Qalqashandī and in *Nubdha*. In the *anwā'* tradition, as related by Ibn al-Ajdābī (1964), the Black Nights begin on XII:5. Ibn Raḥīq (fol. 6r) remarked in a refreshingly honest passage of his almanac that the dating of the Black Nights varies, but generally they include the twenty days before and the twenty days after Coptic Christmas.

Layālī al-majar (?). The seven nights of *majar* (?) refer to a period at the end of summer from VIII:29 to IX:4. At this hot period, explained al-Malik al-Ashraf (*Tabṣira*, fol. 110r), the late summer rains are plentiful, springs are flowing well, wells are full, and wadis are in flood. Animals now begin to gain weight from the presence of lush pasture, and wood that is cut during this week will not worm. Abū al-'Uqūl added that these nights, which he starts at VIII:27, are accompanied by wind (*nawd*) and cold upon the crops, which contradicts the claim by al-Malik al-Ashraf that these nights stood in opposition to the cold Nights of the Old Woman and represented the last of summer's heat.

The precise term is not clear from the texts, or from the lexical evidence. If the reading of *majar* is correct, this can signify the increase in drinking without being able to quench thirst, according to al-Aṣmaʿī (in Haffner 1905:19). This fits the idea of a hot period, especially given the usage of *nājir* among the Bedouins for a hot period in summer when camels cannot slake their thirst. There is also a Yemeni usage of *majr* in the sense of "rain" (I. al-Akwaʿ 1968). Perhaps the term is a misreading of *nājir* from the *anwāʾ* literature, since *najr* literally means "heat" (*ḥarr*) in classical Arabic (*Lisān al-ʿArab*, *ʿ-l-l*). The idea of a hot period opposite the Nights of the Old Woman brings to mind the *waghra* periods during the summer.[32] The related *waqda* period at the rising of Canopus is a time of intense heat from VIII:26, according to al-Bīrūnī (1879:265). A period of intense heat can be called *waqda* if it lasts for at least seven days (al-Marzūqī 1968:2:71). Later Yemeni almanacs invariably misread this term as *jaḥr*, a term used in Yemen today to signify the hot and dry period in May or June between the spring and late summer rains.

Muʿtadilāt. This was defined in *Tabṣira* (fol. 110r) as a period of temperate weather for about forty days between VIII:14 and IX:22, just before the autumn period referred to as *ṣafarīya*. Quṭrub (1985:100) defined it as a period of forty days after the rising of Canopus with variable temperatures, although he actually equated it with the days of *ṣafarīya*. According to *Tāj al-ʿarūs* (*ṣ-f-r*) this is a pleasant time after the heat has lessened. However, there is some confusion with the similar term *muʿtadhilāt* or *muʿtadhalāt*, which is said to refer to a period of intense heat when people "blame" each other, hence the meaning of the term (Lane 1984:1989). The noted lexical scholar al-Zamakhsharī (1982:296) said this latter term refers to the blazing heat at the summer rising of Canopus. In this sense al-Marzūqī (1968:1:273) cited it as the opposite of the Nights of the Old Woman.

Chapter 4

Environment

EARTH AND WATER SOURCES

The almanac tradition focuses on a number of aspects of the environment as perceived by medieval Islamic scholars. Regarding the earth itself, al-Malik al-Ashraf noted that the underground (*bāṭin al-arḍ*) began to warm after I:12 and cool after VII:15–16. The first date is marked by the entry of the sun into the zodiacal constellation of Aquarius and the second correlates with the beginning of Leo. These dates differ from those usually cited in non-Yemeni almanacs. In the *anwā'* tradition, as reported by Abū Ḥanīfa al-Dīnawarī, the warming starts during the *naw'* of *jabha* at II:14; most almanacs record the event in February. Al-Malik al-Ashraf's date for the cooling is also early. The *anwā'* tradition relates this to the *naw'* of *sa'd al-su'ūd* at VIII:15 and Abū Ḥanīfa added that at this time the ground does not absorb water quickly because of the effect of the summer drought. This date is also said to correspond with the rising of *jabha* and Canopus (*suhayl*). The concept of the warming and cooling of the earth is Greek in origin. However, in the Hippocratic tradition (Hippocrates 1983:338) the underground was said to be cooler in summer than in winter because at this time it was lighter and more porous. The reason given for this was the action of the sun in evaporating moisture as water percolated downward.

Water sources were of vital importance to the inhabitants of the Arabian Peninsula. Medieval scientists determined the dates at which underground water and surface water would generally decrease and increase during the course of the year. According to the almanac, water sources decline between X:8 and III:11. Spring flow is reduced in the summer after VII:10, an event Abū Ḥanīfa al-Dīnawarī associated with the rising of *han'a*. Ibn al-Kalbī (in Ibn al-Faqīh 1967:64) related the decrease to the summer rising of Capella (*ayyūq*). Abū al-'Uqūl and *Fuṣūl* have the reduction in spring flow from VII:12, with the latter source recording a further decrease at X:26. This timing differs from that of al-Bīrūnī, who noted at IV:28 that springs are fuller in winter than in summer. The almanac records an increase in overall water supply after IV:1, a day often associated with magical significance for rain. Ibn al-Ajdābī noted that if it rains on IV:1, the year will be productive and fertile.[1] This date is close to the *anwā'* tradition, in which Abū Ḥanīfa al-Dīnawarī noted the increase at the setting of *simāk* on IV:7. The increase in spring flow is cited at V:30 by *Fuṣūl*, a date which fits well with the climatological context of Yemen since by this time the spring rains have come. The term used for a spring in the *Fuṣūl* reference is *ghayl*, the common term in Yemeni dialect.[2]

In addition to the general state of the water supply, which obviously varied across the expanse of the medieval Islamic world, the Rasulid almanacs contain valuable information on the stages of the Nile, Euphrates, and Tigris rivers. The most important river in the entire almanac tradition is the Nile,[3] a river extolled by Arab writers in prose and verse as having water sweeter than honey, whiter than milk, and more aromatic than camphor (Ibn Iyās 1982:32; al-Ibshīhī 1981:374). The water from the Nile was in fact a popular medicant in the traditional medicine of the medieval Islamic world (Ibn Qayyim al-Jawzīya 1957:307). The Nile was said to be one of the original rivers of Paradise and, as a Greek historian had long before noted, the very lifeblood of Egypt. While there is no biographical evidence that al-Malik al-Ashraf ever visited Egypt, there were numerous sources and individuals he could have consulted.

The range of information on the Nile in this almanac is extraordinary for a non-Coptic almanac. A distinction is made between the time when the floodwaters of the Nile begin to recede (*tanṣarifu*) on X:2 and when the Nile formally decreases (*tanquṣu*) on X:19. A similar distinction was made in the almanac of al-Qazwīnī. According to the author the first date is when the Egyptians begin to plant; this is a date widely circulated in the almanac tradition. The Çoptic almanac of al-Qalqashandī refers to this day as the marriage (*'urs*) of the Nile. *Fuṣūl* dates the planting in Egypt at X:5, perhaps a copyist error. The major Coptic almanacs place the decrease in the Nile from about X:16 (19 *Bābih*).

With the decrease in the Nile it carries less sediment. The almanac notes that the water becomes clearer (*taṣfā*) at I:20, a date also recorded in *Fuṣūl*. Abū al-'Uqūl mentioned this at I:21, which corresponds exactly with the date in the Coptic almanac of al-Maqrīzī. A few months later, at the beginning of its rising, the Nile fills with sediment and turns a murky green color. Ibn Riḍwān (1984:85) attributes the green color to "the large quantity of stagnant and putrid water that contains duckweed [*armaḍ*] and water moss – whose color is very green on account of their corruption." At this time it is not safe to drink.[4] The reason for this, according to some medieval authors, was that wild beasts such as elephants and hippopotami plunged into the waters of the Upper Nile to escape the torrid heat of summer and in the process dirtied the water (Qāsim 1978:14). Al-Malik al-Ashraf (*Tabṣira*, fols. 110r–110v) simply pointed out that the water becomes murky because of the plentiful rainfall near its source. By the time the floods rose, they contained a large amount of eroded soil changing the color to red.

The murkiness of the waters is referred to in the Coptic sources with the verb *tawḥamu*, although Pellat (1979:181, 1986:274) prefers a rendering of *tawaḥḥumu* with the sense of "envie de femme en ceinte." In reference to this change in the Nile, the Rasulid sources read *tawkhumu*, presumably with the sense of becoming unhealthy or difficult to digest. Al-Mas'ūdī (cited in Ibn Iyās 1982:35) explained that at the beginning of the increase the Nile water becomes green and murky (*takhḍaru*). The almanac of Saray (fol. 1) refers to this change as *taghayyur*. Al-Malik al-Ashraf dated this event at VI:8, but the Coptic sources usually place it at least a week earlier, for example, V:28 (3 *Ba'ūna*) in the reckoning of al-Qalqashandī.

The increase in the Nile to flood stage was the most important event in the agricultural cycle of Egypt. The Yemeni astronomer al-Fārisī (*Mumtaḥan*, fol. 5r) wrote that this occurred in the Coptic month of *Ba'ūna* (VI). Al-Malik al-Ashraf placed the flooding of the Nile lands at VI:23, while *Fuṣūl* has VI:19 and Abū al-'Uqūl noted VI:22. Several dates are recorded in the Coptic almanacs, depending on the event being described during the process of rising. The most common date in the non-Coptic almanacs is VI:29, when a magical rite is described for foretelling the success or failure of the year's crops. Al-Qazwīnī, for example, said that the alchemists in Egypt go out on this night and check for dew on plants, because the presence of dew will indicate a high flood stage. This is a reference to the famous Night of the Drop (*laylat al-nuqṭa*), during which medieval Egyptians believed a miraculous drop would fall on the Nile and cause the floods to rise. In the Coptic reckoning this usually occurs at the Festival of St. Michael, on VI:5–6 (11–12 *Ba'ūna*). This belief is derived from an ancient Egyptian myth about the tears of the goddess Isis, the wife of Osiris, that fell on the Nile at the summer solstice (Amīn 1953:91). The actual dating of the flood stage varied and would be announced each year following measurements and various ceremonies. However, this generally occurred around the summer solstice and the midsummer rising of Sirius, the latter astronomical event signaling the start of the agricultural year in ancient Egypt. After the formal announcement that the flood stage had reached 16 *dhirā'* (ca. 10.5 meters), the ruler in Cairo would impose the *kharāj* tax (al-Maqrīzī 1926:1:60, 273).

There is no mention in the Rasulid almanacs of the breaking of the canals near the end of the flood stage in the month of *Tūt* (September).[5] According to the Coptic almanacs, the canal draining took place in stages. Most canals were opened at the Festival of the Cross (17 *Tūt*) in order to drain the land for planting. The Nile was famous for the variety of its fish (Ruffer 1919:32–42). *Salwa* and Taymūr mention an increase in the number of fish after IX:30, after the floods had abated and there was less sediment in the flow. The Coptic almanac of al-Makhzūmī (Pellat 1989:94) notes that small fish in the Nile increased during *Bābih* (October). Ibn Riḍwān (1984:97) warned against the adverse health consequences of eating fish caught in the Nile during the autumn.

The Euphrates, the well-known river flowing through Syria and Iraq, was also considered one of the rivers of Paradise.[6] Al-Malik al-Ashraf said that the Euphrates reached flood stage at IV:24, the date also recorded by al-Bīrūnī. *Fuṣūl* records this as IV:25, *Salwa* at IV:8 (27° Aries), and Taymūr at IV:10. In the *anwā'* tradition, according to Abū Ḥanīfa al-Dīnawarī, the flood stage began at the setting of *ghafr* on IV:13. At V:31, in the reckoning of al-Malik al-Ashraf, sailing was no longer possible on the Euphrates because of the flooding. He recorded the end of the flood stage at VII:22 and the lowering at VII:24. The former date was cited by Abū al-'Uqūl for the lowering of both the Euphrates and the Tigris. However, Abū al-'Uqūl noted the last flooding of the Euphrates at I:28 and *Salwa* at I:16 (14° Aquarius).

The author also mentioned the Tigris (Dijla), which he claimed lowered from VII:24 along with the Euphrates.[7] Abū al-'Uqūl placed this at VII:22. The Tigris reaches maximum flood stage in IV, a month before the Euphrates, because of the major snowmelt in the north where it originates. A number of legends were current in the medieval period about the Tigris, including the idea that the prophet Daniel was responsible for digging it and channeling water from it to the Euphrates. In the medical tradition it was claimed by some (e.g., Ibn Iyās 1982:23–24) that drinking the water of the Tigris reduced the libido of men but drove women wild. *Allāhu a'lam.*

PLANTS

Yemen has the richest biodiversity of flora on the Arabian Peninsula, since it is located at the crossroads between Africa and Asia and is characterized by substantial geographical variation.[8] The Rasulid sources describe many of the plants, especially those with ornamental or practical uses in the society. The most important herbal from this period is that of al-Malik al-Muẓaffar Yūsuf ibn 'Umar (1982), the father of al-Malik al-Ashraf. This text draws on the previous botanical tradition in Islam, especially the pivotal text of Ibn al-Bayṭār (1291/1874). The herbal contains almost almost no information from Yemeni folklore, although there is a valuable appendix of Yemeni plant names.[9] The Rasulid agricultural texts, including the almanacs, provide important information on some of the local flora, especially herbs and aromatics.

The almanacs note the various stages of growth of plants, trees, and foliage. The basic term for "plants" in Arabic is *shajar* (*ashjar*, plural). This refers to any plant with a stalk (*sāq*), including trees (Ibn Qutayba 1982:98). The Arabic concept is broader than the English usage of "tree," a common translation of *shajar*. Branches are generally called *furū'* and roots are called *'urūq*, standard usage in classical Arabic. The sap in a tree is *mā'*, which literally refers to water.

Sap is said to begin flowing from the roots upward to the branches at I:1, and it seeps from the wood at II:1, according to al-Malik al-Ashraf. The former date was noted by Abū al-'Uqūl and in the *Bughya*, while *Fuṣūl* has I:4. Abū al-'Uqūl and *Fuṣūl* gave the latter date as II:3. This differs from the *anwā'* tradition in which the sap flows during the rising of *sa'd al-su'ūd*, as noted by Ibn al-Ajdābī for II:18. None of the Rasulid almanacs mention the time when sap flows back down to the roots, an event usually indicated in the almanac tradition as occurring in IX.

One of the most common references in the almanacs is to the loss of leaves of deciduous plants. This was important in the Greek tradition as well. Theophrastus (1916:1:67) noted that "the fall of leaves in all cases takes place in autumn or later, but it occurs later in some trees than in others, and even extends into the winter." Leaves are said to turn yellow in the autumn at IX:21, according to al-Malik al-Ashraf and Abū al-'Uqūl, although *Fuṣūl* lists this for IX:23. This is the start of a period known as *ṣafarīya*, which is mentioned in the almanac. By X:22 leaves begin to fall and by XII:15 trees are bare of leaves. The first appearance of leaves is after I:14, but most come after II:6 according to the almanac. Abū al-'Uqūl and *Fuṣūl* added that buds appear at the latter date. This correlates with the *anwā'* tradition, where trees are said to bud under the *naw'* of *jabha* at II:18 according to Ibn al-Ajdābī. By III:11 the trees are said to be fully dressed with leaves. As early as II:22, according to the almanac and Taymūr, plants that grow from permanent roots spring to life. *Fuṣūl* gives this as II:18 and *Salwa* has it at II:24 (13° Pisces). *Salwa* and Taymūr note that blossoms last until VI:11 (28° Gemini).

An important use of trees in Yemen has long been as firewood; indeed much of the country was probably deforested by the medieval period (Hepper and Wood 1979). Ibn al-Mujāwir (1954:81), who traveled in Yemen shortly before the time of the author, named several coastal wadis where wood was commonly cut. Important wooded areas of Yemen are also described in the earlier geographical text of al-Hamdānī (1884–91, 1983). The almanac notes that the best time to cut wood is between IX:1 and X:5. This is the time indicated by *Fuṣūl* for Yemen, while wood is said to be cut from X:7 in Syria. Abū al-'Uqūl dated the cutting of wood from X:3, while *Salwa* places the cutting between X:2 (17° Libra) and XI:2 (18° Scorpius). According to the *Bughya*, wood was cut in Yemen during the month of October. All of these dates correlate with the *anwā'* tradition, where Ibn al-Ajdābī mentioned cutting of wood at the *naw'* of *baṭn al-ḥūt* on X:1.

The seasons for cutting wood were related to the scientific knowledge regarding the life cycle of trees. Theophrastus (1916:1:187) said it was good to cut wood in summer when bark was easily shed. Medieval authors also were familiar with earlier astrological folklore, such as the comment by Ibn al-Mujāwir (1954:81) that wood cut on a bright night or when the moon was waning would not become wormy. Theophrastus (1916:1:421) recommended cutting wood when the moon had set, because wood was thought to be "harder" then. In a practical sense it was important to pick times in which the wood would dry quickly and not be readily infested by worms or termites. While there was clearly a local tradition of knowledge about cutting wood, the almanac references are derived from classical Greek science. As early as Hesiod (1973:72) it had been noted that wood cut during the autumnal rains in October, as well as that cut during the midsummer rising of Sirius, would not become wormy. Al-Malik al-Ashraf said that wood cut during the nights of *majar* from VIII:29 to IX:4 would not have worms. The almanac of al-Qazwīnī recorded that wood cut at X:3, virtually the same date as in the Rasulid almanacs, would not become wormy. Al-Qazwīnī also noted that wood cut on X:13 would not be attacked by the termite (*araḍa*), which is sometimes called the white ant and is a major agricultural pest in Yemen (Niebuhr 1792:1:270, 2:336; Serjeant 1974a:39). The scholar al-Bīrūnī said that the reason for this was that on this day there was a peculiar mixture of air. For Islamic Spain Ibn al-'Awwām (1802:2:435) said that wood cut at I:27 would not worm. On the other hand, Abū al-'Uqūl cautioned against cutting wood during February, because sap was flowing in the wood at this time.

The natural plants (i.e., those plants that were not cultivated herbs and ornamentals) mentioned in the almanac are discussed in alphabetical order:

'Arm. The term *'arm* is a colloquial term for the carandas plum, or *Carissa edulis* (Forssk.) Vahl (Bedevian 1936:146; Schweinfurth 1912:88), which is a sprawling, tangled shrub with pale pink flowers, a strong sweet scent, and black fruit (Collenette 1985:51). The term *'arm* is apparently unique to Yemeni dialect in the southern highlands near Ta'izz.[10] Al-Hamdānī (1983:247) said that the feminine form of this word could be used as a woman's name in Yemen. In the biographical text of the Yemeni al-Burayhī (1984:80), a certain man was known as *Ṣāḥib al-'arma*, because he came from

an area in Mikhlāf Ja'far where this plant grew. Al-Malik al-Afḍal (*Bughya*, fol. 107r) said the shrub was found at Ṣan'ā', Dhubḥān, Ṣabir, and al-Dumluwa. He also claimed that it was called *qarnaṣ* (?) in Ta'izz and *ḥarīqa* (?) or *maḥriqa* (?) in the mountains. Other terms used in Yemen for this plant include *la'dh* and *lū'* (al-Hubaishi and Müller-Hohenstein 1984:191; Great Britain Admiralty 1946:601; Schweinfurth 1912:162). In Yemeni dialect the terms *aywān* and *shadn*[11] are said to be synonyms of *'arm* (*Ta'rīb*). The fruit of *'arm* ripens in IX in the mountains at the time that sorghum is parched, according to al-Malik al-Ashraf. The almanac records the opening of the flower at IV:18, while *Salwa* records this for III:15 (3° Aries). Today, at Jabal Ṣabir near Ta'izz the stalk of this tree is shredded and used for wrapping wounds; the black berry is eaten.

Al-Malik al-Ashraf and al-Malik al-Afḍal (*Bughya*, fol. 106r) equated *'arm* with classical *amīr bārīs*, which is generally used for the barberry (*Berberis vulgaris*), a plant which originated in India and is not native to Yemen. There is considerable confusion in the herbals regarding this term. The published editions of the herbals of al-Anṭākī (1951:1:57), al-Dhahabī (1984:77), Ibn al-Bayṭār (1291/1874:1:54), and Yūsuf ibn 'Umar (1982:8) have *amīr bārīs*, while Bedevian (1936:106) records *anbar bārīs*. The correct term should be *ambar bārīs* (al-Khatib 1978:34; al-Khawārizmī 1984:192; Levey 1973:156). The barberry was also known as *'ūd al-rīḥ* (al-Anṭākī 1951:1:57; Ducros 1930:94) in Arabic, *zirrishk* (Ibn al-Bayṭār 1291/1874:1:54; Levey 1973:156; Yūsuf ibn 'Umar 1982:8) in Persian, and *athrār* in Berber (Ducros 1930:32). The barberry is hot and dry in the humoral system and its edible fruit was an important medicant in the medieval period. One of the remedies using it was called *ḥaḍāḍ al-hindī*, made by boiling the wood of the plant until completely soft (al-Khawārizmī 1984:192).

'Asaqī. This is a Yemeni term for a variety of acacia, of which there are some sixteen species identified for Yemen (Dubaie and Al-Khulaidi 1991:43). The *'asaq* variety was first identified by the eighteenth-century botanist Forskal, who called it *Acacia asak*, a term still in vogue. It is a relatively small tree up to four meters in height with white-creamy flowers and short, glabrous thorns (Dubaie and Al-Khulaidi 1991:48–49). It is common in the foothills above 500 meters (Deil and Müller-Hohenstein 1985:2). As is the case for most of the acacia varieties, it has a wide variety of uses as lumber, firewood, fodder, and charcoal. According to al-Malik al-Ashraf, the honeycomb made primarily from blossoms of this tree was available in the mountains from VII:13. This variety of honey was collected in al-Ma'āfir and Dhubḥān from VIII:1. The term *'asaq* can also be applied to the wild rose in Yemen, while in classical Arabic it had the additional meaning of a rotten palm branch (*al-*

Muḥīṭ, *'-s-q*).

Bān. The well-known term *bān* refers to the ben-oil or horse-radish tree *Moringa peregrina (Forssk.)* Fiori.[12] This tree was also known in the Yemeni dialect of the Sarāt region as *shū'* (Ibn al-Bayṭār 1291/1874:1:79; Ibn Qutayba 1982:100; Yūsuf ibn 'Umar 1982:275, 567) or *shuwū'* (al-Aṣma'ī 1972:36). Al-Malik al-Afḍal said in the *Bughya* that this tree grew wild in Yemen, especially on the road between Ta'izz and Aden. It was also recorded as growing near Dhofar (al-Qalqashandī 1913–19:5:15). The seed of this plant resembles the cowpea (*lūbiyā'*) and yields an oil considered hot and dry or, by some, hot and wet (al-Anṭākī 1951:1:67). Freya Stark (1940:123, 318) observed in the Ḥaḍramawt that this seed was soaked in water and used to reduce swelling, while the leaves were beneficial for healing a snakebite. Watchmakers also used ben oil in southern Arabia (Great Britain Admiralty 1946:591).

The almanac says that the seeds were available after VI:1. According to al-Qazwīnī, the ben-oil tree was planted at XII:1, apparently in reference to the northern Levant. However, al-Bīrūnī said this was the date for a fair held in Damascus to celebrate the cutting of the ben nut. In Egypt ben oil was used in cooking and cosmetics (Manniche 1989:122). The ben nut was also imported from India and Ceylon.

Ḍāl. This term is the equivalent of *sidr* in classical Arabic (al-Anṭākī 1951:1:226; al-Aṣma'ī 1972:23; al-Ḥimyarī 1980:243; Ibn Qutayba 1982:100; *Kifāya*, fol. 95r), although Ibn al-Bayṭār (1291/1874:3:92) called it the fruit of *sidr*. *Ḍāl* refers to both the christ's-thorn tree (*Ziziphus spina-christi* L. Willd) or *Ziziphus nummularia* in Yemen. Al-Malik al-Ashraf appears to make a distinction between *ḍāl* as a highland term and *ilb* (i.e., *'ilb*) as a coastal term for the same tree. Abū Ḥanīfa al-Dīnawarī (in Ṣāliḥīya and al-'Amd 1984:201) said that *ḍāl* was a wild variety without resin (*ṣamgh*) and with small fruit. Al-Bīrūnī (1973:1:180) quoted Abū Ḥanīfa to the effect that *ḍāl* refers to the spring variety of *sidr*. The term *ḍāl* can also apply to the jujube tree (*Z. jujuba* Lam.) in Yemen and to the lotus tree (*Z. lotus*) in Egypt and North Africa (Bedevian 1936:625).

Al-Malik al-Ashraf said the honeycomb made primarily from this plant's blossoms was available in the mountains after XII:16. According to the same author in *Mughnī*, this was not a useful tree for camel fodder in the mountains, although today the christ's-thorn is generally considered a useful fodder plant in Yemen.

Ilb. At I:8, according to the almanac, the honeycomb from the blossoms of a plant called *ilb* is available in the mountains. This term is in fact a dialectical transformation of the classical *'ilb*, which refers to the *sidr* tree, or christ's-thorn (*Ziziphus spina-christi*). In the Tihāma and coastal foothills the letter *'ayn* is commonly softened to a *ḥamza*, a trait known for centuries (Rabin 1951:31). Classical *'ilb* is widely noted in Yemeni sources as the christ's-thorn (I. al-Akwa' 1984:2:939; al-'Arashī 1939:430; Beeston et al. 1982:15; al-Hamdānī 1938:35; al-Hubaishi and Müller-Hohenstein 1984:204; Jastrow 1983:114; Landberg 1901:1:344; Schweinfurth 1912:95). The term *'irj* also refers to *Ziziphus spina-christi* in the Tihāma, as noted by al-Hamdānī (1938:35).

The local term for the fruit of the *'ilb* is *dūm* (Bury 1911:311; Rossi 1939:167), which should not be confused with *dawm* in reference to the wild doum palm (*Hyphaene thebaica* Del. Mart).[13] In the tradition of the Prophet's medicine (*al-ṭibb al-nabawī*), al-Dhahabī (1984:198) claimed that this was the forbidden fruit that Adam ate in Paradise. The term *nabq* also refers to the fruit of christ's-thorn and jujube; this is hot and dry in the humoral system. In the south this fruit ripens in March and is dried on rooftops (Bury 1911:311). When other sources of food are scarce, this fruit is combined with milk in the diet of Yemeni Bedouins (Van der Meulen and von Wissmann 1932:48). The leaves of this plant are used as an antiseptic and antipruritic in Yemen (Fleurentin and Pelt 1982:96–97) and also for washing the hair (Serjeant 1962a:498).

Abū al-'Uqūl said that the first appearance of *dūm* or *nabq* was at I:8 and that it became plentiful at I:16. This is about the same time as it appears in Egypt. Grohmann (1930:1:108), however, noted that this fruit ripened in Yemen at the end of March. In Ḥaḍramawt the blossoms of this plant are very important for honey, which is collected from July through August (Bury 1911:311; Ingrams 1936; Great Britain Admiralty 1946:513). This timing differs considerably from the reference in the almanac. The green leaves of this tree are important for fodder in the coastal region, according to al-Malik al-Ashraf. This is also true today, for example, in the Ḥaḍramawt (van der Meulen and von Wissmann 1932:49). Freya Stark (1940:123) documented a folk belief in the Ḥaḍramawt that spirits live in this tree and will comb out and beautify the hair of those who sleep in the tree's shadow.

Kama't. One of the most important uncultivated food plants to the Bedouins of the desert was the truffle, or *Tuber* sp. (*kama't*), of which there are numerous varieties on the peninsula.[14] The Prophet Muḥammad even referred to it as a type of manna, especially useful for eye diseases (Ibn Qayyim al-Jawzīya 1957:279). In the humoral system it was defined as cold and wet. Al-Malik al-Afḍal (*Bughya*, fol. 109r) described a type of truffle found at al-Tha'bāt near Ta'izz. This resembled the heads of turnip plants, but the leaves were like those of cowpea (*dijr*). It grew up in moist areas after rain and was eaten.

The almanac mentions the appearance of truffles in the spring at IV:14. Early spring was the major season for truffles for most of the peninsula, especially under the *naw'* of *jabha* at II:14, according to Abū Ḥanifa al-Dīnawarī. *Fuṣūl* mentions truffles in Iraq at III:23. Al-Qazwīnī recorded the gathering of truffles between II:16 and V:16, while the Coptic almanac of al-Qalqashandī notes their presence at IV:17 (22 *Barmūda*). The Rasulid almanac of *Mīqāt* said that there would be plenty of truffles in the spring if the Yemeni *wasmī* rain in February was accompanied by thunder (i.e., lots of rainfall).

Qushār. This term is a Yemeni variant for the classical *'ushar*, or the Dead Sea apple (*Calotropis procera* Willd. R. Br.), although *qushār* has not been recorded in the available lexicons. It is unclear if this is a dialectical transformation or based on the term *qishr* (literally, "husk"). The form *'ushār* is found in Yemeni dialect (Bādhīb 1991:24; al-Hubaishi and Müller-Hohenstein 1984:191). *Calotropis* produces a pod which is an important medicant, defined as hot and dry. It is toxic but is used in Yemen today as a local anesthetic and antiseptic for skin infections (Fleurentin and Pelt 1982:98). Al-Hamdānī (1983:318) mentioned that in Najrān a type of sugary liquid descended from the sky onto the leaves of this plant, perhaps in reference to the sugary sap of the plant used as a medicant (al-Bīrūnī 1973:1:185; Ibn al-Bayṭār 1291/1874:3:123). The white extract from this plant was apparently used as a substitute for flour at times (Great Britain Admiralty 1946:600). An ancient legend was recorded by al-Qazwīnī (1981:295) in which this plant was used in a rite to determine the fidelity of women.

The almanac mentions the collection of honey made from this plant at IX:16. The reference is probably to the coastal region and foothills, where this is a common plant. It is also common in the Eastern Plateau of Yemen (Scholte et al. 1991:55).

Ṣuyyāb. The term *ṣuyyāb* refers to *Euphorbia inarticulata* Schweinf. in Yemen (al-Hubaishi and Müller-Hohenstein 1984:195; al-Khulaidi 1989:113), which is commonly found at lower elevations. The latex from this plant is used in Yemen against camel mange and verruca (Fleurentin and Pelt 1982:94–95). According to al-Malik al-Ashraf, the honeycombs made from the blossoms of this and *'ilb* were collected at I:8 in Surdud.

Ẓubba. Al-Malik al-Ashraf mentioned the presence of the honeycomb made from this tree at II:18 in the mountains; Abū al-'Uqūl noted this for II:19. In Yemen this term refers to *Acacia mellifera* (Vahl) Benth., the most common species of acacia at lower altitudes (Great Britain Admiralty 1946:590; al-Hubaishi and Müller-Hohenstein 1984:188; al-Khulaidi 1989:112; Scholte et al. 1991:30; Schweinfurth 1912:159; Wood 1985:17). This variety of acacia is a round-crowned, single-trunked tree up to four or five meters in height with small hooked thorns in pairs and white, sweet-scented flowers (Dubaie and al-Khulaidi 1991:55). In classical Arabic *ẓubba* can also refer to ebony (Yūsuf ibn 'Umar 1982:558), but this tree was certainly not cultivated in Yemen. Alternative Arabic terms for this type of acacia include *qatād*[15] and *sanṭ 'asalī* (al-Khatib 1978:44). The almanac at I:27 notes a synonym *ḥmja* (?), but this term is unclear from the text and has not been identified in the lexicons or major Rasulid sources.

ANIMALS

Many of the references in the almanac relate to animals, including valuable information relevant to Yemen[6] as well as the general animal lore recorded in the almanac genre. The southwestern corner of the Arabian Peninsula has a wide diversity of fauna, as it does of flora, because of its unique position bordering the African continent. A number of important species were apparently hunted out in historic times.

The almanac notes that wild animals (*wuḥūsh*) are sexually aroused at II:23. Abū al-'Uqūl placed this at II:22, while *Salwa* and Taymūr give II:16 (6° Pisces) as the time for this arousal. According to *Fuṣūl*, however, wild animals bear their young at II:11. These dates are derived from the *anwā'* tradition, in which Abū Ḥanīfa al-Dīnawarī mentioned the excitement of animals at II:27 under the *naw'* of *zubra*. According to al-Hamdānī (1983:240–41, 307), Yemen was noted for the baboon (*qird*),[17] hyrax (*wabr*), and lion (*asad*).[18] During the medieval period there were also plenty of ibex (Serjeant 1976) and gazelles. At least one species of gazelle, the so-called Queen of Sheba gazelle, is unique to the area (Groves 1989).

Birds

There are more references to birds than to any other kind of animal in the almanac.[19] This no doubt reflects royal interest at the time in falcon hunting, with references in the almanac to both birds of prey and some of the birds commonly hunted.[20] Al-Malik al-Mu'ayyad Dāwūd, brother of the author of the almanac, is credited with an abridgement of a text on falcon hunting, although no known copy of this exists today (I. al-Akwa' 1980:155). A published edition exists of a Rasulid hunting text by Ḥamza ibn ʻAlī al-Nāshirī (1985) entitled *Intihāz al-furaṣ fī al-ṣayd wa-al-qanaṣ.* Another Yemeni falcon hunting text was written by a certain Yaʻqūb ibn Ismāʻīl; this is called *Nuzhat al-mulūk al-akhyar fī al-iqtināṣ bi-anwāʻ al-aṭyār.* As noted in the almanac the primary hunting season was in the autumn, when hundreds of thousands of migratory birds flew by Yemen to escape the cold of the northern climes. The primary raptors involved in the migration over Yemen are buzzards and steppe eagles (Porter and Christensen 1987:122). This was the time when falcons and sparrow hawks were captured and then used for the hunting season.

This annual appearance of certain bird species, especially the hoopoe (*hudhud*), was noted by farmers as a seasonal marker. During planting and harvesting times farmers often had to protect their seeds and crops from a variety of bird species, as is commonly reflected in Yemeni proverbs (I. al-Akwaʻ 1984:2:883,961,1201; al-Baraddūnī 1985:8–9,38; Varisco 1985b:64). Among the chief avian culprits were pigeons, ravens, sand grouse, and partridges. It is not uncommon today to see heaps of stones raised and decorated with scraps of old clothing as scarecrows. In the past boys used to sit atop perches near harvest time and use slings to battle the birds.

According to the almanac of Abū al-ʻUqūl, birds mated at the start of *Shubāṭ* (II:1), and according to *Salwa* at II:3 (22° Aquarius). This information is taken from the earlier *anwāʼ* tradition, as is, for example, the reference by Ibn al-Ajdābī regarding the mating of birds at the *naw'* of *ṭarf* around II:5. The relatively recent Yemeni almanac of al-Ḥaydara (1974) mentions the mating at II:6. Many of the almanacs explain that this is in reference to small birds (*ʻaṣāfīr*).

Al-Malik al-Ashraf did not mention the mating of birds, but he did provide hatching times at IV:8 and V:15. The former time is given as IV:7 (25° Aries) in *Fuṣūl* and *Salwa*. The non-Yemeni almanacs record a range of dates for egg hatching, but generally about a week later than indicated by al-Malik al-Ashraf. The *anwāʼ* tradition places this under the *naw'* of *ghafr* at IV:16 according to Ibn al-Ajdābī. The reference here is to birds in general, but primarily small birds. The ostrich (*naʻām*) is said to lay its eggs on IX:23 (8° Libra), according to the Rasulid almanac of *Salwa*. This is similar to the date given in the *Calendar of Cordova* (IX:25). The ostrich was said to lay its eggs at the beginning of the autumn *wasmī* rains (al-Marzūqī 1968:2:145). However, Musil (1928:38) said the ostrich laid its eggs in March or April and these eggs hatched about three weeks later.

Among the specific birds mentioned in the almanac are the following:

Abū fuṣāda. This is an Egyptian term for the wagtail (*Motacillidae*). The yellow wagtail, which is more common in Yemen, is *Motacilla flava* and the white variety is *M. alba*. The citrine wagtail (*M. citreola*) and grey wagtail (*M. cinerea*) are also known in Yemen (Brooks et al. 1987:47). The more common name in Arabic is *dhu'ara*, in reference to the fact that it always wags its tail back and forth so that it appears to be fearful or in a frenzy (al-Ma'lūf 1932:163). This bird is called *hazār al-dhayl* in the Ibb area and *ṭayr al-baqar* at Abyan ('Ubādī 1989:144). Its presence was noted by al-Ḥajrī (1984:4:804) in the Tihāma foothills. The Iraqi term for this bird is *zīṭa*.

According to the almanac the wagtail arrives in Egypt at the same time as the crane (*kurkī*) on X:9, although *Fuṣūl* records the arrival of the crane at X:8. This reference is to the winter migration southward of these birds from Egypt. The specific mention of the wagtail is unique in the Rasulid texts; most non-Yemeni almanacs refer to either the kite (*ḥidā'*) or vulture (*rakham*) as arriving in October, as in the early almanac of Abū Ḥanīfa al-Dīnawarī at X:2. The author has clearly derived this reference from an Egyptian source; the wagtail appears somewhat later in Yemen and heads north again in the spring.

Badrī. Al-Malik al-Ashraf mentioned the last departure of this bird at IX:2, while *Salwa* and Taymūr place this at IX:16 (1° Libra). This is in reference to its migration south to escape the cold of winter in the north. It is not clear whether this information is being copied from another source or is meant for Yemen. The term *badrī* refers in Arabic to a type of hunting falcon (*buzāt*, plural) as explained in the almanac of Abū al-'Uqūl. This term is known from the medieval texts (e.g., Viré 1967:54), where it referred to a variety with round eyes according to the important hunting text of Kushājim (Ṣāliḥīya 1985:56). The term may be derived from *badr* for the full moon (Phillott 1908:52, note 3). Al-Malik al-Ashraf and Abū al-'Uqūl said that the *badrī* falcon was used for hunting, along with the sparrow hawk (*bāshiq*) and merlin, at I:3.

Bawāshiq. The term *bawāshiq* is the plural of *bashiq* or *bashaq*. In the plural it can refer to a variety of "beasts of prey," the literal rendering of *sibā'* (al-Ḥimyarī 1980:206), although it was commonly used for the European sparrow hawk (*Accipiter nisus nisus*) in hunting texts (al-Ma'lūf 1932:2; Viré 1977:141). The author probably meant sparrow hawks in his usage, since he made a distinction between *bawāshiq* and *jawāriḥ*, the latter being an obvious generic for birds of prey. The term *bawāshiq* was derived from Persian (al-Damīrī 1906:1:230).

The sparrow hawk was especially popular in Persia as a hunting bird in royal circles. It was considered one of the lightest and fastest rising birds for hunting. This bird is not generally used for hunting on the Arabian Peninsula today (Allen and Smith 1975:118), but it was apparently important in the hunting of the Rasulid court. Sparrow hawks can be found on the peninsula between early October and late March (Meinertzhagen 1954:368). The earliest arrival date in Yemen is mid-September (Brooks et al. 1987:17). As a medicant the flesh of this bird was hot and dry, although the Prophet forbade the eating of birds of prey. Al-Malik al-Ashraf said that these birds, probably in reference to sparrow hawks, were used in hunting along with the merlin at I:3. According to later Coptic almanacs, such as *Nubdha* and al-Khalījī, the *bawāshiq* arrived in Egypt at VIII:22 (30 *Misrā*) as part of the southern migration.

Dajāj. The chicken (*dajāj*) is a popular domestic fowl which rates only a few references in the medieval almanacs. The herbalist al-Anṭākī (1951:1:151, 2:69) claimed that this was the best-tasting fowl, having a light meat defined as hot and wet. Both the author and Abū al-'Uqūl said that chicks (*farārīj*) were plentiful after VIII:17. Chicken eggs increase at X:18, according to the author, and at X:17 in the reckoning of Abū al-'Uqūl. This is said to be due to increased grain from the autumn harvest and the intensity of the sun at this time. However, *Salwa* and Taymūr mention this increase at X:3 (18° Libra), earlier in the cool autumn. The later Yemeni almanac of al-Thābitī claims that the increase was between X:3 and X:18; the dates in the almanac probably represent the end of the increase in eggs. Eggs and young chicks are part of the traditional diet for new mothers in Yemeni society (Adra 1983:21), although they were probably quite rare as food for the general populace in medieval Yemen. When chickens are louder and more noisy than usual, this is a sign for rain, according to the *Bughya* (fol. 24r).

Hudhud. One of the birds most frequently mentioned in the almanacs is the hoopoe, or *Upupa epops epops*. In Arabic this is the *hudhud*, about which there is considerable folklore in Arab tradition (Wensinck 1971:541–42). Legend has it that wise King Solomon made the hoopoe king of the birds (*mālik al-ṭuyūr*), hence the visible crown on its head. When Solomon visited the Queen of Sheba, he found the hoopoe sitting next to her.[21] The Prophet forbade Muslims to kill the hoopoe, although the meat was considered hot and dry as a medicant.

The term *hudhud*, like a number of older bird names in Arabic, is said to be based on the sound that the bird makes. In Yemeni dialect there are a number of variants, including *yudyud*, *yubyub*, and *yumyum*. Among the numerous Arabic epithets for this bird are *abū al-akhbār*, *abū 'ibbād*, *abū al-rabī'*, *abū al-rīḥ*, *abū sajjār*, and *abū thumāma* (al-Nāshirī 1985:184). Among the Rwala Bedouins, according to Musil (1928:40), it is known as the one who butchered its mother and father (*dhābiḥ ummih wa-abūh*).

The almanac and Abū al-'Uqūl recorded its departure at I:16, while *Salwa* and Taymūr note this at I:14 (3° Aquarius). The almanac of al-Shayzarī places this event during February. The reference here is to its departure southward to Yemen. The hoopoe is a marker of spring in Yemen, especially the time for the spring rains (M. al-Akwa' 1979:123; Serjeant and al-'Amrī 1981:427, note 362). In al-Ḥujarīya of the southern highlands it is time to plant sorghum when the hoopoe sings its song. Tribespeople in the central highland valley of al-Ahjur claim this bird issues a warning about the presence of snakes, a belief noted in the medieval literature (al-Mustawfī al-Qazwīnī 1928:91–92). The later Yemeni almanac of al-Sirājī claims that the hoopoe lays its eggs in late January. Meinertzhagen (1954:293) notes that it lays eggs in the Persian Gulf region during April and May.

Jawāriḥ. The term *jāriḥa* (*jawāriḥ*, plural) may refer to any beast of prey (al-Nāshirī 1985:113; al-Tha'ālibī n.d.:13), although in the almanac the reference is exclusively to hunting birds. Among the important birds of prey on the peninsula in the medieval period were falcons, hawks, eagles, vultures, ravens, kites, and owls. The female goshawk (*bāz*) was exported from Yemen during the Abbasid period (Ahsan 1979:216). Al-Malik al-Ashraf mentioned hunting with these birds between IX:14 and X:21, although *Salwa* notes this for IX:15 (1° Libra). This is the season of major migration from the north, when these birds prey on the numerous small birds involved in the migration. The reference in the almanac indicates hunting of sea birds and thus in the coastal Tihāma rather than in the mountains. Autumn and early winter were the primary times for hunting with birds on the peninsula. One of the favorite victims of these birds would have been the bustard (*ḥubāra*), or *Ardeotis arabs*, which is still found in coastal Yemen. The hunting birds were also capable of catching hares and occasionally gazelles. In the early spring around mating time the falcons and hawks that had been caught for the hunting season would be returned to the wild. The Coptic almanac of al-Maqrīzī notes the hatching of young birds of prey on I:19 (24 *Ṭūba*).

Kurkī. The common crane (*Grus grus grus*) is generally called *kurkī* (*karākī*, plural) in Arabic, although it can also be referred to as *ghurnūq* (al-Jāḥiẓ 1968:5:149) and *rahw* (al-Ma'lūf 1932:75). This was a favorite game bird, especially in Egypt. The meat was considered hot and dry, with Ibn Qayyim al-Jawzīya (1957:297) suggesting that the meat sit a day or two before being eaten. Among its qualities, the meat was considered a powerful aphrodisiac.

According to al-Malik al-Ashraf and Abū al-'Uqūl the crane arrived in

Egypt with the wagtail (*abū fuṣāda*) on X:9, although *Fuṣūl* places this at X:8. No mention is made of its presence in Yemen, although it has been observed in the winter (Brooks et al. 1987:22). Ibn Mammātī said that the crane begins to arrive in Egypt about the time of the Festival of the Cross at IX:14 (17 *Tūt*), while al-Maqrīzī cited this arrival at X:5 (8 *Bābih*). The crane was said to winter in Egypt and points south, and to summer in Iraq and to the north (al-Ibshīhī 1981:362). The information in the almanac is derived from Egyptian sources, although it was widely disseminated in the region. Long before, the Greek historian Hesiod (1973:73) cited the arrival of the crane in Greece during October as a marker of the chilly autumn rains and time for ploughing. Aelian (1971:21) said that cranes carried stones as ballast for their journey from Greece to Egypt, where "they fall in with the Egyptians as they are sowing their fields, and in the ploughlands they find, so to speak, a generous table, and though uninvited partake of the Egyptians' hospitality." Sailors in the Indian Ocean claimed that the sight of a crane meant that land was near (Shihāb 1982:194).

Qaṭā. This is the sand grouse (*Pterocles* sp.), one of the birds hunted in the medieval period. Both the crowned sand grouse (*Pterocles coronatus*) and the chestnut-bellied sand grouse (*P. exustus*) are found in Yemen, with the latter being the more common ('Ubādī 1989:100, 102; Brooks et al. 1987:35). The Arabic term is said to be derived from the sound of the bird's call of *qaṭāqaṭā*. The singular form is *qaṭāh*, with plurals of *qaṭawāt* and *qaṭayāt*. In Thamūd of southern Yemen the crowned sand grouse is called *barā'iṭ* ('Ubādī 1989:100). In Arabic the crowned sand grouse is often called *kudrī*; it is dust-colored with a yellow throat, multicolored breast, and short tail. The chestnut-bellied variety is known as *jūnī* and has a dust-colored breast, black belly, and larger body (al-Nāshirī 1985:162). The young of the sand grouse are called *nahār* (Ibn Qutayba 1982:155) or *sulk* (al-Batalyūsī 1984:571), and their nests are designated *afḥūḍ* (al-Tha'ālibī n.d.:190). The sand grouse is said to always fly in a flock (*sirb*).

Ibn Qutayba (1949:69) claimed they always laid eggs in lots of odd numbers. The eggs are laid in wasteland far from water sources and potential predators (Musil 1928:39) in April and May (Meinertzhagen 1954:459). These birds are quite fond of grain and thus are considered pests by farmers. According to Ibn Qayyim al-Jawzīya (1957:298), the meat was not recommended, although he thought it a useful medicant for dropsy (*istisqā'*). The Romans considered the brain of sand grouse an aphrodisiac that led women to grant sexual favors. The price of sand grouse in Yemen was listed in a royal account book of al-Malik al-Muẓaffar (*Shāmil*) as being eighteen *dirham* in 691/1292.

According to al-Malik al-Ashraf the sand grouse was present in Yemen between XI:25 and III:9. Abū al-'Uqūl said that it left the north on XI:3, arrived in Yemen on XI:24, and departed Yemen on III:9. *Salwa* simply notes its presence in Yemen between XI:7 (23° Scorpius) and III:11 (28° Pisces). Although al-Ḥajrī (1984:4:804) claimed it was only found in the Jawf region of eastern Yemen, it was certainly present in the wider area under Rasulid control.

Simmān. The common quail (*Coturnix coturnix*) was referred to as both *salwa* and *simmān* in the almanac. The former term was in reference to the biblical story of the manna and the quails, which were said to fall between VIII:25 and XI:4. The latter term is Egyptian colloquial for the classical *sumāna*. In classical rendering the singular is *sumānah*, with plurals of *sumānayāt* and *samāmīn*. The quail is called *furwat* in al-Ḥujarīya and *'ifrada* in Abyan ('Ubādī 1989:52). The quail is also known as *farī* and *muray'ī* in the Levant. The author's father, Yūsuf ibn 'Umar (1982:241), identified the quail as *qatīl al-ra'd*, because some thought it would die when it heard the sound of thunder (*ra'd*); this was a common tradition in the medieval sources (al-Damīrī n.d.:2:26). The harlequin quail (*C. delegorguei*) is also found in Yemen as a migrant.

According to the author the quail was present in Yemen until III:9, with Abū al-'Uqūl noting that it arrived in Yemen at XI:3. *Salwa* and Taymūr place it between XI:7 (23° Scorpius) and III:10 (28° Pisces). Quails can be found in Arabia between mid-September and early May (Meinertzhagen 1954:568). Ibn al-Mujāwir (1954:277–78) quoted a curious legend that said no one knew where the quails at Dimyāṭ in Egypt came from. Ibn Mammātī said that the quail migrated north again from Egypt on III:23 (27 *Baramhāt*). The quail was a popular game bird, especially in Egypt. Ruffer (1919:30) claimed that the quail were so exhausted from their journey south that they were easily caught on the Mediterranean seacoast. He added that they were quite tasty, "having just gorged on the excellent grapes of Greek islands." According to *Shāmil* the price of its meat in Yemen during 691/1292 was eighteen *dirham*, the same as for sand grouse. The meat was considered hot and dry in the humoral system and had a number of medicinal uses.

Yu'yu'a. In his discussion of sparrow hawks at I:3, al-Malik al-Ashraf also mentioned hunting with a bird noted in the text as *lu'lu'a*, which is probably a miscopying of *yu'yu'a*, a well-known term for the merlin (*Falco columbarius aesalon* Christiani-Ludovici), also known as *jalam* in Syria (al-Baladī 1983:55) and Iraq (Kushājim in Ṣāliḥiya 1985:59). This bird was like the *ṣaqr* falcon, although it was smaller. Musil (1928:35) describes it as a fierce predator which is especially fond of sand grouse. Abū al-'Uqūl at I:4 defined it as a type of *bazāt*, or hunting falcon. The *yu'yu'a* was also called *yuthaq* and *abū al-riyāḥ* (al-Baladī 1983:55).

Insects

Like other medieval almanacs the text of al-Malik al-Ashraf records a number of references to common insects, especially to the seasonal appearance and disappearance of certain bugs. None of this information is derived from the Yemeni folk tradition, apart from the mention of honey seasons. Some of the common timing is still relevant to Yemen, which has its fair share of creepy crawlers and noxious vermin.[22] As the modern Kuwaiti author Ayyūb Ḥusayn (1984:66) reminisces, insects were much more a part of everyday existence in the past when houses were made of unfinished wood or mud. In the nineteenth century, Didier (1985:54–55) claimed that flies were such a problem at the port of Yanbu in Saudi Arabia that a camel had to be brought in to attract them and carry them off. "You eat them, you drink them, you breathe them; they are a scourge comparable with the seven plagues of Egypt," he exclaimed. They were also an intimate part of sea travel in the medieval period and later. Another nineteenth-century traveler, named Osgood (1854:159), once traveled on a pilgrim boat from Aden to Mocha. He had difficulty sleeping because in the next room there were about fifty women, "who, suffering from the annoyances of the swarms of mosquitoes, nail-gnawing cockroaches and vermin, which infested the vessel, kept the air resonant with shrill squalling." While on a voyage down the Nile, Madden (1829:294) lamented that his boat was "literally a Noah's ark" because of the vermin and flies.

The specific insects mentioned in the almanac include:

Barāghīth. This is the standard Arabic term for fleas (*Pulex* sp.), which were no doubt endemic in medieval Yemeni bedding. In Yemeni dialect fleas are generally known as *qummāl* (I. al-Akwa' 1984:2:827; Rossi 1939:230), as noted by Ibn Jaḥḥāf in his almanac for X:7. Medieval scholars thought that fleas only lived for five days, during which time they feasted on lice (al-Mustawfī al-Qazwīnī 1928:36). The herbals are full of recipes and charms to ward off fleas.

Al-Malik al-Ashraf noted the stirring or increase in fleas after the heat of summer at VII:21, a timing given as VII:20 in *Fuṣūl* and VII:19 by Abū al-'Uqūl, who claimed that the mosquito (*baqq*)[23] also stirred at this time. The fleas begin to decrease after X:9 according to the almanac, or X:6 according to *Fuṣūl*. The reference here is for Yemen, where fleas increase with the late summer or early autumn rains. For Egypt, however, fleas were more common in the winter, with al-Anṭākī and al-Maqrīzī noting their appearance at XII:9 (13 *Kiyahk*). Mosquitos, on the other hand, increase in Egypt at X:19 with the beginning of the decrease in the Nile flow. In areas of the Middle East where there is a spring rain the fleas appear at this time as well, as noted in the almanacs of Ibn Māsawayh and al-Qazwīnī for II:20.

Al-Dhubāb al-azraq. This is the dreaded blue fly, a dangerous variety of horsefly that appears in Egypt and near Damascus every spring, according to the author. Both Abū al-'Uqūl and al-Malik al-Ashraf claimed that these could actually kill a camel when agitated. The name appears to have been reserved primarily for flies that could severely harm camels (al-Jāḥiẓ 1968:3:390). Ibn Qutayba (1982:193) said that the term *qama'a* also referred to a large blue fly. A swarm of these was referred to as *sha'arā'* (al-Aṣma'ī in Haffner 1905:113). The almanac and Abū al-'Uqūl noted the appearance of these blue flies at III:15, about the time of the spring equinox. The date is given as III:17 in *Fuṣūl*. The Coptic almanac of al-Qalqashandī notes their presence at III:23 (27 *Baramhāt*), the same date recorded by Ibn Māsawayh. The reference in the almanac of Ibn al-Bannā' to "cowflies" (*dhubāb al-baqar*) at III:15 is probably a synonym for these blue flies.

The season for flies (*Musca* sp.) in general is not indicated by the author, although Taymūr mentions the generation of flies at III:4. This timing is at least a month later than the time recorded in the *anwā'* tradition, as for example the date of II:1 under the *naw'* of *ṭarf* according to Abū Ḥanīfa al-Dīnawarī. In Yemen flies are mainly a problem during the summer rains and there are very few in winter. Al-Hamdānī (1938:11) claimed that flies were never a serious problem in Ṣan'ā', although the same could not have been said about the hot coastal town of Zabīd. Flies were also abundant in Mecca and a constant bane of the pilgrim (al-Muqaddasī 1989:145).

The medieval scholar thought that flies were spontaneously generated by a corrupt mixing of air and soil and that flies could not fly in cold wintry air (al-Musṭawfī al-Qazwīnī 1928:72–73). The maximum life of a fly, according to al-Jāḥiẓ (1968:3:315), was only forty days. The health problem created by flies was known by some medieval practitioners of the medical discipline, who noted that the Prophet Muḥammad said it was necessary to wash a vessel on which a fly landed. Another tradition of Muḥammad said that the fly carried disease on one wing and a cure on the other (al-Suyūṭī 1986:199). The fly was hot and wet in the humoral system; it was forbidden to eat it.

The three late Yemeni almanacs of Ibn Jaḥḥāf, al-Thābitī, and *Tawqī'āt* referred to the appearance of a red fly at V:23. It was called *mubashshir al-'inab* (announcer of the grapes) because its arrival coincided with the ripening of grapes in Yemen. This usage survives in the central highland valley of al-Ahjur, where this type of fly is called *bishārat al-'inab.*

Dūd al-qazz. The mention of silkworm, commonly called *dūd al-qazz* in the almanacs, does not refer to Yemen. The silkworm was known in some parts of the Arab world to the north, although information also filtered in from the east. The eggs were said to be smaller than poppy seeds. It is recorded in some sources that in the spring women would tie them up under their breasts to assist the incubation. Then they would put the silkworms on a tray and scatter bits of mulberry leaves over them. Al-Malik al-Ashraf noted the stirring or mating of silkworms at II:4, while Abū al-'Uqūl and *Fuṣūl* mentioned this at II:3. A distinction is made between this reference to the beginning of the larvae stage and the emergence of the silkworm at III:10. The Coptic almanacs place the latter event at III:12 (16 *Baramhāt*). The Rasulids imported silk for their royal clothing and banners.

Hawāmm. The common term *hawāmm* refers to a variety of creeping insects, perhaps best translated as "noxious vermin."[24] Ibn Sīda (1965:8:100) claimed that this term referred to any animal that crept (*dābba*)[25] on the ground and was not eaten; thus he excluded the locust. It is odd that the Rasulid almanacs do not in fact mention the appearance of the locust (*jarāda*), which was a scourge to Yemeni farmers. Ibn Māsawayh noted in his almanac that *hawāmm* could be used for worms, flies, and locusts. The major vermin in Yemen, according to al-Hamdānī (1983:308), were various snakes (*thu'bān* and *af'ā*), scorpions (*'aqrab*), a type of black ant called *qa'ṣ*, mosquitoes (*ba'ūḍ*), cockroaches (*banāt wardān*), beetles (*khunfasā'*), and bedbugs (*kattān* or *baqq*).

Al-Malik al-Ashraf said that these various vermin disappeared from view (i.e., underground) at I:4, but this is certainly a copyist error. *Salwa* and Taymūr, for example, place the disappearance at XI:9 (26° Scorpius) and XII:8 (25° Sagittarius). The non-Yemeni almanacs usually record it for the month of November, although some relate this to the setting of *sa'd al-akhbiya* in late August (e.g., al-Shayzarī for VIII:26). Abū Ḥanīfa al-Dīnawarī said they went underground at the *naw'* of the Pleiades on XI:15. Al-Bīrūnī noted that some people claimed that all animals without bones, i.e., insects of this type, perished on XI:20. In his typical candor, however, he quickly noted that this was a relative statement because he had been "molested by gnats" while in the region of Jūrjān during January!

The almanac notes the emergence of noxious vermin at II:16, as distinct from their appearance at III:15. *Salwa* records the appearance at III:27 (15° Aries). According to Ibn 'Āṣim, they first come out of the ground at the rising of *sa'd al-akhbiya* at II:25 after having been in the ground for the three months of winter. Their appearance is noted under the rising of *al-fargh al-mu'akhkhar* or setting of *'awwā*, according to Abū Ḥanīfa al-Dīnawarī and Ibn Māsawayh. In this sense the reference to the appearance signifies when they were abundant.

Naḥl. The honeybee in Yemen is *Apis mellifera yemenitica*, generally known as *naḥl* in classical Arabic but more commonly as *nūba* in Yemeni dialect (I. al-Akwa' 1984:2:714). Honeybees in Yemen are small bodied with a gentle but excitable nature (Jaycox and Karpowicz 1990:1). Abū al-'Uqūl said that bees would not make honey if there was rain on IX:6, an obvious reference to the earlier magical lore of either the Syriac or Greek traditions. None of the Rasulid almanacs mention bees, although the seasons for collecting various types of honey are noted in some detail. Honey, which is hot and dry in the humoral tradition, was probably the most important medicant in Islam, since it figures prominently in several traditions of the Prophet Muḥammad.[26] Besides the many benefits for people, honey was also deemed to be an aphrodisiac for camels. The Prophet Muḥammad forbade the killing of honeybees (Ibn Qutayba 1949:64). Another tradition refers to an alcoholic drink in Yemen called *bit'*, which was made from honey (al-Rāzī al-Ṣan'ānī 1974:255).

Yemen is recognized throughout the region for the quality of its honey.[27] One of the earliest sources on honey production in Yemen is the tenth-century A.D. geographical text of al-Hamdānī (1983:311), who noted a variety of honey called *shuhd* from Jabal Ḥaḍūr in the central highlands that was so thick it had to be cut with a knife. In the important honey-producing area of Jabal Hinawm, al-Hamdānī reported that a beekeeper might have up to fifty hives. The Yemeni term for a beehive is generally *jabḥ* and the honeycomb is called *shabk*, the latter term being mentioned in the almanac. Yemeni beekeepers used reed cylinders coated with mud and dung, hollowed-out wooden hives, and modified clay storage jars. No doubt there were migrant beekeepers in the medieval period as in Yemen today in order to take best advantage of the various flowering seasons.

There are several ways of defining honey varieties in Yemen. Qāḍī Muḥammad al-Akwa' (1979:153) has reflected on the types of honey from his childhood days. One of these was called *duhnī*, because it was like butter or thick oil; another was called *sukkārī* because it was white and clear like sugar. Al-Malik al-Ashraf, however, mentioned the type of honey by the main flowering plant that bees frequented in making the honey. Six separate references are made to plants which define honey types ranging from collection in midsummer to early spring. The honey from *Acacia asak* (*'asaqī*) was collected in the mountains at VII:13 and in the southern highland towns of al-Ma'āfir and Dhubḥān at VIII:1. The recent Yemeni almanac of al-Ḥaydara notes that honey is plentiful at VIII:20. Several species of acacia are important for honey production in Yemen; these include *salam* (*A. ehrenbergiana* Hayne) in Wādī Surdud (Arab League Institute 1977a:5), *samur* (*A. tortillis* Forssk. Hayne) in Daw'ān (Serjeant 1954:451, note 68), and *ẓubba* (*A. mellifera* Vahl Benth.) or *ḥmja* (?). According to al-Malik al-Ashraf the honey from *ẓubba* was collected in the mountains of Surdud at I:27 and in the mountains in general at II:18. This was the best variety of honey, according to the almanac. The flowering times for different acacias vary considerably, especially given the wide range of elevation in the country.

The almanac places the early autumn harvest of honey from the Dead Sea apple, or *qushār* (*Calotropis procera*), in the mountains between IX:16 and X:24. Autumn honey is the most common in Yemen, due in large part to the flowering after the late summer rains (M. al-Akwa' 1981:12; Gingrich in Dostal et al. 1983:67). Serjeant and Lewcock (1983:556) claim that in the northern highlands red autumn (*'allānī*) honey is preferred to white spring honey. In this the Yemenis differ from the classical tradition, in which spring honey was generally considered the best (Abū Ḥanīfa al-Dīnawarī 1974b:132; al-Anṭākī 1951:2:69; Ibn Sīna 1983:23; al-Tamīmī in Marín and Waines 1989:128), a tradition quoted by the father of the author (Yūsuf ibn 'Umar 1982:324).

Another major tree important in honey production is the christ's-thorn (*Ziziphus spina-christi*), which is called both *ḍāl* and *ilb* in the almanac. The term *ḍāl* appears to be for a mountain variety, the honey of which was collected in the mountains at XII:16 at the coldest part of winter. Honey from the christ's-thorn is prized today in the Ta'izz and Ibb areas (Karpowicz 1983:8), as well as in the Ḥaḍramawt. Yemeni *ilb* is dialectical for classical *'ilb* and was used primarily in the coastal region and perhaps in the foothills of Wādī Surdud. The recent almanac of al-Ḥaydara places honey from the christ's-thorn at XI:16. In Daw'ān of the Ḥaḍramawt this type of honey was collected in the autumn (Serjeant 1954:451, note 68), as is also the case in Bayt al-Faqīh of the Tihāma. Al-Malik al-Ashraf indicated there was a mixed honey of *'ilb* and *ṣuyyāb* (*Euphorbia inarticulata* Schweinf.) collected in the mountains of Surdud at I:8. In Yemen today the honey from *ṣuyyāb* is said to burn the throat. *Euphorbia* species are important sources of pollen for bees in Yemen (Jaycox and Karpowicz 1990:7).

One other type of honey is noted in the almanac for XI:15. This is from an unidentified plant, *mtsha* (?). Perhaps it refers to the *ṭunub* tree (*Cordia africana*), which Abū al-'Uqūl noted blossomed at X:13. Another possibility is that this is a misreading of *mazz*, a type of wild pomegranate which al-

Aṣma'ī (1972:36) claimed was very important for making an excellent variety of honey in the Sarāt region of Yemen. Al-Malik al-Ashraf defined the honey of this unidentified type as white, excellent tasting, sticky, viscous, and one that does not harden.

Naml. The ant (*Formica* sp.) is referred to as *naml* in the almanac, although the more common term in Yemeni dialect is *dharr* (Rossi 1939:161). In classical usage *dharr* generally refers to a small ant (al-Tha'ālibī n.d.:25). The term *nashsh* can also refer to an ant in Yemeni dialect, as noted by Rossi for the western highlands. Another term for the ant in Yemen is *qa'ṣ*, which al-Malik al-Ashraf described in *Milḥ* as a natural enemy of the date palm moth. The ant is hot and dry in the humoral system, but it should not be killed according to the Prophet. The so-called white ant, or *araḍa* (*Microerotermes diversus* Silvestri), is in fact a termite.[28]

According to al-Malik al-Ashraf ants disappeared underground at XI:4, although *Fuṣūl* places this at XI:3. The later Rasulid almanac of *Salwa* notes that ants enter their hives at XII:8 (24° Sagittarius). These two events are commonly referred to in the almanacs. The first is the disappearance of ants underground, which is usually cited a month or two before they are said to actually enter their hives. Ibn Mammātī, for example, said that ants go underground on X:24 (27 *Bābih*) and enter their hives on XII:7 (11 *Kiyahk*). The almanac and *Fuṣūl* record the emergence of ants at II:12, while Abū al-'Uqūl placed this at II:11 and *Salwa* and Taymūr at II:8 (28° Aquarius).

Reptiles

The only animal of this category mentioned by name in the almanac is the snake, of which there are many varieties in Yemen.[29] The term used in the almanac is *ḥayya*, which is usually reserved in Arabic for small snakes (Musil 1928:42). A large snake is called *thu'bān* in Yemen. There are numerous legends concerning snakes in Yemeni folklore. It is often said that snakes will not enter through the gates of certain towns, such as Ṣan'ā' and Nā'iṭ (al-Hamdānī 1938:12, 32), Dhamār (Ibn al-Mujāwir 1954:190), and Kawkabān. The same holds true for certain shrines, such as the legendary tomb of the prophet Shu'ayb on Jabal al-Nabī Shu'ayb, the highest point in Yemen. The same claim is sometimes made for other dangerous animals, such as scorpions.

According to the almanac and *Fuṣūl* snakes lose their sight at XII:10, although Abū al-'Uqūl gave this as XII:7 and *Salwa* as XII:6 (22° Sagittarius). This is a common reference in the non-Yemeni almanacs and reflects a belief that snakes lose their sight when they hibernate underground in the winter.

When they reappear in the spring they are still blind and need to rub their eyes with a certain plant, such as fennel, *shamār* in Arabic (al-Damīrī 1906:1:635; al-Ibshīhī 1981:341). Al-Qazwīnī claimed that if it was still cold when it was time to come out, they would congregate underground until the weather warmed. The almanac and *Fuṣūl* reported that snakes come out and regain their sight at III:8. Abū al-'Uqūl mentioned this at III:4 on the last of the Nights of the Old Woman. The timing in *Salwa* is for III:6 (23° Pisces). The non-Yemeni almanacs also place this emergence from hibernation during March.

Domestic Animals

Although Yemen was primarily an agricultural country, domestic animals were extremely important in the economy.[30] In parts of the coastal region and in the eastern part of the country there were pastoralists, including camel nomads. Sheep and goats formed the main source of meat for the Yemeni diet. Draft animals in agriculture consisted of Zebu cattle in the richer areas and donkeys or camels in the poorer areas. Donkeys and camels were the main pack animals, especially for the long journey from the coastal region to the highlands. During the Rasulid period there was a standing cavalry and the sultans took a lively interest in horses.

Bahā'im. The term *bahā'im* (*bahīma*, singular) refers in general to quadrupeds, although in the almanac the primary reference is to large domestic animals such as cows, donkeys, sheep, and goats (al-Damīrī n.d.:1:158). In Ṣan'ānī dialect *baḥīma* refers to a donkey and *baḥma* to a female calf (Rossi 1939:163). The general term for larger domestic beasts is *qurāsh* in Yemeni Arabic. Cows in general are called *baqar*, the classical term. The bull is *thawr* and the young bull is *tabī'*. A male calf is referred to as *'ijl*. The generic term for sheep is *ghanam* or *kharūf*, while a ram is called *kabsh* or *barbarī*. The collective for goats is the classical *ma'az*, while a billy goat is called *tays*. Small sheep and goats are called *tallī* (Landberg 1901:1:605; Rossi 1939:162).

According to the almanac, domestic animals gained weight from VIII:17, an obvious reference to the coming of autumn and new pasture. This date is given as VIII:17 in *Fuṣūl* and VIII:16 by Abū al-'Uqūl. This is a common reference in the non-Yemeni almanacs. The magical *Sirr al-asrār*, attributed to Aristotle (1983:45), notes that beasts fatten in summer. According to the almanac, Abū al-'Uqūl, and *Fuṣūl* these animals begin to lose weight from I:11, with *Fuṣūl* adding that this continues until III:11. A different tradition is recorded in *Salwa*, where beasts and people are said to lose weight from

X:23 (8° Scorpius). This reference cannot be for Yemen, since Abū al-'Uqūl noted the pasturing of cattle and other domestic beasts in the coastal region from X:16.

According to al-Malik al-Ashraf, the last availability of *samn* (ghee, or clarified butter) was at XII:5 in Mikhlāf Ja'far. The times that domestic beasts give birth are not specified in the almanac, apart from details on horses and camels, discussed below. The later Yemeni almanacs of Ibn Jaḥḥāf and al-Thābitī mentioned the birth of *bahā'im* at IX:24. The Coptic almanacs place the birth of domestic beasts during *Bābih* (X). Abū al-'Uqūl said that sheep bore their young for two months after X:12.

Ibl. The camel, that paragon of traditional Arabia, permeates Arab folklore like no other beast.[31] The Yemeni camel is of the one-hump variety, *Camelus dromedarius*, as are its kindred on the Arabian Peninsula. The term *ibl*, used in the almanac, is the collective. A mature camel in general is *jamal*, while the mare is *nāqa*; although there are numerous terms for camels at different stages of life. The major varieties of camels in Yemen during the Rasulid period were *mas'ūdīya, manṣūrīya, al-'irḍīya al-Yamānīya* (from Jabal Shamīr near Mawza'), *al-'irḍīya al-jabalīya, 'udhrīya, ḥalwīya* (from Ḥalī), *muwallada*, and *yamānīya* ('Alī ibn Dāwūd 1987:384–86).

The camel was an important animal for transport and draft power in Yemen. During the Rasulid era the primary places of camel raising were in the coastal region and the area of al-Sha'bānīya near Ta'izz. In the eastern part, or Jawf, not under Rasulid control, there were scattered camel nomads who ranged into the Empty Quarter of the Arabian desert.

According to al-Malik al-Ashraf the camel was sexually aroused at XI:26, a date certainly copied from the earlier almanac tradition as reported in Ibn Qutayba's *anwā'* text and by Ibn 'Āṣim, who associated this day with the rising of *harrārān* (the joint rising of Antares and Vega). Abū al-'Uqūl noted the arousal of camels at XI:28. A different tradition is cited by *Salwa* and Taymūr, which indicate the rutting of both camels and elephants at XI:20 (7° Sagittarius).[32] This same dating can be found in the Coptic almanac of *Nubdha* and in Saray at XI:19. The main rutting season for camels is during the cold months of December and January, as noted in most of the Coptic almanacs, for the Rwala (Musil 1928:332) and in Najd (al-Suwaydā' 1983:97), although this can occur as late as March (al-Ḥabartī 1988:49). The recent Yemeni almanac of al-Ḥaydara places the rutting at II:8.

The process of two camels in the act of procreation has engendered many comments from both Arab and Western authors. The Victorian English cum Latin translation of al-Damīrī (1906:1:30) notes that the male "covers the female only once a year, *sed diu initum prorogat et pluries semen in feminam immittit*, and on that account it is subsequently affected with languor and weakness." In less obtuse prose, the Frenchman Daumas (1971:99) declares that "it drools, it spumes, it bulges, a sort of bladder of flesh extrudes from its mouth, it no longer wants to eat, it loses its belly, it is often in erection, as it always stales to the rear, it frequently pisses on its tail." Yet for all of this it remains a favorite archetype in the romantic poetry of Arab tribesmen.

The female bears in about a year, although there are slight regional differences. According to the old Bedouin lore reported by Ibn Qutayba (1956:95), camels born in the winter after X:26 were called *ruba'* and were said to be weak because of the intense cold at the time. The best birthing season in the opinion of Ibn Qutayba was between I:17 and II:12. The camels born in late spring after IV:6 were called *huba'* and were also considered weak because of the impending summer heat.

In Rasulid Yemen, according to al-Malik al-Ashraf, there were two main birthing seasons. The winter season between IX:25 and I:27 in the areas south of Ta'izz and in al-Sha'bānīya yielded the *ṣirbīya* variety. The term derives from the name for the time of the autumn harvest (*ṣirāb*), which was also the name of the Himyaritic month of October.[33] Abū al-'Uqūl said the major time for production in the coastal region was at XII:3. *Salwa* placed the production of *ṣirbīya* camels at I:19 (7° Aquarius), apparently in reference to the end of the season. The offspring from IV:11 to VII:26, especially at V:7, were called *ṣayfīya* in the areas south of Tai'zz and in al-Sha'bānīya according to the almanac. This is in reference to the late spring and early summer season of *ṣayf* in Yemeni usage. Ibn al-Ajdābī said that camel production in the Hejaz was common at the rising of Canopus on VIII:9. Al-Malik al-Ashraf said in *Mughnī* that camels should be watered morning and evening during the hot period of *jaḥr* before the summer rains.

The almanac refers to the young as *fuṣlān*, a term which generally refers to a young camel (*faṣīl*) still nursing or just able to graze and drink water (Abū Zayd in Ibn Sīda 1965:7:20). Al-Malik al-Mujāhid (*Aqwāl*, fol. 109r) defined *faṣīl* as a camel in its second year but not yet ridden. Abū al-'Uqūl noted at V:6, however, that the use of *fuṣlān* referred to sheep and goats. Al-Malik al-Ashraf said that V:7 was the time of greatest availability of *fuṣlān* and that they were good to eat. Despite the comment in Abū al-'Uqūl, whose almanac exists in later error-prone copies, al-Malik al-Ashraf is probably referring to the eating of young camel meat. Camel meat was considered hot and dry in the humoral system and an aphrodisiac, among other things.[34] Camel was an important source of meat for the Bedouins of the Arabian Peninsula. The Rwala Bedouins did not eat a camel calf less than three months old (Musil 1928:97). Daumas (in Marsh 1856:79) considered camel meat a delicacy, noting "all the flesh is good, and the hump is the choicest dish a host can offer to guests of distinction." The Prophet Muḥammad is said to have required Muslims to perform the ablutions before eating camel meat (al-Dhahabī 1984:184). It is interesting to note that the patriarch Jacob is said to have forbidden eating camel meat because "he felt himself to be transported with unknown desires for women" (Daumas 1971:107).

Khayl. The only reference to horses (*khayl*) in the almanac is for Egypt. The author said that XII:27 was the start of two months of pasturing for horses in Egypt. This was because the clover (*qurṭ*) had ripened by this time (*Tabṣira*, fol. 110r). According to *Fuṣūl* this refers to the Coptic months of *Ṭūba* and *Amshīr*, although this statement cannot be corroborated from the available Coptic almanacs. Al-Qalqashandī said horses go to pasture at II:27 (23 *Amshīr*), while *Nubdha* records this for XI:30 (4 *Kiyahk*). The *Calendar of Cordova* mentions pasturing of horses at II:16 and grazing on cropland in III.

The Rasulid almanac of Abū al-'Uqūl records the bearing of horses on III:20, while *Salwa* and Taymūr indicate this at III:19 (7° Aries). This correlates well with the dating in the Coptic almanacs, for example al-Maqrīzī for III:18 (15 *Baramhāt*). A second time for the birth of horses is indicated in the almanac of Abū al-'Uqūl at IV:13 and in Taymūr at IV:18. The dating in *Salwa* of V:16 (4° Gemini) is probably a simple copyist error. April is apparently the end of the season. The *Calendar of Cordova* and al-Shayzarī mentioned horse production between III:15 and IV:15. All of these dates appear to be derived from the classical tradition, in which Qusṭūs (fol. 92v) said that the best time for horse production was during the last part of March because of the temperate weather. In the Najd region of Saudi Arabia there is no special season for breeding, but spring is preferred by the Arabs (al-Suwaydā' 1983:119).

Medieval Yemen was renowned for its horse breeding.[35] The names of at least eighteen horses owned by al-Malik al-Ashraf have been recorded (*Aqwāl*, fol. 106r; 'Alī ibn Dāwūd 1987:343). The cavalry was a vital part of the Rasulid army and great attention was paid to the training and upkeep of horses, as is noted in the surviving Rasulid texts on veterinary practices. At the time of al-Malik al-Mu'ayyid Dāwūd, the successor of al-Malik al-Ashraf, the Rasulid cavalry was said to number about 2,000 (Ibn al-Mujāwir 1954:167; al-'Umarī 1974:47). Few of the common people would have had access to horses. It is reported that at one time before the Rasulid period a certain Ja'far ibn Ibrāhīm forbade the people in the Tihāma to ride horses ('Umāra 1976:49).

There was a brisk trade in horses through the ports of Aden and al-Shiḥr on the southern coast of Yemen. According to Abū al-'Uqūl the horses to be exported from Aden arrived in al-Janad from Ṣan'ā' on VII:21 and left al-Janad for Aden at VII:26. The season for sale of horses to merchants in Aden began on VIII:13 (29° Leo) according to *Salwa* and Taymūr, while *Ma'rifa* places this at VIII:15. Marco Polo (1958:264, 309) described the horse trade between the Arabian Peninsula and India at the end of the thirteenth century. Horses were exported to India from Aden, al-Shiḥr, Dhofar, Hormuz, and Qays. A certain king of the Coromandel coast was said to import some 2,000 horses a year, although most of them died after arrival. The shrewd merchant Polo added, "You can take it from me that the merchants who export them do not send any veterinaries or allow any to go, because they are only too glad for many of them to die in the king's charge." Ibn Baṭṭūṭa (1980:259) was amazed that horses in Dhofar were fed a steady diet of sardines.

Magical Creatures

Arab authors often classified various types of spirits or mythical beasts as animals. Al-Malik al-Ashraf said that on XI:30 the *quṭrub* stirred in Egypt. He also mentioned in *Tabṣira* (fol. 111r) that this spirit appeared during the time of hot *khamsīn* winds after IV:20. Both the author and Abū al-'Uqūl defined the *quṭrub* as a type of evil spirit (*ghūl*), although the latter placed its stirring at XII:7. This legend is certainly derived from the Coptic tradition. The almanac of al-Khalīji records the appearance of the *quṭrub* in Egypt at XI:24 (29 *Hatūr*). It would appear that the Coptic date has been transposed on the Syriac reckoning used in the almanac.

The *quṭrub* is defined in the lexicons as a male *ghūl* (al-Tha'ālibī n.d.:16) or a small spirit (*al-Muḥīṭ, q-ṭ-r-b*). In pre-Islamic Arabia some said that it was a creature part beast and part human and that it could assume different shapes. This spirit is said to only come out at night (al-Damīrī n.d.:2:256), when it is especially dangerous. It was said to be found in the outlying areas of Egypt and Yemen (al-Ibshīhī 1981:325; Padwick 1924:430). People generally gave it a wide berth, although al-Damīrī noted that some bold and clever people paid no attention to it. If the *quṭrub* has sex with someone, it possesses the body and eventually worms develop and consume the body of the victim. Al-Hamdānī (1983:378) described several places in Yemen where spirits (i.e., *jinn*) could be found readily.[36]

Chapter 5

Agriculture

GENERAL

The dominant theme of the Rasulid almanacs is agriculture, for which an extraordinary amount of information has been documented in the seasonal cycle. The sultans were patrons of agriculture and horticulture to an unprecedented extent in the history of Yemen. In addition to the almanacs at least four important treatises were written on the agriculture of the time (Varisco 1989c). These combine information on agriculture in Yemen with advice from previous authors, including the major text of Cassianus Bassus, known to the Arabs as Qusṭūs. The earliest of the Rasulid agricultural treatises is *Milḥ al-malāḥa fī ma'rifat al-filāḥa* by al-Malik al-Ashraf, the author of the almanac published here. The brother of al-Ashraf, al-Malik al-Mu'ayyad Dāwūd, is credited with a treatise called *al-Jamhara fī al-filāḥa*, but no copy exists. Similarly there is no known copy of the text by al-Malik al-Mujāhid 'Alī entitled *al-Ishāra fī al-'imāra.* The longest and most important agricultural treatise from the Rasulid period was written by al-Malik al-Afḍal al-'Abbās, *Bughyat al-fallāḥīn fī al-ashjār al-muthmira wa-al-rayāḥīn*, which quotes extensively from *Milḥ* and *al-Ishāra fī al-'imāra.* This same sultan wrote a number of smaller treatises which have been preserved in a mixed Rasulid manuscript from his royal library.

In addition to showing scholarly interest, the Rasulids were avid gardeners and established state control over agricultural production in parts of the country. Royal gardens were tended at Tha'bāt (Serjeant 1974a:35–36; Smith 1974), just to the east of the town of Ta'izz. This appears to have been the favorite vacation spot of the sultans, who built palaces here and established a royal mint. During the Ayyubid period in the early twelfth century A.D. the famous Saladin sent fruit trees from Syria to be planted at the gardens in Tha'bāt. In the coastal region near Zabīd there was a royal garden at Rāḥa (al-Ḥibshī 1980:41). Al-Malik al-Mujāhid was credited with having introduced the coconut tree into Yemen in his gardens at Zabīd, as noted by Ibn

Baṭṭūṭa (1980:262). According to al-Malik al-Afḍal (*Bughya*, fol. 124v), this occurred in 731/1330–31. Diplomatic delegations from east and west brought exotic plants to the Rasulid sultans. A delegation from Sind (Pakistan) in 768/1366–67 brought plants for al-Malik al-Afḍal, author of the *Bughya*. In 800/1397–98 a delegation from Ceylon brought mango (*'anbā*) trees for planting. In 820/1417 a large fleet of Ming dynasty ships arrived in Aden from China (Ma Huan 1970). The sultans also experimented in their gardens with grape varieties and roses, as noted by al-Malik al-Afḍal. Al-Malik al-Mujāhid introduced rice at al-Jahmalīya in the coastal region.

It is interesting to note that several important crops in Yemen's later history are not mentioned in the Rasulid sources. It seems that both coffee (*bun*) and *Catha edulis* (*qāt*) became popularized at the end of the Rasulid period and were thus not mentioned in the texts of al-Malik al-Afḍal and his predecessors. The fourteenth-century historian Ibn Faḍl Allāh al-'Umarī (in Rodinson 1977:77) claimed that the *qāt* shrub was introduced into Yemen during the reign of al-Malik al-Mu'ayyad Dāwūd in the early fourteenth century A.D. According to his account, the sultan thought ill of the plant and said it should not be grown. Ibn Baṭṭūṭa visited Zabīd and Ta'izz in A.D. 1320, but did not mention the presence of either coffee or *qāt*, two exotic items which certainly would have sparked his interest. If either were being grown by the time of al-Malik al-Afḍal, they would surely have been mentioned in the *Bughya*. The almanacs fail to mention three important cash crops in medieval Yemen: *wars* (*Memecylon tinctorium*),[1] from which a yellow dye was extracted; *fuwwa* (*Rubia tinctorium*), or madder, which yielded a red dye; and *nīla* (*Indigofera* sp.), or indigo, the source of a blue dye. All were trade items from Yemen and are described in other texts. There is also no mention in the almanacs of the incense trees for which South Arabia is justly famed.

The Rasulid sultans were entertained by agriculture in a number of ways. The major nonreligious holiday in medieval Yemen was probably the celebration of ripe dates at the coastal town of Zabīd. When the first dates ripened, generally in May, the people would celebrate a festival called *sabt al-subūt*. This term is apparently derived from the Jewish holiday of the Festival of Weeks, celebrating the harvest some seven weeks after Passover.[2] However, the term *sabt* literally means "rest" (Nashwān ibn Sa'īd 1953:2:357) and this is more likely the origin of the term for this holiday of rest under the palms. The Rasulid sources date the start of this Yemeni holiday from the first Saturday in *Ayyār* (V); thus the exact date differed from year to year. Al-Ashraf's almanac places the *sabt al-subūt* at V:2, a Saturday. In another part of his astronomical treatise (*Tabṣira*, fol. 62r) he recorded a specific date for *sabt al-subūt* as 10 *Jumādā al-Ūlā*, 677, which is equivalent to September 30, 1278. *Fuṣūl* adds that this festival began during the first ten days of the month and could include two Saturdays. Abū al-'Uqūl and *Taqwīm* indicate that the last day of the celebration was at VIII:2, which includes the main period of the date harvest. Similar medieval celebrations of the date harvest were observed at Mecca (Ibn Jubayr 1984:99) and Hormuz (Marco Polo 1958:66).

The Rasulid historian al-Khazrajī (1906–18:3:142, 4:291; 1981:279) described the *sabt al-subūt* outing of al-Malik al-Ashraf during 695/1296; this was in fact his last celebration. As befits a royal retinue, some three hundred camel-borne litters carried dancing girls and provisions for entertainment of the court and the people under the palms. Ibn Baṭṭūṭa (1980:247) described the festivities only a few decades later, saying: "They go out on every Saturday to the palm plots in the days when there are *busr* and fresh ripe (*ruṭab*) dates. None of the inhabitants remain in the town, not even visitors. The musicians go out and venders go to sell their fruits and sweets. The women go out on camel litters." Ibn Baṭṭūṭa was quite stricken by the beauty of Zabīdī women, whom he thought had far more spirit and freedom than women in other regions he had visited. Ibn al-Mujāwir (1954:79) said this was a great party season lasting for two or three months and people came to Zabīd from all over the region. He also mentioned the drinking of date wine (*faḍīkh*) and sexual encounters under the swaying palms. An anonymous Yemeni poet was quoted by Ibn al-Mujāwir as saying:

> This is the reddening and the pollenating, while the spadix has already opened,
> O maidens, spin [your charm] that the dates may be edible.
> (*hadhā al-shaqḥ wa-al-laqḥ wa-al-ṭal' minih qad iftataḥa,*
> *yā ghāzalāt aghzalū fa-al-nakhl ṣār balaḥ.*)

Later Yemeni historians condemned some of these practices as immoral (Yaḥyā ibn al-Ḥusayn 1968:1:494).[3]

Although the almanacs provide a basis for reconstructing the seasons of agricultural activities, there is little information on the wider folklore associated with cultivation and harvest. The formal agricultural treatises discuss a number of magical rites associated with agriculture, but these all appear to be derived from earlier non-Yemeni sources. Much of the astrological information mentioned in the *Bughya* is taken from the agricultural treatise of Ibn Waḥshīya, who included a great deal of magical lore from the Syriac tradition. Al-Malik al-Afḍal, for example, noted in the *Bughya* (fol. 18r) that it is better to plant wheat when the moon is waxing than when it is waning; in this he draws from the lore of Ibn Waḥshiya. Al-Malik al-Ashraf recorded magical information in *Tabṣira* (fol. 52) relating to the lunar stations, such as the notion that it is better not to plant if the moon is in the station of *buṭayn*, one of the stations in Aries. This magical lore on the stations is ultimately derived from India, perhaps via Persian texts. It is doubtful that Yemeni farmers held beliefs regarding the timing of agricultural activity according to the lunar stations or solar zodiac, since this was largely a textual tradition. There was certainly a tradition of magical lore, as evidenced in the ethnographic data, but this is virtually impossible to reconstruct for the practical world of medieval Yemen.

Contemporary ethnographic research in Yemen does provide relevant information about agriculture in its local seasonal contexts. For example, farmers in rain-fed areas become very concerned when an expected rain does not come. Within Islam there is a prayer, known as *istisqā'*, to invoke rain from God.[4] In much of Yemen this is accompanied by the sacrifice of an animal, such as a camel, which is in fact a pre-Islamic practice surviving in local custom. When rain is too plentiful, the farmer fears flooding and erosion of his fields. There is also the constant threat of locusts, which sweep across Yemen from time to time and wreak havoc on subsistence production.[5]

TAXES

The Rasulid sultans would have been unable to patronize the sciences to the extent they did without an effective tax collection system, referred to as the *dīwān al-kharāj al-sultānī* (*Mulakhkhaṣ*, fol. 8r). Several surviving texts show that the Rasulids developed an efficient system of administrative divisions with regular reports sent to the court from the various districts in the country. The details of this system are outlined in the *Mulakhkhaṣ al-fitan* of al-Ḥasan ibn 'Alī al-Ḥusaynī (died ca. 815/1412), briefly described by Cahen and Serjeant (1957), and the important tax document from the reign of al-Malik al-Muẓaffar Yūsuf (see *Shāmil*).[6] There are clear parallels between the Yemeni texts and tax terminology applied earlier in Ayyubid Egypt (see Frantz-Murphy 1986), which is not surprising given the origin of the Rasulids as retainers to the Ayyubids. Taxation at Aden during the Ayyubid period is discussed by Ibn al-Mujāwir (1954) and in Löfgren (1950:58–66).

Rasulid Yemen was divided into three main administrative divisions for tax purposes (al-Ḥibshī 1980:33-34). The mountains were divided between the higher mountains (*al-bilād al-'ulyā*) bordering the Zaydī area in the north and the southern mountainous region (*al-Yaman al-khaḍrā'*) around Ta'izz. The second zone consisted of the coastal area, or Tihāma, where seasonal flood irrigation was practiced along the main wadis. Finally, there were the main ports, especially the major commercial center of Aden, which garnered substantial tax revenues from the active port trade.[7] Abū al-'Uqūl, in his almanac, noted that the tax revenues (*māl al-'ushūr*) from Aden were taken to the treasure city of al-Dumluwa at II:6. During the Ayyubid period four main tax collections were taken from Aden to Ta'izz: after the arrival of the Indian fleet; after the receipt of the madder (*fuwwa*) crop at Aden; after the departure of horses for India; after the departure of the Indian fleet (Ibn al-Mujāwir in Löfgren 1950:65). For the year 802/1399 al-Khazrajī (1906–18:2:277) said the tax from Aden "was of great amount, with large sums of money, both gold and silver, several lacs in all, besides wearables and perfumes in great quantity."

During the Rasulid era there was an elaborate administrative network of royal clerks, referred to as *kuttāb* (*Mulakhkhaṣ*, ch. 2). These clerks kept records of activities on royal estates, recorded the amounts and products paid as tax, and were involved with *waqf* documents. The tax ledger from the reign of al-Malik al-Afḍal (Varisco 1991b) cites several distinct terms in relation to tax estimation and assessment. The term *mustakhraj* (literally, "tax payment received") used in the tax ledger of al-Malik al-Afḍal is rendered in al-Ashraf's almanac as *istikhrāj*, which appears to be an assessment made during or just after the crop harvest. The generic use of *kharāj* for an agricultural tax is found in the Egyptian Ayyubid text of al-Makhzūmī (Frantz-Murphy 1986:27). The official responsible for *istikhrāj al-amwāl* (tax assessment of agricultural land) was called a *mushrif* (*mashārif*, plural). They were located in major fortified towns (*al-huṣūn al-maḥrūsa*), such as Ta'izz and al-Dumluwa.

Another term found in the texts is *misāḥa*, referring to estimation by sight survey. According to Waṭyūṭ (fol. 42v) this system was a Rasulid innovation in Yemen. Abū al-'Uqūl defined the *massāḥ* as *khāriṣ*, one who assesses or surveys the harvest. As Serjeant (1958:9) notes, in Yemen the term *khāriṣ* is often used for the tax collector as well. The related term *khirāṣa* was used to specify a tax estimate on a crop. The usage in Yemen is not confined to dates and grapes, as in earlier classical usage (e.g., al-Khawārizmī 1984:87).

Several major tax periods for major crops in Rasulid Yemen are mentioned in the Rasulid almanacs, although these do not represent a complete listing. These periods are discussed below in the chronological order in which they appear in the almanacs:

Shabb sorghum. The almanac places the tax assessment on *shabb* sorghum in Wādī Surdud and Wādī Mawr at XI:11 after the harvest of this crop between XI:3 and XI:10. *Ma'rifa* says that this tax was collected at the district center of al-Maḥālib along Wādī Mawr during October.

Sābi'ī sorghum. According to Abū al-'Uqūl, the tax on *sābi'ī* sorghum was estimated at XII:25 and assessed at XII:30. The reference here is clearly to Zabīd, where Abū al-'Uqūl placed the harvest at XII:10–23.

AGRICULTURE

Ghalla. Al-Malik al-Ashraf mentioned a tax on crop yield (*ghalla*) for I:15. The use of *ghalla* was generic in Rasulid Yemen for one of the three types of taxable land (*Mulakhkhaṣ*, fol. 11v). This term was also used in the tax system of Ayyubid Egypt (Frantz-Murphy 1986:39).

'Ushr. The term *'ushr* refers to the standard tithe or payment of a tenth on production. According to both al-Malik al-Ashraf and Abū al-'Uqūl this tax was assessed in al-Mahjam along Wādī Surdud at V:11.

Ghaḍīr. Abū al-'Uqūl said there was a tax called *ghaḍīr* on horses, camels, cows, and sheep at V:16 for al-Jaba', al-Ma'āfir, Ẓabāb, and al-Janad. This would have been assessed after the major bearing period for each of these animals.

Mustaftaḥ. This appears to have been the major crop tax for the mountains in the Rasulid period. The term is not explained in the almanacs. It probably refers to the opening, or beginning, of the tax period (see al-Khawārizmī 1984:86). In his Coptic almanac al-Maqrīzī referred to the beginning of the tax in *Ṭūba* (I) as *iftitāḥ al-kharāj*. However, it should be noted that crops grown by means of surface flow (*fatḥ*) were subject to the *'ushr* tax (*Lisān al-'Arab*, *f-t-ḥ*). According to al-Malik al-Ashraf, assessment of the *mustaftaḥ* tax began on VII:14, whereas *Fuṣūl* has VII:12, and *Salwa* and Taymūr read VII:15 (30° Cancer). Abū al-'Uqūl said the tax at VII:14 applied to the mountains and Mikhlāf Ja'far. *Ma'rifa* places the tax for Mikhlāf Ja'far at VII:11 and for al-Janad, Ta'izz, and al-Sha'bānīya at VII:21. Abū al-'Uqūl indicated this tax on sesame in the coastal foothills of al-Ḥawāzz at VII:28.

'Uṭb (cotton). The tax on cotton production began on VII:28, according to al-Malik al-Ashraf. Abū al-'Uqūl said the tax on VII:27 was for al-Mahjam. The tax on cotton at Zabīd was assessed on VI:17 according to *Taqwīm*, but on VI:29 according to Abū al-'Uqūl. *Ma'rifa* cites a second tax period for Zabīd, Fashāl, and al-Kadrā' during *Tishrīn al-Awwal* (X), with the tax in Abyan during *Kānūn al-Awwal* (XII) and in Laḥj during *Ayyār* (V).

Nakhl. The coastal date plantations provided substantial tax revenues for the Rasulid sultans. According to al-Malik al-Ashraf the transport of the date tax to Zabīd was at VIII:14. *Taqwīm* refers to this event in early VIII. The reference in the almanac is to the raising of the *rasm*, a term which refers to the tax collection bound for the royal treasury (*ṣundūq*).[8] This event occurred near the end of the availability of fresh dates, when their taste began to change. This was also near the end of the celebration of *sabt al-subūt*, a festival season before the harvest. In 624/1227, according to Ibn al-Mujāwir (1954:80), the annual date tax reached 110,000 dinars for the Ayyubid dynasty.

The times of assessment on date palms varied from place to place in the coastal region. Both *Taqwīm* and *Bughya* note the assessment for the trees in Zabīd at VI:17. Abū al-'Uqūl placed this at VI:24, and *Ma'rifa* at VI:22. *Salwa* and Taymūr record the harvest earlier at VI:12 (29° Gemini). According to *Ma'rifa*, the tax on date palms was levied in *Ayyār* (V) for Laḥj but in *Ḥazīrān* (VI) for the coastal towns of al-Kadrā', al-Ṣulay, al-Qaḥma, and al-Shiḥr.

Ghalla. A tax on crop yield was assessed for the southern highland areas of al-Janad, Ta'izz, and al-Sha'bānīya during *Aylūl* (IX) according to *Ma'rifa*. This differs from the tax on crop yield noted in the almanac at I:15.

Ṣayf sorghum. The tax on sorghum sown during the spring (*ṣayf*) in the Tihāma was assessed at IX:8 according to al-Malik al-Ashraf and Abū al-'Uqūl. *Ma'rifa* records the tax on *ṣayf* sorghum during *Tishrīn al-Awwal* (X) for Zabīd, al-Ṣulay, Fashāl, al-Shiḥr, Mawza', and Ḥays but during *Kānūn al-Thānī* (I) for al-Kadrā'.

AGRICULTURAL CYCLE

The year for medieval Yemeni farmers was linked to their agricultural activities, the necessities of providing food for their families and meeting the sometimes stiff tax burdens imposed by the state. The area under Rasulid control encompassed a variety of environmental zones with different crops and cropping seasons. The primary distinction was between the coastal zone (Tihāma), with its hot and humid climate virtually year-round, and the mountains and central highland plains, where frost often occurred in the winter. The almanacs provide details for most of the major coastal wadis as well as the region near the southern highland capital of Ta'izz. Much of the information relates to production on land owned by the sultans. However, there is little information about the area of Ṣan'ā' and north to Ṣa'da apart from several references to grape production. Thus, the portrait of the agricultural cycle that emerges is far from complete for the whole region and does not cover the more marginal rain-fed farming areas in the north of the country.[9]

Al-Malik al-Ashraf (*Tabṣira*, fols. 115r,116v) provided a general summary of the main planting and harvesting seasons in Yemen apart from the references in his almanac:

Times for planting: Know that the first time for planting sorghum, wheat, barley, and sweet pea (*'atar*) as well as for harvesting emmer wheat (*'alas*) and *qiyāḍ* [wheat and barley] in the mountain areas and districts is mostly during the ten select [days], the last five in *Nīsān* (IV) and first five in *Ayyār* (V). It is called select because of the planting. This includes planting of white *shurayjī*[10] sorghum in temperate districts. Before this is the planting of red sorghum in the mountains and cold areas; after this is the planting of white *ra'īsī* sorghum in the wadis and hot areas. The first planting [of sorghum] in the cold areas is in the middle of *Ādhār* (III) at the time of the *qiyāḍ* harvest, while the last planting in the hot areas of the wadis is at V:23 with the first planting of wheat [in the mountains].

The select time for planting wheat and barley is during the last ten days of *Ḥazīrān* (VI), at which time *ḥabashī* and *wasnī* wheats are both planted in temperate areas. Before this is the planting of *'arabī* wheat, barley, and the first of *ḥabashī* [wheat] in the mountains and cold areas. After this the *wasnī* [wheat] is planted in the wadis and hot areas,[11] as well as emmer wheat and sweet pea. The first planting of wheat is on V:28 and the last in the middle of *Tammūz* (VII). The first availability of parched *muqādim* [wheat and barley][12] in the mountains is at the rising of the third (*thālith*) star of Ursa Major. The first harvest of wheat and barley, little by little, is in the middle of *Aylūl* (IX). The first harvest of sorghum, little by little, is in the middle of *Tishrīn al-Awwal* (X). The select time for planting *dithā'* [wheat] in its areas is during the Nights of the Old Woman at the *naw'* for the rising of *sa'd al-akhbiya* in the cold areas. After this is the last of the planting, when it is the last of the rain.

Times for harvesting: The first harvest of wheat and barley is at the arrival of the sun in Libra. This is little by little on account of the successive nature of the planting, as has been mentioned. The first harvest of sorghum is at the arrival of the sun in Scorpius. This is little by little on account of its planting, as has been mentioned. The first planting of *qiyāḍ* [wheat] is in the middle of *Kānūn al-Awwal* (I) and its first harvest is with the first planting of sorghum in the middle of *Ādhār*.

The Rasulid corpus as a whole describes the seasons and methods of cultivation for virtually every crop known in medieval Yemen. For the mountain areas the dominant summer crop was sorghum, which was sown during a period described as the "ten select" (*al-'ashr al-mukhtāra*) days. This referred to a period of ten days at the end of April and beginning of May. Al-Malik al-Ashraf (*Tabṣira*, fol. 109r) defined it further, saying: "This is a known period among farmers of the [mountain] districts. Whoever starts sowing ten days before this sows in the first of the period; whoever follows it by ten days sows in the last of the period. This is because most of the planting is for a month and the ten select [days] are in the middle of this, except in the upper parts of the cold mountain areas where they precede it and in the hot areas where they follow it." Abū al-'Uqūl added that this period was relevant for the mountains, Mikhlāf Ja'far, al-Ta'kar, and similar areas. The designation of a ten-day period may be the author's own usage, since this is a common designation for an agricultural period in the classical text of Cassianus Bassus, with which the Rasulids were familiar. It also brings to mind the deccans of Greek astronomy. Although April is in fact the main sowing month for sorghum in the mountains today, reference to *al-'ashr al-mukhtāra* has not been documented in recent ethnography. The Yemeni poet al-Zumaylī (Serjeant and al-'Amrī 1981:414) put it this way:

April is the sowing season of fame
most suitable for all of the grains.
(Nīsān waqt al-matlam al-mashhūr
bih ṣalāḥ jumlat al-budhūr)

The specific seasons for the crops mentioned in the almanac are discussed in detail by crop name in the next section.

Considerable attention was paid in the Rasulid texts to horticulture, in no small part because of the royal gardens near Ta'izz and Zabīd. Al-Malik al-Ashraf recommended the planting of trees between I:20 and II:20. Abū al-'Uqūl placed this from I:13 to II:18, while *Fuṣūl* notes the planting from I:6 at the beginning of the third forty-day period until II:21. According to the *Bughya*, trees were planted in Yemen from I:4, although there was also a planting from XI:15 mentioned by al-Malik al-Mujāhid as quoted in the same text. *Salwa* mentions a planting at XII:12 (28° Sagittarius) and at XII:21 (7° Capricornus), with the last planting at II:18 (7° Pisces). The date of XII:12 appears to be a direct copying of the date mentioned by Ibn Waḥshīya, a text quoted in reference to this date by al-Malik al-Afḍal in the *Bughya*. The Rasulid almanac *Mīqāt* notes the planting of trees in February.

During the Rasulid era a number of measures were used for agricultural crops, as described in detail in *Shāmil*.[13] The basic unit for grain was the *zabadī* (*azbūd*, plural), which differed from era to era and region to region in medieval Yemen. The *zabadī* was said to be equivalent to the amount of grain eaten by an individual in a month's time. It should be noted that the specific measure would often vary in actual weight according to the product being measured. Ibn al-Mujāwir (1954:89) listed the weights used in Yemen in the Ayyubid period, which immediately preceded the Rasulid era, as follows:

1 *mudd* = 32 *thumn*
32 *thumn* = 32 *zabadī*
1 *zabadī* = 1 *mann* = 2 *raṭl*
1 *raṭl* = 120 *dirham*
1 *dirham* = 13 *qīrāṭ*

The Rasulid historian al-Khazrajī (1906–18:3:148) said that the Ta'izz *zabadī* was worth eight Egyptian *raṭl*, apparently in reference to the year 663/1264–65. According to *Shāmil* the Ta'izz *zabadī* at the end of al-Malik al-Muẓaffar's reign was equal to four and one-half *ṣunqurī* units of *zabadī*. The term *ṣunqurī* derives from the name of the Ayyubid ruler Sayf al-Dīn Ṣunqur ibn 'Abd Allāh al-Ātabik of the early thirteenth century A.D.

CEREAL CROPS

Sorghum and Millet

The dominant subsistence crop for all of Yemen has long been sorghum (*Sorghum bicolor*).[14] The geographer al-Muqaddasī (1989:135) noted that sorghum and millet were the staple food crops at Zabīd in the tenth century A.D. Sorghum is a very useful plant which can be grown in hot and cold areas on either rain-fed or irrigated land. The general term for sorghum in Arabic is *dhura*, which is distinct from *dukhn*, a term applied to various millets in Yemen. Sorghum was also known simply as *ṭa'ām* (Grohmann 1930:1:211; Hirsch 1897:279; Manzoni 1884:17).[15] Numerous terms for sorghum varieties were recorded for Yemen, at least twenty-two of which were mentioned by the author in the almanac. The basic distinction was by the color of the grain, either red (*ḥamrā'*), white (*bayḍā'*), or yellow (*ṣafrā'*). The bulk of the coastal crop appears to have been white varieties, based on the Rasulid texts and later travelers (e.g., di Varthema 1928:25). Both sorghum and millet grains were defined as cold and dry in the humoral system. Yemenis traditionally make a variety of breads and a porridge called '*aṣīd* from sorghum grain. The stalks and leaves serve as valuable fodder for cows and camels.

According to al-Malik al-Ashraf the time for sowing sorghum in the mountains is between III:16 and V:28, particularly during the so-called ten select days at the end of *Nīsān* and start of *Ayyār*. Al-Malik al-Ashraf and *Fuṣūl* begin the sorghum planting at III:16 at the time of the harvest of *qiyāḍ* wheat. Both *Fuṣūl* and Abū al-'Uqūl placed the sowing until V:28, when it was time to begin sowing wheat in the mountains. *Salwa* refers to the last planting of sorghum in the mountains at VI:16 (4° Gemini), although Taymūr places this at V:18. This reference is probably for Ṣan'ā', as noted by al-Malik al-Ashraf for V:18. In the warmer areas of the wadis the last sowing was at V:23, according to the author's description provided earlier. The early Arab almanacs of Abū Ḥanīfa al-Dīnawarī and Ibn Māsawayh note the sowing of sorghum in the Tihāma of Yemen and in Nubia at V:24.

According to the *Bughya*, in the mountains the ground was ploughed three times during the winter. It was thought best to sow while the ground was midway between wet and dry. After the furrows were ploughed, the grain was sowed by dropping a few grains at a time into the bottom of the furrow. The sower then walked on and dropped more grains further along in the furrow. Some people buried the grain with soil turned over by the foot and others cast it without stepping on it. A ploughing of the field about forty days after the sowing was possible. It was evidently quite common to interplant various vegetables among the sorghum plants, such as cowpeas, sweet peas, cucumbers, melons, and sesame (al-Hamdānī 1983:318).

The almanac of al-Malik al-Ashraf cites the start of the sorghum harvest at X:17, saying in another place that this was at the start of Scorpius. This was also the start of the harvest in Wādī 'Udayna. Abū al-'Uqūl and *Salwa* mention the harvest at X:4 (19° Libra), and Taymūr at X:5. The timing of the sorghum harvest was what gave rise to the use of the term *ṣirāb* (harvest) for the Himyaritic month of October. The time for stripping (*sharf*) the leaves from the sorghum plant in many parts of the country comes about a month before the harvest, although this was not discussed by the author. Just before the harvest the still immature heads could be eaten after parching (*jahīsh* or *farīk*).[16] According to al-Malik al-Afḍal (Serjeant 1974a:47), "the ears are placed in this fire and covered over with some of the burning embers–when they are cooked one takes them out and they are rubbed together in the hand–which is best–or beaten out with a stick in a coarse cloth, and one clears them of twigs and stems and cleans them."

Some varieties of sorghum were capable of being ratooned, thus having successive harvests. Al-Malik al-Afḍal (Serjeant 1974a:48) said the first cropping was for parching, the second was called *'aqb*, the third was called *khilf,* and the rare fourth cropping was referred to as *jinnīya*. In *Mughnī* al-Malik al-Ashraf said that the first cropping was called *jāda* and the second *'aqb*.[17]

The royal ledger of al-Malik al-Muẓaffar (*Shāmil*) records the sorghum yields in the Ta'izz area for 692/1293. On land of good quality the yield for sorghum grain was said to be 4,000 *azbūd* for every 10 *azbūd* of grain sown, or an increase of 400-fold. On average land the yield from 10 *azbūd* was 1,500 *azbūd*, while on poor land the yield was only 900–1,000 *azbūd*. The yield of sorghum stalk on good land was said to be 200 packloads for every 10 *azbūd* of seed sown. On average land the yield would only be 30 packloads. Interestingly enough, the stalk yield on poor rain-fed land was 50 packloads, although the grain yield was much more limited than on good or average land. Good land in this context means access to irrigation, while average land indicates the rain-fed areas with plentiful rainfall and adequate soil. The poor land was dependent on limited rainfall and in some years was unproductive.

The fodder value of sorghum stalk differed according to variety, as described by the author in *Mughnī*. The best stalk for camels came from *sābi'ī* sorghum in the coastal region. A distinction was made between *wakhim*, sorghum that has reached the time for heads to show but that has either very immature or no heads, and *mashraf*, sorghum that has heads but without any grain formed. These were more valuable as fodder than stalks on which grain had already appeared in the heads. Similarly, stalks from a first cropping were superior to those of a ratooning. The *jaḥrī*, *baynī*, and *khāmisī* varieties were not as good as the *sābi'ī* but were still in great demand. The stalk of *kharajī* was suitable fresh, but it was said it should not be given dry to camels. Camels should not feed on stalks from either *zi'ir* or red *sābi'ī* because these could burn their stomachs. Millet stalks were said to be suitable as fodder. In the mountain areas the best sorghum stalk is that defined as *wakhim*, especially from the *ra'īsī* and *shurayjī* varieties. These stalks were mixed with fresh alfalfa (lucerne) for the best diet of camels.

The term used in the almanac for millet is *dukhn*, although it is not always possible to identify the precise millet meant.[18] The most common millet in Yemen appears to be *Pennisetum americanum* (= *P. glaucum*), which is bulrush or pearl millet (Blatter 1933:491; Landberg 1901:1:295; Serjeant 1974a:38; Steffen et al. 1978:2:10). Wigboldus (1991b), however, believes that pearl millet was not introduced into Yemen until the fourteenth century. *Dukhn* was planted on sandy soil after V:22 according to al-Malik al-Afḍal in the *Bughya* (fol. 23v). *Salwa* notes the sowing of millet in the mountains at V:23 (11° Gemini) and at Laḥj on VI:19 (6° Cancer). *Salwa* further notes that millet was sown at al-Mahjam at VIII:15 (30° Leo). Taymūr cites the best time for sowing millet in the coastal region at V:20 and for the mountains at V:25. Abū al-'Uqūl said that millet was planted at Laḥj and Abyan at VI:8 and in the foothills of the Tihāma after VIII:10. Serjeant (1974a:38) observed millet being sown in Wādī Jīzān from the middle of September. The recent almanac of al-Ḥaydara notes the sowing of millet in the Ta'izz area around V:20. Many of these dates are near that mentioned much earlier by Abū Ḥanifa al-Dīnawarī in his almanac: V:24. Al-Malik al-Ashraf noted the harvest of millet at al-Mahjam at III:3, while *Salwa* and Taymūr place this at III:2 (19° Pisces).

The specific varieties of sorghum mentioned in the almanac are discussed below in alphabetical order:

Bājisī. This coastal variety was sown around the summer rising of Sirius, called *bājis* in the Tihāma. Al-Malik al-Ashraf, Abū al-'Uqūl, and *Fuṣūl* placed the sowing at VII:10, while Taymūr mentions the planting from VII:9 to VII:16.

Baynī. According to the *Bughya* (Serjeant 1974a:48), this refers to a variety of sorghum sown between (*bayna*) the rising of the third and seventh stars of Ursa Major. This would make it similar to a *khāmisī* sowing. The timing corresponds with that of the contemporary almanac of al-Ḥaydara (Serjeant 1954:454), who mentions this variety at IX:4 after the rising of the third star of Ursa Major. This reading does not make sense, however, for the references in the Rasulid almanacs. Al-Malik al-Ashraf placed the sowing at I:5–25, several months after the time for the dawn rising of the third star of Ursa Major. However, this does correlate with the evening rising of these stars at the end of January, and this would appear to be the intended meaning. Taymūr notes the sowing in Wādī Mawr, undoubtedly in reference to al-Maḥālib, from I:7 to 27. *Ma'rifa* equates the sowing of *baynī* at al-Maḥālib with that of *jahrī* during XI. The almanac notes that in Wādī Mawr this variety was parched at III:19 and harvested at III:28, the latter date also being referenced by Abū al-'Uqūl. Taymūr, however, places the harvest in Wādī Mawr at IV:21, perhaps a misreading of the earlier texts.

Bukr. The term *bukr* literally refers to the first of something, such as the date palm the first year that it bears fruit (*Bughya*, fol. 82r). According to the *Bughya*, this was a white variety sown at Laḥj and Abyan. In al-Dathīna *bukr* can also refer to a red variety known as *ḥaymar* (Serjeant 1954:450, note 56). The term *bakūr* has also been noted for a variety of wheat or barley sown in October near Dhamār (Grohmann 1930:1:215). The related term *bukkār* is used in parts of Yemen for broomcorn, or *Panicum* sp. (Schweinfurth 1912:176; Scott 1942:187). The almanac records the sowing of *bukr* at Laḥj on VIII:2. Abū al-'Uqūl placed this between VIII:19 and VIII:28, while *Ma'rifa* has the sowing in Laḥj at VIII:20 and in Abyan at VIII:25. Al-Malik al-Ashraf, *Fuṣūl*, and *Ma'rifa* all place the harvest in Abyan at XII:1. In the *Bughya* (fol. 93r) the harvest of *bukr* at Laḥj and Abyan is said to occur on XII:10, 355 days after the Indian *nayrūz* in the latter part of the *naw'* of *han'a*. This is a well-known variety in Laḥj (Hunter et al. 1909:4; Maktari 1971:156).

Ḥamrā'. Several sorghum varieties are considered red (*ḥamrā'*) in Yemen. The almanac notes a sowing of red sorghum in the coastal region at

XI:23 after the sowing of *kharajī* sorghum. *Milḥ* indicates that red sorghum was sown at the same time as white sorghum in Zabīd, Rimaʿ, and nearby areas. According to the *Bughya*, there was a sowing of red sorghum in the cold mountain areas at the middle of March, with a harvest in nine months. Abū al-ʿUqūl mentioned the harvest of a red variety in Sharʿab during December.

ʿIshwī. This famous variety of sorghum was sown around the time of the evening rising (*ʿishā'*) of the Pleiades, which the author placed at X:14. The sowing of this variety is indicated at X:7 (22° Libra) by al-Malik al-Ashraf and *Salwa*. *Fuṣūl* records it for X:5, while *Maʿrifa* mentions its sowing in Zabīd at X:8. In the *Bughya* the date for the sowing is X:16. *Taqwīm* also records the sowing near the beginning of October. In *Milḥ* this variety is said to be sown at X:16 in Wādī Rimaʿ. The evening rising of the Pleiades in the middle of October is an important agricultural marker in Yemeni folklore (al-Iryānī 1980:62; Varisco 1989b).

Another sowing is indicated at V:4 by al-Malik al-Ashraf, but this may be an error for another variety. Perhaps the usage here is by extension, since it is the time for the dawn rising of the Pleiades.

Jaḥrī. This term is derived from the hot and dry summer period of *jaḥr* in Yemen. Al-Malik al-Ashraf defined this in *Mughnī* as the crop which comes at the time of the ripe dates (*alladhī ya'tī zarʿatan ayyām al-tamr*). *Taqwīm* includes a description of *jaḥr* as the hot period in *Ayyār* (V) when melons ripen in the coastal region. The term *jaḥr* in classical Arabic refers to a very dry and barren year (al-Ḥimyarī 1980:231), hence its application to this period in Yemeni dialect. This period of *jaḥr* is frequently mentioned among Yemeni farmers today (Serjeant 1974a:31; Varisco 1982a:112). Al-Malik al-Ashraf recorded a sowing of *jaḥrī* (!) at XII:9 for the Tihāma, but this is a mistake for *kharajī*, as noted below.[19] According to *Taqwīm* white *jaḥrī* was sown as part of the *nasrī* sowing from I:20 to I:28 in Wādī Zabīd. The sowing of red *jaḥrī* proper was from II:10 to II:20, while a red variety also called *tamrī* was sown from III:1 to III:8. Abū al-ʿUqūl noted the sowing of the red variety at II:2 at the same time as melons and cucumbers.

Jawzī. This variety was sown at V:15 in the coastal region according to the almanac, but at V:14 in *Fuṣūl*. Abū al-ʿUqūl defined it as a variety of millet sown on VI:11 in the coastal region. The later almanac poem of al-Zumaylī also records the sowing in *Tammūz* (VI) (Serjeant and al-ʿAmrī 1981). The reference is obviously to the zodiacal constellation of Gemini (*jawzā'*), which was said to begin at V:14 in the reckoning of the almanac. It should be noted that *jawzā'* can refer to Orion in other contexts.

Khāmisī. This variety was named for a sowing at the rising of the fifth star (*khāmis*) of Ursa Major, which rose on IX:14 according to the almanac. This reference was for Zabīd, where the author and Abū al-'Uqūl said *khāmisī* was sown at IX:2; this is given as IX:1 in *Milḥ*. A general sowing in the coastal region was also indicated for VIII:4 according to the almanac, but at VIII:5 in *Fuṣūl* and *Ma'rifa* and at VIII:8 (23° Leo) in *Salwa* and Taymūr. The author noted that in Wādī Mawr and Wādī Surdud the *khāmisī* sowing for VIII:10 was called *shabb*. A sowing of red *khāmisī* is recorded for VIII:8 in *Taqwīm*. According to the later almanac poem of al-Zumaylī (Serjeant and al-'Amrī 1981:417) this was called *badhanjā* and sown on VIII:25. The term *khāmisī* was used in Mawr, Rima', and Zabīd, according to the *Bughya*. The same term has also been recorded for a wheat variety which ripened at the rising of *khāmis 'allān* in the contemporary Yemeni marker system (Serjeant 1974a:30).

Kharajī. This important coastal variety is not clearly identified in any of the Rasulid sources and is at times confused with *jaḥrī* sorghum. The Cairo edition of the *Bughya* reads the reference to *kharajī* in *Milḥ* as *jaḥrī*. Even the copyist of the almanac, which was copied in the Rasulid period, appears to have been unfamiliar with the term and does not provide diacriticals, nor has it been recorded in contemporary usage. Later almanacs sometimes render the Rasulid term as *jirjīr* (watercress), which is totally out of place. The reading of *kharajī* is based on use of the term in the royal ledger (*Shāmil*) of al-Malik al-Muẓaffar, where the term is used to indicate "a common variety" of something, such as slaves and clothing.[20]

In *Milḥ* al-Malik al-Ashraf said that red and white varieties of *kharajī* were sown in the coastal region, the latter at XII:1–10, with the harvest in three months. The author also equated it with *nasrī* sorghum sown at XI:16. *Salwa* and Taymūr note the sowing in Zabīd at XI:3 (19° Scorpius) and a red variety between XII:4 and XII:10 (20°–26° Sagittarius). For Wādī Zabīd *Taqwīm* records a sowing of the white variety for eight days in October and the red variety for November in the upper part of the wadi. Abū al-'Uqūl mentioned a sowing of this in Mawza' at X:7, while *Salwa* and Taymūr have this for X:12 (27° Libra). In Wādī Nakhla, according to the *Bughya*, this variety with black husk and crooked ears was sown ten days after *sābi'ī* sorghum (i.e., in November). The tax for *kharajī* was assessed along with that for *sābi'ī* sorghum, according to *Ma'rifa*.

Nasrī. The dawn rising of Vega (*al-nasr al-wāqi'*), noted at I:8 in *Tabṣira* by al-Malik al-Ashraf, or that of Altair (*al-nasr al-ṭā'ir*) at I:21 would appear to be the candidates for the naming of this sorghum variety. *Taqwīm* notes this was an alternative name for white *jaḥrī* sorghum planted between I:20 and I:28. *Salwa* places the sowing in the Tihāma at XII:15 (30° Sagittarius). The sowing in Zabīd is said to be at XII:10, according to *Ma'rifa*, with a harvest in February. However, the other references in the almanacs do not relate to this time. Al-Malik al-Ashraf said it was sown on XI:16 and called *kharajī* in the coastal region. The white variety was sown in Laḥj at XI:16 and the red variety five days later, according to *Milḥ* and the *Bughya*; the harvest was in three months. *Ma'rifa*, on the other hand, records the sowing in Laḥj at VIII:1, with the harvest in XII. Taymūr records a sowing at V:2, but this may be an error for another variety.

Ra'īsī. This was a white variety sown in the mountains during the ten select days, according to *Milḥ* and the *Bughya*, which also mention that it had loosely packed heads. Abū al-'Uqūl said it was planted at al-Janad and al-Jaba' on V:17 and harvested in the mountains at X:4. In *Ma'rifa*, however, a second cropping (*'aqb*) of this variety is noted for Ḥaraḍ in June, although this seems early. This sorghum name was recorded by von Maltzan (1873:391) for the area of al-Ḥujarīya and is still used in Dhamār (Serjeant 1974a:67, note 109).

Rub'ī. The derivation of this sorghum name is from the rising of the fourth star of Ursa Major, which the almanac places at VIII:30. It should be noted, however, that Ibn Sīda (1965:11:118) described dates that mature in the heat of summer as *rib'ī*. *Salwa* and Taymūr mention the sowing of this variety in Ḥaraḍ from VIII:11 to VIII:24 (25° Leo –9° Virgo), with a harvest at XI:19. Al-Malik al-Ashraf said that this variety was parched in al-Dathīna at XII:3 and harvested at XII:29. *Salwa* noted the harvest for XII:29 (16° Capricornus), but *Fuṣūl* has this at I:1.

Sābi'ī. This variety was named for the rising of the seventh (*sābi'*) star of Ursa Major, which the author said rose at IX:30. This formed the bulk of white sorghum grown in the coastal region and benefited from the late summer rains. According to the author the stalks of *sābi'ī* sorghum were considered the best for camel fodder in the Tihāma (*Mughnī*). Abū al-'Uqūl defined this variety as a grain of the Israelites. In the *Bughya* al-Malik al-Afḍal said this sowing went by a number of different names, including *shabb* in Mawr and Surdud and *bukr* in Laḥj.

The almanac provides more information for this variety than for any other. It is said to be a white variety sown in Zabīd between IX:13 and IX:30, especially at IX:19. This variety was parched at XII:8 and harvested at XII:19. A second cropping could be parched at II:8 and harvested at II:25. The sowings at al-Maḥālib in Wādī Mawr and in Wādī Sihām were said to occur on IX:18. The sowing at Zabīd is for IX:14–30 according to *Fuṣūl,* with the harvest at XII:19, while *Ma'rifa* records the sowing here at IX:16, with the harvest in *Kānūn al-Thānī* (I). *Salwa* notes the sowing at IX:15 (30° Virgo), as does the *Bughya* (fol. 21v). *Taqwīm* also places the sowing for Zabīd at IX:15, as the sun enters Libra, and adds that this was along the lower and middle parts of the wadi. The grain was said to appear in seventy days, with the harvest in ninety days. Abū al-'Uqūl said the parching in Zabīd was from XI:21 to XII:8, while the harvest was at XII:10–23. The parching of the second cropping was noted for II:20 (9° Pisces) in *Salwa.*

In the reckoning of Abū al-'Uqūl, the sowing in Banī Sayf and Bilād al-Rakab was at X:2, with a harvest from II:4 to II:21. *Ma'rifa* places the sowing in al-Mahjam at VIII:27, with the harvest at XII:22, while *Salwa* notes the sowing here from VIII:27 to IX:5 (12°–20° Virgo), with the harvest at XI:3 (19° Sagittarius). The sowing in al-Qaḥma and al-Kadrā' was at IX:16 according to *Ma'rifa,* with the harvest in *Kānūn al-Thānī* (I).

Ṣawmī. In *Milḥ* the author defined *ṣawmī* sorghum as the only mountain variety to be ratooned for a second and third harvest. It was said to have red grain which was coarse, dry, and not very palatable, according to the *Bughya.* The origin of the term is unexplained, but it may apply to a particular area near Ta'izz.[21] Al-Malik al-Ashraf mentioned in the almanac and *Milḥ* that the sowing of this variety was from X:1 to X:15, with a harvest in four months at II:5. Abū al-'Uqūl noted the planting at X:1 and the harvest at II:6. *Salwa* and Taymūr mark the sowing between IX:23 (7° Libra) and X:14 (24° Libra). It was sown in Mikhlāf Ja'far at the rising of the seventh (*sābi'*) star of Ursa Major, according to *Milḥ* and *Ma'rifa.* At this time chick-peas (*ḥimmaṣ*) were interplanted with the *ṣawmī* variety.

Ṣayfī. A sowing of sorghum and millet in the spring (*ṣayf*) gave rise to this name in the coastal region. This is a common crop name both in Yemen and in other parts of the Arab world.[22] Al-Malik al-Ashraf said that *ṣayfī* sorghum was sown at IV:19 and especially after V:20. *Fuṣūl* records the first planting in the Tihāma at IV:6. Abū al-'Uqūl said the planting was at V:3 and V:4 at al-Mahjam. According to *Taqwīm*, white and red varieties were sown during V:1–10. The select time for sowing *ṣayf* millet was at V:19 (7° Gemini), according to *Salwa.* The *Bughya* places this sowing at the start of *Ḥazīrān* (VI), with a harvest in four months, but it also notes a sowing of *ṣayfī* called *wasmī* in Mawr and Surdud as early as the middle of *Ādhār* (III). The term *ṣayfī* is also applied in the Rasulid sources to the *thālithī* and *khāmisī* sowings, according to *Taqwīm.* This explains the references in *Ma'rifa* to the following *ṣayfī* croppings: for Zabīd a planting at VIII:9 and a harvest in *Tishrīn al-Thānī* (XI); for Mawza' a planting at VIII:9 and a harvest in *Tishrīn al-Awwa* (X); for al-Qaḥma a planting in *Āb* (VIII) and a harvest in *Tishrīn al-Awwa* (X); for Laḥj, Abyan, and Aḥwar a planting in *Tishrīn al-Thānī* (XI) and a harvest in *Shubāṭ* (II).

Shabb. The origin of this term is not explained in the sources, although there are several possibilities. Perhaps it refers to the dusty color of alum (*shabb*), for which Yemen was famous. Another usage is suggested by the verb *shabba* as found in the almanac of Ibn Mammātī. In his discussion at III:30 (24 *Baramhāt*) *shabba* refers to the maturing growth of a crop as the ears develop. Abū al-'Uqūl said the *shabb* variety was also called *jāda*, a term usually associated with the first cropping of sorghum. The term *shabb* has survived to the present in the Yemeni Tihāma and in Wādī Jīzān. Forskal (1775b:cxxiii) cited the term as *shabb sa'īdī* .

The almanac and *Milḥ* place the sowing of *shabb* (called *khāmisī*) in Surdud and Mawr at VIII:10, with the parching at X:12 and the harvest between XI:3 and XI:10. *Shabb* was a white variety also sown as *sābi'ī*, according to the *Bughya*. Abū al-'Uqūl mentioned the parching at X:11 and the harvest from XI:1 to XI:10. At al-Mahjam the planting was at VIII:1, according to *Ma'rifa*, or VIII:13 (28° Leo) in the reckoning of *Salwa* and Taymūr. At al-Maḥālib it was planted VIII:9 and harvested in *Tishrīn al-Awwal* (X), according to *Ma'rifa*. The recent Yemeni almanac of al-Sirājī places the sowing of *shabb* in *Ḥazīrān* (VI) under the rising station of *nathra*. In modern Jīzān *shabb* is sown in mid-June at the rising of *dhirā'*, according to Serjeant (1974a:29), who adds that local farmers sometimes use *shabb* to refer to the rising star at this time.

Shurayjī. This term is miscopied in the text as *rḥy* (!). Serjeant (1974a:45) reads the reference in the *Bughya* as *shurayḥī* for the southern Yemeni place name, but this should be corrected to *shurayjī* in reference to al-Shurayj, an area southeast of Ta'izz and famous for its sorghum even today ('Umar ibn Yūsuf 1985a:181, note 5). According to *Milḥ* and the *Bughya*, the grain was harder than *ra'īsī* and between white and yellow in color. Al-Malik al-Ashraf said that this was planted in temperate areas during the ten select days and harvested in seven months. It was planted on V:1 in Mikhlāf Ja'far according to *Ma'rifa*.

Tamrī. The almanac places the planting of this variety at II:1 in the coastal region. In *Taqwīm*, however, the term is used for a sowing of *jaḥrī* sorghum from III:1 to III:8, with a note that what is planted after this time will not bear grain. According to the *Bughya*, this was sown as a variety called *ḥaddār* in Mawr and Surdud on III:19, while a later sowing was noted some ten days before *sābi'ī* sorghum in Ḥays, Mawza', Rasyān, and the coastal foothills.[23] This variety is said to be so named because of the fact it ripens when dates (*tamr*) are mature in the coastal region.

Thālithī. This variety was named for a sowing at the rising of the third (*thālith*) star of Ursa Major, which the almanac places at VIII:21. In *Milḥ* the author described it as a white variety sown at the beginning of VIII in Zabīd and Rima' but at VIII:10 in Surdud. The almanac notes the sowing in the coastal region at VII:31, while Abū al-'Uqūl gave this as VII:29. *Taqwīm* records the sowing of white *thālithī* from VII:15 and red *thālithī* later up until VIII:8. According to *Salwa* the sowing in Zabīd was at VII:27 (11° Leo), while Taymūr notes this from VII:27 through VIII:6. *Ma'rifa* includes the sowing at al-Kadrā' on VIII:9, with a harvest in *Kānūn al-Thānī*, while at al-Qaḥma it was also planted in *Āb* (VIII). This was said to be equivalent to a *shabb* sowing in Mawr and Surdud, according to the *Bughya*.

Thawrī. This variety was said to be sown at V:I when the sun was in the zodiacal constellation of *thawr* (Taurus). The almanac also noted a rain period called *thawr* at V:19. In the contemporary system of agricultural marker stars in Yemen there is a star period of *thawr* in May. The recent almanac of al-Sirājī, however, notes a sowing of this sorghum variety in *Aylūl* (IX) in Wādī Mawr.

Zi'ir. This is a white variety sown at III:29 in Surdud and Mawr, according to the author in *Milḥ* and the almanac. The abridged *Bughya* mentions *zi'ir* as a sowing on III:20 in Surdud, Mawr, Rima', and Mawza'; this was apparently harvested when the *sābi'ī* sorghum was sown. Taymūr notes that it was sown between III:17 and III:30 at al-Mahjam, while *Salwa* places the sowing from III:15 to III:30 (5°–18° Aries). Both sources note the sowing at Ḥaraḍ from III:25 to IV:3 (13°–22° Aries). According to *Ma'rifa*, the sowing at al-Mahjam was at III:17, while the sowing in the mountains was at III:12. The harvest of the second cropping of *zi'ir* at al-Mahjam was at VIII:22 (7° Virgo) according to *Salwa*. This same variety was also sown at XII:10 in Zabīd, with a harvest during *Shubāṭ* (II), as well as at XII:15 in al-Kadrā' and al-Qaḥma, according to *Ma'rifa*. The recent almanac of al-Sirājī notes a sowing at XII:12 under the rising of the star *na'ā'im*, as well as a sowing in *Shubāṭ* (II) under *muqaddam*. The origin of the term *zi'ir* is not explained in the sources.[24] Serjeant (1974a:69, note 139) records this term for the Ṣubayḥī territory of the south and in Wādī Jīzān of the Tihāma.

AGRICULTURE

Wheat and Barley[25]

Wheat (*Triticum* sp.) and barley (*Hordeum* sp.) were important crops in the Yemeni highlands and Ḥaḍramawt, although they could not be produced on the hot coastal plain. Ibn al-Mujāwir (1954:63), however, claimed he saw wheat growing at Fashāl in 623/1226. The almanac cites the usual Yemeni word for wheat, which is *burr* or *birr* (*burra* or *abrār*, plurals). This is a Hebrew cognate also found in the South Arabic dialect of Sabaic (Serjeant and Lewcock 1983:542). In the edition of a relatively recent historical text by al-'Arashī (1939:149) this word is said to be derived from the Latin *far*, a claim which seems a bit farfetched given the antecedent use in Hebrew. Al-Wāsi'ī (1982:149) notes that *burr* is the Yemeni equivalent of *ḥinṭa* or *qamḥ*, terms used outside Yemen. According to al-Bīrūnī (1973:1:133), Yemeni wheat was also called *hīsh*. There are numerous terms used for specific croppings, as noted in the discussion below. In the humoral system wheat is considered hot and wet, while barley is cold and dry. Several types of bread are made in Yemen, as well as porridge.

In his general discussion of planting seasons described earlier, al-Malik al-Ashraf said that wheat was planted between V:28 and VII:17 in the mountains, with the select time being the last ten days of *Ḥazīrān* (VI). *Fuṣūl* notes that wheat was sown until VII:18. Al-Malik al-Mujāhid was quoted in the *Bughya* as mentioning the planting of wheat from *Ayyār* (V) until the start of Cancer in the middle of *Ḥazīrān* (VI). According to *Salwa* the best time for planting wheat was at VII:2 (17° Cancer), with the last sowing at VII:25 (10° Leo). According to Taymūr the best time for planting came at VII:4, with the last sowing at VII:26. In *Milḥ* the sowing of barley is placed from the middle of *Ḥazīrān* (VI) until VII:1. Although the major period for planting wheat was in late spring and early summer, there was also a winter season as discussed below under *qiyāḍ*. *Fuṣūl* notes that wheat was planted in Egypt at XI:1.

The heads of wheat could be parched after three months, while the harvest was generally after four months. Al-Malik al-Ashraf, Abū al-'Uqūl, and Taymūr all placed the wheat and barley harvest at IX:17, although *Fuṣūl* mentions IX:16, as the sun enters Libra, a point also made by al-Malik al-Ashraf. The harvest proceeds in stages, since not all the varieties ripen at the same time. *Salwa* and Taymūr place the last of this harvest at X:18 (2° Scorpius), after which the sorghum harvest begins in the mountains. The royal ledger of al-Malik al-Muẓaffar (*Shāmil*) cites the yield for wheat in the highland area near Ta'izz. On good land this was 150 *azbūd* for every 10 *azbūd* of seed planted. Each *zabadī* in Ta'izz at this time was equivalent to about 8 *raṭl* units. On average land the yield was 100 *azbūd* for every 10 sown. For barley on good land the yield was less than wheat, only 100 *azbūd* for every 10 sown. If the wheat stalk was cut at the ground, it was said to yield 2 *shabaka* (i.e., bundle) of straw for every 100 *azbūd* of grain, while barley yielded only a single *shabaka*.

The specific varieties of wheat mentioned in the almanac are discussed below in alphabetical order:

'Alas. This is the classical term for tetraploid emmer wheat (*Triticum dicoccum*).[26] In Yemeni dialect this was *nusūl*, according to al-Malik al-Ashraf. This is usually considered the best type of wheat in Yemen (I. al-Akwa' 1984:2:949; M. al-Akwa' 1971:67; al-'Arashī 1939:439; Ibn Rusta 1892:111; al-Wāsi'ī 1982:149). Nashwān ibn Sa'īd al-Ḥimyarī (1916:75) claimed that it was the favorite food of the Himyarite kings in Yemen. In his history of Ṣan'ā', al-Rāzī al-Ṣan'ānī (1974:450) called it the basic food of the people of Ṣan'ā'. Ibn Baṭṭūṭa (1980:260) compared it to the *sulṭ* variety of barley.

In *Milḥ* al-Malik al-Ashraf said the white variety of emmer wheat was sown from VII:1 and stood three months, while the red variety stood three and one-half months. The grain of the white variety was red, but the color of the husk was white, hence its distinction as white. There was said to be a sowing of *nusūl* at VII:1. According to al-Malik al-Mujāhid, as quoted in the *Bughya*, the red variety was sown at the same time as *'arabī* wheat. *Salwa* and Taymūr indicate the planting at VIII:20 (5° Virgo). The recent almanac of al-Ḥaydara puts the sowing at VII:15 and the harvest in three months, although there is relatively little production of this variety in Yemen today. According to *Shāmil*, the yield of emmer wheat on good land is 100 *azbūd* for every 10 sown, but only 40 *azbūd* on average land and 20 *azbūd* on poor land. For every 100 *azbūd* of grain, a yield of up to 2 *shabaka* of straw was possible.

'Arabī. This was a common term for a wheat or barley variety in the Arab world (Abū Ḥanīfa al-Dīnawārī in Ibn Sīda 1965:11:61; Clement-Mullet 1865:193). The term literally means "Arabic." In Yemen this refers to a white and small-eared variety of wheat grown in the mountains. Al-Malik al-Ashraf noted in *Milḥ* that the sowing of this variety was from VI:10 to VI:20, with a harvest after four months during the *ṣirāb* harvest. *Fuṣūl* cites the last time for planting this variety at VI:14. The sowing is in the first half of *Ḥazīrān* according to *Milḥ* and the *Bughya*. There is also a sowing of *'arabī* called *dithā'* as noted below.

Dithā'. The term *dithā'* refers to a late winter cropping or early spring sowing. The seasonal reference to the early spring rains is common in Yemen today. Some sources also associate it with the Himyaritic month name for

January. Al-Malik al-Ashraf and *Fuṣūl* note the sowing at II:28 during the Nights of the Old Woman. In *Milḥ* it is said to be a weak variety of *'arabī* wheat sown at Jabal Ṣabir and Mikhlāf Ja'far after the *wasmī* rain. There was also a sowing called *'aqar* after the *wasmī* rain in the mountains of al-Shā'ir, al-Ḥaqūl, and al-Shawāfī. According to the Rasulid sources, *dithā'* is considered the weakest variety of wheat.

Ḥabashī. This term is no doubt derived from *ḥabashī* (Ethiopian) in reference to the dark color of this variety. Ibn Sīda (1965:11:61) defined a similar usage for a black variety of barley. It is possible, however, that the term is derived from the place name of Jabal Ḥabashī (al-Ḥajrī 1984:2:227), which is located in the southern highlands. In *Milḥ* the author said it was medium-sized, mixed red and white in color, and sown on VI:15–30. It was considered to have a quality between that of *'arabī* and *wasnī* varieties. He also stated in *Tabṣira* that both *ḥabashī* and *wasnī* wheats were sown during the select time for sowing wheat in the last ten days of *Ḥazīrān* (VI). Al-Malik al-Mujāhid noted that a variety of this was called *samrā'* (brown). The term *samrā'* is used for wheat grown in the Ṣa'da region today (Serjeant 1974a:65, note 76).

Halbā. Al-Malik al-Ashraf said in *Milḥ* that this was a short-grained white variety without a husk. It was sown at VI:15 after the *'arabī* wheat and stood three and one-half months. The almanac places the harvest of *halbā* wheat in Ba'dān and Mikhlāf Ja'far at XI:11, while *Salwa* and Taymūr note this at XI:12 (29° Scorpius). Abū al-'Uqūl said the harvest was at XI:25. A wheat variety with this name is found in modern Najd (al-Suwaydā' 1983:79).

Muqādim. This term was not defined in *Milḥ* or the *Bughya*. The term refers to an early cropping, as in the case of *miqdām* for early date varieties. The almanac mentions its sowing at V:18, the same time as the general sorghum planting in Ṣan'ā'. *Fuṣūl* defines *muqādim* at V:17 as a type of barley. Al-Malik al-Ashraf noted that barley could be planted in the mountains as early as the *al-'ashr al-mukhtāra* around the start of *Ayyār* (V). The almanac states that it was first parched at the rising of the third (*thālith*) star of Ursa Major, an event which was timed at VIII:21. The harvest was at IX:12 in al-Ashraf's almanac, IX:11 in the almanac of Abū al-'Uqūl, and IX:10 (26° Virgo) in *Salwa* and Taymūr.

Nusūl. This is a Yemeni term for emmer wheat (*'alas*), as noted earlier. Al-Malik al-Ashraf said in *Milḥ* that this literally referred to the grain once it was separated from its envelope. The Yemeni *qāḍī* al-'Arashī (1939:425,

439) reads the pronunciation in the measure of *dukhūl*, although Serjeant (1974a:40) renders it as *nasūl*.

Qiyāḍ. This term refers to a winter cropping of wheat or barley, a usage still found in Yemen today (M. al-Akwaʻ 1971:61; al-ʻAnsī 1980; Dresch 1989:297; Glaser 1885:89; Messick 1978:146; Rossi 1939:151, 1953:360; Serjeant 1954:445). The lexicons refer to *qiyāḍ* as a crop that is harvested in summer (*qayẓ*), but this is not the usage in Yemen. Al-Malik al-Ashraf in *Milḥ* defined it as wheat and barley sown at the start of winter after the main sorghum harvest was in. According to the almanac and *Salwa*, this took place on XII:17 (2° Capricornus). *Fuṣūl* notes the sowing at XII:15 along with the evening rising of Sirius (*ʻalib*). In the *Bughya* reference is made to a *qiyāḍ* sowing of *ʻarabī* wheat on irrigated land in *Kānūn al-Awwal* (XI); this was harvested in three months. The almanac poem of al-ʻAffārī places the *qiyāḍ* sowing at the *mihrajān* on XI:28 at the end of the *wasmī* rain. The almanac places the harvest at III:16 as sorghum begins to be planted in the mountains. *Fuṣūl* gives a date of III:15 and Taymūr has III:9. The reading of II:6 (25° Aquarius) in *Salwa* is a month too early and is either a copyist error or was meant for the harvest of *quṣaybī* wheat. The later almanac of *Tawqīʻāt* mentions a *qiyāḍ* sowing of barley at I:13.

Quṣaybī. This obscure reference in the Rasulid almanacs is for *wasnī* wheat sown in the area of al-Quṣayba in the southern highlands, as noted in *Milḥ* and *Maʻrifa*. Later almanac compilers were not familiar with this term and usually copied it as *qayḍī* (!). This was considered the best variety of red thick-grained *wasnī* wheat in Yemen. According to the almanac it was planted between X:1 and XI:18, with the best time from X:10 to X:25. Abū al-ʻUqūl said it was planted between X:1 and X:25, with X:10 as the best time. According to *Milḥ* and the *Bughya*, the sowing of this irrigated variety at al-Quṣayba was from X:15 to XI:15, with the harvest after three and a half months. *Salwa* and Taymūr record the sowing of this wheat variety at X:10 (25° Libra), with the last of the sowing at X:31 (16° Scorpius) according to *Salwa*. This may be the variety referred to by Abū Ḥanīfa al-Dīnawārī as being planted in Yemen at X:10.

The almanac places the parching of this variety at I:26, while Abū al-ʻUqūl noted I:24 and *Salwa* has I:22 (10° Aquarius). The almanac records the harvest between II:5 and III:24, while Abū al-ʻUqūl said it was harvested at II:6 along with *ṣawmī* sorghum.

Ṣirbī. The almanac of al-Malik al-Ashraf is the only extant Rasulid source that correctly identifies this variety of wheat. The available copies of the almanac of Abū al-'Uqūl read this as *ṣabrī*, no doubt in reference to the important site of Jabal Ṣabir, but this reading is corrupt. The almanac places the harvest of this variety at Qā' al-Ajnād, probably near Ta'izz, on X:30. This is clearly a reference to the season of *ṣirāb*, which begins at this time, as reflected in the Ḥimyaritic month name for *Tishrīn al-Awwal* (X). In the *Bughya* it was noted that the main sowing of *'arabī* wheat in the mountains during *Ḥazīrān* (VI) was also known as *ṣirāb* because of the time at which it was harvested in the autumn. The term survives in contemporary usage in the northern highlands for summer crops harvested before sorghum in the late autumn (Dresch 1989:296).

Wasnī. In *Milḥ* al-Malik al-Ashraf called this the best variety of wheat and said it was red and thick-grained. It was sown in a number of places, including al-Quṣayba, as discussed above, Ta'izz, and Mikhlāf Ja'far. In Yemen today this variety is sometimes called *bawnī* (al-Mujāhid 1980:218) in reference to Qā' al-Bawn in the central highlands north of Ṣan'ā'. Al-Malik al-Ashraf said it was sown during the select days for planting wheat at the end of *Ḥazīrān* (VI) at the same time as *ḥabashī* wheat. In Mikhlāf Ja'far this occurred in VII, according to *Ma'rifa*, although the *Bughya* would seem to indicate the sowing here during the autumn *ṣirāb* period. This variety was parched after eighty days, although most wheat varieties required three months before parching. The harvest was said to be after three and a half months.

Rice

The standard term for rice (*Oryza sativa*) in the almanac is *aruzz*, although this is usually shortened to *ruzz* or *rizz* in dialect.[27] This grain was generally considered hot and dry in the humoral system, although some scholars claimed it was cold and dry (al-Dhahabī 1984:73). Although rice was an important food crop in other parts of the Arab world, it was never cultivated in Yemen on a significant scale due to the relative lack of permanent water sources. The comment of al-'Umarī (1974:48) that rice was a common crop in Yemen is surely in error, if the text is correctly edited. Both Ibn al-Mujāwir (1954:142) and Ibn Baṭṭūṭa (1980:260) said that rice had to be imported to Aden from Egypt and India. Marco Polo (1958:309) remarked that some rice was grown in southern Arabia, but most had to be imported. In many parts of the highlands rice was not available in the past. Some tribesmen looked down on rice as inferior to sorghum, wheat, and barley. This is reflected in a Yemeni proverb quoted by al-Adīmī (1989:774): If rice brings strength, then an Indian has tribal honor (*idhā kānat bi-al-ruzz quwwa, kān bi-al-Hindī murūwwa*).[28] However, rice was given high marks by the Prophet Muḥammad (al-Suyūṭī 1986:366) and considered an aphrodisiac in the herbal tradition.

Al-Malik al-Ashraf described the cultivation of rice in Yemen in *Milḥ*. This required a great deal of irrigation water. Seven days after sowing, the rice shoot was said to appear, and irrigation water was let out of the plot. The ground must not be allowed to dry out until the harvest some six or seven months later. When the head turned yellow, it was ready to harvest. The planting occurred during the ten select (*al-'ashr al-mukhtāra*) days in spring, and the harvest was in VIII. Al-Malik al-Mujāhid, as quoted in the *Bughya*, said that it was sown in the mountain areas of Ḥarāz, Bura', and al-Lihb at the same time as sorghum. *Salwa* records the first cultivation of rice from IX:18 (3° Libra) until X:8 (23° Libra). Rice was planted by al-Malik al-Mujāhid at al-Jahmalīya in the coastal region. Al-Khazrajī (1906:2:270, 1918:5:300) said that rice was threshed at Zabīd during November–December in 801/1398. Waṭyūṭ (fol. 16v) reported rice growing in Wādī Sihām during the Rasulid period. The modern almanac of al-Ḥaydara mentions the planting of rice at VI:10. Some rice is currently grown near Ḥajja, Bilād al-Sharf, and Ḥajūr in Yemen (M. al-Akwa' 1971:67).

The only mention of rice in the almanac is for the harvest in Egypt at V:20, as is also noted in *Fuṣūl*. *Salwa* and Taymūr refer to a planting, apparently in Egypt, at IX:18 (3° Libra), with the former source citing this through X:8 (23° Libra). However, during the medieval period the primary season in Egypt for sowing rice was in *Bashans* (V), as noted in the Coptic almanacs, with the harvest starting in *Bābih* (X). *Salwa* and Taymūr refer to this harvest in Egypt at IX:14 (29° Virgo).

Sugarcane

Sugarcane (*Saccharum officinarum*) was an important crop in medieval Yemen, since it was the main source of sugar.[29] The term mentioned in the almanacs is *qaṣab al-sukkar*, which al-Malik al-Ashraf identified as *muḍḍār*, a term still in use in Yemen (M. al-Akwa' 1979:129). In Yemen sugarcane was also called *qaṣab al-shīrī* or *qaṣab al-shīrīn* (al-Hamdānī 1983:310) or *la'āṣ* (M. al-Akwa' 1979:129), although the last term was usually reserved for the sugary pulp rather than the plant. Red cane and brown sugar are referred to as *'aṭawī* in Yemen (al-'Arashī 1939:430; al-Wāsi'ī 1982:151–52). The Persian term *qand* may also have been used for sugarcane in medieval Yemen (Ibn al-Mujāwir 1954:86). In the humoral system sugarcane is hot and wet. The Prophet Muḥammad recommended eating sugar before sleeping as a universal cure (al-Suyūṭī 1986:294). Sugar was also thought by medieval Arab scholars to be an aphrodisiac.

In *Milḥ* the author said that sugarcane was planted in the middle month of winter; *Ma'rifa* defines this as *Shubāṭ* (II). The modern almanac of al-Ḥaydara mentions planting of sugarcane at II:15 and II:24. This is about the same time that it was planted in Egypt, according to the Coptic almanacs. Al-Ashraf's almanac records the cutting of cane in Najrān from VIII:1 to VIII:19, but this is given as VIII:4–18 by Abū al-'Uqūl. The last standing of sugarcane on the threshing floors was at IX:8. The almanac and Abū al-'Uqūl noted the availability of cane from XI:16, apparently a reference to a colder area than Najrān, perhaps Jibla. According to the almanac and Abū al-'Uqūl, cane was taken from the threshing floors in Najrān at XI:12. Abū al-'Uqūl also said a red variety was available from IX:1. According to *Salwa* cane was available from X:13 (28° Libra) until II:7 (26° Aquarius). Cane was also grown in Wādī Sihām in the Tihāma (Waṭyūṭ, fol. 16v)

The almanacs commonly refer to the crushing of cane to make sugar, although the timing varies. Al-Ashraf's almanac places this between XII:16 and V:26, while *Fuṣūl* records this from XII:17. According to Abū al-'Uqūl the main period for crushing was on XII:21 for Jibla, 'Anna, and Wādī Nakhla, but the crushing in Najrān was said to be between VIII:4 and VIII:18. The Coptic almanacs note the crushing of sugarcane during *Kiyahk* (XII).

FRUITS, VEGETABLES, LEGUMES, AND CULTIVATED HERBS

The Rasulid texts describe a wide range of fruits, vegetables, and herbs known and cultivated in medieval Yemen. Despite the fact that so many plants were grown to some extent, most were not part of the diet of the common people at this time. The important noncereal plants in the diet included various winter and summer legumes, such as lentils, green peas, cowpeas, and fenugreek, and a limited number of green vegetables and fruits. There were also regional specialties such as sesame in the Tihāma, dates in the Tihāma and Najrān, and grapes in the highlands. Many of the exotic plants were introduced from India and flourished primarily in royal gardens or lands owned by the sultans and their allies. This was not just a Rasulid innovation, for in the tenth-century A.D. al-Hamdānī (1938:22) remarked that even the *jinn* used to bring fresh fruits from India for the kings of Yemen.

The Rasulid agricultural treatises follow the scientific tradition in classifying cultivated plants. The term *qaṭānī* (plural) refers to various legumes and pulses, although sesame is considered one of the grains (*ḥubūb*, plural). Al-Malik al-Afḍal distinguished fifteen varieties of *qaṭānī* in the *Bughya* (fol. 35v). These included, in the order discussed: chick-peas (*ḥimmaṣ*), lentils (*'adas*), mung beans (*māsh*), cowpeas (*lūbiyā'*), broad beans (*bāqillā'*), endive (*hindibā'*), green pea (*'atar*), hyacinth beans (*hurṭumān*), fenugreek (*ḥulba*), watercress (*ḥilf*), mustard (*khardal*), safflower (*qurṭum*), poppy (*khashkhāsh*), flax (*mūma*), and *Nigella sativa* (*al-ḥabba al-sawdā'*).

Various fruits and vegetables are classified as *buqūl* and *khaḍrawāt* (literally, "greens"), although the term used for fruit in general is *fawākih* (plural). According to the *Bughya* (fol. 42r), *buqūl* were planted between XII:2 and I:29 and ripened from the end of *Nīsān* (IV) through the month of *Ayyār* (V). Thirty varieties of *buqūl* were distinguished. These were, in the order discussed: yellow and green melons (*biṭṭīkh*), cucumber (*qiththā'* and *khiyār*), pumpkin (*qar'*), eggplant (*bādhinjān*), carrot (*jazar*), turnip (*lift*), radish (*fijl*), garlic (*thūm*), onion (*baṣal*),Chinese chive (*kurrāth*), ginger (*zanjabīl*), lettuce (*khass*), endive (*hindibā'*), lupine (*turmus*), colocasia (*qulqāṣ*), Swiss chard (*salq*), spinach (*isfānākh*), balsam of kataf (*qaṭaf*), purselane (*rijla*), mint (*na'na'*), pennyroyal (*fūdanj*), common rue (*shadhāb*), parsley (*maqdūnis*), celery (*karafs*), okra (*bāmīya*), asparagus (*hilyawn*), cabbage (*kurunb*), and fumitory (*shāhtarraj*).

In the *Bughya* (fols. 64v–66v) al-Malik al-Afḍal defined several herbs, distinguished as spices rather than foods per se. These were dill (*shibith*), coriander (*kuzbara*), fennel (*rāzayānaj*), and black cumin (*al-kammūn al-ḥabashī*).

Thirty-four tree crops and fruits are classified in the *Bughya* (fols. 81r–129v) as *al-ashjār al-muthmira*, including date palms (*nakhl*), grapes (*'inab*), fig (*tīn* and *balas*), pomegranate (*rummān*), quince (*safarjal*), apple (*tuffāḥ*), plum (*ijjāṣ*), pear (*kumathrā*), peach (*khawkh*), apricot (*mishmish*), mulberry (*tūt*), olive (*zaytūn*), walnut (*jawz*), almond (*lawz*), pistachio (*fustuq*), coconut (*nārajīl*), betel nut (*fūfal*), doum palm (*dawm*), carob (*qaranīṭ*), banana (*mawz*), sugarcane (*qaṣab al-sukkar*), citron (*utrujj* and *ḥummāḍ*), orange (*nāranj*), lemon (*līmūn*), tamarind (*ḥumar*), lebbek tree (*labakh*), christ's-thorn (*sidr*), Indian labarnum (*khiyār shanbar*), ben tree (*bān*), cotton (*quṭn*), madder (*fuwwa*), and turmeric (*hurd*).

Al-Malik al-Ashraf noted for VIII:24 that at this time fruit loses its sweetness and the taste changes. Abū al-'Uqūl cited this for VIII:23 and *Salwa* indicates it for VIII:21 (6° Virgo). In the Coptic tradition, al-Maqrīzī mentioned it for the month of *Misrā* (VIII) due to the encroaching water of the Nile floods. The indication is that after this the fruit will start to spoil. In the legendary history of the prophets there were claims that fruit did not spoil until Cain killed his brother Abel (Ibn Iyās 1982:76). It is doubtful that much fruit was allowed to spoil in medieval Yemen. For a number of practical reasons Yemeni farmers tend to eat fruit while it is still green. This was noticed as well by Wallin (1854:178) as he traveled through Najd, but he couldn't decide if it was "in consequence of the great love which Arabs in general have for immature fruit, or because they have no patience to wait for its maturity."

The specific terms cited in the almanac for various fruits, vegetables, legumes, and cultivated herbs are discussed below in alphabetical order. It must be stressed that numerous other plants were grown and were discussed in detail in the agricultural treatise of the author.

Al-'Atar al-akhḍar. This term refers to the green pea (*Pisum sativum*), which is cold and dry in the humoral system. Other Rasulid sources identify this as *julubbān*, a term still heard in Yemen (I. al-Akwa' 1968:414; al-'Arashī 1939:430; al-Wāsi'ī 1982:150) and equivalent to the common Arabic term *bisilla*, which is derived from Latin. The author stated in *Milḥ* that the green pea was planted at VII:1 and bore after two and a half to three months. Both the almanac and *Salwa* note the availability of this pea at Jabal Ṣabir from IX:7 (23° Virgo), the latter source noting its availability until X:5 (20° Libra). The common practice in Yemen today is to sow it at the same time as wheat and barley in the highlands.

Balas ṣihla. In Yemeni dialect *balas* refers to any type of fig, wild or cultivated. This was the common term for *tīn* used in various parts of Yemen (M. al-Akwa' 1971:70; al-'Arashī 1939:139; Ibn al-Dayba' 1983:48; 'Inān 1980:156; al-Iryānī in 'Afīf et al. 1992:1:164; Manzoni 1884:123; Nāmī 1948:7; Nashwān ibn Sa'īd 1916:7; al-Wāsi'ī 1982:151). The Yemeni scholar Isma'īl al-Akwa' (1984:2:833) says that *balas* refers to the fruit and *balasa* to the tree. Ibn Sīda (1965:11:137) noted that in classical usage *balas* was used for the fruit and *ṭīn* for the tree. It is possible that the term *balas* in the sense of "fig" was used by the Prophet Muḥammad (see *Lisān al-'Arab*, *b-l-s*). The common fig is *Ficus carica*, but *balas* is also used in Yemen for the sycamore fig (*Ficus sycamorus*), which has an edible fruit (Great Britain Admiralty 1946:593). Al-Malik al-Afḍal (*Bughya*, fol. 102v) said the best variety was called *Rūm* (literally, "Roman"), but this is probably not a Yemeni usage.

Although the author mentioned *tīn* in general, this reference is to figs grown in the garden area of Ṣihla near Ta'izz. The almanac and *Fuṣūl* note the presence of the *ṣihla* fig between V:14 and VII:5. Abū al-'Uqūl said it was good to eat at VII:4. According to *Milḥ* (in *Bughya*, fol. 103r), it should be grown only on rain-fed land and bears fruit in three years.

Baṭṭīkh/biṭṭīkh. This is the general term in Arabic for melons of several varieties.[30] The almanac refers to two general types, the yellow melon (*al-baṭṭīkh al-aṣfar*), or *Cucumis melo*, and the green melon (*al-baṭṭīkh al-akhḍar*), or *Citrullus vulgaris*. Melon was a favorite food of the Prophet Muḥammad, who liked to eat it with dates (al-Suyūṭī 1986:173–74).

The yellow melon was known in Egypt as the *'abdallāwī/'abdalāwī* melon, named after 'Abd Allāh ibn Ṭāhir, a governor of Egypt in the early ninth century A.D. at the time of the caliph al-Ma'mūn (Clement-Mullet 1870:102; Watson 1983:89). This term has also been rendered as *'abdallī* (al-Nuwayrī 1935:11:30–31) and *'abdalī* (Pellat 1986:265). The almanac notes the planting of this melon at I:16. The planting time is given as I:31 and II:2 by Abū al-'Uqūl, who said that the *qiththā'*, or snake cucumber (*Ecballium elaterium A.* Rich), was planted at the same time in Zabīd and the Tihāma. The *Bughya* cites I:15, *Fuṣūl* and *Salwa* give I:24 (12° Aquarius), and Taymūr has I:22. According to *Taqwīm*, it was planted in the coastal region during *Shubāṭ* (II) and eaten after sixty-five days at the time of *sabt al-subūt*; this refers to the upper part of Wādī Zabīd (*Bughya*, fol. 22v). The *Bughya* (fol. 22v) also notes that while the *baṭṭīkh* in the Tihāma is said to be eaten between forty and sixty days after ripening in the season of *jaḥr*, melon was eaten at the royal garden of Tha'bāt in only fifty-five days in an experiment of al-Afḍal's father. The recent Yemeni almanac of al-Ḥaydara places the planting of melon at II:7. Both the almanac and *Fuṣūl* cite the availability of this variety between IV:4 and V:10, with it being good to eat at IV:30. Abū al-'Uqūl said it was present in the coastal region around Zabīd and Wādī Nakhla after IV:4, with IV:26 being the time of its greatest availability. *Salwa* and Taymūr mention the presence of this variety somewhat earlier at III:28 (16° Aries) through V:15 (2° Gemini). The same two sources note its presence in Aden and Laḥj at III:18 (6° Aries). Both yellow and green melons were present in Ta'izz, according to al-'Umarī (1974:46).

The green melon, which is similar to watermelon, goes by a number of terms in the Rasulid sources. The most common term in the modern dialect is *ḥabḥab* (M. al-Akwa' 1971:39; al-'Arashī 1939:423; 'Inān 1980:155), which was also cited by Abū al-'Uqūl, the *Bughya*, and *Tāj al-'arūs*. This term was also used in the Hejaz (al-Nuwayrī 1935:11:30). According to Ibn al-Mujāwir (1954:87), the origin of the term stems from a chant by melon hawkers: *ḥabḥab kathīr al-mā' qalīl al-ḥabb* (a *ḥabḥab* melon with lots of juice and few seeds). This type of melon was also called *farqūs* (*Bughya;* al-Sirājī 1959; *Ta'rīb*), a term with known variants of *farqūṣ* (*Bughya*, fol. 107v), *faqqūs* (*Tāj al-'arūs*), and *faqqūz* (Grohmann 1930:1:229).[31] Another term for this melon mentioned in the *Bughya* is *dalas*. In the classical sources this variety may also be called *al-baṭṭīkh al-hindī* (the Indian melon) or *al-baṭṭīkh al-rūmī* (the Roman melon). *Taqwīm* refers to a winter variety sown at IX:13 and eaten at the end of *Tishrīn al-Thānī* (XI). Abū al-'Uqūl said this was available in Zabīd and Ḥays at X:22 and most available at XI:15. According to *Salwa*, this variety was available from X:16 (1° Scorpius) through XI:12 (28° Scorpius). Abū Ḥanīfa al-Dīnawarī claimed that melon was planted in Yemen at VII:20 under the *naw'* of *dhābiḥ*, but this does not appear to be the appropriate timing during the Rasulid period. The modern almanac of al-Ḥaydara notes a planting of melon at VIII:27.

Du'bub. The almanac notes the presence of *du'bub* at XI:27, while Abū al-'Uqūl mentioned this at XI:29 and *Salwa* at XI:26 (12° Sagittarius). This plant was cultivated at Jabal Ṣabir near Ta'izz. Al-Hamdānī (1983:321) said this term means "twisting" in reference to the shape of the plant. The seed could be dried and ground into flour to make bread. It was also possible to make an aphrodisiacal drink from *du'bub*. *Du'bub* appears to be the rushnut or earth almond (*Cyperus esculentus*), because *Ta'rīb* equates it with *ḥabb al-ẓalam*, which is equivalent to *ḥabb al-'azīz* or *fulful al-Sūdān* (Ibn al-Bayṭār 1291/1874:2:4; Yūsuf ibn 'Umar 1982:563). This plant was popular in ancient Egypt and is still cultivated in Egypt today (Manniche 1989:98). Ibn Durayd (in Ibn Sīda 1965:11:64) claimed a bread could be made out of this. *Du'bub* can also be used for *Solanum incanum* (*Tāj al-'arūs*), but this does not fit the context here.

Fūl. The broad bean (*Vicia faba*), or fava bean, is known as *fūl* in Arabic, although the more common Yemeni term is *qillā'* (I. al-Akwa' 1968:414; M. al-Akwa' 1971:67; 'Inān 1980:156; Rossi 1939:164), usually pronounced *qilla* in dialect. This is a shortening of the classical *bāqillā'* or *bāqillā*, which is the term noted in *Milḥ* and the *Bughya*. The Prophet Muḥammad, as noted in *Milḥ*, recommended the eating of broad beans, which are cold and dry in the humoral system.

Al-Malik al-Ashraf recorded a sowing between the sorghum in cold mountain areas during *Nīsān* (IV). These beans were eaten after three months. Abū al-'Uqūl said that broad beans were planted at IV:25 between the sorghum, a practice found throughout contemporary Yemen (Dresch 1989:293). The modern almanac of al-Ḥaydara refers to a sowing at IV:17. The almanac states that the broad beans were finished at VII:31, but this is an error since the other Rasulid almanacs record this as the last time for mulberry (*tūt*). This is clearly a copyist error, since the broad bean is said to be available at VIII:1 in *Fuṣūl*. *Salwa* noted the availability of green *fūl* between VIII:2 (17° Leo) and X:18 (3° Scorpius), and Abu al-'Uqūl cited VIII:4 as the time of availability. There was also an autumn sowing at the end of *Aylūl* (IX), according to *Ma'rifa*. The *Bughya* (fol. 23v) records an irrigated variety sown at the end of XI. Both al-Ashraf's almanac and *Fuṣūl* claim that the beans from this sowing are no longer available at III:31. *Fuṣūl* adds that they are available in Iraq from the rising of the station *mu'akhkhar* at III:23.

Hilyawn/halyūn. Asparagus (*Asparagus officinalis*) was known as *hilyawn* or *halyūn* in Arabic. This hot and wet plant, which was considered an aphrodisiac, was very popular in royal circles (Ahsan 1979:96).[32] A classical variant for asparagus was *aqlām al-dhi'b* (jackel's claws), and the term *ṣūf al-hirr* (cat's hair) has been recorded for Aden (Great Britain Admiralty 1946:600). Al-Malik al-Ashraf and *Salwa* record its availability at al-Janad on XI:25 (10° Sagittarius), while Taymūr mentions XI:23. This was where most of the asparagus in Yemen was cultivated (*Bughya*, fol. 105r). The best time to plant asparagus was during *Aylūl* (IX) and *Tishrīn al-Awwal* (X), according to *Ma'rifa*. Asparagus was planted in Egypt at IX:27 (30 *Tūt*), according to al-Qalqashandī, or XII:13 (17 *Kiyahk*), according to al-Maqrīzī.

Ḥumar. This is the Yemeni term for *tamr hindī*, or tamarind (*Tamarindus indica*), as noted in the *Bughya* (fol. 108r) and in contemporary usage (al-Wāsi'ī 1982:151). A variant Yemeni term is *ḥawmar* (Yūsuf ibn 'Umar 1982:52). Tamarind, which is cold and dry in the humoral tradition, made a popular drink and was used as a laxative. The pods are also an important food source for baboons in the foothills of Yemen. Ibn al-Mujāwir (1954:64) observed that it was exported from a village along Wādī Surdud in his time. The tamarind tree grows wild in Yemen, but it could also be planted in gardens during the month of *Shubāṭ* (II), according to *Ma'rifa*. The ripe pods were available at XII:28, according to the almanac, although in *Milḥ* the tree was said to bear its fruit in *Kānūn al-Thānī* (I). Abū al-'Uqūl said it was available from XII:28, harvested from XII:31 at Shar'ab near Ta'izz, and most available at I:10. *Salwa* and Taymūr mention the availability of the pods at XII:24 (11° Capricornus). The modern almanac of al-Ḥaydara claims that tamarind is collected at II:5.

Ijjāṣ. The term *ijjāṣ* refers to the plum (*Prunus domestica*) in Arabic,[33] although in Yemeni dialect this is rendered as *injāṣ* (M. al-Akwa' 1971:70; Grohmann 1930:1:206; Messick 1978:306; Sharaf al-Dīn 1985:129, note 6). Rossi (1939:166) rendered this as *najāṣ* for Ṣan'ā'. In Yemen it generally refers to the dark (*aswad*) variety. Ibn Rusta (1892:111) said the Yemeni variety differed from that of Khūrasān. The plum tree was planted in *Shubāṭ* (II) and would bear in two years, according to the *Bughya*; *Milḥ* said the plum tree matured in three or four years depending on the quality of the soil. The almanac and *Fuṣūl* note the availability of plums at IV:1, although Abū al-'Uqūl cited V:2. *Salwa* gives a range of IV:11 (30° Aries) through VI:14 (1° Cancer), while Taymūr has IV:13–VI:14. Both the almanac and *Fuṣūl* note that it was good to eat at V:13.

'Inab. One of the most important fruit crops in Yemen has long been that

of grapes (*Vitus vinifera*), especially in the region east of Ṣan'ā'. Both the grape and raisin are considered hot and wet in the humoral system. Fresh grapes were a favorite food of the Prophet Muḥammad (al-Suyūṭī 1986:178). Although wine was forbidden for Muslims, it was made and used by Yemeni Jews.

There are numerous varieties of grapes in Yemen; Ibn Rusta (1892:111) claimed there were at least seventy![34] Vines were planted in the autumn month of *Aylūl* (IX) and in mid-*Kānūn al-Thānī* (I), according to *Milḥ*. Al-Malik al-Afḍal included a long section on cultivation and care of grapes, although some of this information is derived from earlier non-Yemeni sources. According to this discussion, grapevines were planted in Yemen from X:15 to XI:15 or from mid-XI to II:28. Abū al-'Uqūl said vines were irrigated at I:5 and pruned at I:25. Vines were pruned during the first ten days of *Shubāṭ* (II) before being irrigated, according to *Milḥ*. Vines required pruning (*taqlīm*) at I:21 with the rising of Altair, according to *Fuṣūl*. *Salwa* and Taymūr note the pruning between II:2 (21° Aquarius) and II:21 (11° Pisces). According to the *Bughya* (fol. 95r), the soil around vines should be worked in IX, especially at the rising of the stars of Ursa Major, while pruning was recommended for II, along with the cleaning off (*ṭa'zīm*) of the roots. Vines were pruned at I:14 in the year 680/1281 at the Rasulid garden of al-Jannāt, but at II:4 in the lower part of Tha'bāt near Ta'izz (*Bughya*, fol. 21v). The modern almanac of al-Ḥaydara places the pruning at III:5.

Sour grapes (*ḥiṣrim*), an important medicant, were available in Yemen from IV:23 (12° Taurus) through VII:1 (16° Cancer) according to *Salwa*. Grapes were first available at V:23 according to the almanac, Abū al-'Uqūl, and *Fuṣūl*. *Salwa* and Taymūr place this at V:13 (1° Gemini). In contemporary Yemen grapes begin to be ready during the hot season of *jaḥr*, starting in May (I. al-Akwa' 1984:1:366; al-Baraddūnī 1985:56). The almanac notes the presence of grapes in the garden of al-Jannāt for VI:12, VI:22, and VII:3, with the best time for eating at VII:5. Abū al-'Uqūl said grapes were ripe at al-Jannāt at VII:2, while *Fuṣūl* gives VII:5. Al-Malik al-Ashraf said grapes were ready to eat by VIII:1. Grapes were picked at VIII:19 for 'Abadān and areas east of Ṣan'ā', and IX:13–29 for Ṣan'ā'. Abū al-'Uqūl said that the popular red variety known as *'āṣimī*[35] ripened at VIII:12 and was one of the last varieties to ripen in Yemen. The harvest in 'Abadān was at VIII:18–19, as reckoned by Abū al-'Uqūl. *Salwa* and Taymūr place the grape harvest in Ṣan'ā' at VIII:19 (4° Virgo). The same two sources claim fresh grapes were last available at X:7 (21° Libra). Al-Malik al-Mujāhid (*Bughya*, fol. 105r) noted that grapes were eaten in both winter and summer in Dhofar on the southern coast due in part to a special type of pruning practiced there.

The almanac places the first picking of grapes for raisins (*zabīb*) in 'Udayn, al-Ẓāhir, and the Ṣan'ā' region at IX:10, with a second picking at IX:30. Abū al-'Uqūl recorded the picking at IX:10 for Ṣan'ā'. Both al-Malik al-Ashraf and Abū al-'Uqūl said that it was not suitable to pick grapes for raisins at IX:20 and IX:19, respectively, with the rising of the sixth (*sādis*) star of Ursa Major. The main grapes used for raisins in Yemen today are black (*aswad*) and white (*biyāḍ* and *rāziqī*) varieties (Yemen Arab Republic 1984a:38). The grapes are dried for one to two months, often on a wooden lattice. The raisin, which is hot and wet in the humoral system, was considered an aphrodisiac in the medical tradition. The Prophet Muḥammad recommended eating twenty-one raisins a day to keep the doctor away (al-Suyūṭī 1986:290).

Jawz. The term *jawz* refers to the walnut (*Juglans regia*), which is hot and dry in the humoral system. According to *Ma'rifa*, the walnut tree can be planted anytime, but *Milḥ* mentions this for *Shubāṭ* (II). Al-Malik al-Ashraf and Abū al-'Uqūl said walnuts were available from VI:18, while *Fuṣūl* places this at VI:20. The green walnut was available from VI:16 (3° Cancer), according to *Salwa*. The almanac notes the picking of walnuts at VII:16, while *Fuṣūl* has this at VII:15. It was last available at VIII:21, according to Taymūr.

Al-Kammūn al-ḥabashī. This term literally refers to a black (*ḥabashī*) variety of cumin also known as *al-kammūn al-kirmānī* (al-Anṭākī 1951:1:275; Ibn Sīna 1983:100; Ṣāliḥīya and al-'Amd 1984:136). The herb cumin (*Cuminum cyminum*) was cultivated in Kirmān (Colin 1978:522); hence its name in the herbals. Al-Malik al-Afḍal (*Bughya*, fol. 108v) described its medicinal value in Yemen.

Ibn al-Bayṭār (1291/1874:4:82–83) defined this as a wild variety of cumin resembling *shawnīz* (*Nigella sativa*). The reference in the almanac is not to *Nigella sativa* (see Ibn Qayyim al-Jawzīya in al-Suyūṭī 1986:281), known in the herbals as *al-kammūn al-aswad, al-ḥabba al-sawdā'*, or *shawnīz*.[36] The important medicant *Nigella sativa* is hot and dry in the humoral system and was considered useful for curing almost all illnesses (al-Suyūṭī 1986:280; 'Umar 1990). *Milḥ* described the sowing of *Nigella* in *Ādhār* (III) in irrigated gardens, with a harvest in four and one-half months.

According to the almanac, black cumin was planted at XII:13, while *Salwa* and Taymūr note this at XII:12 (27° Sagittarius). According to the *Bughya* (fol. 66r), black cumin was sown as an irrigated variety in *Tishrīn al-Awwal* (X) at the time of the wheat harvest and harvested in four months. It was best planted in direct sunlight. The harvest of black cumin was at IV:16, according to *Salwa* and Taymūr. Abū al-'Uqūl noted a planting at IV:28, with irrigation for five days.

Khawkh. The peach (*Amygdalus persica*) is called *firsik* in Yemeni dialect (I. al-Akwa' 1984:2:1000; *Bughya*; 'Inān 1980:156; Manzoni 1884:68; Sharaf al-Dīn 1985:60, note 5). This term appears to be derived from the Greek word for "Persian" (al-'Arashī 1939:149), although the usage is reported in classical Arabic (Ibn Qutayba 1982:100). Al-Hamdānī (1983:196) said there were three varieties of peaches in Yemen: *ḥimyarī* (Himyarite), *fārisī* (Persian), and *hindī* (Indian). In the humoral system the peach is cold and wet. The flower buds produce an aromatic oil used in Yemen against headaches (Fleurentin and Pelt 1982:96–97).

Al-Malik al-Ashraf noted that peaches were available from VI:1 to VIII:12 and good to eat at VII:18. Peaches were said to be available in al-Jannāt at VI:12. Abū al-'Uqūl referred to the availability of peaches from V:31 to VIII:13 and *Fuṣūl* from VI:1 to VIII:11. *Salwa* places the first peaches at V:17 (5° Gemini), with the best eating from VII:8 (3° Leo).

Kishd. The term *kishd* refers to the hyacinth bean (*Dolichos lablab*), also referred to as *hurṭumān*[37] in the Rasulid texts. In *Milḥ* al-Malik al-Ashraf said that the hyacinth bean was interplanted with sorghum in *Nīsān* (IV) and was ready in three months. However, in the almanac *kishd* was said to be available at Jabal Ṣabir at X:4, in the coastal foothills at XI:23, and in al-Mahjam up to XII:22. For al-Mahjam Abū al-'Uqūl said it was present at I:9 and especially at I:12. This bean was said to last until *Shubāṭ* (II), according to the *Bughya*.

Labakh (?). The almanac mentions the presence of a plant in the coastal region at I:9. Unfortunately the text is smudged and none of the other almanacs shed significant light on the plant intended. A possible reading is *labakh* (*Albizia lebbeck*) for the lebbek tree, which is an important medicant. Among other things, *labakh* was said to be an antidote to poison (*Bughya*, fol. 124v). This Arabic term is also used for *Mimusops laurifolia* (Forssk.) Friis, an important tree in ancient Egypt (Manniche 1989:121). *Salwa* records the presence of *labakh* at IX:13 (28° Virgo) in the Tihāma. It was planted in Yemen during *Shubāṭ* (II), according to *Ma'rifa*. *Milḥ* notes that it matures in six or seven years. This plant is cultivated in gardens in southern Yemen (Gifri and Gabali 1991:93); it grows best in the shade (Bādhīb 1991:79).

Another possible candidate for the term in the text is the turnip (*Brassica rapa*), called *lift* or *saljam* in Arabic. This was planted during IX through XI, according to the *Bughya* (fol. 23r). *Salwa* said turnips were present at IX:19 (4° Libra). According to al-Maqrīzī, the turnip was ready in *Kiyahk* (XII) in Egypt, the same time as in Greece (Qusṭūs, fol. 84r).

Lūbiyā'. The term *lūbiyā'* refers to green cowpeas (*Vigna sinensis*), although the usual term in Yemen is *dijr/dujr* (Goitein 1934:24; Landberg 1901:1:570; Leslau 1938:122; Maktari 1971:154), a term noted in the Rasulid sources and widely known on the peninsula.[38] The white variety was called *wāthiba*, according to *Milḥ*. The term *thāmir* has also been noted for this bean in Yemen (*Ta'rīb*). Cowpeas are hot and wet in the humoral system.

In *Milḥ* the author said this term referred to red and white cowpea varieties sown among the sorghum at the rising of the seventh (*sābi'*) star of Ursae Majoris at IX:30 in the coastal region. Abū al-'Uqūl said that cowpeas were first available in the coastal region at I:8, with the harvest at I:18. There was also a sowing at V:4, according to the same source. This is referred to in the *Bughya* as a sowing between the sorghum in midspring with a harvest after two and one-half months in the Tihāma and after four months in the mountains. Al-Ashraf's almanac notes the harvest of green cowpeas at Jabal Ṣabir on IX:7, as does the almanac of Abū al-'Uqūl.

al-Mawz al-hindī. The banana (*Musa cavendishii*) is known as *mawz* in Arabic.[39] Bananas have been grown in Yemen for some time; al-Hamdānī (1983:139,310) noted its presence in the coastal foothills during the tenth century A.D. Bananas were also grown at Dhofar, according to Ibn Baṭṭūṭa (1980:262). This hot and wet fruit, considered an aphrodisiac, could only be grown in areas with heat and a plentiful supply of irrigation water. According to *Milḥ*, there were two varieties: *hindī* (Indian) and *baladī* (local). The *hindī* variety had a long stalk, while the *baladī* was larger, thicker, and sweeter. The *Bughya* (fol. 118r) records a variety from Mogadishu as well. In Ṣan'ā' today large bananas, mostly imported, are referred to as *baqar* (cows) and small bananas as *ghanam* (sheep).

According to the almanac, bananas were available in al-Dumluwa, one of the treasure cities of the Rasulids, between IV:25 and XI:7. *Milḥ* notes that the Indian variety was planted from shoots in *Ādhār* (III). *Ma'rifa* records that bananas could be planted at any time of the year, but al-Ḥaydara places the planting of bananas at III:11. In Yemen today the *laḥjī* (i.e., for Laḥj in the south) variety of banana is planted during June and July (Yemen Arab Republic 1984a:14–15). According to Ibn Rusta (1892:111) the banana could be kept for up to forty days after picking.

Mishmish. The general term for apricot (*Prunus armeniaca*) is *mishmish* in Arabic, but the common term in Yemeni dialect is *barqūq/burqūq* (*Bughya*; Ibn Rusta 1892:111; Rossi 1939:163; Sharaf al-Dīn 1985:129, note 4; al-Wāsi'ī 1982:151). The term *barqūq* is apparently derived from the Latin *praecox* (al-'Arashī 1939:153) and was later adopted by the Spanish as *albarcoque*.[40] The apricot is cold and wet in the humoral system. According to the *Bughya*, apricot trees were planted in *Shubāṭ* (II). Al-Malik al-Ashraf and *Fuṣūl* note the availability of apricots from IV:1, with the best eating at V:13. Abū al-'Uqūl cited the presence of apricots at V:12, while *Salwa* indicates the range from IV:4 (23° Aries) through V:27 (15° Gemini). At Mikhlāf Ja'far, according to the almanac, there were apricots at IX:1.

Nakhl. The date palm (*Phoenix dactylifera*) is to the agriculture of the Arabian peninsula what the camel is to its stock raising.[41] Dates were cultivated mainly in the coastal region, especially near Zabīd, along parts of the southern coastal region and in Ḥaḍramawt and Najrān. Before the appearance of Islam there was a festival at Najrān centering on worship of palm trees (al-Alūsī 1882:1:347). Ibn al-Mujāwir (1954:78) recorded a legend that dates were first planted in the Tihāma by Abyssinian soldiers in the early Christian era. The general term in Arabic for the tree is *nakhl*, while the vocabulary for date varieties and stages of growth is extensive in both the formal language and dialects. The palm is also important for lumber in construction.

According to the detailed discussion in *Milḥ* and the *Bughya*, there were two main types of date palms in medieval Yemen. The first was called *thi'l*, which yielded a white date three years after planting. The origin of this term may be related to the meaning of tooth or an extra teat from the classical *thu'l* (al-Aṣma'ī in Haffner 1905:82). The term is still used in the Tihāma (Yemen Arab Republic 1984a:32) and has been reported for the Hejaz (Popenoe 1973:177), where it is defined as "warty." The *thi'l* type was said to come from Mecca originally and was considered the better of the two varieties grown in Yemen. The second major type of date palm was called *muwallad*, which was said to bear in four or five years. Unlike the first type, the *muwallad* dates did not change color as they matured. The *muwallad* date could be planted from seed, but the *thi'l* was only cultivated from shoots.

There were numerous terms for local date varieties in Yemen according to shape, size, color, or location. Among the *muwallad* dates were *dakhr*, *miqṣad*, and *dhābil*, according to *Milḥ*. Ibn al-Mujāwir (1954:79) listed the names of ten varieties in the Tihāma. The contemporary Yemeni historian Muḥammad al-Akwa' (1971:69) estimates that at least fifty varieties are distinguished in Yemen.[42] In medieval Yemen the best was considered to be the *farḍ* date cultivated near Aden. Its seed was the size of a barley grain, according to the *Bughya* (fol. 87v). *Farḍ* was also known in the classical tradition (al-Sijistānī 1985:92) and is an important variety today in Oman (Popenoe 1973:218–19), where it is used in local medicine (al-Anqar 1980:62). The dates that matured earliest were called *miqdām* in the Rasulid sources, a term also known in Oman.[43] Dates with no value were called *khashaf*, according to the *Bughya* (fol. 90r); this is a term also used today.

The almanacs record a variety of information on the cultivation and harvest of dates in Yemen. The young shoot (*fasīl*) of the palm was planted at I:18, according to Abū al-'Uqūl. The planting times for a number of major Rasulid towns were given in *Ma'rifa*: II:11 for al-Kadrā'; II:21 for Zabīd, Fashāl, and al-Ṣulay; *Tishrīn al-Thānī* (XI) for Laḥj.

The growth of the date begins with the emergence of the spadix (*ṭal'*), a process known as inflorescence. The spadix was white, pure, lustrous, round, uniform, similar in appearance to a pure pearl, and not unlike the white teeth of a maiden, according to al-Ḥimyarī (1980:241). If the tree is female, the spadix will develop into dates, while the spadix of the male will be used to pollenate the female trees or be eaten fresh. The *ṭal'* was considered cold and dry in the humoral system and had several medicinal uses. According to the almanac, the spadix of the early variety (*miqdām*) appeared at X:29. *Taqwīm* places the *miqdām* spadix from XI:25, as *sābi'ī* sorghum is being harvested, until XII:25. *Salwa* and Taymūr note inflorescence of the early variety at XI:4 (20° Scorpius). Abū al-'Uqūl gave XII:13, which is close to the date of XII:12 noted by Abū Ḥanīfa al-Dīnawarī for inflorescence in the *anwā'* tradition. The spadix of other varieties came out after XII:18 according to the almanac, *Salwa*, and Taymūr; although *Fuṣūl* notes this at XII:16. According to *Taqwīm*, at Zabīd both the *muwallad* and *thi'l* varieties yielded the spadix after XII:25 and through the month of *Shubāṭ* (II). Abū al-'Uqūl said the inflorescence of *thi'l* dates was at II:3, while *Salwa* refers to this at II:28 (17° Pisces). Some varieties are capable of producing *ṭal'* twice a year, according to the *Bughya*. The period of inflorescence was said to last two months.

Female date palms will not produce without pollenation (*talqīḥ*) either through the natural action of the wind or by artificial means (see Popenoe 1922). Pollenation generally occurred about ten days after the spadix had split open and the flowers were exposed to view. Estimates vary on the number of female trees that the spadix of a male tree can serve; this can be from thirty to forty (al-Jarwān 1987:115) to over one hundred. Artificial pollenation requires great skill, because if the spadix is inserted for too long a period of time, it can "burn" the fruit of the female so that it will fall off before it fully ripens. This type of spoiled date was generally called *shīsh* or *shīṣ*. The winds which assisted in pollenation at this time were called the Pollenating Winds (*al-riyāḥ al-lawāqiḥ*), which the almanac placed from I:11 through II:24. *Milḥ* associated these winds with the southern *azyab*. The almanac and *Fuṣūl* record the pollenation of *miqdām* date palms at I:21, with the last of this time at II:26 according to al-Malik al-Ashraf. Abū al-'Uqūl noted pollenation of palms between I:22 and II:24, while *Salwa* and Taymūr give I:15 (4° Aquarius) through II:11 (1° Pisces). *Ma'rifa* lists the following times for pollenation: XII:25 at Laḥj; I:20 at al-Ṣulay; I:25 for Zabīd, al-Kadrā', Fashāl, and al-Shiḥr. According to the *Bughya* (fol. 93r), pollenation lasts forty days from XII:10 until the falling of the First Coal (*jamra*).

At III:27, according to the almanac, date palms are ascended with ropes, a process indicated by the verb *yurqā* in Arabic. This verb was defined by al-Sijistānī (1985:6) as "climbing up" (*yuṣ'ada 'alayh*) and was derived from the term *mirqā*, the rope used in doing this. The reason for climbing the tree may have been to place a straw basket or cover to protect the dates, a practice still widely found in the Ḥaḍramawt (van der Meulen and von Wissmann 1932:119; Serjeant 1981a:318). In addition to protecting the dates from birds, bats, and wind, a basket or bag may aid the ripening process (Popenoe 1973:104). *Salwa* places this activity at III:29 (17° Aries).

The next stage in development of the date was called *balaḥ* [44] in classical usage and was said to be equivalent to the sour-grape (*ḥiṣrim*) stage for grapes. The fruit at this stage is considered sweet and slender, according to the *Bughya*. Abū al-'Uqūl noted that *balaḥ* dates increased around Zabīd at IV:13, while *Salwa* places this at IV:2 (21° Aries). The last stage before being fully ripe was known as *busr*. This is when the date begins to turn yellow and red, a process indicated by the verb *yuzhī* in Arabic. This occurred at V:14, according to the almanac, but at VI:13 in *Fuṣūl*. Abū al-'Uqūl placed the *busr* stage of the early *miqdām* variety at IV:29. According to the *Bughya* (fols. 92v, 93r) the *busr* appeared with the arrival of the sun in the zodiacal sign of Cancer (*saraṭān*) and in Qalhāt at VI:14. This stage was said to last for thirty days.

The fresh ripe date in Arabic is *ruṭab*, which is hot and wet in the humoral system. In southern Yemen today fresh dates are sometimes called *maḥū* (Serjeant 1981a:317, note 72) or *faḍaḥ* (Arab League Institute 1977b:5). The *ruṭab* date could come in red, yellow, or green varieties (Ibn al-Mujāwir 1954:79). Ibn Jubayr (1984:99) claimed that *ruṭab* dates in Mecca, to the north of Yemen, were the best tasting and sweetest he had ever tried. The ripening of dates at Zabīd was the occasion for a festive season known as *sabt al-subūt*, as discussed earlier. Fresh ripe dates were first available at VI:1, according to the almanac and *Fuṣūl*. Abū al-'Uqūl said *muwallad* dates were ready at V:14, other dates at V:31, and *thi'l* dates at VI:6. *Salwa* noted the presence of fresh ripe dates at IV:16 (5° Taurus), clearly in reference to the *miqdām* dates. The *thi'l* variety was ready at VI:22 (9° Cancer), according to *Salwa*, which records the last availability of *ruṭab* dates at VI:22 (9° Cancer). Fresh ripe dates were present at the rising of the Pleiades in the middle of *Ayyār* (V) according to *Taqwīm*. This is in reference to the *anwā'* tradition and a famous *ḥadīth* of the Prophet Muḥammad.[45] In the hot areas of the Arabian Peninsula dates began to dry on the trees as early as May, a fact noted by Marco Polo (1958:67) for Hormuz. Abū al-'Uqūl noted that the clusters of dates hung low on the trees at Zabīd by VI:17. The almanac notes that the best eating of *thi'l* dates is at VI:21, while *Fuṣūl* gives this as VI:22.

The date harvest (*ṣirām*)[46] began at VII:19, according to al-Malik al-Ashraf and Abū al-'Uqūl. *Salwa* and Taymūr cite this at VII:22 (7° Leo). In Yemen today the main date harvest is during August. The fully ripe date is generally called *tamr* when it begins to dry on the tree and was considered hot and dry in the humoral system, as well as a major medicant. A tradition of the Prophet Muḥammad, for example, states that a woman who eats dates will bear a mild-mannered child (al-Dhahabī 1984:88). The almanac and Abū al-'Uqūl noted that at VIII:14 the taste of the date begins to change and starts to spoil, although *Fuṣūl* gives this for VIII:12. The *Bughya* (fol. 87v) correlates this to the rising of Canopus.

While most of the information provided in the almanac is for Yemen, there is also a reference to the reddening of dates in the Hejaz and coastal region at IX:26. This dating is also given by Abū al-'Uqūl and *Salwa*, although *Fuṣūl* has IX:25 and Taymūr reads IX:27. This dating is somewhat late compared to non-Yemeni sources. Abū Ḥanīfa al-Dīnawarī claimed that dates ripen at the rising of *nathra* on VII:19, while Ibn al-Ajdābī said they redden at the rising of *nathra*. According to an early tradition recorded by al-Sijistānī (1985:79), dates were red at the rising of Sirius, that is, about the middle of July, and were harvested about forty nights later. Ibn al-Ajdābī said that dates were ripe everywhere by IX:10 at the *naw'* of *mu'akhkhar*.

Qurṭ. The term *qurṭ* refers to Egyptian clover (*Trifolium alexandrinum*), which is generally called *birsīm* in Egypt (Muller-Wodarg 1957:41). All the references in the Rasulid almanacs are to the cultivation of this major fodder plant in Egypt. In Yemen the main fodder crop was alfalfa (lucerne; *Medicago sativa*), known locally as *qaḍb*. This is found at all elevations and is invariably irrigated. According to *Milḥ*, Yemeni alfalfa was planted anytime except during the autumn rains and could last for up to ten years.

Al-Malik al-Ashraf said *qurṭ* was planted in Egypt at X:12, after the floods began to recede from the land, and was ready by I:22. *Fuṣūl* notes the planting at X:10 and the maturing at I:22. It was available at I:29 (17° Aquarius), according to *Salwa*. The Coptic almanacs place the planting in Egypt during *Bābih* (X). Ibn Mammātī said it was available in *Kiyahk* (XII), although al-Qalqashandī cited this for 2 *Ṭūba* (XII:28).

Rummān. The pomegranate (*Punica granatum*) was available in sweet (*ḥulw*) and sour (*ḥamīḍ*) varieties. The sweet variety was considered hot and wet, but the sour was cold and dry. Ibn al-Mujāwir (1954:62) observed the sour variety growing at al-Qaḥma along Wādī Rima'. It was said that pomegranate trees produced better if interplanted with *ās*, which is myrtle (Ṣāliḥīya and al-'Amd 1984:170). The husk of pomegranate is called *khashab* in Yemeni dialect (*Tāj al-'arūs, kh-sh-b*). The peel of the fruit held medicinal value in Yemen, especially as an antiseptic for healing wounds and as an antidiarrheal (Fleurentin and Pelt 1982:98-99).

According to al-Malik al-Ashraf, Abū al-'Uqūl, and *Fuṣūl*, the sweet variety blossomed at III:5; while *Salwa* and Taymūr place this at III:6 (24° Pisces). The almanac notes that pomegranates are available at VII:1 along with quince. Along the coast the pomegranate was available at IX:5 in the reckoning of al-Malik al-Ashraf and Abū al-'Uqūl. The harvest in this region was at X:23, according to the almanac, or X:22 according to Abū al-'Uqūl. Pomegranates were picked in Ṣan'ā' at X:23, according to the almanac, but at X:26 (12° Scorpius) according to *Salwa* and Taymūr. Abū al-'Uqūl said that pomegranate was cut along with quince at IX:12, the same date mentioned in the Coptic almanac of Ibn Mammātī. The greatest availability of pomegranates was at XI:7 for Zabīd and Rima', according to Abū al-'Uqūl.

Safarjal. Quince (*Cydonia vulgaris* L. Pers.) was available in sweet and sour varieties. Canaan (1928:163) suggested that the term *safarjal* is derived from a combination of the Arabic words *safar* (journey) and *jalā'* (emigration). The quince was considered cold and dry in the humoral system. One of the medicinal uses of the leaves in Yemen was as a treatment for acne (Fleurentin and Pelt 1982:96–97).

In *Milḥ* al-Malik al-Ashraf said quince trees were planted in either *Aylūl* (IX) or *Ādhār* (III). Al-Malik al-Ashraf, Abū al-'Uqūl, and *Fuṣūl* note the availability of quince at VII:1. *Salwa* gives a range between V:8 (26° Taurus) and IX:12 (27° Virgo) for quince. Abū al-'Uqūl said that the last of the harvest was at IX:12, along with the picking of pomegranate. The *safarjal* was grown in Ta'izz during the Rasulid era (al-'Umarī 1974:46).

Simsim. The general Arabic term for sesame (*Sesamum indicum*) is *simsim*, a cognate found in Aramaic, Coptic, and Hebrew, ultimately derived from Old Babylonian (Kraus 1968:113). The more common terms in Yemeni dialect are *juljulān* (*Bughya*; Ibn al-Mujāwir 1954:88; Manzoni 1884:68; *Milḥ*) and *juljul/jiljil* (al-'Arashī 1939:129; Grohmann 1930:1:221; Ingrams 1936:55). Al-Anṭākī (1951:1:198) claimed that *juljulān* is an Ethiopian term; however it was known in the classical tradition (Ibn al-Bayṭār 1291/1874:1:166; Ibn Sīda 1965:11:62), where it could also refer to dried coriander (al-Bīrūnī 1973:1:278).

The port of Mocha was famous for sesame in the early medieval period (al-

Muqaddasī 1989:136). The *Bughya* describes two varieties of sesame in medieval Yemen. The *baladī* variety was white and considered the best for eating and for oil. The *ṣīnī* (Chinese) variety was black and slightly bitter in taste. The seeds of sesame are ground to make oil (*ṣalīṭ*) or a paste (*ṭaḥīna)*. Sesame is hot and dry in the humoral system. The Prophet Muḥammad used to wash his face with sesame oil. A tradition also notes that a certain man who applied sesame oil to the appropriate part of his body was able to satisfy seventy women (al-Suyūṭī 1986:387). In Yemen sesame oil was rubbed on the flower of the date palm at the time of pollenation to prevent infestation.

In the warm areas of the mountains sesame was sown at V:1 according to al-Malik al-Ashraf, at V:2 according to Abū al-'Uqūl, and at V:3 (21° Taurus) according to *Salwa* and Taymūr. Abū al-'Uqūl noted the sowing of the black (i.e., *ṣīnī*) variety in the mountains at IV:27. In *Milḥ* the author also noted a sowing from X:10 to XI:15, with the harvest after three months and ten days. Al-Malik al-Mujāhid, as quoted in the *Bughya*, mentioned the sowing during the middle ten days of *Tishrīn al-Awwal* (X), with the flower appearing in forty-three days and the harvest after one hundred days. *Taqwīm* refers to the sowing in Zabīd from XI:2 to XI:10 and in Wādī Rima' from XII:4 to XII:10. According to *Taqwīm*, sesame blossomed in forty-three days and the seed appeared after fifty-three days. Abū al-'Uqūl said the sowing in Zabīd was at XI:14. *Salwa* places the sowing in Zabīd from XI:8 (24° Scorpius) through XI:25 (11° Sagittarius), while Taymūr gives this as XI:7–27. The modern Yemeni almanac of al-Ḥaydara notes the sowing in the coastal region at II:17. In the contemporary Ḥaḍramawt the branches of *ithab* (*Ficus* sp. [*salicifolia*?]) are placed in irrigation channels of sesame fields in order to increase the yield (Varisco et al. 1992).

Tīn. The almanac distinguishes between *tīn*, the general term for fig (*Ficus carica*), and *balas ṣihla*, a variety of fig cultivated in the southern garden area of Ṣihla. The fig, which is hot and wet in the humoral system, is almost as important as the date in Arabic folklore.[47] The Prophet Muḥammad said that it was a fruit sent down from Paradise (Ibn Qayyim al-Jawzīya 1957:225).

Fig trees were planted in the autumn month of *Aylūl* (IX) or in mid-*Kānūn al-Thānī* (I), according to *Milḥ*. According to al-Malik al-Ashraf, as recorded in the *Bughya* (fol. 21v), the fig was sown from seed or grafted from the middle ten days of *Shubāṭ* (II) to IV:10. Al-Malik al-Ashraf said figs were available at V:17, were good to eat at VI:16, and lasted until VII:24. *Salwa* notes the availability of figs (*balas*) between V:7 (25° Taurus) and VI:29 (14° Cancer), while in Taymūr this is given as V:8–VII:23. *Fuṣūl* mentions the last figs in Mikhlāf Ja'far at VII:23. The reference of Abū al-'Uqūl to the eating of figs at V:15 is probably for the *ṣihla* variety. The later almanac of Ibn

Jaḥḥāf records the last of figs in Ṣan'ā' at VIII:31. Al-Malik al-Afḍal (*Bughya*, fol. 100v) claimed to have eaten figs from the gardens at al-Jahmalīya in the month of *Shubāṭ* (II).

Tuffāḥ. According to al-Malik al-Ashraf in *Milḥ*, there were three varieties of apple (*Malus communis*), or *tuffāḥ*: sweet, sour, and Meccan (*makkī*). The apple was said to be cold and dry in the humoral system. Apple trees were planted in *Shubāṭ* (II) along with most other fruit trees. Both the almanac and *Fuṣūl* record the presence of apples at IV:1, while Abū al-'Uqūl gives this as IV:2. *Salwa* and Taymūr note the apple at III:8 (26° Pisces), which seems somewhat early. According to the later almanac of *Tawqī'āt*, apples were ready in Ṣan'ā' at IV:1.

Tūt. The mulberry tree (*Morus nigra*) is referred to as *tūt* in Yemen and in most other Arabic dialects. The *Bughya* also notes the classical synonym *firṣād* (see Ibn al-Bayṭār 1291/1874:3:162; Yūsuf ibn 'Umar 1982:53). Another Yemeni term for the mulberry is *ḥubūb al-mulūk*, apparently because of its popularity in royal circles (Great Britain Admiralty 1946:593).

Al-Malik al-Ashraf said mulberries were available at Jibla from V:23, while Abū al-'Uqūl gave this as V:22 and *Fuṣūl* as V:24. The berries were good to eat at VI:29 according to the almanac, at VI:28 according to Abū al-'Uqūl, and at VI:27 according to *Fuṣūl*. Abū al-'Uqūl added that the last mulberries were at VII:30.

Yaqṭīn. According to the discussion in the *Bughya*, the term *yaqṭīn* was equivalent to *qar'*, which generally refers to the common gourd (*Cucurbita maxima* Duch.). The lexicons define the generic *yaqṭīn* as a plant without a stalk (*sāq*), that is, a vine. The common term in the Yemeni dialect of the highlands for the gourd itself is *dubbā'* or *dubba*, which is also mentioned in the *Bughya* and the almanac of Abū al-'Uqūl. The gourd, which is cold and wet in the humoral system, was said to be the vine under which the prophet Jonah sat.[48] The Prophet Muḥammad liked a soup made from gourd (al-Suyūṭī 1986:163). One of the medicinal uses of the seeds of *dubbā'* in Yemen is as an anthelmintic (Fleurentin and Pelt 1982:98-99).

The author and Abū al-'Uqūl said that it was good to plant gourds at III:2. The *qar'* ripened in forty days, according to the *Bughya* (fol. 22v). They were available until X:14, according to the later Yemeni almanac of *Tawqī'āt*.

Zaytūn. The olive tree (*Olea* sp.) was referred to as *zaytūn* in Arabic. There is no evidence that it was cultivated in Rasulid Yemen, although the climate would appear to be suitable in the highlands. Al-Malik al-Afḍal

(*Bughya*, fol. 111r) said that it was not known in Yemen, but that there was a wild tree resembling the olive near the fortress site of al-Dumluwa in the southern highlands. The olive was planted in recent times in Oman and parts of northwest Arabia (Great Britain Admiralty 1946:593). Ibn al-Mujāwir (1954:142) observed that olives were imported to Yemen from Egypt. Olives and olive oil were also imported to Yemen from Syria (al-'Umarī 1974:48).

The almanac, as well as Abū al-'Uqūl and *Fuṣūl*, mentions the picking of olives in Egypt at XI:6. The Coptic almanacs did in fact place the picking of olives during *Tūt* (XI). At this time there were only a few olive trees in Egypt, mostly in Fayoum (al-'Umarī 1986:83). The harvest in Syria was at XI:2, according to Abū Ḥanīfa al-Dīnawarī, or XI:7 according to al-Qazwīnī. Al-Bīrūnī mentioned the pressing of olive oil at XI:23 in Syria. According to *Milḥ* and *Ma'rifa*, the olive tree was planted in *Tishrīn al-Awwal* (X). Qusṭūs (fol. 74v) said that olive trees were planted in Greece during *Tishrīn al-Thānī* (X) and *Kānūn al-Awwal* (XII), as well as in *Nīsān* (IV). The almanac of *Fuṣūl* mentions the planting in Syria for *Kānūn al-Thānī* (I), while there was still ice on the ground.

FLOWERS AND AROMATIC PLANTS

The climatic variation in Yemen allows for the growth of many flowers and aromatic plants both in the wild and in cultivated gardens. As avid gardeners in their own right, the Rasulid sultans introduced a number of exotic species and took great care of these in their royal gardens. The agricultural treatises of al-Malik al-Ashraf and al-Malik al-Afḍal describe a wide variety of *rayāḥīn*, or aromatic plants. In the *Bughya* (fols. 66v–81r) al-Malik al-Afḍal mentioned twenty-four varieties: rose (*ward*), violet (*banafsaj*), marigold (*līnūfar*), Indian jasmine (*al-full al-hindī*), *bādhān* or *bādhām*, narcissus (*narjis*), gilliflower (*khīrī*), jasmine (*yāsamīn*), musk rose (*nasrīn*), white rose (*fsḥ* ?), myrtle (*ās*), sweet basil (*ḥabaq*), marjoram (*mardaqūsh*), *ādhāb* ? (type of basil), bush basil (*nammām*), lavender cotton (*'abayathirān*), screwpine (*kādhī*), chrysanthemum (*uqḥūwān*), camomile (*bābūnaj*), henna (*hinnā'*), sweet trefoil (*ḥandaqūqā*), pasque flower (*shaqā'iq al-nu'mān*), crown imperial (*iklīl al-mālik*), and white mallow (*khaṭmīya*).

The specific flowers and aromatics mentioned in the almanac were widely cultivated, especially in the coastal region. These are discussed below in alphabetical order:

Balasān. One of the most important medicants in medieval tradition was balsam of Mecca, or balm of Gilead. The scientific name for the common variety of *balasān* is *Commiphora opobalsamum*. The wood of this plant was considered hot and dry in the humoral system, with the lotion especially valuable against diseases defined as hot. The variant term *balsam* is also found in some Arabic sources. According to Glaser (in Grohmann 1930:1:155), it was called *bishām* in the Jawf.

The reference in the almanac is to the pressing of the resinous lotion from balsam at III:30, which must be for Egypt, as can readily be seen by comparing the similar dates in the Coptic sources. Abū al-'Uqūl gave the same date, but *Salwa* and Taymūr noted this pressing at III:26 (14° Aries). However, al-Anṭākī (1951:1:82) said the lotion should be pressed at the rising of Sirius in midsummer. According to the last two Rasulid sources the incising of balsam to remove the sap occurred around XI:18 (5° Sagittarius). This is only one day earlier than the time mentioned by al-Qalqashandī in his Coptic reckoning.

At the time of the author, balsam was apparently grown only in the Arab world at 'Ayn Shams (Heliopolis) in Egypt, a fact frequently referred to in the medieval sources (Ibn al-Bayṭār 1291/1874:1:106; Ibn al-Wardī 1939:153; *Tāj al-'arūs*; al-'Umarī 1985:128; Yūsuf ibn 'Umar 1982:23). Balsam was generally planted in Egypt during *Bashans* (May), according to the Coptic almanacs. Al-Maqrīzī said that 24 *Bashans* (V:19) was the Coptic Festival of Balsam, celebrating the arrival of the Virgin Mary into Egypt.

Kādhī. This aromatic plant is the screwpine (*Pandanus tectorius* Sol. or *P. odoratissimus*). It is also known as *kadar* (*Ta'rīb*; appendix to Yūsuf ibn 'Umar 1982:570) and *'ūd al-dhi'b,* or "wolf's wood" (Great Britain Admiralty 1946:598), in Yemen. The Indian name is *kiyūra* (Smith 1989:114). This tropical plant can reach 6–8 meters in height. A lotion made from the sap was used as a medicant, for which it was defined as cold and dry (Ibn al-Mujāwir 1954:82). Al-Hamdānī (1983:321) claimed this plant produced the most prized scent in Yemen. Ibn al-Mujāwir (1954:81) recorded a legend that the heads would not form unless there was lightning. According to the *Bughya* it was planted like a banana tree and reached maturity in two or three years. This aromatic was planted primarily in the coastal region and foothills, where it can still be found. In the upper parts of wadis this plant was used as a windbreak on coffee plots in later centuries (Grohmann 1930:1:160). Al-Malik al-Ashraf, *Salwa*, and Taymūr mention the availability of the aromatic heads from V:10 (27° Taurus), while Abū al-'Uqūl had this at V:9. The almanac notes the presence of these heads until XI:29.

Khashkhāsh. The poppy (*Papaver somniferum*, var. *album*) was valued primarily for the opium (*afyūn*) derived from the flower.[49] This gave rise to the popular name of *abū al-nawm* (literally, "father of sleep") in Egypt (al-Anṭākī 1951:1:140). This cold and dry flower had a number of medicinal uses apart from the drug, which was considered *ḥarām* by most legal scholars. The cultivated variety had white seeds, while wild varieties had black or yellow seeds (Yūsuf ibn 'Umar 1982:127–28). In *Milḥ* al-Malik al-Ashraf said that the poppy was planted in *Ḥazīrān* (VI), at the same time as *'arabī* wheat, and harvested in five months. *Ma'rifa* also records this planting in *Ḥazīrān*. The almanac and Abū al-'Uqūl note the planting at V:19. Taymūr records a planting at I:10, but this may be in reference to Egypt, since Ibn Mammātī listed a planting at I:9 (14 *Ṭūba*). According to the author and Abū al-'Uqūl, the poppy was harvested at XI:9. The Coptic almanacs also record a sowing in late spring, with a harvest in November.

Narjis. The narcissus (*Narcissus poeticus*) was considered hot and dry in the humoral system. In the *Bughya* the wild variety is called *'abhar* and the cultivated variety is called *maḍā'af*, both terms derived from the classical tradition (Ibn al-Bayṭār 1291/1874:3:116). According to the almanac, this was planted at X:14, although *Fuṣūl* claims this was for Egypt, as is confirmed in the Coptic almanacs. According to the *Bughya*, it was planted in Yemen during *Aylūl* (IX), blossomed in fifty days, and was harvested in seventy days. Ibn Māsawayh claimed that the rose and narcissus were planted in Yemen at V:22. This would be the planting relevant for the blossoming of narcissus at IX:10 according to the almanac and IX:9 according to *Fuṣūl*. *Salwa* records the blossoming at V:4 (22° Taurus), while Taymūr gives V:6; these would result from a planting in autumn.

Shāhtarraj. Fumitory (*Fumaria officinalis*) was said to be available at al-Janad on IV:5. This was where most of the fumitory in Yemen was cultivated during the Rasulid period (*Bughya*, fol. 105r). *Salwa* notes its presence at IX:3 (18° Virgo), while Taymūr records this at VIII:30. The Coptic almanac of *Nubdha* cites the presence of fumitory along canal banks at XII:30 (5 *Amshīr*).

This hot and dry medicant had a bitter taste. According to *Ta'rīb*, it was also known as *baqlat al-malik* or *sulṭān al-buqūl*, no doubt because of its importance as a medicant. It was planted in *rabī'*, which al-Malik al-Afḍal (*Bughya*, fol. 148v) defined as *Kānūn al-Awwal* (XII) through *Shubāṭ* (II), and was harvested in four months.

Ward. The common term for rose in Arabic is *ward*, which is often used as a woman's name in its feminine form. This cold and dry flower has a variety of medicinal uses, as well as for the flavoring of rose water. The wild variety in Yemen is *Rosa abyssinica* (Fleurentin and Pelt 1982:96; Scott 1942:94). One of the common Yemeni terms for the rose is *ḥawjam*.[50] Abū

Ḥanīfa (in Ibn al-Bayṭār 1291/1874:4:189) said this referred to the red rose. Al-Malik al-Afḍal in the *Bughya* called the rose the "sultan of all aromatic flowers" (*sulṭān al-rayāḥīn*). In *Milḥ* al-Malik al-Ashraf distinguished between the local (*baladī*) variety, which was said to be red, and the Syrian (*sha'mī*), or white rose. However, the white rose can be found growing wild in Yemen today. Al-Malik al-Ashraf said domestic roses were planted in *Aylūl* (IX) or at mid-*Kānūn al-Thānī* (I), while *Ma'rifa* notes the planting in *Aylūl* or at XI:15. The almanac and *Fuṣūl* record the blossoming of roses at III:1, with the greatest availability at IV:9 according to the almanac and Abū al-'Uqūl. Abū al-'Uqūl also noted that roses were present at Jabal Ṣabir and Mikhlāf Ja'far at I:11, while *Salwa* records this same information for I:23 (11° Aquarius). The rose was last available at V:21 according to Abū al-'Uqūl, whereas *Salwa* and Taymūr cite this for V:16 (3° Gemini). The contemporary almanac of al-Ḥaydara records the presence of roses from I:25 to IV:15. The white Syrian variety was said to blossom in the autumn as well.

Yāsamīn/yāsimīn. In the *Bughya* a distinction is made between *yāsamīn* for the white jasmine (*Jasminum officinale* L.) and *full* or *zanbaq* for the yellow jasmine (*J. sambac* Ait.). In addition, *J. gratissimum* Defl. and *J. multiflorum* Roth have been recorded for Yemen (Fleurentin and Pelt 1982: 98). The white variety was the most common in Yemen and the yellow may have been introduced by the Rasulids or Ayyubids. The term *full/fill* is used in contemporary Yemeni dialect for the white variety as well (al-Waysī 1962:89) and for *Nyctanthes sambac* L. of the *Verbenacea* (Fleurentin and Pelt 1982:100). The term *zanbaq* is also used for the lotion (*duhn*) extracted from jasmine (Yūsuf ibn 'Umar 1982:168, 207). The seeds of jasmine produce an aromatic oil used in Yemen for urinary infections, kidney stones, and eczema and as a tranquilizer (Fleurentin and Pelt 1982:98–99).

According to *Ma'rifa* the white variety could be planted anytime, but the yellow was planted at II:16 or in *Ādhār* (III). Al-Malik al-Ashraf and Abū al-'Uqūl said that *yāsamīn* blossoms at V:27 and the flowers become plentiful at VII:27. According to *Salwa* the yellow variety blossomed at V:4 (22° Taurus) along with the narcissus, while the white variety was present at V:24 (12° Gemini). Taymūr records the presence of the yellow variety at V:6 and the white at V:29.

FABRIC PLANTS

The almanac mentions two plants cultivated in Yemen for making fabric: flax and cotton. Production appears to have been limited, however, since there was a brisk trade in cotton cloth from India and linen from Egypt (Goitein

1967:120).

Kattān. Flax (*Linum usitatissimum* L.) was important in the medieval Arab world for linen and as a medicant.[51] The seed was known as *mūma*, as noted in the *Bughya*, or *bizr al-kattān* (al-Anṭākī 1951:1:74). The lotion (linseed oil) from the seed was called *duhn al-sarrāj* in Yemen (*Ta'rīb*). The seed was considered hot and dry in the humoral system. It had a number of medicinal uses, especially as a laxative and anti-inflammatory (Fleurentin and Pelt 1982:94–95).

According to al-Malik al-Ashraf in *Milḥ*, flax seed was sown broadcast during *Ḥazīrān* (VI) and *Tammūz* (VII) at the same time as *'arabī* wheat. Flax had to be irrigated and was ready in four months. The references in the Rasulid almanacs, however, are to the cultivation of flax in Egypt. Al-Malik al-Ashraf and Abū al-'Uqūl noted the harvest in Egypt at IV:23. *Fuṣūl* gives this as IV:21, and *Salwa* as IV:12 (1° Taurus). The Coptic almanacs note the harvest in *Baramhāt* (III) and *Barmūda* (IV). The harvest in Yemen would have been in the autumn.

'Uṭb/'uṭub. The most important fabric crop in Yemen was cotton (*Gossypium arboreum)*, referred to in Arabic as *'uṭb/'uṭub* or *quṭn/quṭun*.[52] In Dhofar there was also a wild variety of cotton known as *G. stocksii* (Great Britain Admiralty 1946:595). In addition to providing thread for cloth, the fiber of the cotton plant could be used as stuffing or to make paper. Cottonseeds were also used to produce a cooking oil.

Fuṣūl recorded one sowing at III:2 and a later sowing in Abyan at VII:25. The contemporary almanac of al-Ḥaydara notes a sowing at II:7, and al-'Affārī (Varisco 1989b) mentioned the planting of cotton under the rising of *balda* at I:10. In the coastal region, today, cotton is generally planted in July and August and picked after 130–150 days. The Coptic almanacs record the sowing in Egypt during *Baramhāt* (III) or *Barmūda* (IV).

There were two major harvest seasons for cotton. One was known as *ṣayfī* because it took place in the spring (*ṣayf* in Yemen) at the start of *Ayyār* (V), as noted in *Shāmil*. The almanac refers to this harvest at al-Mahjam for V:29. The second harvest season was designated *ṣirbī* because it took place at the harvest (*ṣirāb*) of *sābi'ī* sorghum, according to *Shāmil*. The almanac and *Fuṣūl* note the harvest at Abyan on XII:1, Abū al-'Uqūl gave this as XII:2, and *Salwa* and Taymūr record XII:7 (23° Sagittarius). Abū al-'Uqūl said that cotton was most plentiful at XII:19, the date mentioned in the almanac for the *ṣirbī* variety.

Chapter 6

Health, Humors, and Sex

As an almanac highlighting seasonal phenomena, reference is made to the changing states of human health throughout the year. Medieval medical knowledge among the Arabs was based primarily on the Greek tradition as embodied in the writings attributed to Hippocrates (ca. 5th century B.C.) and Galen (2nd century B.C.).[1] This tradition defined health and life in general as a function of the four humors with implications for each season on proper diet, hygiene, and suitable medical practices. Al-Malik al-Ashraf was knowledgeable in medicinal science, as is evidenced by the inclusion of at least three titles on medicine among his known works. His father, al-Malik al-Muẓaffar Yūsuf, compiled a major herbal based on important earlier sources, especially that of the Iraqi Ibn al-Bayṭār, who died in 646/1248. Ibn al-Bayṭār (1291/1874) collected information on some 1,400 simples from over 150 authorities. A number of the Rasulid sultans wrote about medicine and herbal remedies. The mixed Rasulid manuscript from the library of al-Malik al-Afḍal contains numerous medical treatises and charts relating treatment to astrology.

Some of the formal scientific knowledge on medicine also appears in a genre known as *al-ṭibb al-nabawī*, which consists primarily of traditions from the Prophet Muḥammad on a range of health and hygiene matters.[2] The compilers of this genre quote Galen and Hippocrates, as well as other non-Arab sources, in explaining some of the traditions of Muḥammad. Among the Arabs there was a long-standing knowledge of the humoral system, as for example the belief that Adam was created from the four humors (al-Suyūṭī 1986:102). The great contribution of this genre, however, is the principle that medicine was a worthwhile pursuit. One of the most famous sayings of Muḥammad notes that God did not make any disease without providing a cure for it (*mā anzala Allāh dā' illā anzala lih shifā'*), the only exception being death or perhaps certain poisons (al-Suyūṭī 1986:97). In another tradition it was noted that virtually every plant has a medical use, much of this having been revealed to Solomon and the Prophet Muḥammad himself. This fits in well with the local practice in Yemen of using the rich variety of plants for cures and practical needs.[3]

HUMORAL SYSTEM

In the classical system of medicine each season of the year has a specific health regime. Indeed, knowledge of the climate in a specific environment was a prerequisite for medical practice. In the Hippocratic writings, for example, the doctor was urged to learn as much as he could about meteorology and astronomy. The changes of the seasons, said Hippocrates (1983:213), "are especially liable to beget diseases, as are great changes from heat to cold, or cold to heat in any season. Other changes in the weather have similarly severe effects." Knowledge of seasonal change was necessary for proper prescription and treatment. A cure proposed in the heat of summer, for example, might be deadly during the cold of winter. The most critical times of the year from the medical perspective were thus those in which there was a mixing of the seasons (*imtizāj al-faṣlayn*), as noted in the almanac for XI:30, [II:28],[4] V:31, and VIII:31. In Islamic folklore the times of seasonal change are sometimes viewed as inappropriate for performing certain activities (Masse 1954:259).

Each season of the year has a dominant humor (*khilṭ*), which controls the health and diet regime for the season. The humor was defined according to its nature as either hot or cold, wet or dry. The dominant humor of spring is blood (*dam*), which is hot and wet, in keeping with the season which it represents. The seat of the body's blood in medieval reckoning was the liver (*kabid*) rather than the heart. Blood was considered the best humor, and correspondingly spring the best season of the year. During summer the humor of yellow bile (*al-mirra al-ṣafrā'* or *al-ṣafrāwī*) stirs in the body. This hot and dry humor was linked with the gall bladder (*marāra*), which regulated body temperature among other things. Black bile (*al-mirra al-sawdā'* or *al-sawdāwī*), which is hot and cold, dominates the autumn. Black bile was located in the spleen (*ṭiḥāl*) and was thought to regulate fear in human psychology. For the winter season the cold and wet humor of phlegm (*balgham*) is in control. This humor was said to be located in the lungs (*ri'a*) and affected the emotion of sadness.

The humoral concept constitutes a holistic approach to human health which defined most medical science in the East and the West until the Enlightenment in Europe. Although it was not accurate by modern standards, it did accommodate a number of practical observations and could be adapted to successful practice. There are three basic principles which define the humoral concept as applied in medieval Arab science. First, all living phenomena can be broken down into basic characteristics of hot or cold, wet or dry, so that seemingly disparate elements of nature can be linked in a single classification system. The medieval herbals define each plant, animal, or mixed medicant according to these characteristics, including in some cases the stage or degree of the characteristic, for example, whether something was hot in the first or second degree. Second, each season has its unique health and hygiene regime based on its nature, as noted above. This meant that diet and activity had to be adapted to the particular season. The almanacs provided practical details on this matter. Third, health is defined as a balance of the humors within the body and disease as an imbalance. In the words of Hippocrates (1983:262), "Health is primarily that state in which these constituent substances are in the correct proportion to each other, both in strength and quantity, and well mixed." This placed a premium on preventive health care, a major thrust in the Hippocratic and Islamic medical traditions, especially for diet and hygiene. Treatment, when necessary, becomes a way of returning to the natural balance. Here a sort of epidemiological isostasy comes into play where balance is restored by using an opposite. For diet, one eats cold and dry foods in a hot and wet season; for disease, one finds a treatment that counteracts the imbalance created by too much of a particular humor. In general, if the disease is considered hot and dry, the remedy must be cold or wet.

ILLNESS AND TREATMENT

Given the logic of the humoral system, it follows that some diseases will be more common in a certain season than others. Hippocrates (1983:213–15), who was writing for the climate of Greece, claimed that the healthiest season was spring and the most dangerous season healthwise was autumn. This was not necessarily the case for parts of the Arab world where the climate differed from Greece, despite the theory behind the humoral system. However, the almanacs reflect the scientific perspective derived from the classical tradition and validated in general for the Arab world. Yemen was by and large a healthy place, at least in medieval terms. Arab geographers remarked on the perfect climate of Ṣan'ā', while the Rasulid capital at Ta'izz was considered a sort of garden paradise. This is no doubt due in part to the lack of rain during the cold of winter. There is little reference to particularly unhealthy areas along the Yemeni coast, although later writers often mention the danger of fevers in parts of the Arabian Gulf (e.g., Wallin 1854:174). By contrast, in Kuwait during the summer there was "damp heat which seems to penetrate their very bones, and brings out ailments of every description" (Dickson 1951:254).

Infectious disease (*wabā'*) was said to be a problem from IX:9 through

XI:13, according to al-Malik al-Ashraf. Abū al-'Uqūl began this at IX:6, while Taymūr adds that it lasts until XII:30 in Egypt. It was commonly thought that there would be more disease if the winter was not cold (al-Suyūṭī 1986:230). The term *wabā'* (*awba'* or *awbi'a*, plurals) in this context relates to a variety of common illnesses which spread through infection (al-Khawārizmī 1984:190; al-Tha'ālibī n.d.:84). It was distinguished in the almanac tradition from the term *ṭā'ūn* (*ṭawā'īn*, plural), which refers to pestilential disease or the bubonic plague.[5] Al-Malik al-Ashraf said that the season for pestilential disease with swelling (*waram*) and sores (*qurūḥ*) was between III:20 and VII:8. Abū al-'Uqūl gave the range as III:19–VII:6. This information is clearly derived from the *anwā'* tradition, in which Abū Ḥanīfa al-Dīnawarī noted the end of the plague period at VII:7 with the rising of *dhirā'*. A similar dating is found in the Coptic almanacs. Lane (1973:2) observed that the "plague" was most severe in Egypt during the spring, especially when the *khamāsīn* winds blew. Diseases, in general, were said to be less after I:12, according to the almanac.

The common cold (*zukām*) was most common at IV:10 (28° Aries), according to the almanac and *Salwa*, although Abū al-'Uqūl and *Fuṣūl* place this at IV:12. *Salwa* and Taymūr note the increase in colds at XII:21 (8° Capricornus). The later almanac of *Tawqī'āt* adds that there are also coughs (*su'āl*) and nasal drainage (*nazālāt*). Stark (1940:63) observed that coughs and fevers were common in the Ḥaḍramawt during winter. Most non-Yemeni almanacs mention colds for the late summer and autumn (e.g., al-Qazwīnī on VIII:28). It is interesting to note that Arab scholars believed a person could catch a cold by sleeping under moonlight (al-Nuwayrī 1923:1:56).

Eye diseases have always been a major health problem in the Arab world, especially in very hot environments with sandstorms and a bountiful supply of flies.[6] Hippocrates claimed that spring was the worst season for opthalmia, an observation also relevant for most of the Arab world. Al-Malik al-Ashraf noted the prevalence of eye diseases (*awjā' al-'ayn*) between IV:10 and VII:11. According to *Fuṣūl*, eye inflammation (*ramad*) was a problem at IV:12. For Egypt, eye disease increased when the Nile rose, as noted by Ibn Māsawayh at V:7.

Almost all Arab almanacs mention the time when it is suitable or not suitable to use a purgative (*mushil*), an important medical practice in the medieval period. According to al-Bīrūnī, purgatives and hot medicinal drinks should not be taken at VII:18. He quoted Hippocrates, who was said to have prohibited this and the regular use of bleeding for twenty days before and twenty days after the midsummer rising of Sirius. The *Calendar of Cordova* notes this ban by Hippocrates for VII:8 and relates it to the rising of Sirius (see Hippocrates 1983:159). The reason is that at this time the heat of summer is so strong that it will dissolve wet substances. Thus, the use of purgatives, unless absolutely necessary, would lead to a dangerous imbalance and probably bring on fever. Al-Malik al-Ashraf referred to this ban as being between VI:27 and VIII:10, while *Fuṣūl* begins it at VI:22 and *Salwa* at VI:25 (12° Cancer). Abū al-'Uqūl also cautioned against the use of purgatives in *Shubāṭ* (II), *Tishrīn al-Awwal* (X), and *Tishrīn al-Thānī* (XI). The Rasulid almanacs recommend the use of purgatives at III:14 or shortly thereafter with the coming of spring; this is also derived from the Hippocratic tradition. *Salwa* places the use from ca. III:12 (2° Aries). Abū al-'Uqūl said that one should use purgatives in *Nīsān* (IV) and *Ayyār* (V). The Rasulid almanac *Mīqāt* indicates that purgatives are suitable in *Aylūl* (IX) and *Tishrīn al-Awwal* (X). As the Hippocratic tradition noted, purgatives were suitable in both spring and autumn because of the change in seasons.

One of the most common treatments in the medieval period was bleeding, or bloodletting *(faṣd)*, and the related practice of cupping (*ḥijāma*).[7] Al-Malik al-Ashraf did not refer to bleeding in the almanac, but elsewhere he noted that it should be done in *Adhār* (III). Both the Greek tradition and the Prophet Muḥammad prescribed bleeding as an important remedy for the stirring of blood in the spring. Abū al-'Uqūl said that bleeding should be avoided in *Kānūn al-Thānī* (I), *Shubāṭ* (II), *Tishrīn al-Awwal* (X), and *Tishrīn al-Thānī* (XI). The later Yemeni almanacs of Ibn Jaḥḥāf and *Tawqī'āt* caution against bleeding at X:9. Abū al-'Uqūl recommended both bleeding and cupping at IV:6. Circumcision (*khitān*) was especially appropriate at III:29, according to Abū al-'Uqūl, since blood was dominant at this time. This idea was also noted at III:24 by al-Bīrūnī, who related it to the blowing of the Pollenating Winds at the time. In addition to the season of the year, some times were considered more propitious than others for bleeding and cupping. As al-Suyūṭī (1986:253) commented, it was better to bleed in the latter half of the lunar month because blood was not so active at this time. Even days of the week were good or bad for this, with Thursday generally considered a bad day for bleeding.

In addition to specific diseases and treatments, recommendations are often given in the almanacs for preventive medicine. According to al-Malik al-Ashraf (*Tabṣira*, fol. 117v), it was advisable to enter a hot bath (*ḥammām*) during *Kānūn al-Thānī* (I) and *Tishrīn al-Awwal* (X). Abū al-'Uqūl recommended a hot bath in *Nīsān* (IV) and *Kānūn al-Awwal* (XII), but advised a cold bath in the hot month of *Ḥazīrān* (VI). Public baths were built in the main cities of medieval Yemen, and no doubt the Rasulid sultans regularly availed themselves of the luxury of a hot bath and rubdown.[8] The use of oils or lotions on the limbs of the body was recommended by the author in *Tammūz* (VI) and *Tishrīn al-Awwal* (X). Certain scents were also suitable or not suitable seasonally. Al-Malik al-Ashraf recommended the scents of rose (*ward*) and camphor (*kāfūr*) during *Ayyār* (V), since these were cold scents, but not during the cold month of *Kānūn al-Awwal* (XII). Strenuous exercise was all right in *Kānūn al-Thānī* (I) but not in *Nīsān* (IV).

PREVENTIVE DIET

In order to maintain a healthy balance of humors in the body, it was necessary to adapt the diet for each season.[9] While some foods were more or less suitable almost any time of the year, several should be increased or decreased according to the season, and others should be avoided in certain seasons. The herbals record the nature and degree, where relevant, of each food so that a proper diet can be achieved. Ideally one eats the opposite food from the nature of a season. Thus, a hot spice like ginger should be avoided in summer, whereas cold and wet fruits are especially beneficial in summer. Foods defined as temperate, neither hot nor cold to a great degree, were especially suitable for the temperate seasons of spring and autumn.

The earliest formal almanacs, especially the text of Ibn Māsawayh and the *Calendar of Cordova*, provide a great deal of information on seasonal diet by month. Despite minor variations, similar advice on diet was made by al-Malik al-Ashraf (*Tabṣira*, fols. 117v–119r) and Abū al-'Uqūl. Al-Malik al-Ashraf argued that eating should be reduced in the month of *Ḥazīrān* (VI) due to the heat, and in the month of *Āb* (VIII) because this was a time for weak digestion. His dietary advice is summarized below according to each month of the year. The recommended foods are indicated to the left and the foods to be avoided are listed to the right:

Recommended Foods	Foods to be Avoided
Tishrīn al-Awwal (October)	
hot, wet, fatty foods	beef
most meat, e.g., goat, fowl	dry pulses, e.g., lentils
dates	sumac
walnuts	sour grapes
	things that constipate (i.e., *qawābiḍ*)
Tishrīn al-Thānī (November)	
hot and wet foods	hot and dry or hot and wet foods

Recommended Foods	Foods to be Avoided
chicken	spicy foods (*ḥarīfāt*)
suckling lamb	dry legumes
chick-peas	beef
Swiss chard (*salq*)	game
boiled sweet pudding with milk	cheese
ginger	melons
garlic	*tharīd* (dish of sopped bread)[10]
Chinese chive (*kurrāth*)	

Kānūn al-Awwal (December)

hot and dry foods	cold and wet foods
dishes with honey	fish
dates	sour milk (*laban*)
sweets	cold pulses
ginger	
garlic	
Chinese chive	

Kānūn al-Thānī (January)

hot and dry foods	cold and wet foods
hot water	citrons (*utrujj*)
clarified butter (*samn*)	snake cucumbers (*qiththā'*)
fowl	
goat	
dried fruits	
onions	
celery	
parsley	
hot pastries (*ma'ājīn*)	
walnuts	
almonds	
pistachios	
hazelnuts	

Shubāṭ (February)

temperate foods	
sour grapes	
sumac	
sweets	

Recommended Foods	Foods to be Avoided
game, including sandgrouse (*qaṭā*)	
honey	
cumin	
***Ādhār* (March)**	
mild food	food producing blood in body
sour food	salty food
sumac	fatty meat
lentils	game
vinegar	garlic
sweet drinks	Chinese chive
***Nīsān* (April)**	
cold and wet foods	sweets
food that calms the blood	fruit drinks
sour food	tamarind
vinegar	bananas
goat, sheep, fowl	spicy food
	onions
	garlic
	Chinese chive
***Ayyār* (May)**	
cold and mild foods	hot and dry foods
goat, suckling lamb, fowl	salty food
fish	
sour milk	
snake cucumbers (*qiththā'*)	
***Ḥazīrān* (June)**	
cold and wet foods	spicy food
fresh fish	honey
fresh and sour milk	garlic
lettuce	onions
endive	Chinese chive
cucumbers (*khiyār*)	
grapes	
dates	

Recommended Foods	Foods to be Avoided
plums	
bananas	
peaches	
lemons	
sour pomegranates	
Tammūz (July)	
cold fruits	hot and spicy food
sour apples	gourds (*qar'*)
quince	
sour pomegranates	
plums	
Āb (August)	
hot and cold, sweet, and sour foods[11]	hot and dry foods
mild food	spicy food
fatty meats	some pulses
oily food	
Aylūl (September)	
hot and wet foods	cold and dry foods
lamb, goat, and fowl	salty food
	spicy food
	sour food
	things that constipate
	beef

Much of this advice would have been irrelevant to farmers in Yemen at this time. However, since a number of the recommendations in the herbals are based on practical experience, certain aspects of the "scientific" diet may have been present in the folk tradition. The population subsisted primarily on sorghum, supplemented by millet grain in the coastal zone and wheat and barley in the mountains. A few fruits were available in season, especially melons and grapes. In rural Yemen few green vegetables were grown or eaten, the main ones in recent history being Chinese chive, onion, and long white radish (*fijl*). Pulses were an important part of the diet. It is not clear if fenugreek (*ḥulba*) was as important in the diet during the Rasulid period as it is today in Yemen. Ceretainly milk products would have been important domestic foods as well as part of the local trading network.

SEX

Health and hygiene also include sexual activity, both in marriage and in the case of concubines for the court. Sex was a form of preventive medicine in and of itself and was considered a cure for certain illnesses, including madness (al-Anṭākī 1951:2:70). Al-Malik al-Ashraf said that sexual desire (*shahwat al-bāh*) was aroused at VI:7. This is a common reference in the almanacs, given as VI:9 (15 *Ba'ūna*) by al-Qalqashandī in his Coptic almanac. However, sex should be avoided during the intense heat of summer. The almanac of al-Bīrūnī cautions against coitus at VII:25 because of the heat. The idea that sex during the hottest part of summer could be injurious to bodily health was expressed by the Prophet Muḥammad. This was quite an ancient concept, reported even as early as the time of Hesiod (1973:77), who said of the midsummer rising of Sirius:

> Women are full of lust, but men are weak
> Their heads and limbs drained dry by Sirius.

According to Abū al-'Uqūl, sex is recommended in Tishrīn al-Awwal (X), *Tishrīn al-Thānī* (XI), and *Kānūn al-Awwal* (XII). However, al-Bīrūnī at XII:11 claimed that copulation was not appropriate in autumn or at the beginning of winter because of the presence of infectious diseases. The Rasulid almanac *Mīqāt* notes that sex is favorable in *Kānūn al-Thānī* (I), *Nīsān* (IV), *Āb* (VIII), and *Tishrīn al-Awwal* (X), but cautions against it in *Ayyār* (V) and *Ḥazīrān* (VI). Abū al-'Uqūl said sex should be avoided or decreased during *Nīsān* (IV), *Ḥazīrān* (VI), *Tammūz* (VII), and *Āb* (VIII).

The changing seasons were not, of course, the primary reasons for choosing to have or not have sex.[12] After saying one should not make love on XII:11, al-Bīrūnī explained that the conditions of sexual intercourse depend on a variety of factors, including age, time of day, place, custom, physical characteristics of the body, diet, desire, the readiness of female genitals, and so on. In the medicinal lore attributed to the Prophet Muḥammad these conditions are amplified in detail. Sex with an old woman (*'ajūz*) or a maiden before puberty was not advised, apart from the issue of social sanctions. Some scholars recommended sex on Thursdays and Fridays, both regarded as propitious days for conception. The best time for lovemaking was after food had been properly digested and the individual was not too exhausted.[13] It was not wise to drink hot water after the heat of sex, nor was it considered a healthy activity in the *ḥammām* (al-Damīrī n.d.:2:125; Ibn Jawzī 1987:26). For those familiar with astrology, it was important to look at the zodiacal signs, planets, and lunar stations. It is doubtful whether the pedantic musings of medieval scholars reflected the practices of the common man and woman in Yemen. However, there were certainly folk customs, especially where there was contact with foreign traders.

The medieval herbals are replete with concoctions said to have aphrodisiacal qualities. Indeed, in reading through an herbal it often appears that every other plant seems to have some function related to sex. For example, al-Dhahabī (1404/1984:36,49) remarked in his account of *al-ṭibb al-nabawī* that citron (*utrujj*) and carrot (*jazar*) were aphrodisiacs. The carrot is not an unusual choice, since its phallic resemblance led to its symbolic power in a number of societies. Not all the recipes were vegetable in origin. Wild fowl were considered to aid the lover, especially the wild pigeon. Ibn al-Wardī (1939:199) claimed that a cow's horn, burnt to an ash and mixed in a drink, aroused sexual desire. Al-Damīrī (1906:1:33) said that both camel flesh and camel urine were aphrodisiacal, the latter perhaps more effective if undisclosed to the recipient. Aphrodisiacs were sometimes said to be gender specific, as in the case of henna being an enticement for men (al-Suyūṭī in Elgood 1962:60). Other remedies were claimed for reducing sexual desire and for aborting children (see al-Nuwayrī 1937:12:132-216).

The geographer al-Muqaddasī (1989:157) reflected a common belief in the medieval period that adultery was "overpracticed" at the cosmopolitan port of Aden. If Ibn al-Mujāwir is to be believed, some of those attending the *sabt al-subūt* celebration at the start of summer's heat were not very concerned about the advice laid down in the almanacs about the suitable times for sexual activities. Ibn al-Mujāwir was particularly intrigued by the sexual customs he encountered in his travels. He noted that the long white radish (*fijl*) was forbidden to be sold whole in Ṣan'ā'. It was sold quartered so that women could not use it as a dildo (Ibn al-Mujāwir 1954:186). One of his more unusual bits of erotica was that of the people at Jabal Kudummul in the northern Tihāma. Rex Smith (1989:119–20) has provided a translation, which reads as follows:

> From the time she reaches puberty until she gets married, they do not allow the girl to remove [her pubic hair]. Rather the hair grows longer and longer as time goes on. She allows it to grow until she [is able to] plait it into a tress (*dabbuqah*). It is said that it, that is the hair, is greased and combed and washed with *sidr* and earth. On her wedding night she plaits her hair in two, each tress being let down (*yusdalu*) on to each of her thighs. She is then displayed to her husband. When he is in private with her and has assumed a man's [normal] position [for intercourse], he then grasps these two plaits and pulls them out by the roots. When he has removed them, he deflowers her. The next morning her female relatives visit her, each bringing a plate of butter. They say to her, "How's it going with your beard (*zubbah*)?!" To which she replies, "Fine, like the seller of the pumpkin (*dubbah*)!" [Each relative] anoints the place with butter

to remove the pain, since [her husband] has pulled out skin along with the hair.

Sexually transmitted diseases appear to have been unknown in the medieval Arab sources. The famous herbalist Shaykh Dāwūd al-Anṭākī stated that syphilis first appeared in Arabia in 807/1404–5, but Serjeant (1965:241) thinks it did not commence until almost a hundred years later. A Ḥaḍramī chronicle refers to a disease called "Persian Fire" for the year 909/1503–4. It is known that some of the Mamlūk troops sent to counter the Portuguese presence in the Red Sea in 921/1515–16 complained of the so-called Frankish chancre (*al-ḥabb al-Ifranjī*). By the seventeenth century Yemeni jurists were issuing statements about the impact of syphilis on marriage contracts.

Chapter 7

Navigation

GENERAL

The Rasulid almanacs provide extensive details on sailing seasons between East and West in the Indian Ocean and Red Sea.[1] The biographical sources are silent as to whether or not al-Malik al-Ashraf ever traveled by sea. His father went by ship for the pilgrimage to Mecca in 659/1261. In 677/1278 his father outfitted a military expedition to subdue Dhofar on the southern Yemeni coast (Smith 1988:29–31).

During the medieval period Aden was one of the primary stopping points along the sea route between India and Africa. Consequently most of the Arab geographers and travelers paid a great deal of attention to it. The two main Arab travelers who visited and described Aden just before and during the Rasulid period were Ibn al-Mujāwir and Ibn Baṭṭūṭa. The famed merchant of Venice, Marco Polo, also came near in A.D. 1295, but he did not actually visit Aden. These are the main sources for information about navigation in the Indian Ocean and around the coast of Yemen until the informative navigational poems and treatise of Ibn Mājid (1971) written in the last half of the fifteenth century A.D.[2] Similar navigational texts no doubt existed in the Rasulid period, since Marco Polo (1958:303) mentioned "the maps and writings of the practised seamen who ply in these waters." Information on sailing in this region is also provided in the later texts of Sulaymān al-Mahrī (1925; Khūrī 1970) and Sidi Çelebi (Hammer-Purgstall 1834–39; Bittner and Tomaschek 1897). In the fifteenth century the Ming dynasty in China sponsored a trade expedition which called at the port of Aden (Ma Huan 1970) and there is a brief description of the visit.

Before the coming of the Portuguese into the Indian Ocean in A.D. 1498, the ships of the region were primarily variations of the so-called Arab dhow, probably not too dissimilar from the contemporary Kuwaiti *būm* (Tibbetts 1971:49).[3] The dhow was characterized by a long stern and sharp bow, which allowed it to run well with the wind. One of the unique features of the dhow was the triangular lateen sail, which gave it great maneuverability in the wind. The larger ships had two masts. During the Rasulid period ships were constructed entirely of wood, primarily Indian teak (*sāj*) and coconut, and stitched with palm fiber. The ships in the Indian Ocean were caulked and daubed with fish oil, mostly shark (*qirsh*) or whale, or clarified butter (*samn*) rather than pitch. As a result there was much damage to the hull from barnacles and other sea life and the ships had to be beached frequently for cleaning.

There is a legend, recorded by al-Idrīsī (1970:1:50), that no ships with iron nails (*al-marākib al-musammara bi-al-ḥadīd*) could pass through the straits of Bāb al-Mandab into the Red Sea, because there was a magnetic mountain there which would attract all the nails and thus cause the ship to sink. This legend was no doubt inspired during the fervor of the Crusades. There was, in fact, good reason to fear the coming of European ships even during the Rasulid period, since Guillaume Adam proposed in the fourteenth century A.D. that Crusader ships blockade the entrance to the Red Sea and cut off the sea trade from India to Egypt.

The ships were adequate for long-distance trade, but considerable destruction at sea made commerce here a rather hazardous undertaking. After commenting on how fragile the ships were at Aden, Hormuz, and Qays, Marco Polo (1958:308) remarked that "if the sea there were as rough and boisterous as in our part and as often wrecked by storms, not a vessel would ever complete her voyage without suffering shipwreck." Thus, it is understandable why so much attention was paid to the proper seasons for sailing so as to avoid those times when winds were contrary or the sea was likely to be rough due to monsoon storms. This also explains why it was important to have safe harbors along the sea route for protection from inclement weather in and out of season.

Different styles of ships served several purposes among the ports and coastal villages of the Indian Ocean and African coast. The almanac simply uses the generic terms *markab* and *safīna*. One of the common terms for the boats that sailed to Aden from the Red Sea was *jalba* (*jilāb*, plural), as noted by Ibn Baṭṭūṭa (1962:361) and Ibn Jubayr (1984). It is important to note that by the beginning of the Rasulid period, in the thirteenth century A.D., the carrack had already appeared in the Mediterranean and would soon develop into the basic oceangoing ship of western Europe. This would have a major impact on the sea trade with the eventual arrival of Portuguese galleons at the end of the fifteenth century.

There were two basic ways of sailing in the Indian Ocean. One was to sail in sight of land during the day; this was called *dīrat al-mūl* by Ibn Mājid. The second was an unfettered course using fixed bearings, referred to as *dīrat al-*

maṭlaq. Coordinates for sailing at night, especially when out of sight of land, were based on the altitudes of certain stars, primarily the northern circumpolar stars. The local method described in some detail by Ibn Mājid was based on the *ṭirfa*, defined as the distance traveled on a fixed bearing to raise the latitude by one *iṣba'* (literally, "finger") unit. This was about the length of a day's sailing. The method was similar to the later European use of "raising the Pole" (Tibbetts 1971:299).

As early as the tenth century A.D., navigators in the Red Sea and Indian Ocean had defined a star compass of thirty-two rhumbs, based on the rising and setting points of sixteen stars.[4] This star compass, as defined by Ibn Mājid, is identified below. The direction indicated by the rising point (*maṭla'*) of the star is shown to the left, and the direction of the setting (*mughīb*) is shown to the right:

Rising		Setting
N	*jāh* (Polaris)	N
N by E	*farqadān* (β γ Ursae Minoris)	N by W
NNE	*na'sh* (α β γ δ ε ζ η Ursae Majoris)	NNW
NE by N	*nāqa* (parts of Cassiopeia and Andromeda)	NW by N
NE	*'ayyūq* (Capella)	NW
NE by E	*al-nasr al-wāqi'* (Vega)	NW by W
ENE	*simāk* (Arcturus)	WNW
E by N	*thurayyā* (Pleiades)	W by N
E	*al-nasr al-ṭā'ir* (Altair)	W
E by S	*jawzā'* (Orion's belt)	W by S
ESE	*tīr* (Sirius)	WSW
SE by E	*iklīl* (β δ π Scorpii)	SW by W
SE	*'aqrab* (Antares)	SW
SE by S	*ḥimārān* (α β Centauri)	SW by S
SSE	*suhayl* (Canopus)	SSW
S by E	*sulbār* (Achernar)	S by W
S	*quṭb suhayl* (Canopus as Pole)	S

The magnetic compass, or lodestone, was not widely used in the Rasulid period, based on the available textual evidence, but it was known in the Persian Gulf as early as A.D. 1232, when it was mentioned in a Persian text (Tibbetts 1971:290). Ibn Mājid (Tibbetts 1971:75) claimed it was invented by King David of old, Alexander the Great, or the Quranic legendary al-Khiḍr, thought to be a servant of Moses.

In addition to the threat of natural disaster, an ever-present danger during the year, ships sailing in the region sometimes had to contend with pirates and inhospitable tribesmen along the coast. Marco Polo (1958:292, 298) warned about the threat of pirates off the island of Socotra and on parts of the Indian coastline. The Persian Gulf, especially around the Musandam Peninsula of Oman, was apparently a haven for corsairs even in the medieval period (Ibn Mājid in Tibbetts 1971:213), which was a strong incentive for ships to sail together as commercial fleets, this being the implication of the references to distinct sailing seasons in the almanacs. Ships sailing alone and outside the main season did so at risk.

The travelers and Ibn Mājid provide clues as to the makeup of the crew on a sailing ship in the Rasulid period. The owner of the ship was called the *nākhūdhā*.[5] The captain of the ship was the *rubbān* (Ibn Baṭṭūṭa 1980:245; Ibn Jubayr 1984:50). In addition to being knowledgeable of the sea and practical astronomy, the captain also had to be a leader and skilful in dealing with port and customs officials. The other skilled position on board was the pilot or navigator (*mu'allim*), who was usually in charge of fitting the ship and putting the crew together. Ibn Mājid (Tibbetts 1971:77) advised that the pilot be "a patient man in time of fatigue and capable of distinguishing between movement and haste, knowledgeable and learned in many things, steady and constant, gentle in his speech, just, never complaining of one man before another, steadfastly obeying his Lord, and fearing God."

THE PORT OF ADEN

The site of Aden was a major port even in the pre-Islamic period when a fair was held here at the end of the lunar-solar month of *Sha'bān*. It had a well-protected harbor and easily defended city. This was a more or less mandatory stop along the major east-west and south-north trade routes by sea. Ibn Faḍl Allāh al-'Umarī (1985:157) claimed that a week did not go by without merchant ships calling at Aden. Ibn al-Mujāwir (1954:144) claimed that seventy or eighty ships put into Aden each year, but this figure seems low. A later source indicates that there were about forty ships present in Aden harbor in 1513 when the Portuguese attacked (Serjeant 1974c:47). In the Rasulid period it must have been a large town with a cosmopolitan population including Indians and Africans, as documented for later periods. It is doubtful that the population in A.D. 1295 was 80,000, as claimed rather fancifully by Marco Polo. But there is no reason to doubt that Aden was not the largest city in southern Yemen.

Aden was, in fact, the jewel in the tax-driven crown of Rasulid rule in Yemen. As Marco Polo (1958:308) put it, "I assure you that the sultan of Aden derives a very large revenue from the heavy duties he levies from the merchants coming and going in his country. Indeed, thanks to these, he is one of the richest rulers in the world." According to Ibn al-Mujāwir (1954:144), there were four major shipments of revenues each year from Aden to Ta'izz for the royal court. These coincided with the first arrival of the Indian ships, the entry of the madder (*fuwwa*) crop in Aden, the export of horses to India, and the return sailing of ships for India. Each shipment was estimated at about 150,000 dinars in 625/1228. Ibn Baṭṭūṭa (1962:372) described the merchants here as being very wealthy, so much so that some of them owned their own ships. There were also Indian (Bāniyān) and East African merchants or trading agents resident in Aden.

The Rasulids developed an elaborate administrative structure to coordinate the customs activities of Aden, as described in detail in *Shāmil* and *Mulakhkhaṣ al-fitan* (see Serjeant 1974b:211–13). Virtually all products from India and Iraq were taxed. Among the specific items discussed in the *Mulakhkhaṣ al-fitan* (fol. 17v) were perfumes, slaves, aromatic wood, amber, camphor, and musk. There was also a "protection" tax (*shawānī*) that ships had to pay because of the presence of guard ships outside the harbor to keep pirates away from the shipping lanes. Ludovico di Varthema (1928:27), speaking of Aden less than a century after the Rasulid period, said: "As soon as a ship comes into port, the officers of the Sultan of the said city board it, and desire to know whence it left its own country, and how many persons there are on board." He added that the customs officials took the precaution of taking a ship's masts and sails ashore to ensure the proper customs would be paid. Vessels trading at the port usually sought the services of a broker (*dallāl*), whose fee was regulated by the Rasulid state.

Commerce was the raison d'être of life in Aden. According to the historian al-'Umarī (1974:51), Yemen had to import a great deal of materials from Egypt and Syria. The products that passed through here were imported from as far away as China and Madagascar. A Chinese trading expedition in Aden during the mid-fifteenth century brought precious stones, large pearls, coral, golden amber, rose water, and exotic animals (Ma Huan 1970:154). From the East, according to al-Idrīsī (1970:1:54) the trade goods included silk, cotton cloth, ivory, pearls, mother-of-pearl, iron swords, saddles, lead, ebony, incense, musk, camphor, cloves, nutmeg, cinnamon, cardamom, pepper, coconuts, bamboo, and various other plants. From Africa the most important trade items were ivory, rhinoceros horn, animal hides, slaves, ambergris, lumber, clothing, gold, turtles, and other rare species. Yemen also exported goods, especially agricultural products and live animals. At the close of the ninth century A.D. Ibn Khurradādhbih (1889:71) noted that Yemen's commercial products included various types of clothing, amber, the yellow dye *wars*, mules, and donkeys. Ibn Jubayr (1984:110) noted that Mecca received grains, clarified butter (*samn*), raisins, almonds, and fruits from Yemen. No doubt considerable commercial fishing was based in Aden and the small villages on the southern coast of Yemen.

NAVIGATION

SAILING SEASONS

Although sailing was theoretically possible along the coast at almost any time of the year, there were certain well-defined sailing seasons between major ports according to the direction of the dominating winds and turbulence of the sea. Al-Malik al-Ashraf said in his almanac that the sea is locked up (*yanghaliqu*) and unsafe for shipping at XI:19. Abū al-'Uqūl specified that this was a reference to the Mediterranean (al-Baḥr al-Māliḥ, which Ibn Jaḥḥāf called Baḥr al-Rūm). The date in *Fuṣūl* is XI:23, at which time violent winds were said to blow.

Reference to the closing of the Mediterranean Sea to sailing in the winter is quite common in the Arab almanacs. Abū Ḥanīfa al-Dīnawarī mentioned this at XI:25, after noting that the sea became rough at the setting of the Pleiades on XI:15. The Coptic almanac of al-Qalqashandī places the closure of the sea at XI:24 (28 *Hatūr*). The *Calendar of Cordova* refers to this closure of the Mediterranean as the gale (*naw'*) of *ḥandīs*.[6] In the early thirteenth century, Ibn Jubayr (1984:288) was caught in violent seas off the island of Crete on XI:7. According to al-Bīrūnī (1879:236) navigation was suspended from the port of Alexandria at XI:13, since "the sea has certain days when it is in uproar, when the air is turbid, the waves roll, and thick darkness lies over it." The North African Ibn al-Bannā' was slightly more poetic in noting that this was the time when the Devil (Iblīs) farts over the sea.

The almanac references were clearly taken from earlier classical sources, although the shipping seasons on the Mediterranean would have been no secret to the Rasulids with their extensive contacts in Egypt. As early as the eighth century B.C. Hesiod (1973:78) warned: "Gales of all winds rage when the Pleiades, pursued by violent Orion, plunge into the clouded sea. Then keep your ships no longer on the wine-bright sea." The Roman writer Vegetius (Casson 1971:270) placed the closing of the sea from the third day before the ides of November to the sixth day before the ides of March. Throughout the classical, early Christian, and medieval periods, the Mediterranean was basically closed to long-distance navigation from November to April. The violence of the winds and gales was far worse here than in the Indian Ocean, despite the presence of the monsoon winds in the latter. To sail on the Mediterranean during this period not only risked natural disaster but also increased the threat of piracy and thus made it more difficult to raise capital and finance the cargo.

Al-Malik al-Ashraf and *Fuṣūl* indicated that ships sail again in the western Mediterranean (al-Baḥr al-Maghrib) after IV:29 and that the whole sea is opened at V:19. This was primarily with an easterly wind. Abū Ḥanīfa al-Dīnawarī said that sailing began at the rising of the Pleiades, which he cited at V:16; this is clearly the tradition on which the second date is based. The non-Yemeni almanacs begin the period for sailing in the Mediterranean, at least from Egypt, as early as the spring equinox. Al-Maqrīzī said that ships sail in *Baramhāt* (III) to Egypt from western Europe. However, there was still turbulence on the sea, as noted by Abū Ḥanīfa al-Dīnawarī at III:27 and al-Qazwīnī at III:25.

The Rasulid almanacs record the name for a period in the spring when sailing was difficult on the Mediterranean. This is called *bakhnīṭas*, a term Arabized from the Greek (παχνιτμ) for foggy weather at sea.[7] This term was garbled in a number of earlier and later almanac texts, but with the Rasulid manuscripts the original term can now be identified. The earliest reference to the term in Arabic is in the *Calendar of Cordova*, where the Arabic is rendered *maknīṭas* and translated into Latin as *magnetis*. The next known reference occurs in the Geniza almanacs from ca. A.D. 1130–60 (Goldstein and Pingree 1979:167; 1983) as *baknīṭas* or *baknīs*. In the published edition of the thirteenth-century A.D. almanac of Ibn al-Ajdābī (1964:154), the editor renders the term mistakenly as *tajbīs* (!) and then proceeds in a lengthy and contorted footnote to justify this term as referring to violent spring rains that create clay (*jibs*), but this argument clearly does not hold water. In the almanac of Ibn al-Bannā' the term is rendered as *bakhnas* or *bakhānis*, while the anonymous Andalusian almanac (Navarro 1990:183) cites *bajānīs*. The published Coptic almanac of al-Falakī and Būz Bāshā (1893–94:64) identifies the term *takhtīṭas*, in reference to these weeks, as a Coptic religious festival. The correct form *bakhnīṭas* is indicated in a relatively recent Coptic almanac (Ṭal'at, fol. 19r) located in the Egyptian National Library.

The *Calendar of Cordova* (Dozy 1961:55) correctly indicates that this period was a time in the Greek calendar when ships did not enter the sea. Al-Malik al-Ashraf obviously had access to a reliable source, because he was able to provide a reasonably accurate rendering of the Greek into Arabic. He may have derived his information from the famous *zīj* of al-Fārisī (*al-Mumtaḥan*, fol. 5r), where the term is defined as *musabba'*, apparently in reference to the fact that it consists of seven weeks. Al-Malik al-Ashraf also referred to an extra week called *al-bakhnīṭas al-masīḥ* (the *bakhnīṭas* of the Messiah, i.e., Christ), which indicates that this time must have developed a religious significance in the Greek Church; the only other almanac to mention this extra week is that of Ibn al-Ajdābī. The timings of the Rasulid almanacs for the weeks in this period are listed on the next page:

Week	*Tabṣira*	Abū al-'Uqūl	Taymūr	*Salwa*
1	III:24	III:25	III:23	III:23
2	III:31	III:31	III:29	III:29
3	IV:7	IV:7	IV:6	IV:6
4	IV:14	IV:14	IV:15	IV:15
5	IV:21	IV:21	IV:20	IV:20
6	IV:28	IV:29	IV:30	IV:28
7	V:5	—	V:5	V:4
masīḥ	V:12			

This dating is very close to the dating in the Geniza texts and that of Ibn al-Ajdābī. The *Calendar of Cordova* and the derivative almanac of Ibn al-Bannā' and the anonymous Anadalusian almanac (Navarro 1990:178) begin these weeks at III:1. In the Greek calendar the dating is III:25–V:18 (Koukoulez 1952:5:375); al-Malik al-Ashraf clearly had access to an accurate source.

The almanac does not refer to the Red Sea, Persian Gulf, or Indian Ocean specifically, although the sailing times are given for some of the main ports in the region. In the medieval period the Red Sea was generally known as Baḥr al-Qulzum, so named from ancient Clysma near Suez (Becker and Beckingham 1960:931). The southern part of the Red Sea was sometimes referred to as Baḥr al-Yaman. Ibn Baṭṭūṭa (1980:245) said that ships did not travel by night on the Red Sea because of the numerous sandbars, reefs, and strong currents. The main port on the Red Sea coast during the Rasulid period was 'Aydhāb, which was linked to the Nile town of Qūs. Another port of call for ships from Rasulid Yemen was the port of Quṣayr al-Qādim, where Yemeni ceramics from the period have been found (Whitcomb 1988:186). It took about one month to sail the length of the Red Sea between Egypt and Bāb al-Mandab. The winds parallel the coasts in the Red Sea. The north wind dominates above 18° latitude. During the monsoon season from October through April the southeast (*azyab*) wind is dominant in the southern part. In addition to the ships used for commerce, especially the Kārimī merchant fleet, there was a great deal of activity on the sea during the pilgrimage period. No mention is made in the almanac of any of the Rasulid ports along the Tihāma coast, one of the most important being al-Ghulayfiqa near Zabīd.

The Gulf of Aden was known as either Baḥr al-Barbarā or Khalīj al-Barbarā in the medieval period, in reference to the African coastal area of Berbera. The predominant wind in the Gulf of Aden is northeasterly, except for a light westerly wind from June to September. The sea around Aden was closed to shipping in July and August (Serjeant 1974c:178, note Z). Baḥr al-Hind referred to the Indian Ocean near the coast of India, while Baḥr al-Fāris appears to have been used for the Persian Gulf. This latter term was often used

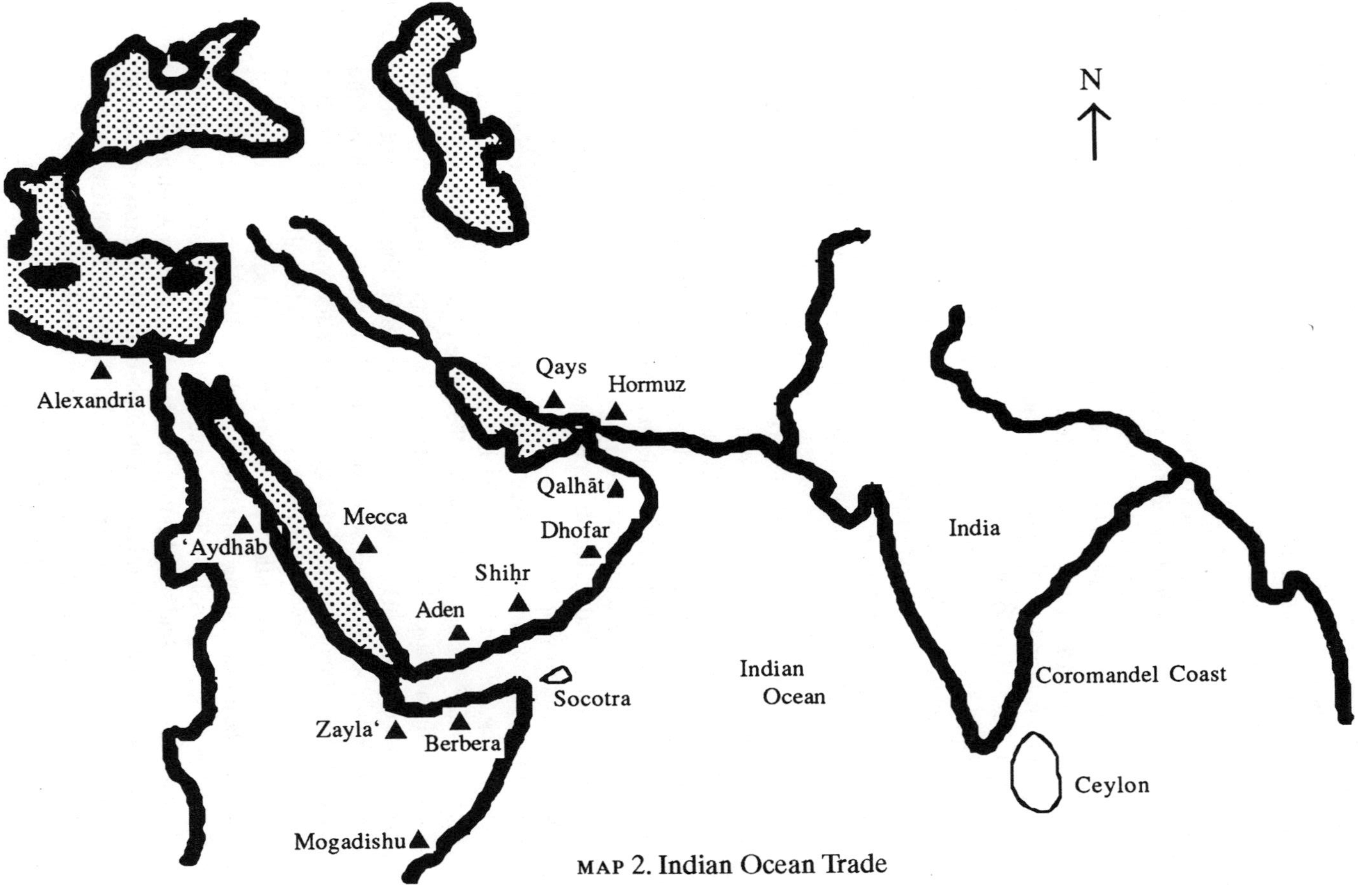

MAP 2. Indian Ocean Trade

for a greater area of the Indian Ocean. Al-Mas'ūdī (1982:1:127) claimed that travel was difficult on Baḥr al-Fāris between mid-August, when the sun entered Virgo, and mid-February, when the sun entered Pisces. This is apparently in reference to the autumn monsoon, which was in fact the major sailing period west. Al-Qazwīnī referred to rough seas on Baḥr al-Fāris at XI:13. Al-Malik al-Ashraf mentioned violent sea winds (*'awāṣif*) at II:23, apparently in reference to the Indian Ocean.

Every port along the Indian Ocean had three basic seasons. The first was when ships sailed from the port on a defined wind; the second, when the ships returned from a foreign voyage; and the third, when the port was closed due to rough seas or lack of wind. A port that was closed (*ghalq*) might still receive ships, but the home fleet would be beached for repair and cleaning. The sailing season was labeled *mawsim*, or *mūsim*, a term used in pre-Islamic Arabia to refer to the period of pilgrimage or time for a regional trade fair (*sūq*). In modern usage *mawsim* is used for the monsoon. The almanac defines the main sailing seasons and a number of specific periods when fleets set out for a specific port. Several ships would set sail together for protection, including the danger of pirates. The main season (*al-mawsim al-kabīr*) is used in the almanac for the major southwest monsoon that dominated travel in the Gulf of Aden and Indian Ocean at the start of autumn. This monsoon strikes earlier in the south and lasts longer. The main season began on VIII:21 (day 230 of the *nayrūz* calendar at the time of al-Malik al-Ashraf) and ended at IX:13 (about day 250 of the *nayrūz* calendar). This was the season for most travel from Aden to India. The author equated it with the *tīrmāh* sailing at the end of the southwest monsoon.

The first part of any major sailing season was often called "First of the Season" (*awwal al-zamān*) and the last part was known as "Last of the Season" (*ākhir al-zamān*), paralleling the usage of *ākhir al-waqt* in North Africa for the month of *Aylūl* (IX) in the Geniza letters (Goitein 1967:1:482) in reference to sailing at the end of the business season. Thus, the First of the Season for the southwest monsoon would have begun in the autumn, and the Last of the Season in spring. Ibn Mājid used a parallel expression of the first and last parts of the *kaws* wind for this monsoon. In fact, the usage of First of the Season and Last of the Season is relative to a particular season. For example, the *dīmānī* sailing from Aden to India at III:26 is called First of the Season by al-Malik al-Ashraf. This is actually in reference to the return of the *dīmānī* ships which had sailed at the First of the Season from Aden in *Tishrīn al-Awwal* (X). The ships still arriving in India from Aden at this time would in fact be Last of the Season, as noted by Abū al-'Uqūl in his reference to the Last of the Season when the sun was in Taurus in mid-April.

NAVIGATION

The Rasulid almanacs mention seventeen specific sailing periods. The term *safar* is usually used for the departure of the fleet or group of ships bound for a particular port or region. Each of the sailings referred to in the almanac is discussed below:

Barbarī. Al-Malik al-Ashraf and Abū al-'Uqūl noted the sailing from Aden for Berbera (Barbara), which is now Bandar 'Abbās on the Somali coast, at IX:13. This would have been on the north wind before the blowing of the south or southeast wind in October. The nineteenth-century traveler Osgood (1854:157) noted that this African coastal town teemed with people from October through March, when the ships came and went, but otherwise was virtually empty. Ibn Mājid and Sulaymān al-Mahrī placed this sailing during *Āb* (VIII). Ibn Mājid (1971:110) said that Yemeni boats sailed for Berbera when they saw Altair and Vega at midheaven. Ibn Baṭṭūṭa (1980:252) observed that the trip from Aden to Berbera took about four days. The Rasulid texts may also have in mind a stop at Socotra on the way to Bandar 'Abbās, because this island was sometimes called Barbara. The island of Socotra was famous for its local varieties of aloe (*ṣabr*),[8] which was collected in July, dried in August, and then marketed (al-Idrīsī 1970:1:50), and dragon's blood (*dam al-akhwayn*),[9] also an important medicant. In 890/1485 a large typhoon hit the island of Barbara and twenty-six ships in port sank (Ibn al-Dayba' 1983:197).

Dīmānī. The term *dīmānī* or *dāmānī* was generally used for the southwest wind or monsoon.[10] The ships of this *dīmānī* sailing went to India from Aden between III:22 and III:26, at IV:17, and at V:6 (day 120 of the *nayrūz* calendar), according to the almanac. Abū al-'Uqūl mentioned the departure from Aden at III:22, while Ibn Jaḥḥāf and al-Thābitī gave this as III:21. *Fuṣūl* marks the last of this sailing at IV:5 and *Ma'rifa* records the sailing at IV:23. According to *Salwa*, the *dīmānī* ships leave Aden up to IV:17 (6° Taurus).[11] According to al-Malik al-Ashraf the return sailing from India was at X:16 as First of the Season. This is in reference to the northeast monsoon beginning at that time. Al-Malik al-Ashraf added that the *dīmānī* ships reach Aden between XI:1 (day 300 in the *nayrūz* calendar) and XII:21 (day 350). The *dīmānī* sailing in the Rasulid sources differs from that given in the later works of Ibn Mājid and Sulaymān al-Mahrī, who cited *dāmānī* for the sailing from Aden to India in late August after the main season of *kaws* (Tibbetts 1971:367).

Hindī. A distinction is made in the almanac between the generic Indian (Hindī) sailing and specific fleets such as the *dīmānī* and *tīrmāh*. The term

Hindī was used primarily for the western coast of India, since the eastern coast figures in the Ṣūliyān sailing. Travel from Aden to Calcutta took about one month in the early fifteenth century (Ma Huan 1970:154). The Malabar coast was very dangerous from May to September because of the local strength of the monsoon. The main sailing period from India to Aden was with the northeast monsoon, which begins in early October in Bengal and reaches Zanzibar on the African coast at the end of November. This was called First of the Season and began on X:16, according to al-Malik al-Ashraf. Al-Malik al-Afḍal in the *Bughya* (fol. 19r) said that ships from India and China came to Aden during *Tishrīn al-Awwal* (X) on the *azyab* wind blowing south from the northeast. *Fuṣūl* and *Salwa* record the sailing from India for Aden at X:17 (3° Scorpius). The First of the Season ships reached Aden from XI:6 until 21 (day 320 of the *nayrūz* calendar) according to the almanac.

The later sailing continues until III:8–16 as Last of the Season, according to al-Malik al-Ashraf. Abū al-'Uqūl cited the date of III:8 as Last of the Season. The Last of the Season ships arrive in Aden at IV:15 (day 100 of the *nayrūz* calendar), according to the almanac and *Fuṣūl*. *Salwa* notes that Indian ships reached Aden until VI:28 (13° Cancer). Ibn Jaḥḥāf and al-Thābitī dated the last arrival to between IV:10 and VI:4.

The Indian fleet returned to India from Aden in late summer with the start of the southwest monsoon. *Fuṣūl* indicates the first departure from Aden at VIII:18 or VIII:26 on the north wind, with the last departure at IX:2–13. Al-Malik al-Ashraf said the last departure from Aden was between IX:6 and IX:13, and the first sailing from Dhofar was at IX:6. Ibn Jaḥḥāf and al-Thābitī noted that the Indian boats left Aden at V:6 and at VIII:18 in reference to the two stages of the southwest monsoon. The first part of the southwest monsoon was referred to as *dīmānī* in the Rasulid sources. Ibn Mājid said that ships left Aden for India when Altair and Vega were at midheaven. The specific products arriving at Aden on these Indian ships are listed by Ibn al-Mujāwir (1954:142-43).

Hurmuzī. Hormuz was the major port on the Persian coast in the medieval period. At the time of the almanac the site of Hormuz was on the mainland. The city of New Hormuz was founded just after A.D. 1300 on the island of Jarūn; it was this city that Ibn Baṭṭūṭa visited. Marco Polo (1958:61) wrote that "merchants come here by ship from India, bringing all sorts of spices and precious stones and pearls and clothes of silk and of gold and elephant's tusks and many other wares." Horses were important as a trade item in Hormuz. Ibn Baṭṭūṭa (1962:400) reported that the people here made ornamental vessels and lamp stands from a local type of salt.

The ships bound for Hormuz left Aden between V:6 and VI:5 as First of the Season. Abū al-'Uqūl recorded this departure at VI:3. Ibn Mājid noted that the sailing from Aden to Hormuz was in early VI at the end of what he termed the first *kaws* season. There was another sailing from Aden at IX:3 as Last of the Season, according to the almanac, and IX:13, according to Abū al-'Uqūl. The arrival of ships from Hormuz at Aden was at XII:11, according to al-Malik al-Ashraf. Ibn Mājid recorded the sailing from Hormuz to Aden primarily between XI and I for the coastal route.

Kārim/Kārimī. The Kārimī merchants of Egypt were very important during the twelfth to fifteenth centuries in the Ayyubid and Mamluk periods (Ashtor 1983:270; Fischel 1937; Labib 1975).[12] The Rasulid sultans held the Kārimī merchants in great esteem as international bankers and as liaison to the sultans in Egypt. For example, in 688/1289 several Kārimī merchants were invited to a banquet at the Rasulid court (al-Khazrajī 1906:1:261). Among the major items traded by them were spices, pepper, sugar, wheat, rice, cloth, weapons, precious stones, and slaves. In later Yemeni almanac copies the word Kārimī is usually garbled, often by adding a *mīm* in front. Al-Malik al-Ashraf said they left Egypt for Aden at VI:30. Abū al-'Uqūl also recorded VI:30, but *Fuṣūl* reads VI:29. *Salwa* mentions the Kārimī at VII:3 (18° Cancer), apparently in reference to their arrival in Aden. Ibn Jaḥḥāf and al-Thābitī mentioned the arrival in Aden at VII:13. The fleet sailed as *ṣā'iḥ* from X:16 until XI:21. Although a much later source, al-Thābitī said the Kārimī returned to Egypt at IX:1.

Maqdashī. After the expulsion of the Banī Mājid in 554/1159 from Yemen to Mogadishu, Zayla', and Dhofar (Trimingham 1975), the East African port of Mogadishu became one of the most important trading partners for Aden. Serjeant (1972:10) has noted that the references in the Yemeni almanacs are probably to shipping from the whole Swahili coast via Mogadishu rather than just ships from the port itself. According to Ibn al-Mujāwir (1954:117), there was a sailing from Aden to Mogadishu, then from there to Kilwa, and finally down to Madagascar (Qumar). The principal exports from Mogadishu included cinnamon, tortoiseshell, and slaves (Cerulli and Freeman-Grenville 1986:128), but it was also known for its camels and sheep. The ships left Mogadishu for Aden at IX:25 (9° Libra) according to *Salwa* and Taymūr. The date was recorded as IX:26 in the almanacs of Ibn Jaḥḥāf and al-Thābitī. Ibn Mājid placed the sailing from Mogadishu at the end of September. The voyage from Mogadishu to Aden took about twenty days via Zayla', according to Ibn Baṭṭūṭa (1980:253). Al-Malik al-Ashraf noted the arrival of these ships in Aden at X:13 (day 280 of the *nayrūz* calendar). This was given as X:8 in *Fuṣūl*. *Salwa* and Taymūr record the arrival at XII:29 (17° Capricornus).

Ibn Jaḥḥāf and al-Thābitī placed the arrival of Mogadishi boats in Aden at X:10, XI:23, and XII:31. According to *Ma'rifa*, there was a sailing to al-Shiḥr from Mogadishu at III:15. Sulaymān al-Mahrī recorded this sailing to al-Shiḥr at the end of IV.

The almanac mentions the departure of ships from Aden for Mogadishu at VI:4, VI:6, XI:22, and XII:16. Abū al-'Uqūl noted the departures at VI:4 and XII:17, while *Fuṣūl* reads VI:5 and XII:16. The dates in *Salwa* are VI:5 (22° Gemini) and XI:14 (30° Scorpius). The sailing is at VI:7 in the reckoning of *Ma'rifa* and at VI:6 according to Taymūr, Ibn Jaḥḥāf, and al-Thābitī; the latter two sources also record a sailing from Aden at VIII:4.

Maṣrī. There are several references in the almanac to the sailing periods between Aden and Egypt. All of this concerns travel on the Red Sea, with no specific mention by al-Malik al-Ashraf of sailing on the Nile or from Alexandria in the Mediterranean. Abū al-'Uqūl said ships sailed from Alexandria at IX:29. According to the Geniza documents (Goitein 1967:316), ships did not sail from Egypt on the Mediterranean from November to March.

Because of the strength of the north wind, ships could sail south and reach the Gulf of Aden only between May and September. Al Malik al-Ashraf said the first ships from Egypt arrived in Aden between IV:15 and V:6, whereas the last Egyptian ships reached Aden between VII:25 and VIII:14. *Salwa* refers to the earlier arrival as Last of the Season and the later arrival as First of the Season, but the reason for this is not clear. Taymūr notes the arrival in Aden at VII:14, while Ibn Jaḥḥāf and al-Thābitī placed the arrival between IV:10 and VII:27. The Kārimī merchants arrived at the end of this season, as noted above. Ibn al-Mujāwir (1954:142) observed that among the products imported to Yemen from Egypt were wheat, flour, sugar, rice, soap, olives, olive oil, and honey.

There were two main sailings to Egypt as defined by al-Malik al-Ashraf. The main sailing period was at the end of the northeast monsoon, which turned into the southeast *azyab* in the Red Sea. This sailing was called *ṣā'iḥ* by al-Malik al-Ashraf, who said it started at X:16. *Fuṣūl* and *Salwa* place this at X:17 (3° Scorpius), while *Ma'rifa* notes it at X:15. The term *ṣā'iḥ* is not explained in the Rasulid texts. *Ma'rifa* reads this as *ṣāliḥ*, which would indicate it is the "proper" period for sailing. There was a *lāḥiq* sailing from Aden to Egypt up until IV:17, according to the almanac, Abū al-'Uqūl, and *Salwa*. *Fuṣūl* places this at IV:15 and *Ma'rifa* at IV:7. Al-Malik al-Ashraf recorded another *lāḥiq* sailing from Aden between V:6 and V:26. The origin of this term is not clear. The term literally means "attached," and in this sense the days of intercalation in the Coptic almanac are sometimes called *lawāḥiq*. According to *Salwa* and Taymūr ships sailed from Aden for 'Aydhāb at the top of the Red Sea at I:13 (2° Aquarius).

Nbṭī (?). Al-Malik al-Ashraf mentioned a sailing at IX:13 from Aden. This was for the Barbarī and Nbṭī (?) ships, although the rendering of the latter term is not clear in the manuscript and is not found in the other Rasulid texts. The context would indicate a sailing southwest to the African coast. Perhaps this is a miscopying for Baṭā or Baqāṭī on the East African coast. This is the time when ships would sail from Aden to Socotra.

Qalhātī. This was the major port commanding the entrance to the Persian Gulf. The next major port on the Arabian side of the Gulf coast was Musqat. Sailing in the Gulf was possible virtually year-round. At the time of the almanac, Qalhāt was under control of the king of Hormuz. Marco Polo (1958:311) called it a good harbor with an active trade in spices, dates, and horses. A nearby village was famed for its bananas, which were exported to Hormuz and other places. Ibn Baṭṭūṭa (1962:396) tasted the best fish he had ever tried in this town, but he was perplexed by the local dialect of Arabic.

According to the almanac, the ships of Qalhāt left Aden as First of the Season between V:16 and VI:5, whereas the Last of the Season ships left at IX:3. Abū al-'Uqūl noted the departure from Aden at VI:11, apparently referring to the end of the season. *Fuṣūl* and *Salwa* place the departure of Qalhātī boats as a *dīmānī* sailing at V:6 (23° Taurus). Ibn Mājid (1971:225) mentioned the best sailing to Qalhāt at VI:10. The almanac indicates that the ships of Qalhāt arrived in Aden between XII:11 and II:28, with the main arrival at I:9, on the winds of the northeast monsoon. *Salwa* and Taymūr recorded the arrival in Aden at I:5 (24° Capricornus).

Qaysī. Ships bound for the island of Qays left Aden between V:16 and VI:5 and again at IX:3, according to the almanac. Abū al-'Uqūl cited the sailing from Aden between V:24 and VI:23. *Fuṣūl* places the departure at V:16, but *Salwa* has V:20 (8° Gemini) and Taymūr has V:23. Those ships which left Qays in *Aylūl* arrived in Aden at XI:6 and XII:11, according to the almanac. *Fuṣūl* has XI:13, *Salwa* reads XI:23 (9° Sagittarius), and Taymūr notes XI:21.

Sayalān. The ships for Ceylon left Aden at VIII:20 along with those bound for the Coromandel coast (al-Ṣūliyān), according to the almanac and *Fuṣūl*. The date in *Salwa* is VIII:16 (1° Virgo). Among the trade items brought from Ceylon were pearls, precious stones, ivory, silk, and cinnamon (Ibn Mājid 1971:220–21). Yemeni ships sometimes stopped in Ceylon for coconut palms used in rope fiber (al-Idrīsī 1970:1:74).

Al-Shiḥr. The port of al-Shiḥr on the southern Yemeni coast was the site of an important pre-Islamic fair. This area was famous for its incense (*lubān*), which was the main reason ships put in here.[13] In addition, it was an important site for camels (Minorsky 1937:148). Marco Polo (1958:309–10) claimed that there was a 400 percent markup on incense for the merchant ships buying here. According to the *Mulakhkhaṣ al-fitan* (fol. 17v), the items taxed at al-Shiḥr included amber, camphor oil, pearls, silk, gold rings, Indian servant girls, and the wild cat (*waḥsh al-zabad*). This port has long been an important market for export of salted fish (Serjeant 1970:199). It was also the main port of emigration for Ḥaḍramī merchants who went to India and East Africa.

Al-Malik al-Ashraf said that the ships of al-Shiḥr arrived in Aden at IX:28 on the winds of the northeast monsoon. *Fuṣūl* mentions this at IX:29, whereas *Salwa* and Taymūr record IX:26 (10° Libra). The sailing to Socotra was primarily in X and XI, according to Sulaymān al-Mahri, with the return sailing to al-Shiḥr in early III. Ships left Aden for al-Shiḥr at IV:25–27, according to *Ma'rifa*. By the time of Sulaymān al-Mahrī, the Shiḥr ships left Aden in mid-June. A number of sailings from various ports to al-Shiḥr are recorded in *Ma'rifa:* from India at III:8, from Mogadishu at III:15, and from Dhofar at IV:17. It was a day's journey by sea from al-Shiḥr to the island of Socotra (al-Bīrūnī 1973:2:197).

Al-Ṣūliyān. The almanac uses this term to refer to the Coromandel coast, from Cape Camorin to the delta of the Kistna and Godavari rivers, of eastern India. Later Yemeni almanacs often garble this term as Ṣawmānī (!). The main port here would have been Ballin, from whence ships sailed on to China. Marco Polo (1958:264) said that there was a brisk trade here in horses from Yemen. Among the products available here in the medieval period were elephants, sapphires, moonstones, pearls, rubies, diamonds, onyx, emeralds, coral, cardamom, cloves, sandalwood, camphor oil, and musk (Stein 1965:51). The almanac and *Fuṣūl* place the sailing from Aden to the Coromandel coast and Ceylon at VIII:20, while in *Salwa* this is at VIII:16 (1° Virgo). The sailing from this region to Aden was at III:16, according to *Fuṣūl*.

Tīrmāh. This term is derived from a Persian month name, originally in the summer, but it was also used for a wind.[14] According to al-Malik al-Ashraf the *tīrmāh* ships sail from Aden to India at VIII:21 as First of the Season. *Salwa* and Taymūr place this at VIII:17 (2° Virgo). This usage parallels that of Ibn Mājid (Tibbetts 1971:367). The last of the *tīrmāh* ships reach Aden from India at VI:5, according to the almanac.

Ẓafārī. Ẓafār is Dhofar, the term used for the area and main town of the southern coast of Yemen bordering Oman near the entrance to the Persian Gulf. The town was captured by al-Malik al-Muẓaffar Yūsuf in A.D. 1278, not long after the almanac was originally compiled. It was especially famous for its horses (Ibn Baṭṭūṭa 1980:259; Marco Polo 1958:310; Serjeant 1974c:167, note B). The Chinese expedition of the Ming dynasty found frankincense, dragon's blood, aloe, myrrh, and even ostriches for sale at Dhofar (Ma Huan 1970:152–53). Ibn Baṭṭūṭa (1962:387) complained that the *sūq* here was full of fleas, because of the quantity of fruits and fish sold. He also noted that bananas, coconut, and betel had been brought from India and grew in the vicinity of Dhofar. The dominant wind here was usually the southwest, except during December and January (Ibn Mājid in Tibbetts 1971:226). From here it took a month or less to reach India, if winds were favorable. The overland route to Ḥaḍramawt took about sixteen days, overland to Aden took a month, and the route to Oman took twenty days.

The almanac records the sailing from Aden to Dhofar at III:23 and VIII:24. Ibn Jaḥḥāf and al-Thābitī said the departure was at IX:3. *Salwa* and Taymūr record the arrival of the first ships from Dhofar in Aden at X:25 (10° Scorpius). *Fuṣūl* has X:31 as the arrival date. The almanac and Abū al-'Uqūl noted that these ships arrived in Aden until XI:20. The ships of Dhofar sailed to the African coast from XI through I, according to Ibn Mājid. According to *Ma'rifa*, ships from Dhofar sailed to al-Shiḥr at IV:17.

Ziyāli'. This term is the plural of Zayla', which referred to the kingdom of Ifāt on the East African coast. The ships bound here left Aden at X:21, according to the almanac; Abū al-'Uqūl gave this as X:19. The journey from Aden to Zayla' took about four days. Ibn Baṭṭūṭa (1929:110) was not impressed by Zayla', which he described as "the dirtiest, most abominable, and most stinking town in the world." Uncharacteristically, this seasoned traveler preferred to stay on ship rather than spend a night in the town. He did, however, note that the sheep here were famed for their fat.

Notes

INTRODUCTION

1. There is no up-to-date survey of Rasulid Yemen. Smith (1969, 1978:2:83–90) discusses the origins of the dynasty and al-Ḥibshī (1980) provides a loose survey of the literature and culture during this time. A short survey by al-'Amrī (in 'Afīf et al. 1992:1:173-76) includes a chart of the dynasty. The major historical texts, which have been published, include Ibn al-Dayba' (1977, 1983), al-Janadī (1983–89), al-Khazrajī (1906–18, 1981), Tāj al-Dīn 'Abd al-Baqī (1965, 1985), 'Umāra (1976), al-'Umarī (1985), a poorly edited work attributed to Yaḥyā ibn al-Ḥusayn (1968), and an anonymous work edited by both al-Ḥibshī (1984) and Yajima (1974). The important text of Badr al-Dīn Muḥammad ibn Ḥātim, edited by Smith (1974–78), was written right around the time that al-Malik al-Ashraf 'Umar became sultan. A number of the published editions of Yemeni texts on the Rasulids are poorly edited and must be used with caution. Smith (1990:132) argues that knowledge of this era is still so incomplete "that we are nowhere near a situation in which we can even begin to contemplate a general history of the Yemen of the early and medieval periods."

2. For general information on the geography of Yemen, see Kopp (1981) and Steffen et al. (1978). A very general history of Yemen is available in Stookey (1978). The most comprehensive treatment of Yemen through the nineteenth century is the useful compilation by Grohmann (1930–34). The recent Arabic encyclopedia of Yemen ('Afīf et al. 1992) has much valuable and up-to-date information, but it is selective in the topics covered. For example, there is no article on Zabīd!

3. According to legend this mountain range was created as the backbone of the earth. The literal meaning of *sarāt* is the "back" (*ẓahr*) of something, according to *al-Muḥīṭ*. Ibn Jubayr (1984:110) quoted the Yemeni Ibn 'Alī al-Ṣayf to the effect that the Sarāt was so called because it was like the "back" (i.e., backbone) of a man.

4. There have been several studies on the tribes in Yemen. The best modern sources are Abū Ghānim (1985), Adra (1982, 1985), and Dresch (1989). For the basic Yemeni sources on tribes in the region, see al-Ḥajrī (1984), al-Hamdānī (1884–91, 1983), Luqmān (1985), and al-Maqḥafī (1985).

5. A valuable survey of the Jews of Yemen has been provided by Klein-Franke (1989). During the Rasulid period most Yemeni Jews lived in the south, especially in the areas of Ta'izz and Aden (al-Ḥibshī 1980:47).

6. I am currently preparing a history of the Arab almanac.

7. In modern published almanacs the common terms are either *taqwīm* or *natīja*. Both refer primarily to the arrangement of the material rather than the content.

8. In a pioneering study of almanac lore in North Africa, Bourdieu (1977:98) has argued that the writing down of an oral calendar necessarily alters its purpose. Inconsistencies appear in a written form that are not regarded as problematic in the oral tradition.

9. Information about the Nile and Egyptian agriculture is found in almost all medieval Arab almanacs. Much of this was no doubt derived from earlier Coptic almanac sources, although the impact of the Coptic tradition on the formation of the almanac genre in Arab science has not yet been analyzed.

10. This text has been edited, albeit with numerous errors, by Muḥammad al-Akwaʻ (1981) based on a manuscript in the Gharbīya library of the Great Mosque in Ṣanʻāʼ.

11. For manuscript copies of this almanac poem, see King (1983a:22).

12. For manuscript copies of this almanac poem, see King (1983a:36).

13. Abū al-ʻUqūl also composed an excellent poem on Arabic terminology; this is located in ms. *majāmīʻ* 193, fols. 75v–103r, of the Gharbīya library of the Great Mosque in Ṣanʻāʼ. This poem was dedicated to al-Malik al-Muẓaffar and was probably written shortly before the sultan's death.

14. This mixed Rasulid manuscript will be published in facsimile by Varisco and Smith for the Gibb Memorial Trust. The zodiacal almanac will be published by Varisco and King (forthcoming).

15. For the available biographical information on the author, the best sources are the texts of al-Khazrajī (1913:4:284–98, 1981:276; *ʻAqd*, 2:65v–66r), al-Waṭyūṭ (fol. 43r), and Bā Makhrama (in Löfgren 1950:181–83).

16. A discussion of the architectural works sponsored by al-Malik al-Muẓaffar is given by I. al-Akwaʻ (1980:84–92). For some of the poetry in praise of this long-lived monarch, see al-Ḥibshī (1980:201ff.). The achievements of al-Malik al-Muẓaffar are discussed in Varisco (1993b).

17. A legend about the stormy relationship between the two royal brothers is described by Luqmān (1978:91–93).

18. Most of the work on this mosque and school was apparently done by a later al-Malik al-Ashraf. For more information, see I. al-Akwaʻ (1980:140–43), al-Ḥibshī (1980:79), and Lewcock (1983).

19. The *zīj* genre is described in detail by Kennedy (1956) and King (1975). Several important collections of astronomical tables were compiled in the Rasulid period, most notably the *Mumtaḥan* of al-Fārisī. The mixed Rasulid manuscript from the library of al-Malik al-Afḍal contains excerpts from numerous Yemeni and non-Yemeni *zīj* sources.

TEXT

(Notes are arranged according to the day for which information is recorded.)

Tishrīn al-Awwal (X)

1 Later copies of Rasulid almanacs usually read *quṣaybī* as *qayḍī* (!).

8 *Bad'* is rendered as *badw* in the text, with the *wāw* indicating the *ḥamza*. This occurs elsewhere in the text.

13 The *ḥamza* is missing in *mi'atayn*.

14 *Thurayyā* is rendered *jawzā* (!) in the text. The correction is from Abū al-'Uqūl and *Fuṣūl*.

18 Abū al-'Uqūl's almanac reads *li-kathra* for *kathra*. The sun's rays would be considered weaker during a period of rain.

21 The text appears to read *mirmāk* (?), but the meaning is unclear. I tentatively interpret this as a copyist error for the *mirām* wind mentioned in *Fuṣūl* at X:17. It could also be a reference to the roughness of the sea, sometimes indicated in almanacs as *rāmis* or *rawāmis*. The preposition *min* would seem more suitable than *'alā* after *yaṣlūna*.

23 The information on the ground appears to have been copied from the Coptic tradition rather than for Yemen. Al-Maqrīzī noted the term *shaqqa* in reference to ploughing at X:9 (12 *Bābih*); Ibn Mammātī placed it in the month of *Bābih* (X).

Tishrīn al-Thānī (XI)

1 The term *rabī'* is rendered *rab'* (!) in the text.

2 The form *zubānān*, in which the final *nūn* is added, appears to be unique to the Yemeni sources.

4 *Fuṣūl* adds *fī mawāḍi'ih* (in its places) after *salwā*.

6 Al-Qaysī is Qaysī (!) in the text. *Fuṣūl* has *marākib* Qays.

9 *Shahrī* (in construct) is rendered *shahr* (!) in the text. The reference should be to two months.

12 *Makhzān* is a Yemeni variant for *makhzan* (Serjeant 1974a:62, note 24). The preposition *bihī* would seem better replaced by *fīhī*.

14 The reading after *kharīf* is problematic. For XI:15 *Fuṣūl* reads: *tatashabaku al-jānifa 'alā wajh al-arḍ*. For I:16 my reading in al-Malik al-Ashraf's almanac is *inqishā' al-jānifa 'an al-arḍ*, while in *Fuṣūl* at I:15 the reading is *infisāḥ tashbīkat al-jānifa 'an wajh al-arḍ*. The interpretation of these passages is not clear from the Rasulid sources, but it would appear to be in reference to frost on the ground. *Fuṣūl* mentioned XI:15 as the start of the frost (*ḍarīb*) in the mountains. The reference may be taken from the *anwā'* tradition, since Abū Ḥanīfa al-Dīnawarī mentioned ice on the

ground surface (*yuqa'a al-jalīd fawq al-arḍ*) at XI:15 with the setting of the Pleiades. The use of *tatashabaka* may refer to a spreading effect like a net, an appropriate image for the frost lacing the ground.

15 The term *mtsha* (?) is unclear from the text and not documented in the other sources; it is probably a local plant name. The Bughya (fol. 108r) notes that *Nigella sativa* (*al-ḥabba al-ṣawdā'*) is brought from al-Madāra, so perhaps it is in reference to this plant.

16 *Matnam* is the local dialect term for *matlam* in the coastal region. The term *kharajī* is rendered in the text without diacriticals; this is sometimes confused with *jaḥrī*, another variety of sorghum in the Tihāma.

18 *Al-Samā'* is missing in the text.

25 *Simmān* is dialectical for *sumāna*.

Kānūn al-Awwal (XII)

1 *Janā* is written in the text with an *alif maqṣūra*, a common practice in the medieval Yemeni sources.

9 The term *jaḥrī* has no diacriticals in the text.

24 The words between parentheses have been added by a different hand.

Kānūn al-Thānī (I)

6 *Bula'* is shortened from *sa'd bula'*. For Epiphany the text reads *al-ghitāsh* (!).

8 The term *ilb* is dialectical in the coastal region for *'ilb*.

9 The reading of *labakh* is tentative, since the original is smudged and unclear.

16 See the note for XI:14.

19 *Al-Dhābiḥ* is shortened from *sa'd al-dhābiḥ*.

27 The term *al-ḥmja* (?) has not been identified, but it must be a local plant name.

29–30 This discussion of the *anwa'* is not connected with an event at this time in the almanac. It seems as if the sight of *al-anwā'* in the line above prompted the author to switch to the somewhat similar sounding *al-anwā'*.

Shubāṭ (II)

6 The *ḥamza* is missing for al-Ṣābi'īn in the text.

10 The words between parentheses are written in the margin by the same hand.

13 The letter *bā'* refers to the number 2 and the letter *zā'* refers to 7. This is the *abjadīya* ordering of the Arabic alphabet for numerical documention, the common usage in astronomical tables.

14 *Al-Su'ūd* is shortened from *sa'd al-su'ūd*.

26 The words between parentheses have been added by a different hand.

Ādhār (III)

3 The text and Abū al-'Uqūl read *al-dijr*, but the correct term should be *dukhn* as in *Salwa* and Taymūr.

6 The writer did not record the name of the star.

10 The words between parentheses are written in a different hand.

12 The words between parentheses have been copied over in a different hand.

14 The original reads *al-balghamī* (!), but the reference should be to the humor of blood.

15 The letter *rā'* is missing from *ẓuhūr* in the text.

24 The almanac does not provide the diacriticals for *al-bakhnīṭas*.

30 The verb *ya'ṣaru* is miscopied by a later hand; this reading is based on the almanac of Abū al-'Uqūl.

Nīsān (IV)

3 The reference to the Pleiades is also found in the almanac of Abū al-'Uqūl. This must have been copied from an earlier non-Yemeni source, since the almanac records the setting (*naw'*) of the Pleiades at V:16. This is the general time for the disappearance of the Pleiades, as noted at IV:6.

4 This dating for Easter is inaccurate; the correct day should be IV:5 for my dating of the almanac.

14 The words in brackets complete the formula used elsewhere in the almanac.

22 Where this zenith occurred is not clear in the almanac. Abū al-'Uqūl simply mentioned this for Yemen.

24 The words between parentheses are in a different hand.

27 The rendering of *al-sharqīya* is *al-sharqī* (!) in the text.

Ayyār (V)

6 The words between parentheses are written in the margin in the same hand.

8 The verb *taghzuru* would fit the meaning better than *taghuru* (!) in the text.

11 The crop or plant name has been recopied and smudged, but it appears to be *du'bub*.

12 The first part of this line is missing; the reading between brackets is based on *Fuṣūl* at V:7.

16 The words between parentheses are written in the margin in the same hand.

21 The term *inqiḍā'* is written with an *alif maqṣūra* in the text.

31 The words between parentheses are written in a different hand. The term al-Furāt is misspelled with a *tā' marbūṭa* in the text.

Ḥazīrān (VI)

6 Note that the almanac repeats similar information found at VI:4.

8 The text reads *tawkhumu*, but this term is rendered *tawhamu/tawahhumu* in the Coptic almanacs.

9 The copyist began the information from day 10 but did not finish it.

11 For *al-mu'taḍadī* the text reads *al-'aḍadī* (!).

Tammūz (VII)

1 The term *al-muqaddam* is shortened from *al-fargh al-muqaddam.*

3 Al-Jannāt is miscopied as *al-khayrāt* (!) in the text.

16 Note that the copyist repeated information from the previous day.

21 In the original the eighth form of the verb is indicated, but this must be an error.

23 The reading of 'Arār is tentative; this place name has not been identified.

29–30 There is a lacuna in the text, as noted. The text reads *rabī'* as *rab'* (!).

31 The text has *fūl* (!) for *tūt*, but Abū al-'Uqūl and *Fuṣūl* provide the correct rendering of *tūt.*

Āb (VIII)

3 The text reads *fī awsāṭ* (!) *al-samā'.*

6 The text does not clearly identify the place, but it is apparently for Ṣan'ā'.

12 In the text *inqiḍā'* is miscopied as *ilqiḍā* (!).

14 *Arba'ūn* is rendered *arba'īn* (!) in the text.

19 The plural *al-makhālif* is rendered *al-makhālīf* in the text; this is a Yemeni variant for the plural.

20 The definite article was dropped for Sayalān in the text.

28 The term *al-akhbiya* is shortened from *sa'd al-akhbiya* .

Aylūl (IX)

9 The text reads *shamāl* for *azyab*, but the latter rendering is based on the almanac of Abū al-'Uqūl.

13 The term al-Nbṭī is uncertain. This time should be for a sailing to the African coast or Socotra.

23 The term *Al-Mu'akhkhar* is shortened from *al-fargh al-mu'akhkhar.*

24 The wording here varies from a similar usage at III:17.

CHAPTER 1. CALENDARS

1. The term "Rūm" is ultimately derived from the city of Rome, but it was used for the Byzantine Empire in the medieval period (Miquel 1975:380–81). After the Rasulid period this term was commonly applied to the Ottoman Turks, who made Constantinople their capital. In contemporary Yemeni dialect one of the local terms for maize, or Indian corn, which was introduced from the New World around the sixteenth century, is *rūmī*, no doubt in reference to a belief that the first wave of Ottoman Turks brought this crop to Yemen.

2. *Mumtaḥan*, fol. 4v. For discussion of Dhū al-Qarnayn, see Wall (1978).

3. For a concise description of the history of the Julian calendar and Gregorian reform, see Moyer (1982). Precise correlations are readily available in a number of texts, for example, Mahler and Wüstenfeld (1961) and Schram (1908).

4. The Himyaritic month names are cited in the following almanacs: al-Baḥr al-Na'āmī (M. al-Akwa' 1981), *Bughya*, Ibn Raḥīq, and Ja'far al-Ṣādiq. Beeston (1956, 1974) did the pioneering work on the South Arabic calendar, with revisions by Robin (1981). The South Arabic forms cited in this text are taken mostly from Biella (1982). For more information, see al-Iryānī and 'Abd Allāh (in 'Afīf et al. 1992:1:280-82).

5. It should be noted that al-Baḥr al-Na'āmī records *Dhū al-Dithā* as the name for the month of February. Al-Iryānī and 'Abd Allāh (in 'Afīf et al. 1992:1:280-82) continue to cite the month name as *dithā'*.

6. *Tabṣira*, fol. 109r. Compare the discussion in the almanac at II:10.

7. This is the general interpretation in Yemen today. The earth is said to be adorned with plants at this time because of the spring rains. This proverb has also been recorded by Agaryshev (1968:33; 1986:74) and al-Baraddūnī (1985:52, note 21).

8. *Tabṣira*, fol. 109r. The interpretation by Saliba (1985:717) of this time as a season of winnowing wheat is not accurate for Yemen but is based on usage of the term in the Levant. The common verb for "winnowing" in the Yemeni highlands is *madhaḥa*, although *nasafa* is also heard throughout Yemen (Landberg 1901:1:722).

9. This term is found in the north and south, including the Ḥaḍramawt (Landberg 1901:1:580).

10. *Tabṣira*, fol. 109r. This usage has also been noted by Abū 'Alī al-Marzūqī (1914:1:175) and al-Sijistānī (1985:93).

11. Note the errors of *'allām* in Rossi (1939:151) and *'alān* in Serjeant (1954:437). The term *'allān* is cited in the historical text of al-Janadī (1983:1:500).

12. For correlation of Islamic and Christian dates, the standard sources are Freeman-Grenville (1977) and Mahler and Wüstenfeld (1961). For more information on the Islamic calendar, see Ginzel (1906:1:238–74).

13. The Coptic calendar and its events have been described by Chaine (1925), Ginzel (1914:3:321–26), al-Nuwayrī (1923:1:191–94), Tisserant (1915), and Wassef (1971:23–95, 1991). It is worthwhile examining the interesting historical discussion

of al-Bīrūnī (1879:59). The Arabic renderings of the Coptic terms are subject to variation.

14. This can also be rendered in Arabic as *Hātūr*. Note the error in the almanac of Abū al-'Uqūl at X:28, where *Hātūr* is called the first of the Coptic year.

15. A basic description of the Persian calendar can be found in al-Bīrūnī (1879:52–56), L. H. Gray (1955), and Masse (1954:255ff.). Correlations of the Yazdagird reckoning with the Julian calendar are provided by Mahler and Wüstenfeld (1961).

16. The best source for information on the navigational *nayrūz* calendar is the text of Ibn Mājid (1971), which has been edited and annotated by Tibbetts (1971). The later text of Sulaymān al-Mahrī (1925) also provides *nayrūz* dates. See also the comments by Grosset-Grange (1972:47–48), Serjeant (1974c:174–75, note R), and Shihāb (1983:82–83). This calendar appears to have survived in the recent Gulf Canopus calendar (Varisco 1990) and in Swahili (Knappert 1993:105).

17. In the oral tradition it would not be difficult to adjust the dates periodically when a considerable gap between the calendar reckoning and the best time for the sailing season had accumulated. It must be remembered that this calendar was meant to be a general guide and that the actual sailing depended on the occurrence of the winds, which obviously did not arrive exactly the same day every year. The sailors did not need this calendar to calculate exact sailing times; it was for convenience.

18. There are numerous medieval Islamic descriptions of Christian festivals. A good summary can be found in al-Maqrīzī, available in French (Griveau 1914), as well as in al-Bīrūnī (1879), available in a flawed English translation. Coptic holidays are described in some detail by Wassef (1971). For the Byzantine rite, see Grumel (1958). More citations of Christian holidays can be found in the Rasulid almanac *Fuṣūl.*

19. For details on the Mixed Nights, see chapter 3.

20. This is mentioned in the biblical book of Exodus, chapter 16.

21. For more details on the celebration of Epiphany, see al-Bīrūnī (1879:288–89), al-Mas'ūdī (1982:2:298–99), and Wassef (1971:56, 190–95).

22. The argument for dating of the almanac is presented in detail in the Introduction. It should be noted that most of the almanac information was not tied to a specific calendar year.

23. For general information on Persian holidays, see al-Alūsī (1882:1:348–52) and al-Bīrūnī (1879:199–204). For details on the *nayrūz* celebration, see Ahsan (1979:286–90), al-Alūsī (1882:1:348–52), al-Bīrūnī (1879:199–204), Ferrand (1924), al-Maqrīzī in Griveau (1914:333–43), and Markwart (1937). The celebration of *nayrūz* in Mamluk Egypt is described in detail by Langner (1983:55–62). Al-Muqaddasī (1989:152) discussed the *nayrūz* festival for medieval Aden.

24. For information on Yemeni Jewish holidays, see Brauer (1934) and *Mumtaḥan*, fol. 10v. See also the discussion in al-Alūsī (1882:1:361–62) and al-Nuwayrī (1923:1:195– 97).

CHAPTER 2. ASTRONOMY

1. For a discussion of the significance of medieval Yemeni astronomy, see King (1983b, 1987). A bibliography of Rasulid astronomical texts can be found in King (1983a).

2. On the *zīj* genre, see Kennedy (1956). Among the important *zīj* works of Rasulid origin are those of al-Fārisī, referred to here as *Mumtaḥan*, and Abū al-'Uqūl.

3. Al-Malik al-Afḍal was in fact quoting Qusṭūs (fol. 7v) on Byzantium, but the statement applies equally to Yemen.

4. *Tabṣira*, fol. 111v. It should be noted that Sirius is the brightest star in the sky and was a frequent marker, due to its summer rising, in Arab folklore. For a discussion of this important star, see the section below on *al-shi'rā al-'abūr*.

5. For information on Yemeni folk astronomy and the agricultural marker stars see Varisco (1989b, 1993a).

6. Several relevant traditions of Muḥammad are discussed at length by Ibn Qutayba (1956:14–15). Among these is one which condemns as unbelievers those who say they were "rained upon" (*muṭirnā*) by a given star or asterism rather than by God.

7. A number of the specific correlations are listed in al-Tīfāshī (1980:167ff.), as well as in numerous other sources. The Arab zodiacal system is described by Kunitzsch and Hartner (1990). For a bibliography of relevant Arabic texts, see Sezgin (1979) and Ullmann (1972). A general introduction to the philosophical aspects of Islamic cosmology has been written by Nasr (1978); see also Miquel (1975:3–16). For a short introduction to medieval Islamic astrology, see Pingree (1990). For information on the knowledge of the zodiac in pre-Islamic South Arabia, see Ryckmans (1975–76). Ibn al-Mujāwir (1954:160–61) discusses some of the medieval folklore on zodiacal symbolism.

8. For the definitive study on the use of shadow lengths in Islamic time-keeping, see King (1990).

9. For further information see Varisco (1989a and in 1991a), as well as a future study to be entitled *Anwā' and Manāzil: The Lunar Stations in Arab Tradition*. A bibliography of the early *anwā'* genre can be found in Sezgin (1979:322–70). The published primary sources include Abū Isḥāq al-Zajjāj (Varisco 1989a), Ibn al-Ajdābī (1964), Ibn 'Āṣim (1985), Ibn Qutayba (1956), and Quṭrub (1922, 1985).

10. The modern equivalents are derived from the work of Kunitzsch (1961), which is based on the text of al-Ṣūfī (1954). A French translation of al-Ṣūfī's work was made by Schjellerup (1874).

11. The numbering here follows the standard order of the stations, beginning with the spring equinox, and is included only for ease of identification in the discussion.

12. The Rasulid sources read this as *zubānān*, adding a final *nūn*, but in most classical texts the final radical is an *alif maqṣūra*.

13. This is copied with minor variation from Ibn Qutayba (1956:6). Although there is considerable debate in the lexicons about the meaning of *naw'*, the astronomical definition here became standard in medieval Islamic science.

14. *Tabṣira,* fol. 112v.

15. *Salwa* records VII:30 (15° Leo) for the timing of the midheaven position.

16. *Salwa* notes I:31 (19° Sagittarius) for this station.

17. The reading in *Salwa* is II:6 (25° Sagittarius).

18. The same time is indicated in *Salwa* (29° Gemini).

19. This reckoning system is also found in Palestine (Dalman 1928:1:23ff.) and Afghanistan (Bausani 1974). For a description of the system in Yemen, see Glaser (1885) and Varisco (1989b, 1993a).

20. *Tabṣira,* chapter 24. Ptolemy actually records 1,025 stars in the Almagest (Kunitzsch 1993:98).

21. For information on this legend in Arab folklore, see R. Allen (1963:433), Bailey (1974:583), and al-Bilādī (1982:324).

22. There is some confusion over this terminology; see Kunitzsch (1961:62).

23. For other terms signifying this star group, see Ibn Mājid (Tibbetts 1971:134).

24. This usage is also noted by al-Baraddūnī (1985:38).

25. The term *bājis* was cited by Ibn Mājid, but note the error of *bājīs* in the Arabic text in Tibbetts (1971:546) and the error of *nāḥis* in Kunitzsch (1961:84, 1967:57, note 22).

26. The text reads *al-Yaman al-asfal.* Zabīd is clearly the reference point for the calculation rather than Ta'izz.

27. Among the known Yemeni variants of this proverb are the following: *inna suhayl fī layla sab'īn sayl* (al-Ahjur, Varisco 1985a:64); *suhayl, suhayl fī layla sab'īn sayl* (Goitein 1934:86); *anā suhayl fī laylatī sab'īn sayl ba'd sayl* (M. al-Akwa' 1971:64); *fī shahr al-suhayl fī al-layla sab'īn sayl* (Glaser in Hann 1911:1861); *suhayl fī yawmih miyyat sayl min ghayr sawārī al-layl* (Serjeant 1974a:30). For a variant in the classical tradition, see Ibn al-Ajdābī at VIII:9 and Ibn Māsawayh at VIII:28.

28. Al-Malik al-Ashraf (*Tabṣira,* fol. 53r) noted that for fifteen days after VII:25 Canopus would rise at dawn without seeming to move and not be visible to the eye. The verbal form *'aruḍa* was used for when it rose, moved a little, and then disappeared; thus, it was visible for a brief space of time. The term refers to something that appears or becomes apparent in this context. See the discussion in the almanac for VIII:8.

CHAPTER 3. METEOROLOGY

1. For general information on the climate of Yemen, see Steffen et al. (1978) and Van Enk and van der Gun (1984), as well as the older but valuable reference of Rathjens et al. (1956).

2. There is an important discussion about dew by al-Hamdānī (1977:121–22). For a detailed survey on dew in Arab tradition, see Pirenne (1978), although the conjectures in this source regarding dew condensation and stone structures are not well established. A Chinese source from the fifteenth century remarks on the importance of dew for nourishing plants near Mecca (Ma Huan 1970:176).

3. For details on this proverb, which was quoted in the almanac at V:8, see note 27 to chapter 2.

4. The reference here is to the stars of *rawābi'*, the bier of Ursa Major. These constitute an important marker for the autumn season in Yemeni folklore. A distinction is often made between the first and second *rawābi'*, or the first and second *rābi'īn* (Glaser 1885:97). In the contemporary Ibb region the process of standing up plants blown over by the wind is called *nuwwād*, while the tying of stalks with a cord to avoid wind damage is *aysār* (Messick 1978:440); this occurs in the late autumn.

5. The fifth star is an important marker in Ursa Major. In the contemporary twenty-eight-marker system in Yemen, it defines the start of *'allān* in the fall. In Ibb it is a time of great winds and rain (Messick 1978:440).

6. Ibn Qutayba (1956:79) noted that it was called *su'ūd* because of the good fortune associated with its rising. According to Abū Isḥāq al-Zajjāj, the *naw'* of *sa'd al-su'ūd* marks the breaking of the heat and start of the autumn rains and grazing (Varisco 1989a: 159).

7. Ibn al-Dayba' (1983:93), for example, mentioned a heavy, cold rain that destroyed crops in Yemen during A.H. 695, the year before al-Malik al-Ashraf died. There are several notices of violent rain in the later Yemeni history of al-Wazīr (1985:188–89, etc.).

8. Antoine Lonnet, personal communication.

9. The additional reference in the almanac to this rain at IV:20 is clearly a copyist error.

10. This discussion is found in *Tabṣira* (fol. 116r) at the start of chapter 36. The definition of twelve winds stems from classical tradition (Aristotle 1971:187). For a description of the winds in the *anwā'* literature, see Ibn al-Ajdābī (1964:126–33) and Ibn Qutayba (1956). There is an interesting lexical discussion in the Yemeni text *Kifāya* (fol. 92r).

11. This has been defined as a cold wind which often disperses clouds (al-Alūsī 1882:3:360). It is often referred to as a south or southeast wind (e.g., Ibn Sīda 1965:9:84; al-Nuwayrī 1923:1:98; al-Tha'ālibī n.d.:176), but it in fact blows from north to south.

12. In the lexicons this refers to a cold wind or a loud, violent wind. The term is in fact derived from the variant *ṣirr* (Ibn Sīda 1965:9:75). Al-Malik al-Ashraf defined it as a wind blowing from a higher to a lower point, i.e., a downdraft. In Islamic cosmology this was a wind sent on land as punishment (al-Tha'ālibī n.d.:176), such as in the case of the west wind sent to destroy the wicked tribe of 'Ād (Ibn Kathīr

1979:3:259, 542 for surah 69:5).

13. As noted in the above footnote, this generally refers to a cold wind; Ibn Sīda (1965:9:75) said it meant the intensity of the cold. This is the meaning associated with the usage of the term in the Quran at surah 3:117 (al-Batalyūsī 1984:374; Kratschkovsky 1926:336).

14. Pseudo-Apollonios (1979) and al-Hamdānī (1884) defined this as the northeast wind. The literal meaning is a barren wind, one that does not bring rain or pollenate trees. This was also said to be one of the winds sent on land by God for punishment (al-Ḥimyarī 1980:230; al-Tha'ālibī n.d.:250), and thus similar to the west wind sent to destroy the tribe of 'Ād (al-Hamdānī 1983:300–1; Ibn Iyās 1982:110; Ibn al-Mujāwir 1954:265; al-Ibshīhī 1981:377).

15. The term *nakbā'* literally refers to a wind blowing between the directions of two cardinal winds (al-Hamdānī 1884:1:154; al-Ḥimyarī 1980:230; Ibn Mājid in Tibbetts 1971:143).

16. This is recorded in *Nubdha* for XI:4 (9 *Hātūr*). The Egyptian term is derived from the village of Marīsa in Upper Egypt, i.e. to the south of Cairo. Ibn al-Faqīh al-Hamadhānī (1967:74) said that if this blows in Egypt for thirteen consecutive days, Egyptians unveil their shrouds and prepare for death; this tradition is apparently derived from al-Jāḥiẓ (Bosworth 1968:121). Al-Mas'ūdī (1894:19) compared the ill effects of this wind in Egypt with that of the *bawāriḥ* in Iraq. In Egypt the south wind blew in both summer and winter (Ibn Riḍwān 1984:95).

17. The term *raqīb* is used in the *anwā'* literature to refer to the star setting at dawn and thus opposite to the rising star (Ibn Qutayba 1956:10). This fits the general timing indicated by Abū al-'Uqūl, although it is doubtful if this was a term used by Yemeni farmers.

18. For a medical definition of *buḥrān*, see al-Khawārizmī (1984:205).

19. For more synonyms of this term, see al-Hamdānī (1983:49). The variant *ḍarab* is recorded in classical usage by al-Batalyūsī (1984:229). The term *ḍarīb* can be used for a frost at any time (Ibn al-Ajdābī 1964 at IV:16).

20. This proverb was recorded by I. al-Akwa' (1984:2:736) and al-Baraddūnī (1985:57).

21. For a discussion of this expression, see al-Hamadhānī (1979:257). The *ḥamārra* of summer contrasts with the *ṣabārra* of winter (al-Tha'ālibī n.d.:20).

22. The term *qarāqir* is derived from *qurr* in reference to the cold of winter. The term *qarqār* is used for the sound of the wind (*Lisān al-'Arab, q-r-r*). The seventeenth-century Yemeni calendar of al-Hattār records a period of three days from 15 to 17 *Shubāṭ* as *qarāqir* and *ṣarāṣir* (Varisco 1993a:128).

23. The term *ṣarāṣir* is derived from *ṣirra* in reference to intense cold. The related term *ṣarṣār* can be used for intensification of cold or sound. See notes 12 and 13 above.

24. This is the same explanation for the term *ramḍā'*, according to al-Batalyūsī (1984:273). The Rwala Bedouins use *jamra* for a shooting star (Musil 1928:6),

perhaps because of the resemblance to the light of a falling coal.

25. For a discussion of this meaning, see al-Bīrūnī (1879:71), Ibn Sīda (1965:9:43), al-Jawālīqī (n.d.:140), and al-Mas'ūdī (1982:2:504). Caussin de Perceval (1947:136) was off the mark when he suggested this was a summer month because of the meaning of *jamād* as drought or barrenness.

26. This information is also discussed in al-Marzūqī (1914:1:175). A variant, *qumāḥ,* is recorded by Lane (1984:2561).

27. The term *nājir* was used for a pre-Islamic month name in Arabic (al-Mas'ūdī 1982:2:507), generally in reference to the hot period in June-July (*Lisān al-'Arab, n-j-r*). *Fuṣūl* records this for V:16–VII:16.

28. Note the error of II:24 in Taymūr for the start of this period.

29. There are numerous references to the *'ajūz* legend in Arab folklore and literature. For a general overview with an emphasis on North Africa, see Garland-Pernet (1958, 1960). See also Bourdieu (1977:101) and Westermarck (1926:2:161–62,174–75) for North Africa. Al-Marzūqī (1968:1:272–73) described the usage among the Bedouins.

30. In surah 69:7 *ḥuṣūm* refers to successive days and nights said to be unlucky and ominous (Ibn Kathīr 1979:3:541). This term is quite common in North Africa (Genevois 1975:36–41; Ibn al-Bannā' in Renaud 1948:33; Joly 1905:305; Westermarck 1926:2:174) and Egypt (Pellat 1986:254–55). The first three days at the beginning of *Baramhāt* are referred to as *ḥusūmāt* and defined as inauspicious in the Coptic calendar; Wassef (1991:442) relates this back to the Egyptian legend of Seth's murder of Osiris.

31. The term *kalib* refers to the intensity of the cold (al-Tha'ālibī n.d.:33). However, the association with the dog (*kalb*) of winter is quite common, especially in later almanacs. The Yemeni poet al-Baḥr al-Na'āmī (in M. al-Akwa' 1981:13) played on this dual meaning by saying that the dog of December was the most dangerous of dogs.

32. The *waghra* is a hot period associated with the risings of several stars of summer. Ibn Qutayba (1956:119) claimed there were *waghra* periods at the risings of the Pleiades, Aldebaran, Sirius, Orion, and Canopus, but that these hot periods ended at the rising of Arcturus (*simāk*).

CHAPTER 4. ENVIRONMENT

1. Many non-Yemeni almanacs refer to the rain during *Nīsān*, especially at IV:1, as being fortunate. Ibn 'Āṣim, for example, said that on IV:27 bread made with this rainwater would rise quickly without needing yeast. This idea is probably derived from the *anwā'* tradition, in which the rain at the setting of *simāk* in early *Nīsān* was considered one of the most beneficial of the year. Ibn al-Ajdābī recorded a proverb that reads, "A rain shower in *Nīsān* is better than a thousand years" (*maṭra fī Nīsān*

khayr min alf sān). In contemporary Morocco the rain during *Nīsān* is rich in God's blessing (*baraka*), while the rain during the Days of the Old Woman (*ḥayān*) is considered unfavorable.

2. In the Yemeni highlands *ghayl* refers to spring flow and is often used to refer to the distribution network from a spring (Varisco 1982a:203–4). *Ghayl* can also mean the flowing of mother's milk.

3. There are numerous sources on the Nile; see the entries *miḳyās* and *Nīl* in the second edition of *The encyclopaedia of Islam.* Information in the early Coptic almanacs has been summarized by Pellat (1986:233–34). For a valuable study on the Nile in the medieval period, see Qāsim (1978).

4. Mitchell (1877:18, 1900) placed this at 4 *Ba'ūna* in his translation of a nineteenth-century Coptic almanac. As a careful Victorian living abroad, he observed that it was necessary to filter and boil the water at this time before drinking it. Madden (1829:295) remarked that the Egyptians strained the Nile water through a cloth in order to reduce the "animalculae." Ibn Riḍwān (1984:136) recommended purification of the Nile water with the marrow of apricot pits, among other things.

5. According to Qāsim (1978:19) the canals were drained in stages. The first canals were opened when the flood reached a level of sixteen *dhirā'* in the month of *Misrā* (VIII). This was when the *khalīj* canal near Cairo was opened. The next opening was at the Coptic *nayrūz* (i.e., VIII:29), with the canals being opened called *nayrūzīya*. The canals opened at the Festival of the Cross (*'īd al-ṣalīb*) on 17 *Tūt* were called *ṣalībiyāt*. After this the remaining canals were opened. For more information, see Rabie (1981).

6. For more information on the Euphrates, see Hartmann and de Vaumas (1960) and al-Nuwayrī (1923:1:266–67).

7. For more information on the Tigris, see Hartmann and Longrigg (1960) and al-Nuwayrī (1923:1:268–69).

8. For recent surveys of Yemeni flora, see Bādhīb (1991), Chaudhary and Revri (1983), Deil (1985), Deil and Müller-Hohenstein (1985), Dubaie and Al-Khulaidi (1991), Gifri and Gabali (1991), Hepper (1977), al-Hubaishi and Müller-Hohenstein (1984), Scholte and al-Khuleidi (1989), Scholte et al. (1991), Varisco et al. (1990), and J. Wood (1985, in press). The volume by Collenette (1985) on flowers of Saudi Arabia contains valuable comparative information for Yemen. Earlier botanical discussions must be used with caution, although there is much valuable information; for a basic bibliography, see Miller et al. (1982). For the work of Forskal (or Forsskal), the botanist on the ill-fated Niebuhr expedition in the late eighteenth century, see Friis (1983) and the excellent compilation by Hepper and Friss (1994) from Forskal's notes.

9. The appendix to the herbal of Yūsuf ibn 'Umar (1982:558–72) is similar to *Ta'rīb*. Yemeni plant names are also discussed in the early text of al-Aṣma'ī (1972:36–37). There is an excellent discussion of plant names, including some medicinal uses, in the *Bughya* (fol. 105ff). For contemporary plant designations in

Yemen, see Bādhīb (1991), Chaudhary and Revri (1983), Kessler and al-Khuleidi (1987), al-Khulaidi (1989:112–14), and Varisco (1982a:481–510).

10. The *'arm* plant was identified for me near the Rasulid site of al-Juwwa in 1992 by the local sheikh and confirmed by Dr. 'Abd al-Raḥmān Dub'ī of Ṣan'ā' University and Mr. 'Abd al-Wālī al-Khulaydī of the Agricultural Research Authority. This term was also noted for *Carissa edulis* by Forskal (Hepper and Friis 1994:76).

11. The term *shadn* can also be used for an aromatic plant with a blossom similar to jasmine, according to *Lisān al-'Arab* (*sh-d-n*).

12. The ben-oil tree has been valued in Egypt since at least the Ptolemaic period as a source of oil. Hobbs (1989:40) observes that the Bedouins of the Eastern Desert harvest the seeds of this tree in late autumn. For more information, see the glossary in Ibn Riḍwān (1984:155).

13. Ibn al-Bayṭār (1291/1874:3:5) remarked that *dawm* was the fruit of the *ḍāl* tree.

14. Truffles represent an important food source for Arabian Bedouins and figure prominently in the folklore, especially as so-called manna. For more information, see Abū Ḥanīfa al-Dīnawarī (1974a:71–86), al-Bīrūnī (1973:281–82), Euting (1914:2:58), and M. al-Marzūqī (1981). The most important variety for Bedouins is called *faq'*, although Ibn al-A'rābī (in al-Bīrūnī 1973:1:281–82) said that the white *faq'* variety was the worst to eat.

15. This term was defined as a thorny tree also called *kathīrā'* by Ibn al-Bayṭār (1291/1874:4:4).

16. For basic information on the natural fauna of Yemen, see Varisco et al. (1990) for further references. The early text of Forskal (1775a) must be used with caution, because of its age and the fact it was edited by Niebuhr, who did not collect the specimens. However, it does contain useful descriptive information. The mammals of Arabia are described in great detail by Harrison (1964–72, 1991). For a discussion of Yemeni terms for various animals, see Grohmann (1930–34), Rossi (1939:160–63), and Varisco (1982a:511–28). The basic sources on Arabic animal folklore are al-Jāḥiẓ (1968) and al-Damīrī (n.d., 1906–8), although the translation of the latter is inadequate and incomplete. An introduction to the genre has been provided by Pellat et al. (1971).

17. The term *qird* is generic for "ape" or "monkey." The ape in Yemen is the baboon (*Papio hamadryas arabicus*), which is similar to the species in East Africa. For information on the baboon in nearby Saudi Arabia, see Kummer et al. (1981). The general Yemeni term for this animal is *rabḥ* (*rubāḥ*, plural). This term was defined as a male *qird* by al-Jāḥiẓ (1968:2:179). Rossi (1939:162) also noted the term *maymūn* for the baboon in Yemen.

18. The reference is probably to the South Arabian leopard (*Panthera pardus nimr)*, generally referred to as *nimr* in Yemen.

19. There are numerous sources on birds in Yemen. For more recent sources, see al-'Amrī and al-Ba'dānī (in 'Afīf, et al. 1992:2:603–6), Brockie (1985), Cornwallis

and Porter (1982), Jennings (1991), Meinertzhagen (1954), Parr (1987), Rands et al. (1987), 'Ubādī (1989), and Varisco et al. (1990). For Yemeni bird names, see M. al-Akwa' (1971:95), Rossi (1939:160-63), 'Ubādī (1989), and Varisco (1982a:511–28).

20. For a major Yemeni text on falcon hunting, see al-Nāshirī (1985). Among the important Arabic sources are al-Baladī (1983) and Kushājim (in Ṣāliḥīya 1985). The history of falcon hunting among the Arabs is treated by Viré (1967, 1977). Ahsan (1979:202–42) summarizes information on hunting during the Abbasid era. For an overview of falcon hunting on the Arabian Peninsula, see Allen and Smith (1975) and al-Timimi (1987). The birds of prey used on the peninsula are described by Meinertzhagen (1954:323–84).

21. The *hudhud* legend is mentioned in surah 27 of the Quran. For more information on this legend in Yemen, see Manzoni (1884:284–92), Philby (1981:65–76), and Watt (1974).

22. For information on insects in Yemen, see al-Humiari (1982), Niebuhr (1792:2:325–29), Rathjens and von Wissmann (1934:114–15), and Scott (1942). The expedition of H. Scott and E. B. Britton collected about 27,000 insect specimens for the British Museum. Butterflies are treated by Larsen (1983, 1984). Traditional Yemeni methods of crop protection from insects are discussed in Varisco et al. (1992). Dr. W. Wranik (Universität Rostock) is planning a volume on the insects of Yemen.

23. The term *baqq* can also be used for the bedbug or louse in Arabic.

24. This rendering was suggested by Jayakar in his translation of the text of al-Damīrī (1906:1:527). It has the merit of being descriptive, since there is no corresponding term for *hawāmm* in English.

25. The term *dabā* commonly refers to the young of locusts and hoppers. Musil (1928:112–13) observed among the Rwala Bedouins that it referred to locusts whose wings were just starting to grow and that still crawled on the ground.

26. For detailed discussions on the importance of honey, see Abū Ḥanīfa al-Dīnawarī (1974a:257–94, 1974b), Ibn Sīda (1965:5:14–20), al-Jāḥiẓ (1968:5:426–31), al-Nuwayrī (1935:11:325–30), and al-Suyūṭī (1986:303–7). Somogyi (1957:82) summarizes the discussion on bees and honey from the zoological lexicon of al-Damīrī. An English translation of a medical text on honey is provided by Marín and Waines (1989).

27. Al-Aṣma'ī (in Abū Ḥanīfa al-Dīnawarī 1974a:266) said the whole land of Yemen produced honey. The historian al-'Umarī (1985:154) noted that there was much honey in Rasulid Yemen. During the Abbasid period Yemeni honey was dried into a type of sugar and exported to Mecca and Iraq (Ahsan 1979:102). For information on honey production in Yemen, see Arab League Institute (1977a), Gingrich in Dostal et al. (1983:62–74), Great Britain Admiralty (1946:513–14), Grohmann (1930:1:200–2), Ingrams (1937), Karpowicz (1983), Scott (1942:58–59), and Serjeant (1954:451, note 68).

28. In addition to its destruction of wood and clothing, the termite is a pest of

sorghum and dates (Varisco et al. 1992).

29. Information on snakes in the region is provided in Corkill and Cochrane (1966), Gasparetti (1987), Niebuhr (1792:2:330–32), and Schmidt (1954).

30. Sources on domestic animals and pastoralism in Yemen include Dostal (1967), Great Britain Admiralty (1946:498–99), Grohmann (1930:1:190–200), and al-Mutawwakil (in 'Afīf et al. 1992:1:292-93).

31. The literature on the camel is extensive, but a good entry is provided in the entertaining and informative study of Bulliet (1990). For information on Yemeni camel varieties, see 'Alī ibn Dāwūd (1987:283–95), Dostal (1967), al-Hamdānī (1983:196, 360), al-Mutawwakil (in 'Afīf et al. 1992:1:293-94), and *Mughnī*. Musil (1928:329–70) provides a detailed description of camels among the Rwala Bedouins.

32. However, both al-Damīrī (n.d.:2:227) and al-Ibshīhī (1981:360) said that the elephant mates in the spring.

33. There is apparently no relation between this usage and the term *ṣarbay* recorded for a camel with its milk dried up or its ears split, or whose milk was only for idols (Lane 1984:1674).

34. A legend regarding the origin of eating camel flesh was given by al-Ḥarīrī (1867:2:516–17). The preparation of camel meat is discussed by Musil (1928:96).

35. For information on Yemeni varieties of horses, see *Aqwāl*, al-Hamdānī (1983:320–21), al-Mutawwakil (in 'Afīf et al. 1992:1:294–95), and al-Wazīr (1985:183). A thirteenth-century A.D. Yemeni author (Ibn Ḥamza 1979) wrote a general treatise on the Arabic terminology for the horse, but this is not specifically oriented toward Yemen.

36. Luqmān (1980:96–97) records stories about the *ghūl* in Yemen. For mention of a story concerning a *quṭrub* in Egypt for the year 433/1041–42, see Langner (1983:149). The idea of spirits inhabiting a wasteland is a common motif in the biblical literature (e.g., Isaiah 13:21, 34:14).

CHAPTER 5. AGRICULTURE

1. Yemen was famous for the yellow dye from this plant (see Grohmann 1930:1:266–70). Al-Hamdānī (1983:319), apparently quoting al-Aṣma'ī, claimed that *wars* was only found in Yemen, although it was apparently exported in the medieval period from Socotra and Ethiopia (al-Bīrūnī 1973:1:335). 'Umāra (1976:58–59) noted its presence in the Rasulid town of al-Mudhaykhira. Al-Bīrūnī (1973:1:335) and al-Nuwayrī (1935:11:329) noted a legend in which *wars* is considered a type of manna and falls from heaven onto leaves and dries to a reddish color in the sun. It should be noted that *wars* sometimes means "saffron" in Arabic.

2. Both al-Ḥibshī (1980:42) and 'Inān (1980:208) claimed that this Jewish festival was the origin of the term, but the reasons for this are not given. The later Yemeni

historian al-Wazīr (1985:279) noted that the Jews celebrated this festival in *Jumādā al-Ūlā*, 1082/1671. For a discussion of the Yemeni literature on *sabt al-subūt*, see the interesting study by al-Ḥaḍramī (1992). In the Yemeni highlands *sabt al-subūt* is later used for a period in autumn. Ibn Jaḥḥāf and al-Thābitī mentioned this *sabt al-subūt* at IX:23 for the start of winter and the start of sheep and goat production in Yemen. The almanac poem of al-'Affārī mentions this period at IX:14 at the rising of the fifth (*khāmis*) star of Ursae Majoris, when it was not good to plant at Ṣan'ā' because of expected frost. The modern almanac chart of al-'Ansī places the three days of *sabt al-subūt* in October.

3. The modern author al-'Aqīlī (1958:189–90) vilified Ibn al-Mujāwir for recording information about immoral practices during the *sabt al-subūt* celebration. However, al-Ḥaḍramī (1992:193) defends this social institution. The medieval traveler al-Muqaddasī (1989:157) noted that adultery was "over-practiced" in Aden. For a discussion of sexual attitudes in South Yemen, see Serjeant (1962b, 1965).

4. For descriptions of rain invocations in Yemen today, see Serjeant (1974a:32) and Varisco (1982a:105–7). The legendary 'Alī ibn Zāyid in Yemeni folklore was involved in a rain invocation (Varisco 1988:504–5). The Rasulid chronicles record a major drought in 673/1274–75 during the reign of al-Malik al-Muẓaffar.

5. Locust devastations are frequently noted in the Yemeni chronicles; see Ibn al-Dayba' (1983:93), al-Khazrajī (1906:1:245), al-Kindī (1991:120), and al-Wazīr (1985). The worse problem is from hoppers (*dabā*) rather than from flying locusts, because the hoppers move close to the ground and may last up to a month (Abū Ḥanīfa al-Dīnawarī 1974a:62).

6. Additional tax information for the Rasulid period is provided in *Ma'rifa* (Varisco 1989c) and in the mixed Rasulid manuscript from the library of al-Malik al-Afḍal, under preparation in facsimile by Smith and Varisco.

7. Port taxes at Aden are discussed by Serjeant (1974b). A comprehensive account of the port taxes appears in *Shāmil*. For details on the items traded through the port of Aden, see chapter 7.

8. The term *rasm* was used in Ayyubid Egypt for a basic agricultural tax (Frantz-Murphy 1986:87). The original meaning of the term was "column" (*jadwal*) and later was shifted to meaning "tax," because the tax records were kept in columns. It should be noted that in Yemeni dialect today the term *marsūm* refers to a property deed or receipt.

9. For Yemeni sources that cover agriculture in the area north of Ṣan'ā', see al-Sirājī (1959) and al-Zumaylī (in Serjeant and al-'Amrī 1981).

10. This term appears as *rḥy* (!) in the text. The reading of *shurayḥī* by Serjeant (1974a:45) and in Varisco (1985a:77) should be corrected.

11. The reference must be to the eastern wadis, since wheat is not planted in the coastal region.

12. The term refers to its early ripening. Note the parallel with *miqdām* for a date

palm variety.

13. For details on measures, see the *Bughya* (fol. 108v ff.), al-Muqaddasī (1989:150), and *Shāmil*. The discussion by Mortel (1990) for Mecca is also useful. For nineteenth century Aden, see Manzoni (1884:263–64).

14. For the description of sorghum production in Yemen, with a list of variety names, see Varisco (1985a). The section on sorghum from the *Bughya* has been translated by Serjeant (1974a:45–53). Watson (1983:9–14) discusses the early history of sorghum in the Arab world. Arabic terms for sorghum and millet are discussed at length by Clement-Mullet (1865:217–24), based primarily on the Andalusian agricultural treatise of Ibn al-'Awwām. Note that older sources often refer to *Sorghum bicolor* as *Sorghum vulgare*; the main variety in the Middle East is also called *Sorghum durra* (Watson 1983:12).

15. *Ṭa'ām* is literally "food" or "grain." This usage parallels the use of *'aysh* (bread) for sorghum in the Sudan (Löw 1926:1:742).

16. It appears that *jahīsh* was the coastal term and *farīk* the highland term, or else *jahīsh* was used primarily for sorghum. The parching of wheat was an important biblical custom (Van Lennep 1875:91), as noted in I Samuel 17:17, 25:18, and Ruth 2:14.

17. These terms vary in different contexts. In Wādī Mawr today the first cropping is called *jadda*, the second *khalf*, and the third *'aqb* (Mitchell et al. 1978:202). Forskal (1775a:174) recorded *'aqb* for the third cropping. Serjeant (1974a:68, note 14) and al-'Aqīlī (1958:44) said *khalf* was for the second cropping in Wādī Jīzān. The term *khilfa* was used in reference to a second cropping of sugarcane in twelfth century Egypt (Frantz-Murphy 1986:42). In Ḥaḍramawt Hunter et al. (1909:69) reported the first cropping as *āb* (father), the second as *'aqb*, and the third as *'aqb al-'aqb*.

18. The Arabic *dukhn* is derived from Hebrew (Löw 1926:1:738–39). This term may apply to sorghum in some contexts. There is some confusion over the types of millet found in medieval Yemen. In the *Bughya* (Serjeant 1974a:51) a distinction is made between Rūmī *dukhn*, which is fine and has a loose head, and Yemeni *dukhn*. The former is said to be broomcorn millet (*Panicum miliaceum*; Grohmann 1930:1:211), which is sometimes called *gharib* in Yemen (Steffen et al. 1978:Pt. II:10). The latter is apparently *Pennisetum glaucum*, which is pearl or bulrush millet (Serjeant 1974a:52). This is sometimes called *bajrī*, an Indian term (Great Britain Admiralty 1946:482). Wigboldus (1991b), however, thinks that pearl millet was only introduced into Yemen via Ethiopia in the mid-fourteenth century. A related term for one of the millet varieties is *jāwarsh*, which Dietrich (1981:249) believes is *Panicum miliaceum*. This is the equivalent of *jowar* or *jowari* in India (Rachie 1970:336). Ibn al-Mujāwir (1954:89) mentioned that *juwārī* was present in Zabīd in the early 13th century. Areas where millet was grown in Yemen are listed in Grohmann (1930:1:210–11).

19. Serjeant (1974a:51) reads a quote of al-Ashraf's passage in the *Bughya* as *jaḥrī* (!), following the indication in the Cairo ms., but this must be an error for *kharajī*. A

planting at this time would be too early for a harvest in the hot period of *jaḥr*.

20. This reading was suggested by Muḥammad 'Abd al-Raḥīm Jāzm, based on its usage in *Shāmil*. It is possible that the word may be *juraḥī*, referring to the area of Sūq al-Jurāḥī near Zabid in the coastal region; however, this seems unlikely from the context. It should be noted that al-Muqaddasī (1989:137) mentioned sorghum growing at al-Jurayḥ in the Tihāma. The reading of *kharajī* should be corrected for *ḥarjī* (!) in Serjeant and al-'Amrī (1981:417) and in Varisco (1985a:75).

21. This variety of sorghum is apparently known in southern Yemen (Serjeant 1954:455). There is a confusing mention of *ṣawmī* at VII:23 in the almanac, where it appears along with a reference to wheat and barley.

22. For Yemen, see Grohmann (1930:1:211), Maktari (1971:56), and Serjeant (1954:450, note 56). For Palestine, see Löw (1926:1:743). For Egypt, see Naẓīr (1969:183).

23. Note the printing error of Rasbān (!) in Serjeant (1974a:48).

24. According to al-Rāzī (1979:271) *za'ar* refers to a small amount of hair. Perhaps this was used in a descriptive sense for the head of this variety.

25. The section on wheat and barley in the *Bughya* has been translated by Serjeant (1974a:39–44). Watson (1983:20–23) discusses wheat production in the early Islamic world. For Arabic terms, see Clement-Mullet (1865:190–213). Grohmann (1930:1:215) mentions the following terms for barley in Yemen: *ḥabīb, shilb, saqla, samra,* and *bakūr*.

26. Clement-Mullet (1865:196, 199) argued that Arabic *'alas* was equivalent to Greek *zea* in reference to *T. dicoccum*. Serjeant (1954:445, note 39) translates this as "rye."

27. For the discussion in the *Bughya* on rice production, see Serjeant (1974a:53–55). Watson (1983:15–19) discusses production in the early Islamic period and Müller-Wodarg (1957:22–24) describes rice production in medieval Egypt. For Arabic terms, see Clement-Mullet (1865:224–26). The medical discussion by Ibn al-Bayṭār of rice as a food has been translated into French by Ferrand (1913:1:237–39).

28. Serjeant (1974a:72, note 182) found a similar proverb in Mukallā.

29. The production of sugarcane in the Islamic world is discussed by Ahsan (1979:101–2), Canard and Berthier (1976), and Watson (1983:24–30). For medieval Egypt, see Müller-Wodarg (1957:45–48).

30. For more information on the terminology and production of melons, see Clement-Mullet (1870:98–106), Löw (1926:1:529–30), and Watson (1983:58–61).

31. In Egypt *faqqūs* referred to the snake cucumber (Ibn Riḍwān 1984:156; Müller-Wodarg 1957:34). The term *faqqūsa* was also used for an unripe melon (*Lisān al-'Arab, f-q-s*).

32. For a poem in praise of asparagus, see Arberry (1967:160). See also Ahsan (1979:96).

33. This term can also be used for pears or peaches (al-Anṭākī 1951:1:38; al-

Dhahabī 1984:72). Piamenta (1990:1:3) is confusing in his discussion of this term, because he refers only to an obscure usage for "cotton" of this well-known term.

34. For names of Yemeni varieties, see M. al-Akwa' (1971:68), Great Britain Admiralty (1946:593), Grohmann (1930:1:237), al-Hamdānī (1938:42–43, 1983:314), Sharaf al-Dīn (1985:28, note 3), al-Thawr (1972:69, note 1), al-Wāsi'ī (1982:41, 150–51), and Zabāra (n.d.:663–73). Traditional Yemeni grape cultivation is discussed by Barakāt (in 'Afīf et al. 1992:2:695-99) and Dostal (1985:287–93).

35. This is the term for a red variety in medieval Syria (al-Muqaddasī 1906:181) and for a white variety in Yemen (Grohmann 1930:1:237). The term *'āṣimī* is also used for a sorghum variety in the northern highland valley of al-Ahjur. The term is said to derive from Wadi 'Āṣim (Piamenta 1991:2:330).

36. A number of sources confuse cumin and black cumin. Ducros (1930:117), for example, notes that "Ethiopian cumin" refers to *Nigella sativa.*

37. This term is also used for oats (Clement-Mullet 1865:213). Ibn al-Bayṭār (1291/1874:4:195) defined it as a pea (*julubbān*). In *Ta'rīb* it is related to *turmus* (lupine) and *al-bāqillā' al-maṣrī.*

38. The term *dijr* is in use in Dhofar and Oman (James A. Mandaville, personal communication). This term is also mentioned in a *ḥadīth*, where the eminent religious scholar al-Shāfi'ī equates it with *lūbiyā* (al-Dimyāṭī 1965:56).

39. For information on bananas in the early Islamic world, see Watson (1983:51–54).

40. The term *barqūq* was used for a type of *ijjāṣ* (plum?) in Syria (Ibn al-Bayṭār 1291/1874:1:89) and Egypt (Müller-Wodarg 1957:71).

41. For general information on date palms in Yemen, see Grohmann (1930:1:230-34) and Serjeant (1981a). The classical terminology is described in the important text of al-Sijistānī (1985).

42. For the date varieties of Zabīd, see Ibn al-Dayba' (1983:48) and Ibn al-Mujāwir (1954:78–81). Al-Malik al-Ashraf (*Milḥ*, p. 70) listed the varieties in Najrān. For varieties in the Ḥaḍramawt, see Arab League Institute (1977b:23) and Popenoe (1973:172–73.)

43. This voweling is indicated in *al-Muḥīṭ* (*q-d-m*). It was so named because it was the first to mature, according to *Tāj al-'arūs* (*q-d-m*). The first dates to mature in the coastal region today are called *khuḍarī* and *tubakī* (Yemen Arab Republic 1984a:32).

44. This term is sometimes applied to ripe dates or dried dates (Lane 1984:246).

45. This *ḥadīth* is widely quoted in the *anwā'* literature (e.g., Ibn Qutayba 1956:31). One of the variants recorded in *Lisān al-'Arab* reads: *Idhā ṭala'a al-najm irtafa'at al-'āha* (When the Pleiades has risen, the blight has risen up). This is said to occur at the morning rising of the Pleiades in May, when the date is in the *busr* stage. For an explanation of variations of this tradition, see al-Suyūṭī (1986:150–52).

46. Although *ṣirām/ṣarām* is the general term for the date harvest throughout the peninsula, the Rasulid almanacs have *inṣirām ayyām al-nakhl.* This is an unusual

usage, as it would literally imply the cutting off of the time for dates, but it clearly means the harvest time, as noted by Abū al-'Uqūl.

47. For some of the folklore on figs, see Ibn al-Wardī (1939:183–84) and al-Nuwayrī (1935:11:153–50).

48. This is mentioned in surah *al-ṣaffat* 37:146 in the Quran and in the biblical book of Jonah.

49. For more information on opium, see Dubler (1960). A *fatwa* on the use of opium was given by Ibn Ḥajar al-Haytamī (1890–91:4:226). Manzoni (1884:220) said that poppy was not used as an external medicant when he visited Yemen.

50. According to *Tāj al-'arūs* this term was originally *jawḥam*. Forskal (1775b: cxiii) recorded the term *ḥawjam* in Yemen.

51. For more information on flax, see Ashtor (1978). Müller-Wodarg (1957:35–38) discusses this plant in medieval Egypt.

52. Grohmann (1930:1:260–62) provides information on cotton cultivation in Yemen. For more information on cotton in the Islamic world, see Inalcik (1982) and Watson (1983:31–34). Müller-Wodarg (1957:38–39) discusses cotton in medieval Egypt. Bādhīb (1991:95) identifies present-day Yemeni cotton varieties as *Gossypium barbadense* (L.) and *G. hirsutum*.

CHAPTER 6. HEALTH, HUMORS, AND SEX

1. The transfer of this knowledge and subsequent development in Islamic science have been the focus of numerous studies. For a basic review, see Dols (in Ibn Riḍwān 1984:3–24), Levey (1973:19–29), and Ullmann (1978). Samso (1978:79–80) discusses the impact of the Hippocratic writings on the almanac tradition. Riddle (1985) provides an excellent introduction to the Greek herbal of Dioscorides, a major source for medieval Arab herbals.

2. The basic published texts for *al-ṭibb al-nabawī* are al-Dhahabī (1984), Ibn Qayyim al-Jawzīya (1957), and al-Suyūṭī (1986). A translation of the Persian text of al-Suyūṭī was made by Elgood (1962), but it is not consistent. An English translation of Ibn Qayyim al-Jawzīya's text is in preparation by P. Johnstone. Collections of the *ḥadīth* literature often include a chapter on medicine. Bürgel (1976) gives an introduction to the genre.

3. For discussions of traditional medicine and health care in Yemeni folklore, see Ṭāhir (in 'Afīf et al. 1992:2:593–94), Myntti (1983,1988,1990), and Swagman (1988). A list of plants used in Yemeni medicine is provided in Fleurentin and Pelt (1982), Jāzm (in Varisco et al. 1990), and Schopen (1983). The herbal of al-Malik al-Muẓaffar (1957), which has been partially translated in Schopen (1983), is based almost exclusively on the classical tradition, especially the herbal of Ibn al-Bayṭār (1291/1874), and does not document Yemeni folk practices. A poetic herbal of the 18th-century Yemeni Sha'bān ibn Sālim al-Ṣan'ānī has been edited and translated into

German by Schopen and Kahl (1993), with valuable annotation of terms. Traditional Yemeni healers sometimes consulted the basic herbals, especially the text of al-Anṭākī (1951).

4. This date is missing in al-Malik al-Ashraf's text, but provided in *Fuṣūl*.

5. An excellent discussion of the use of *ṭā'ūn* and *wabā'* in the early texts can be found in Conrad (1982). These terms are sometimes used interchangeably in Arab almanacs. Al-Jāḥiẓ (1968:6:218) said the Arabs attributed *ṭā'ūn* to the Devil. Some of the major plagues in the early Islamic period were listed by al-Khawārizmī (1984:146). Ibn Qayyim al-Jawzīya (1957:28–35) noted the belief that the plague was originally sent by God as a punishment on the Israelites. A tradition of the Prophet Muḥammad states that the bubonic plague would not enter Mecca. Dols (1977) describes the impact of the "Black Death" in the medieval Arab world.

6. Among the diseases of the eye described by medieval Arab scholars were inflammation, redness, white liquid, night blindness, and weak eyesight. The common eye disorders in contemporary Yemen have been documented by al-Jarrāfī (1983). For some of the local cures for ophthalmia in Egypt, see Lane (1973:257).

7. For more information on bleeding and cupping, see Beg (1982). Blood was widely used as a medicant in the medieval period (see Somogyi 1957:68–70).

8. An eighteenth century A.D. Yemeni text on the etiquette of the *ḥammām* has been edited by al-Ḥibshī (al-Kawkabānī 1985). For the hot baths of Ṣan'ā', see Serjeant and Lewcock (1983:501–24).

9. A number of texts describe the diet in Yemen during the Rasulid era, especially the occasional remarks by Ibn al-Mujāwir (1954). For an excellent discussion of popular foods and methods of food preparation in the Ayyubid and Mamluk periods, see the text of Ibn al-'Adīm al-Ḥalabī (1986), especially the editors' introduction (1:355–412).

10. This was a popular dish of meat, broth, and bread. The Prophet Muḥammad claimed that *tharīd* was to other food like his beloved wife 'Ā'isha to other women (al-Suyūṭī 1986:164).

11. Abū al-'Uqūl said that this was a temperate month and that almost anything could be eaten, as was also indicated for the month of *Aylūl* (IX).

12. For more information on attitudes and sexual practices in the medieval period, see Musallam (1983), al-Sayyid-Marsot (1979), and Walther (1993). The important text of al-Ghazālī (1984) on sexual etiquette has been translated into English, although it is not a consistent translation and the original Arabic should be consulted. Despite the rather provocative style, the essay by Sir Richard Burton (1886:10:192–254) is still of value for information on sexual attitudes in medieval Arab literature. The herbals usually record the aphrodisiacal or anaphrodisiacal qualities of various herbs and simples; much of this would be relevant for Yemen as well. Serjeant (1965) discusses sexual diseases in Yemen.

13. This was disregarded for weddings in Yemen. Ethnographic accounts indicate

that the bride and groom may sometimes stay awake for three nights of celebration before consummation. For more information on Yemeni weddings, see Adra (1982) and Dorsky (1986:99–131).

CHAPTER 7. NAVIGATION

1. For further information on navigation in this region during the medieval period, see 'Abd al-'Alīm (1979), Ferrand (1913–14, 1921–28), Grosset-Grange (1972), Lewis (1973), Reinaud (1845), Shihāb (1981,1982,1983,1987), Sultanate of Oman (1979:89–106), Teixeira da Mosta (1963), and Tibbetts (1971,1974). Serjeant (1974c) discusses shipping in the Gulf of Aden during the Portuguese era. A practical discussion of nineteenth century dhow trade is provided by Villiers (1940).

2. Ibn Mājid is the most famous author in the navigational literature. For more information on his life, see Ahmad (1971), Khūrī (1988), and Tibbetts (1971).

3. For information on Arab ships in the medieval period, see Hourani (1951), al-Idrīsī (1970:1:94), Moreland (1939), and Smith (1978:2:124–25). Serjeant (1974c:132–37) provides an excellent discussion of Arabic terminology for European ships from the Portuguese period. The modern dhows in the region are described by al-Ḥajjī (1988), Hawkins (1977), Rowand (1915), Samuel (1844:24–25), and Sultanate of Oman (1979:107–65).

4. For more information on the navigational star compass, see Tibbetts (1971:296–98) and Tolmacheva (1980).

5. The function of the *nākhūdhā*, or *nawkhūdhā*, is described for a more recent setting by Serjeant (1970). This may be rendered as *nākhudhā*.

6. In the Mediterranean region and North Africa the term *naw'* took on the meaning of a sea storm or gale, as in the usage of Ibn Jubayr (1984:9).

7. Information on the Greek term was given to me by Professor Speros Vryonis of New York University.

8. For information on aloe in Yemen, see al-Bīrūnī (1973:196–97).

9. For an excellent discussion of the dragon's blood tree, see Cronk (manuscript) and 'Abd Allāh (in 'Afīf et al. 1992:1:442–43). For photographs of this tree, see Bādhīb (1991, plate 3).

10. For information on the *dīmānī* wind, see chapter 2.

11. This source mistakenly indicates that ships leave for Aden as *dīmānī* at this time, but the opposite is true.

12. The origin of this term has been debated. Both al-Khazrajī and al-Qalqashandī argued that it was derived from the African tribal name Kānim, but this makes little sense for a group of wealthy Egyptian merchants. It has also been suggested that it may be an Amharic word for spice or a word for yellow amber. The earliest mention of the term is from 577/1181 (Fischel 1958:59).

13. For an introduction to the incense trade in South Arabia, see Groom (1981).

Incense was generally harvested in spring and during the heat of summer, with the main export from the ports after September. For a discussion of *lubān* incense from al-Shiḥr, see al-Bīrūnī (1973:1:291).

14. For information on this term for a wind, see chapter 3.

Bibliography

MANUSCRIPT SOURCES

Abū al-'Uqūl — Muḥammad ibn Aḥmad ibn al-Ṭabarī, known as Abū al-'Uqūl (fl. A.D. 1300)
Jadwal al-yawāqīt fī ma'rifat al-mawāqīt.
(M) Milan, ms. Ambrosiana 302, C46,vi,526 (copy from 1106/1694-95, all references are to this copy unless otherwise noted)
(L) London, British Library, ms. Or. 3747, fols. 13-17.
(SH) Ṣan'ā', Great Mosque, Gharbīya, ms. *ḥadīth* 59, fols. 347r–366v.
(SM) Ṣan'ā', Great Mosque, Gharbīya, ms. *majmū'a* 77, fols. 17r–24v. (copy from 1319/1901–2)

'Aqd — Nūr al-Dīn 'Alī ibn Ḥasan al-Khazrajī (died 812/1410)
al-'Aqd al-fākhir al-ḥasan fī ṭabaqāt akābir al-Yaman.
Ṣan'ā', Great Mosque, Gharbīya, ms. ta'rīkh 136. (copy from 801/1398–99 in hand of author)

Aqwāl — al-Malik al-Mujāhid 'Alī ibn Dāwūd (died 764/1363)
al-Aqwāl al-kāfiya wa-al-fuṣūl al-shāfiya fī 'ilm al-bayṭara.
London, British Library, ms. Or. 3830. (see 'Alī ibn Dāwūd 1987)

al-Aṣbaḥī — Ibrāhīm ibn 'Alī ibn Muḥammad al-Janadī al-Aṣbaḥī (died ca. 660/1261–62)
Kitāb al-Yawāqīt fī 'ilm al-mawāqīt.
Cairo, Egyptian National Library, ms. *mīqāt* 948.1.

Bughya — al-Malik al-Afḍal al-'Abbās ibn 'Alī (died 778/1376)
Bughyat al-fallāḥīn fī al-ashjār al-muthmira wa-al-rayāḥīn. (see Meyerhoff 1944 and Serjeant 1974a)
(C) Cairo, Egyptian National Library, ms. *zirā'a* 155. (all references are to this copy unless otherwise noted)
(S) Ṣan'ā', Great Mosque, Gharbīya, ms. *zirā'a* 1. (copy from

1362/1943; author mislabeled as Yaḥyā ibn Ismā'īl al-Ghassānī)
(T) Tarīm, Ḥaḍramawt, private library; copy from 1197/1782. (ms. copied by R. B. Serjeant in 1953–55)
(I) Istanbul, Topkapi Saray, Ahmet III, ms. A. 2432, fols. 177v–225r. (copy from 1001/1592 by a Kurd)
(ABR) Ṣan'ā', private library, 6 ff. (abridged version from the time of the author)

Fuṣūl — Anonymous (eighth/fourteenth century)
Fuṣūl majmū'a fī al-anwā' wa-al-zurū' wa-al-ḥiṣād.
(S) Ṣan'ā', private library, 2 1/2 pp. (copy from private library of al-Malik al-Afḍal; all references are to this copy)
(Y) Yemen, private library of Sheikh Zayd. (copy from ca. seventeenth century A.D.; photocopy provided by R. B. Serjeant)

Ibn Jaḥḥāf — al-Ḥusayn ibn Zayd ibn 'Alī, known as Ibn Jaḥḥāf (fl. seventeenth century A.D. ?)
Kitāb al-Yawāqīt fī ma'rifat al-mawāqīt.
(B) Berlin, ms. Ahlwardt 5784/5769/5720 (= Mq. 733), fols. 1–7r.
(L) Leiden, University of Leiden, ms. 2807.
(LL) Leiden, ms. Landberg-Brill 445.

Ibn Raḥīq — Abū 'Abd Allāh Muḥammad ibn Raḥīq ibn 'Abd al-Karīm (fl. eleventh century A.D.)
Title unknown.
Berlin, ms. Ahlwardt 5664. (treatise on folk astronomy)

Ja'far al-Ṣādiq — Anonymous (attributed to Ja'far al-Ṣādiq ibn Muḥammad, died 148/765)
Mukhtaṣar fī ma'rifat sīnī al-'Arab wa-shuhūrihā.
Ṣan'ā', Great Mosque, Gharbīya, ms. Q 58. (microfilm copy in the Arab League Institute library, Cairo)

al-Khalījī — Aḥmad ibn 'Alī ibn al-Sayyid 'Alī al-Khalījī
Awrāq taḥtawā 'alā ma'rifat khuṣūṣ al-awqāt wa-al-mawāsim wa-al-tawqī'āt . . .
Cairo, Egyptian National Library, Ṭal'at ms. *mīqāt* 132.

Kifāya — Muḥammad ibn Aḥmad ibn al-Ṭabarī, known as Abū al-'Uqūl (fl. A.D. 1300)

al-Kifāya fī al-lugha al-mashhūra bi-al-riwāya.
Ṣan'ā', Great Mosque, Gharbīya, ms. *majmū'a* 193, fols. 75v–103r.

Ma'rifa — al-Malik al-Afḍal al-'Abbās ibn 'Alī
Faṣl fī ma'rifat al-matānim wa-al-asiqa (?) fī al-Yaman al-maḥrūsa.
Ṣan'ā', private library, mixed Rasulid ms., ca. 1 fol. (copy written 773/1371–72; see Varisco 1991b)

Milḥ — al-Malik al-Ashraf 'Umar ibn Yūsuf
Milḥ al-malāḥa fī ma'rifat al-filāḥa.
(V) Vienna, Glaser Collection, no. 247. (all references are to this copy unless otherwise noted)
(Y) Yemen, private library. (see 'Umar ibn Yūsuf 1985a)

Mīqāt — Anonymous
al-Qawl 'alā shuhūr al-Rūm . . .
Cairo, Egyptian National Library, ms. *mīqāt* 817, fols. 67v–68r. (Yemeni almanac for 727/1326–27)

Mughnī — al-Malik al-Ashraf 'Umar ibn Yūsuf
al-Mughnī fī al-bayṭara.
(C) Cairo, Egyptian National Library, ms. Taymūr *ṭibb* 377.
(M) Milan, ms. Ambrosiana B. 33.
(R) Rome, Vatican Library, ms. V 980, 1128.
(B) Berlin, ms. 6195.
(S) Ṣan'ā', Great Mosque, Sharqīya.

Mumtaḥan — Badr al-Dīn Muḥammad ibn Abī Bakr al-Fārisī (died 677/1278–79)
al-Zīj al-mumtaḥan al-Sharwānī al-ma'rūf bi-al-Muẓaffarī
(S) Ṣan'ā', Great Mosque, Gharbīya, ms. *falak* 3. (copy from 1001/1593; all references are to this copy)
(C) Cambridge, Cambridge University Library, ms. Gg. 3.27.

Nubdha — Anonymous
Nubdha falakīya fī al-'amal bi-al-shuhūr al-Qubṭīya . . .
Cairo, Egyptian National Library, ms. *mīqāt* 187, fols. 1–29. (almanac for 1039/1629)

BIBLIOGRAPHY

Qusṭūs — Cassianus Bassus (fl. sixth century A.D.)
Kitāb al-Filāḥa al-Rūmīya.
Istanbul, Topkapi Saray, Ahmet III, ms. A. 2432, fols. 1-114 (copy from 1001/1592 by a Kurd)

Salwa — al-Malik al-Afḍal al-'Abbās ibn 'Alī
Kitāb Salwat al-mahmūm fī 'ilm al-nujūm.
Ṣan'ā', private library, mixed Rasulid ms., 25 pp. (copy from 777/1375–76 from private library of author)

Saray — Anonymous
Taqwīm.
Istanbul, Topkapi Saray, ms. B. 323, fols. 9r–15r. (almanac for 1009/1600)

Shāmil — Anonymous (late seventh/thirteenth century)
Untitled royal court archive (working title: *al-Shāmil li-al-qawānīn al-iqtiṣādīya fī al-Yaman*).
Ṣan'ā', private library. (copy may be from court records of al-Malik al-Muẓaffar Yūsuf)

al-Shayzarī — Abū Ghanā'im Muslim ibn Maḥmūd al-Shayzarī (died 626/1229)
'Adāt al-nujūm wa-'alāmāt al-ghuyūm.
(A) Milan, Ambrosiana (743 D487 II, 232–61, all references are to this copy)
(Ṣ) Ṣan'ā', Great Mosque, Gharbīya, ms. *majāmī' 23* (copied 1076/1665–66)

Tabṣira — al-Malik al-Ashraf 'Umar ibn Yūsuf
al-Tabṣira fī 'ilm al-nujūm.
Oxford, Bodleian Library, Huntington 233 (Uri 905).

Ṭal'at — Anonymous
Untitled almanac.
Cairo, Egyptian National Library, ms. Ṭal'at *majāmī'* 811, fols. 6v–32r.

Taqwīm — Anonymous (eighth/fourteenth century)
Wujūd fī ẓahr taqwīm qadīm.
Ṣan'ā', private library, mixed Rasulid ms., 1 p.

Ta'rīb	Anonymous *Ta'rīb ba'd al-adwīya bi-lughat ahl al-Yaman wa-ghayrih.* (S1) Ṣan'ā', Great Mosque, Gharbīya, ms. *majmū'a* 27, fols. 209v–12r. (S2) Ṣan'ā', Great Mosque, Gharbīya, ms. *majmū'a* 193, fols. 73v–74v. (SH) Ṣan'ā', private library of Qāḍī 'Alī Muḥammad al-Sharafī.
Tawqī'āt	Anonymous *al-Tawqī'āt fī shahr. . .* Yemen, private library of Sheikh Zayd. (copy from ca. seventeenth century A.D.; almanac similar to that of Ibn Jaḥḥāf; photocopy courtesy of R. B. Serjeant).
Taymūr	Anonymous Title Unknown. Cairo, Egyptian National Library, Taymūr ms. *riyāḍiyāt* 274, pp. 102–25. (see Varisco 1985b, 1993c)
al-Thābitī	Muḥammad ibn 'Abd al-Laṭīf al-Thābitī (fl. seventeenth century A.D.) *Jadāwal . . .* Rome, Vatican Library, ms. VAT. AR. 92.
al-Waṭwāṭ	Jamāl al-Dīn Muḥammad al-Waṭwāṭ (died 718/1318) *Mabāhij al-fikr wa-manāhij al-'ibar.* Istanbul, Süleymaniyeh, ms. Yeni Camii 1010. (see al-Waṭwāṭ 1990)
Waṭyūṭ	Waṭyūṭ, al-Ḥusayn ibn Ismā'īl al-Bajalī (fl. fourteenth century) *Kitāb Ta'rīkh al-ma'lam Waṭyūṭ.* Ṣan'ā', Great Mosque, Gharbīya, ms. 2208 (copy of 1333/1915 from 810/1407–8 original)

PUBLISHED SOURCES

'Abd al-'Alīm, Anwar

1979 *al-Milāḥa wa-'ulūm al-biḥār 'inda al-'Arab.* Kuwait: 'Ālam al-Ma'rifa.

'Abdalī, Aḥmad Faḍl ibn 'Alī Muḥsin

1400/1980 *Hadīya al-zamān fī akhbār mulūk Laḥj wa-'Adan.* 2nd ed. Beirut:

Dār al-ʻAwda.

Abū Ghānim, Faḍl ʻAlī Aḥmad

1985 *al-Bunīya al-qabalīya fī al-Yaman bayna al-istimrār wa-al-taghayyur*. Damascus: Maṭbaʻat al-Kātib al-ʻArabī.

Abū Ḥanīfa al-Dīnawarī (died 282/895)

1332/1914 Almanac. (see al-Marzūqī 1914:2:282–92)

1974a *The book of plants (Kitāb al-Nabāt)*. Edited by B. Lewin. Bibliotheca Islamica, 26. Wiesbaden: Steiner.

1974b Kitāb al-ʻAsal wa-al-naḥl wa-al-nabātāt allātī tajrisu minih. *al-Mawrid* 3/1:113–42.

Abū Zayd Saʻīd ibn Aws al-Anṣārī (died 215/830)

1905 Kitāb al-maṭar. *al-Mashriq* 8:209–14, 265–70.

al-Adīmī, Muḥammad ʻUthmān

1989 *al-Tharwa al-Yamanīya min al-amthāl al-shaʻbīya*. Beirut: Mu'assasat al-Ṣabbāgh li-al-Ṭibāʻa wa-al-Nashr.

Adra, N.

1982 Qabyala: The tribal concept in the central highlands of the Yemen Arab Republic. Ph.D. dissertation, Temple University, Philadelphia.

1983 Local perceptions of breastfeeding, fertility and infant care in Ahjur, Yemen Arab Republic. Unpublished field report for The Population Council, Cairo.

1985 The concept of tribe in rural Yemen. In N. S. Hopkins and S. E. Ibrahim (editors), *Arab society: Social science perspectives*, 275–85. Cairo: The American University in Cairo Press.

Aelian [Claudius Aelianus] (died A.D. 230)

1971 *On the characteristics of animals*. Translated by A. F. Schofield. Harvard: Loeb Library.

ʻAfīf, Aḥmad Jābir, et al.

1992 *Al-Mawsūʻat al-Yamanīya*. 2 vols. Beirut: Dār al-Fikr al-Maʻāṣir.

Agaryshev, A.

1968 *Aqwāl ʻAlī ibn Zāyid*. Moscow. (in Arabic and Russian)

1986 *Aqwāl ʻAlī ibn Zāyid*. 2nd ed. Ṣanʻā': Al-Maktaba al-Yamanīya.

al-Ahdal, al-Ḥusayn ibn ʻAbd al-Raḥmān (died 855/1451)

1986 *Tufḥat al-zaman fī ta'rīkh al-Yaman*. Beirut: Manshūrāt al-Madīna.

Ahmad, S. M.

1971 IBN MĀDJID. In *The encyclopaedia of Islam*, 2nd ed., 3:856–59.

BIBLIOGRAPHY

Ahmad, S. M., et al.

1971 HIND. In *The encyclopaedia of Islam*, 2nd ed., 3:404–54.

Ahsan, M.

1979 *Social life under the Abbasids*. London: Longman.

al-Akwaʻ, Ismāʻīl ibn ʻAlī

1288/1968 *al-Amthāl al-Yamānīya*. Vol. 1. Cairo: Maṭbaʻat al-Madanī.

1400/1980 *al-Madāris al-islāmīya fī al-Yaman*. Manshūrāt Jāmiʻat Ṣanʻā', 1. Damascus: Dār al-Fikr.

1405/1984 *al-Amthāl al-Yamānīya*. 2nd. ed. 2 vols. Ṣanʻā': Maktabat al-Jīl al-Jadīd.

al-Akwaʻ, Muḥammad ibn ʻAlī

1391/1971 *al-Yaman al-khaḍrā' mahd al-ḥaḍāra*. 2nd ed. 2 vols. Cairo: Maṭbaʻat al-Saʻāda.

1399/1979 *Ṣafḥat min ta'rīkh al-Yaman al-ijtimāʻī wa-qiṣṣat ḥayātī*. Damascus: Maṭbaʻat al-Kātib al-ʻArabī.

1981 Qaṣīdat al-Baḥr al-Naʻāmī fī al-ashhār al-Ḥimyarīya. *al-Iklīl* (Ṣanʻā') 1/3–4:9–17.

ʻAlī ibn Dāwūd, al-Malik al-Mujāhid (died 764/1363)

1987 *al-Aqwāl al-kāfiya wa-al-fuṣūl al-shāfiya fī al-khayl*. Edited by Yaḥyā al-Jabbūrī. Beirut: Dār al-Gharb al-Islāmī.

Allen, M. J. S., and G. R. Smith

1975 Some notes on hunting techniques and practices in the Arabian Peninsula. *Arabian Studies* 2:108–45.

Allen, R. H.

[1899] 1963 *Star names: Their lore and meaning*. Reprint. New York: Dover.

al-Alūsī, Maḥmūd Shukrī

1314/1882 *Bulūgh al-arab fī maʻrifat aḥwāl al-ʻArab*. 3 vols. Baghdad: Maṭbaʻat Dār al-Salām.

Amīn, Aḥmad

1953 *Qāmūs al-ʻādāt wa-al-taqālīd wa-al-taʻābir al-Maṣriya*. Cairo: Maktaba al-Nahḍa al-Maṣriya.

al-Anqar, Ibrāhīm ibn Sulaymān

1980 *al-Ṭibb al-shaʻbī*. United Arab Emirates: Lajnat al-Turāth wa-al-Ta'rīkh.

al-ʻAnsī, Yaḥyā ibn Yaḥyā

ca. 1980 *al-Dā'ira al-falakīya al-zirāʻīya li-al-Yaman*. Ṣanʻā'. (circular chart)

al-Anṭākī, Dāwūd ibn ʻUmar (died 1008/1599)

1371/1951 *Tadhkirat ūlā al-albāb wa-al-jāmiʻ li-al-ʻajab al-ʻujāb*. 2 vols. Beirut: Dār al-Fikr.

BIBLIOGRAPHY

al-'Aqīlī, Muḥammad ibn Aḥmad 'Īsā

1378/1958 *Min ta'rīkh al-Mikhlāf al-Sulaymānī.* Riyadh: Maṭābi' Riyāḍ.

Arab League Institute

1977a *Dirāsat taṭawwur tarbīya al-naḥl wa-intāj al-'asal bi-al-jumhūrīya al-'Arabīya al-Yamanīya.* Khartoum: Arab Organization for Agricultural Development, Arab League Institute.

1977b *al-Jadwā al-fannīya wa-al-iqtiṣādīya li-taṭawwur intāj al-tumūr fī al-jumhūrīya al-dīmuqrāṭīya al-sha'bīya al-Yamanīya.* Khartoum: Arab Organization for Agricultural Development, Arab League Institute.

al-'Arashī (al-'Arshī), Ḥusayn ibn Aḥmad

1358/1939 *Kitāb bulūgh al-marām fī sharḥ misk al-khitām.* Edited by Anastase-Marie de St. Elie. Reprint. Ṣan'ā': Maktabat al-Yaman al-Kubrā.

Arberry, A. J. (editor)

1967 *Aspects of Islamic civilization.* Ann Arbor: University of Michigan Press.

Aristotle

1971 *On the heavens.* Translated by W. K. C. Guthrie. Harvard: Loeb Library, no. 338.

Ashtor, E.

1978 KATTĀN. In *The encyclopaedia of Islam*, 2nd ed., 4:774.

1983 *Levant trade in the later Middle Ages.* Princeton: Princeton University Press.

al-Aṣma'ī, Abū Sa'īd 'Abd al-Malik ibn Qurayb (died 216/831)

1972 *Kitāb al-Nabāt.* Edited by 'Abd Allāh Yūsuf Ghānim. Cairo: Maṭba'at al-Madanī.

Aubin, J.

1953 Les princes d'Ormus du XIIIe au XVe siècles. *Journal Asiatique* 241:77–138.

al-'Awdī, Ḥamūd

1400/1980 *al-Turāth al-sha'bī wa-'alāqatih bi-al-tanmīya fī al-bilād al-nāmīya.* Ṣan'ā': Markaz al-Dirāsāt al-Yamanīya.

al-Azrāq, Ibrāhīm ibn 'Abd al-Raḥmān ibn Abī Bakr (died ca. 890/1485)

[1889] 1978 *Tashīl al-manāfi' fī al-ṭibb wa-al-ḥikma.* Reprint. Beirut: al-Maktaba al-Sha'bīya.

Bādhīb, 'Alī Sālim

1991 *al-Nabātāt al-ṭibīya fī al-Yaman.* Ṣan'ā': Maktabat al-Irshād.

Badr al-Dīn Muḥammad ibn Ḥātim al-Yāmī al-Hamdānī (died ca. 802/1302) (see Smith 1978.)

BIBLIOGRAPHY

Bailey, C.

1974 Bedouin star-lore in Sinai and the Negev. *Bulletin of the School of Oriental and African Studies* 37/3:580–96.

al-Baladī, 'Abd al-Raḥmān ibn Muḥammad

1983 *Kitāb al-Kāfiya fī al-bayzara*. Beirut: al-Mu'assasat al-'Arabīya li-al-Dirāsāt wa-al-Buḥūth.

al-Baraddūnī (al-Baradūnī), 'Abd Allāh

1985 *Aqwāl 'Alī ibn Zāyid*. Ṣan'ā': Dār al-Kalima.

al-Bāshā, 'Abd al-Raḥman Rāfit

1403/1983 *al-Ṣayd 'inda al-'Arab*. Beirut: Dār al-Nafā'is.

al-Batalyūsī, Abū Muḥammad 'Abd Allāh (died 521/1156)

1984 *al-Farq bayna al-ḥurūf al-khamsa al-zā' wa-al-ḍād wa-al-dhāl wa-al-sīn wa-al-ṣād*. Edited by 'Abd Allāh al-Nāṣir. Damascus: Dār al-Ma'mūn li-al-Turāth.

al-Battānī, Abū 'Abd Allāh Muḥammad (died ca. 287/900)

1899 *Opus astronomicum (al-Zīj al-ṣābi')*. Pubblicazioni del Reale Osservatorio di Brera in Milano 40/3. Milan

Bausani, A.

1974 Osservazione sul sistema calendariale degli Hazāra di Afghanistan. *Oriente Moderno* 54:341–51.

Becker, A. K., and C. F. Beckingham

1960 BAḤR AL-ḲULZŪM. In *The encyclopaedia of Islam*, 2nd ed., 1:931–33.

Bedevian, A. K.

1936 *Illustrated polyglottic dictionary of plant names*. Cairo: Argus and Papazian Presses.

Beeston, A. F. L

1956 *Epigraphic South Arabian calendars and dating*. London: Luzac.

1974 New light on the Himyaritic calendar. *Arabian Studies* 1:1–6.

Beeston, A. F. L., et al.

1982 *Sabaic dictionary*. Beirut: Librairie du Liban.

Beg, M. A. J.

1982 FAṢṢĀD, ḤADJDJĀM. In *The encyclopaedia of Islam*, supplement, 1:303–4.

Biella, J. C.

1982 *Dictionary of Old South Arabic: Sabaean dialect*. Harvard Semitic Series 25. Chico, Calif.: Scholars Press.

al-Bilādī, 'Ātiq ibn Ghayth

1982 *al-Adab al-sha'bī fī al-Ḥijāz*. Mecca: Dār Makka.

BIBLIOGRAPHY

al-Bīrūnī, Abū al-Rayḥān Muḥammad (died ca. 440/1048)

1879 — *The chronology of ancient nations (al-Āthār al-bāqīya).* Translated by C. E. Sachau. London: W. H. Allen.

1923 — *Chronologie orientalischer Völker von Alberuni.* Edited by C. E. Sachau. Leipzig: Harrassowitz.

1973 — *Al-Biruni's book on pharmacy and materia medica.* 2 vols. Edited by H. M. Said. Karachi: Hamdard National Foundation.

Bittner, M., and W. Tomaschek

1897 — *Die topographischen Capitel des indischen Seelspiegels Moḥīṭ.* Vienna.

Blatter, E.

1919–36 — *Flora arabica.* Records of the Botanical Survey of India 8/1–6. Calcutta: Superintendent Govt. Printing Office.

Bosworth, C. E. (translator)

1968 — *The book of curious and enlightening information: The Laṭā'if al-ma'ārif of Tha'ālibī.* Edinburgh: University Press.

Bourdieu, P.

1977 — *Outline of a theory of practice.* Translated by R. Nye. London: Cambridge University Press.

Brauer, E.

1934 — *Ethnologie der jemenitischen Juden.* Heidelberg: Winter.

Brockelmann, C.

1937–49 — *Geschichte der arabischen litteratur.* 5 volumes. Weimer and Berlin.

Brockie, K.

1985 — Wildlife of the Tihamah 1982, with emphasis on avifauna. In F. Stone (editor), *Studies on the Tihamah*, 18–26. London: Longman.

Brooks, D. J., et al.

1987 — The status of birds in North Yemen and the records of OSME expedition in autumn 1985. In Donald Parr (editor), *Sandgrouse* (England) 9:4–66.

Bürgel, J. C.

1976 — Secular and religious features of medieval Arabic medicine. In C. Leslie (editor), *Asian medical systems: A comparative study*, 44–62. Berkeley: University of California Press.

Bulliet, R. W.

1990 — *The camel and the wheel.* Rev. ed. Cambridge: Harvard University Press.

al-Burayhī, 'Abd al-Wahhāb ibn 'Abd al-Raḥmān (died 904/1498–99)

1984 — *Ṭabaqāt ṣulḥā' al-Yaman.* Edited by 'Abd Allāh al-Ḥibshī. Ṣan'ā': Markaz al-Dirāsāt wa-al-Buḥūth al-Yamanī.

Burton, R. F.
1886 *The book of the thousand nights and a night*. Vol. 10. England: The Burton Club.

Bury, G. W.
1911 *The land of Uz*. London: Macmillan.
1915 *Arabia infelix, or the Turks of Yemen*. London: Macmillan.

Cahen, C., and R. B. Serjeant
1957 A fiscal survey of the medieval Yemen. *Arabica* 4:23-33.

Calendar of Cordova (see Dozy 1967)

Canaan, T.
1928 Plant-lore in Palestinian superstition. *Journal of the Palestine Oriental Society* 9:57-69.

Canard, M., and P. Berthier
1976 ḲAṢAB AL-SUKKĀR. In *The encyclopaedia of Islam*, 2nd ed., 4:682–84.

Casson, L.
1971 *Ships and seamanship in the ancient world*. Princeton: Princeton University Press.

Caussin de Perceval, A. P.
1947 Notes on the Arab calendar before Islam. *Islamic Culture* 21:135–53. (Translation of original French in *Journal Asiatique* 1843.)

Cerulli, E., and G. S. P. Freeman-Grenville
1986–87 MAḲDISHŪ. In *The encyclopaedia of Islam*, 2nd ed., 6:128–29.

Chaine, M.
1925 *La chronologie des temps chrétiens de l'Égypte et de l'Éthiope*. Paris.

Chaudhary, S. A., and R. Revri
1983 *Weeds of North Yemen*. Eschborn: GTZ.

Chelhod, J.
1978 Introduction à l'histoire sociale et urbaine de Zabīd. *Arabica* 25:48–88.

Clement-Mullet, J. J.
1865 Sur les noms des céréales chez les anciens. *Journal Asiatique*, Series 6, 10:185-226.
1870 Études sur les noms arabes de diverses familles de végétaux. *Journal Asiatique*, Series, 6, 15:5–150.

Cole, D. P.
1975 *Nomads of the nomads*. Chicago: Aldine.

Colin, G. S.
1978 KAMMŪN. In *The encyclopaedia of Islam*, 2nd ed., 4:522–23.

Collenette, S.

1985 *An illustrated guide to the flowers of Saudi Arabia.* Meteorology and Environmental Protection Administration, Saudi Arabia, Flora Publications 1. London: Scorpion.

Conrad, L. I.

1982 *Ṭā'ūn* and *wabā'*: Conceptions of plague and pestilence in early Islam. *Journal of the Economic and Social History of the Orient* 25:268–307.

Corkill, N. L., and J. A. Cochrane

1966 The snakes of the Arabian Peninsula and Socotra. *Journal of the Bombay Natural History Society* 62:475–506.

Cornwallis, L., and R. Porter

1982 Spring observations on the birds of North Yemen. *Sandgrouse* 4:1–35.

Costa, P.

1979 The study of the city of Ẓafār (al-Balīd). *Journal of Oman Studies* 5:111–50.

1983 The mosque of al-Janad. In R. L. Bidwell and G. R. Smith (editors), *Arabian and Islamic Studies*, 43–67. London: Longman.

Cronk, Q.

n.d. Vernacular plant names in Socotri and the ethnobotany of dragon's blood. Unpublished manuscript.

Dalman, G.

1928–35 *Arbeit und Sitte in Palästina.* 4 vols. Gutersloh: Bertelsmann.

al-Damīrī, Muḥammad ibn Mūsā (died 808/1405)

n.d. *Ḥayāt al-ḥayawān al-kubrā.* 2 vols. Reprint. Beirut: Dār al-Fikr.

1906–8 *Ad-Damīrī's Ḥayāt al-ḥayawān (A zoological lexicon).* 2 vols. Translated by A. S. G. Jayakar. London: Luzac and Co.

Daumas, E.

1971 *The ways of the desert.* Austin: University of Texas Press.

Deil, U.

1985 Zur vegetation der Gebirgstihama am Beispiel des Beckens von At Tur. In H. Kopp and G. Schweizer (editors), *Entwicklungsprozesse in der Arabischen Republik Jemen,* 1:225–35. Wiesbaden.

Deil, U., and K. Müller-Hohenstein

1985 Beiträge zur Vegetation des Jemen. I. Pflanzengesellschaften und Ökotopgefüge der Gebirgstihamah am Beispiel des Beckens von At Tur (J.A.R.). *Phytocoenologia* 13/1:1–102.

BIBLIOGRAPHY

al-Dhahabī, Abū 'Abd Allāh Muḥammad

1404/1984 *al-Ṭibb al-nabawī*. Beirut: Dār Iḥyā' al-'Ulūm.

Dickson, H. R. P.

1951 *The Arab of the desert*. 2nd ed. London: Allen and Unwin.

Didier, C.

[1857] 1985 *Sojourn with the gran sherif of Makkah*. Reprint. New York: Oleander Press.

Dietrich, A.

1981 DJĀWARS. In *The encyclopaedia of Islam*, supplement, 249–50.

al-Dimyāṭī, Maḥmūd Muṣṭafā

1965 *Mu'jam asmā' al-nabātāt*. Cairo: Dār al-Maṣriya li-al-Ta'līf wa-al-Tarjama.

Dodge, B. (translator)

1970 *The Fihrist of al-Nadīm*. New York: Columbia University Press.

Dols, M.

1977 *The Black death in the Middle East*. Princeton: Princeton University Press.

Dorsky, S.

1986 *Women of 'Amrān: A Middle Eastern ethnographic study*. Salt Lake City: University of Utah Press.

Dostal, W.

1967 *Die Beduinen in Südarabien*. Wiener Beiträge zur Kulturgeschichte und Linguistik 16. Vienna. Ferdinand Berger and Sons.

1975 Two South Arabian tribes: al-Qarā and al-Harāsīs. *Arabian Studies* 2:33–41.

1983 Analysis of the Ṣan'ā' market today. In R. B. Serjeant and R. Lewcock (editors), *Ṣan'ā': An Arabian Islamic city*, 241–75. London: World of Islam Festival Trust.

1985 *Egalität und Klassengesellschaft in Südarabien*. Wiener Beiträge zur Kulturgeschichte und Linguistik 20. Vienna: Ferdinand Berger and Sons.

Dostal, W., et al.

1983 *Ethnographic atlas of 'Asīr. Preliminary report*. Sitzungsberichte d. Österreichische Akademie der Wissenschaften, Philosophisch-historische Klasse 406. Vienna.

Doutté, E.

1909 *Magie et religion dans l'Afrique du Nord*. Algiers: Jourdan.

Dozy, R.

1961 *Le Calendrier de Cordoue*. Leiden: Brill.

Dresch, P.
1982 The northern tribes of Yemen: Their origins and their place in the Yemen Arab Republic. Ph.D. dissertation, Oxford University.
1989 *Tribes, government, and history in Yemen.* Oxford: Clarendon Press.

Dubaie, Abdul-Rahman, and Abdul-Wali A. Al-Khulaidi
1991 Studies on the genus Acacia Mill. in Yemen. *Bulletin of the Faculty of Science, Assiut University, D. Botany* 20/1:43–62.

Dubler, C. E.
1960 AFYŪN. In *The encyclopaedia of Islam,* 2nd ed., 1:243.

Ducros, A. H.
1930 *Essai sur le droguier populaire arabe de l'inspectorat des pharmacies du Caire.* Memoires de l'Institut d'Égypt 15. Cairo.

Dunlop, D. M.
1960 BAḪR AL-RŪM. In *The encyclopaedia of Islam,* 2nd ed., 1:934–36.

Elgood, C.
1962 Tibb-ul-nabbi or medicine of the Prophet. *Osiris* 14:33–192.

Euting, J.
1896–1914 *Tagbuch einer Reise in Inner-Arabien.* 2 vols. Leiden: Brill.

Fahd, T.
1969 Retour à Ibn Waḥšiyya. *Arabica* 16:83–88.
1974 Le calendrier des travaux agricoles d'après al-Filāḥa al-Nabaṭiyya. *Orientalis Hispanica* 1:245–72.

al-Falakī, Muṣṭafā Muḥammad, and Aḥmad Zākī Būz Bāshā
1311/1893–94 *al-Hidāya al-'Abbāsīya fī al-tawārīkh al-falakīya.* Boulak: al-Maṭba'a al-Amīrīya.

Ferrand, G.
1913–14 *Relations de voyages et textes géographiques arabes, persans et turks, relatifs a l'Extreme-Orient des VIIIe au XVIIIe siècles.* 2 vols. Paris: Leroux.
1921–28 *Instructions nautiques et routiers arabes et portugais des XVe et XVIe siècles.* 3 vols. Paris.
1924 L'élément persan dans les textes nautiques arabes des XVe et XVIe siècles. *Journal Asiatique* 204:193–257.

al-Fīrūzābādī, Majd al-Dīn Muḥammad (died 817/141)
1382/1952 *al-Qāmūs al-muḥīṭ.* 4 vols. Beirut: al-Mu'assasa al-'Arabīya li-al-Ṭibā'a wa-al-Nashr.
1403/1983 *Taḥbīr al-muwashshīn fī al-ta'bīr bi-al-sīn wa-al-shīn.* Damascus: Dār Qutayba.

Fischel, W.

1937 Über die Gruppe der Kārimī-Kaufleute. In F. Rosenthal et al., *StudiaArabica* 1, 65–82. Rome: Pontificium Institutum Biblicum.

1958 The spice trade in Mamluk Egypt: A contribution to the economic history of medieval Islam. *Journal of the Economic and Social History of the Orient* 1:157–74.

Fleurentin, J., and J.-M. Pelt

1982 Repertory of drugs and medicinal plants in Yemen. *Journal of Ethnopharmacology* 6:85–108.

Forskal, P.

1775a *Descriptiones animalium.* Edited by Carsten Niebuhr. Havniae: Mölleri.

1775b *Flora aegyptiaco-arabica.* Edited by Carsten Niebuhr. Havniae: Mölleri.

Frantz-Murphy, G.

1986 *The agrarian administration of Egypt from the Arabs to the Ottomans.* Supplement aux *Annales Islamologiques* 9. Cairo.

Freeman-Grenville, G. S. P.

1977 *The Muslim and Christian calendars.* 2nd ed. London: Rex Collins Ltd.

Friis, I.

1983 Notes on the botanical collections and publications of Pehr Forsskal. *Kew Bulletin* 34/3:457–67.

Garland-Pernet, P.

1958 La vielle et le légende des jours d'emprunt au Maroc. *Hesperis* 1/2:29–94.

1960 AYYĀM AL-'ADJŪZ In *The encyclopaedia of Islam*, 2nd ed., 1:792–93.

Gasparetti, J.

1987 Snakes of Arabia. *Fauna of Saudi Arabia* 9:169ff.

Gaudefroy-Demombynes, M.

1912 Les sources arabes du Muḥīṭ. *Journal Asiatique* 165:547–50.

Genevois, H.

1975 Le calendrier agraire et sa composition. *Le Fichier Periodique* 125.

al-Ghazālī, Abū Ḥamīd Muḥammad (died 505/1111)

1984 *Marriage and sexuality in Islam.* Translated by M. Farah. Salt Lake City: University of Utah Press.

Gifri, Abdulnasser, and Saeed A. Gabali

1991 Notes on the distribution of shrubs and trees in Aden (Republic of

Yemen). *Fragmenta Floristica et Geobotanica* (Krakow) 35/1-2:89–95.

Ginzel, F. E.
1906–14 *Handbuch der mathematischen und technische Chronologie*. 3 vols. Leipzig: Hinrichs.

Glaser, E.
1885 Der Sternkunde der südarabischen Kabylen. *Sitzungsberichte der Akademie des Wissenschaften der Wien* 91:89–99.

Goitein, S. D.
1934 *Jemenica: Sprichwörter und Redensarten aus Zentral-Jemen*. Leiden: Brill.
1967 *A Mediterranean society*, Vol. 1. *Economic foundations*. Berkeley: University of California Press.
1980 From Aden to India: Specimens of the correspondence of India traders of the twelfth century. *Journal of the Economic and Social History of the Orient* 23:43–66.

Goldstein, B., and D. Pingree
1979 Astrological almanacs from the Cairo Geniza. *Journal of Near Eastern Studies* 38:153–76, 231–56.
1983 Additional astrological almanacs from the Cairo Geniza. *Journal of the American Oriental Society* 103:673–90.

Gottheil, R. J. H. (editor)
1895 Kitāb al-Maṭar, by Abū Zeid Sa'īd 'Aus al-Anṣārī. *Journal of the American Oriental Society* 16:282-317.

Gray, J. M.
1955 Nairuzi or Siku ya Mwaka. *Tanganyika Notes and Records* 38:1-22.

Gray, L. H.
1955 Calendar (Persian). In *Encyclopaedia of religion and ethics*, 3:128–31. New York: Scribners.

Great Britain Admiralty
1946 *Western Arabia and the Red Sea*. B.R. 527. London: Naval Intelligence Staff, Great Britain Admiralty.

Greengus, S.
1987 The Akkadian calendar at Sippar. *Journal of the American Oriental Society* 107:209–29.

Griveau, R.
1914 Les fêtes des Coptes par al-Maqrîzî. *Patrologia orientalis* 10/17:313–43.

Grohmann, A.
1930–34 *Südarabien als Wirtschaftsgebiet*. 2 vols. Brunn: Rudolf.

Groom, N.
1981 *Frankincense and myrrh: A study of the Arabian incense trade.* London: Longman.

Grosset-Grange, H.
1972 Comment naviguent aujourd'hui les Arabes de l'océan Indien? Suivi d'un glossaire de la navigation arabe dans l'océan Indien. *Arabica* 19:47–77.

Groves, C. P.
1989 The gazelles of the Arabian Peninsula. In *Wildlife Conservation and Development in Saudi Arabia*, 237–48. Riyadh: National Commission for Wildlife Conservation Development.

Grumel, V.
1958 *Traité d'études byzantines.* I. *La chronologie.* Paris: Presses Universitaires de France.

Haffner, A. (editor)
1905 *Texte zur arabishe Lexikographie.* Leipzig: Harrassowitz.

al-Ḥajjī, Ya'qūb Yūsuf
1988 *Ṣinā'at al-sufun al-shirā'īya fī al-Kuwayt.* Doha: Markaz al-Turāth al-Sha'bī bi-Duwwal al-Khalīj al-'Arabīya.

al-Ḥajrī, Muḥammad ibn Aḥmad
1404/1984 *Majmū' buldān al-Yaman wa-qabā'ilhā.* 4 vols. Edited by Ismā'īl al-Akwa'. Publication Project 1/16. Ṣan'ā': Y.A.R. Ministry of Information and Culture.

al-Hamadhānī, 'Abd al-Raḥmān ibn 'Īsā (died 320/932)
1979 *Kitāb al-Alfāẓ al-kitābīya.* Beirut: Dār al-Hudā.

al-Hamdānī, Abū Muḥammad al-Ḥasan (died ca. 360/970)
1884–91 *Geographie der arabischen Halbinsel (Ṣifat jazīrat al-'Arab).* 2 vols. Edited by D. H. Müller. Leiden: Brill.
1938 *The antiquities of South Arabia (al-Iklīl).* Translated by N. Faris. Princeton: Princeton University Press.
1940 *al-Iklīl.* Book 8. Cairo. (Reprinted in Beirut, 1983.)
1397/1977 *Qaṣīdat al-dāmigha.* Edited by Muḥammad ibn 'Alī al-Akwa'. Ṣan'ā': al-Maktaba al-Yamanīya.
1983 *Ṣifat jazīrat al-'Arab.* Edited by Muḥammad 'Alī al-Akwa'. Ṣan'ā': Markaz al-Dirāsāt wa-al-Buḥūth al-Yamanī.

Hammer-Purgstall, J. (translator)
1834–39 Extracts from the Moḥîṭ, that is the Ocean, a Turkish work on navigation in the Indian Seas, translated by J. Hammer-Purgstall. *Journal of the Asiatic Society of Bengal* 1834:545–53; 1836:441–68; 1837:805–12; 1838:767–80; 1839:823–30.

Hann, J. von
1911 Ergebnisse aus Dr. E. Glaser's meteorologischen Beobachtungen in Ṣan'â' (el-Jemen). *Sitzungsberichte der mathematischen-naturwissenschaftlichen Klasse den Kaiserlichen Akademie der Wissenschaften den Wien* 120/2a:1833–96.

al-Ḥarīrī, Abū Muḥammad al-Qāsim (died 516/1122)
1867 *The assemblies of al-Ḥarîrî.* 2 vols. Translated by T. Chenery. London: Williams and Norgate.

Harrison, D. L.
1964–72 *The mammals of Arabia.* 3 vols. London: Benn.

Harrison, D. L., and P. J. J. Bates
1991 *The mammals of Arabia.* Kent: Harrison Zoological Museum.

Hartmann, R., and G. E. de Vaumas
1960 al-FURĀT. In *The encyclopaedia of Islam,* 2nd ed., 1:945–48.

Hartmann, R., and S. H. Longrigg
1960 DIDJLA. In *The encyclopaedia of Islam,* 2nd ed., 1:249–51.

Hawkins, C. W.
1977 *The dhow. An illustrated history of the dhow and its world.* Lymington.

al-Ḥaydara, Muḥammad
1946 (see Serjeant 1954)
1394/1974 *Ṭawāli' al-Yaman al-zirā'ī* (!). Ta'izz.

Heinen, A. M.
1978 The place of al-Suyūṭī's *al-Ḥay'at al-sanīya fī al-ḥay'at al-sunnīya* in the history of Arabic science. 2 vols. Ph.D. dissertation, Harvard University, Cambridge.

Hepper, F. N.
1977 Outline of the vegetation of the Yemen Arab Republic. *Cairo University Herbarium* (Giza) 7–8:307–22.

Hepper, F. N., and I. Friis
1994 *The plants of Pehr Forsskal's Flora aegyptiaco-arabica.* Kew: Royal Botanic Gardens.

Hepper, F. N., and J. R. I. Wood
1979 Were there forests in Yemen? *Proceedings of the Seminar for Arabian Studies* 9:65–71.

Hesiod (eighth century B.C.)
1967 *The Homeric hymns and Homerica.* Translated by H. G. Evelyn-White. Loeb Classical Library. Cambridge: Harvard University Press.
1973 *Theogony: Works and days.* Translated by D. Wender. Middlesex: Penguin Books.

Hess, J. J.
1926 Die Namen der Himmelsgegenden und Winde bei den Beduinen des inneren Arabiens. *Islamica* 2:585–89.

al-Ḥibshī, 'Abd Allāh Muḥammad
1977 *Maṣādir al-fikr al-'Arabī al-islāmī fī al-Yaman.* Ṣan'ā': Markaz al-Dirāsāt al-Yamanī. (The index is inaccurate for this edition.)
1980 *Ḥayāt al-adab al-Yamanī fī 'aṣr Banī Rasūl.* 2nd ed. Ṣan'ā': Y.A.R. Ministry of Information and Culture.

al-Ḥibshī, 'Abd Allāh Muḥammad (editor)
1405/1984 *Ta'rīkh al-dawla al-Rasūliya fī al-Yaman.* Damascus: Maṭba'at al-Kātib al-'Arabī.

al-Ḥimyarī, 'Īsā ibn Ibrāhīm al-Rab'ī al-Wuḥāẓī (died 480/1087–88)
1400/1980 *Niẓām al-gharīb fī al-lugha.* Edited by Muḥammad ibn 'Alī al-Akwa'. Damascus: Dār al-Ma'mūn li-al-Turāth.

Hippocrates
1983 *Hippocratic writings.* Edited by G. E. R. Lloyd. Translated by J. Chadwick and W. N. Mann. Harmondsworth, England: Penguin Books.

Hirsch, L.
1897 *Reisen in Süd-Arabien, Mahra-Land und Hadramūt.* Leiden: Brill.

Hobbs, J.
1989 *Bedouin life in the Egyptian wilderness.* Austin: University of Texas Press.

Hourani, G.
1951 *Arab seafaring in the Indian Ocean in ancient and medieval times.* Princeton: Princeton University Press.

al-Hubaishi, A., and K. Müller-Hohenstein
1984 *An introduction to the vegetation of Yemen.* Eschborn: GTZ.

al-Humiari, A. A.
1982 A first guide to the agricultural insect pests of the Yemen Arab Republic and their management. M.A. thesis, University of Arizona, Department of Entomology.

Hunter, F. M.
1877 *An account of the British settlement of Aden in Arabia.* London: Trübner and Company.

Hunter, F. M., et al.
1909 *Account of the Arab tribes in the vicinity of Aden.* Bombay.

Ḥusayn, Ayyūb
1984 *Ma'a dhikrīyātnā al-Kuwaytīya.* Kuwait: Manshūrāt Dhā al-Salāsil.

Ibn al-ʻAdīm al-Ḥalabī, Kamāl al-Dīn Abū al-Qāsim ʻAmr (died 660/1262)

1986 *al-Wuṣla ilā al-ḥabīb fī waṣf al-ṭiyyāb wa-al-ṭīb.* 2 vols. Edited by S. Maḥjūb and D. al-Khaṭīb. Aleppo: Maʻhad al-Turāth al-ʻIlmī al-ʻArabī.

Ibn al-Ajdābī, Abū Isḥāq Ibrāhīm ibn Ismāʻīl (died 650/1252)

1964 *al-Azmina wa-al-anwā'.* Damascus: Wizārat al-Thaqāfa wa-al-Irshād al-Qawmī.

Ibn ʻĀṣim, Abū Bakr ʻAbd Allāh (died 403/1013)

1985 *Kitāb al-Anwā' wa-al-azmina wa-maʻrifat aʻyān al-kawākib.* Frankfurt: Institut für Geschichte der arabisch-islamischen Wissenschaften.

Ibn al-ʻAwwām, Abū Zakarīyā Yaḥyā (fl. seventh/thirteenth century)

1802 *Libro de agricultura (Kitāb al-Filāḥa).* 2 vols. Madrid: La Imprenta Real.

1864–67 *Le livre de l'agriculture d'Ibn-al-Awam.* 3 vols. Translated by J. J. Clement-Mullet. Paris: A. Franck.

Ibn al-Bannā' (see Renaud 1948)

Ibn Baṣṣāl (fl. fifth/eleventh century)

1955 *Libro de agricultura.* Edited by J. M. Millás-Vallicrosa and M. Aziman. Tetuan.

Ibn Baṭṭūṭa (died 770/1368–69 or 779/1377)

1929 *Ibn Baṭṭūṭa: Travels in Asia and Africa, 1325–1354.* Translated by H. A. R. Gibb. London: Routledge and Sons.

1962 *The travels of Ibn Baṭṭūṭa, A.D. 1325–1354.* Vol. 2. Translated by H. A. R. Gibb. Cambridge: Hakluyt Society.

1980 *Riḥlat Ibn Baṭṭūṭa.* Beirut: Dār Bayrūt li-al-Ṭibāʻa wa-al-Nashr.

Ibn al-Bayṭār, Ḍiyā' al-Dīn ʻAbd Allāh (died 646/1248)

1291/1874 *al-Jāmiʻ al-mufradāt al-adwīya wa-al-aghdīya.* 4 vols. Cairo. (reprinted in Beirut, n. d.)

Ibn al-Daybaʻ, ʻAbd al-Raḥmān ibn ʻAlī (died 944/1537)

1977 *Qurrat al-ʻuyūn bi-akhbār al-Yaman al-maymūn.* 2 vols. Cairo: Maṭbaʻa al-Saʻāda.

1983 *al-Faṣl al-mazīd ʻalā bughyat al-mustafīd fī akhbār madīnat Zabīd.* Edited by J. Chelhod. Ṣanʻā': Markaz al-Dirāsāt wa-al-Buḥūth al-Yamanī.

Ibn al-Faqīh al-Hamadhānī, Abū Bakr Aḥmad (died 289/902)

[1885] 1967 *Kitāb al-Buldān.* Edited by M. de Goeje. Leiden: Brill.

Ibn Fāris, Abū al-Ḥusayn Aḥmad (died 395/1005)

1984 *Mujmal al-lugha.* 4 vols. Edited by Z. Sulṭān. Beirut: Mu'assasat al-Risāla.

Ibn Ḥajar al-Haytamī, Abū al-'Abbās Aḥmād (died 974/1567)
1308/1890–91 *al-Fatāwā al-kubrā al-fiqhīya*. 4 vols. Cairo.
Ibn Ḥamza, Aḥmad ibn 'Abd Allāh (fl. seventh/thirteenth century)
1979 *Ta'rīkh al-khuyūl al-'Arabīya*. Ṣan'ā': Y.A.R. Ministry of Information and Culture.
Ibn Iyās, Muḥammad ibn Aḥmad (died 930/1524)
1402/1982 *Badā'i' al-zuhūr fī waqā'i' al-duhūr*. Beirut: Dār al-Kutub al-'Ilmīya.
Ibn al-Jawzī, 'Abd al-Raḥmān ibn 'Alī (died 597/1201)
1400/1980 *Aḥkām al-nisā'*. Beirut: Manshūrāt al-Maktaba al-'Arabīya.
1987 *Mukhtaṣar luqṭ al-manāfi'*. Edited by Aḥmad Yūsuf al-Daqqāq. Damascus: Dār al-Ma'mūn li-al-Turāth.
Ibn Jubayr, Abū al-Ḥusayn Muḥammad (died 614/1217)
1984 *Riḥlat Ibn Jubayr*. Beirut: Dār Bayrūt li-al-Ṭibā'a wa-al-Nashr.
Ibn Kathīr, Abū al-Fidā' Ismā'īl (died 774/1372–73)
1399/1979 *Mukhtaṣar tafsīr Ibn Kathīr*. 3 vols. Edited by Muḥammad 'Alī al-Ṣābūnī. Beirut: Dār al-Qur'ān al-Karīm.
Ibn Khurradādhbih, Abū al-Qāsim 'Ubayd Allāh (died ca. 300/911)
1889 *al-Masālik wa-al-mamālik*. Edited by M. J. de Goeje. Leiden: Brill.
Ibn Mājid, Aḥmad (fl. ninth/fifteenth century)
1971 *al-Fawā'id fī uṣūl 'ilm al-baḥr wa-al-qawā'id*. Damascus: Maṭbū'āt Majma' al-Lugha al-'Arabīya bi-Dimashq. (See Khūrī 1981 and Tibbetts 1971.)
Ibn Mammātī (died 606/1209)
1943 *Kitāb Qawānīn al-dawāwīn*. Edited by A. S. Attiya. Cairo: Imprimerie Misr.
Ibn Manẓūr, Abū al-Faḍl Jamāl al-Dīn Muḥammad (died 711/1311)
n.d. *Lisān al-'Arab*. 15 vols. Beirut: Dār Ṣādir.
1403/1983 *Nuthār al-azhār fī al-layl wa-al-nahār*. Beirut: Manshūrāt al-Maktaba al-'Arabīya. (See al-Tīfāshī 1980.)
Ibn Māsawayh (see Sbath 1932–33, and Troupeau 1968)
Ibn al-Mujāwir, Jamāl al-Dīn Abū al-Fatāḥ Yūsuf (died 690/1291)
1954 *Ṣifat bilād al-Yaman wa-Makka wa-ba'ḍ al-Ḥijāz al-musammāt ta'rīkh al-mustabṣir*. Edited by O. Löfgren. Leiden: Brill.
Ibn Qayyim al-Jawzīya, Shams al-Dīn Muḥammad (died 751/1350)
1377/1957 *al-Ṭibb al-nabawī*. Edited by 'Abd al-Ghānī 'Abd al-Khāliq. Beirut: Dār al-Fikr.
Ibn Qutayba, Abū Muḥammad 'Abd Allāh ibn Muslim (died 276/889)
1949 *The natural history section from a 9th century "Book of Useful*

Knowledge." *The 'Uyūn al-akhbār of Ibn Qutayba*. Translated by L. Kopf. Collection de Travaux de l'Académie internationale d'Histoire des Sciences 4. Paris.

1375/1956 *Kitāb al-Anwā'*. Hyderabad: Maṭba'at Majlis Dā'ira al-Ma'ārif al'Uthmānīya.

1982 *Adab al-kātib*. Edited by Muḥammad al-Dālī. Beirut: Mu'assasat al-Risāla.

Ibn Riḍwān, 'Alī (died ca. 462/1068)

1984 *Medieval Islamic medicine: Ibn Riḍwān's treatise "On the prevention of bodily ills in Egypt."* Translated by Michael W. Dols. Berkeley: University of California Press.

Ibn Rusta, Abū 'Alī Aḥmad ibn 'Umar (died ca. 310/922)

1892 *al-A'lāq al-nafīsa*. Edited by M. J. de Goeje. Leiden: Brill.

Ibn Sīda, Abū al-Ḥasan 'Alī (died 458/1066)

1965 *al-Mukhaṣṣaṣ*. 17 vols. Reprint. Beirut: al-Maktab al-Tijārī li-al-Ṭibā'a wa-al-Tawāzi' wa-al-Nashr.

Ibn Sīna, Abū 'Alī al-Ḥusayn (died 428/1037)

1403/1983 *al-Qānūn fī al-ṭibb*. Beirut: Maktabat al-Ma'ārif.

Ibn al-Wardī, Sirāj al-Dīn 'Umar (died 749/1348)

1939 *Kharīda al-'ajā'ib wa-farīda al-gharā'ib*. Cairo.

al-Ibshīhī, Shihāb al-Dīn ibn Muḥammad (died ca. 850/1446)

1401/1981 *al-Mustaṭraf fī kull fann mustaẓraf*. Edited by 'Abd Allāh Anīs al-Ṭabbā'. Beirut: Dār al-Qalam.

al-Idrīsī, Abū 'Abd Allāh Muḥammad (died ca. 560/1165)

1866 *Description de l'Afrique et de l'Espagne*. Edited and translated by R. Dozy and M. J. de Goeje. Leiden: Brill.

1970 *Opus geographicum. (Nuzhat al-mushtāq fī ikhtirāq al-āfāq)*. Vol. 1. Napoli: Instituto Universitario Orientale di Napoli, Instituto per il Medio ed Estremo Oriente.

Inalcik, H.

1982 ḲUṬN. In *The encyclopaedia of Islam*, 2nd ed., 5:557–66.

'Inān, Zayd ibn 'Alī

1400/1980 *al-Lahja al-Yamānīya fī al-nukat wa-al-amthāl al-Ṣan'anīya*. Cairo: Maṭba'at al-Sa'āda.

Ingrams, H.

1936 *A report on the social,economic and political condition of the Hadhramaut*. Colonial Report 123. London: H. M. Stationery Office.

1937 Beekeeping in the Wadi Du'an. *Man* 37/33:32.

al-Iryānī, Mṭahhar 'Alī

1980 Ḥawl: al-kalimāt al-Yamanīya al-khaṣṣa. *al-Iklīl* 1/1:57–65.

Isaacs, H. D.
1990 Arabic medicinal literature. In M. J. L. Young et al., *Religion, learning, and science in the 'Abbasid period*, pp. 342–63. Cambridge: Cambridge University Press.

al-Jāḥiẓ, Abū 'Uthmān 'Umar (died 255/869)
1387/1968 *Kitāb al-Ḥayawān.* 8 vols. Cairo: Sharikat Maktabat Maṭba'at Muṣṭafā al-Bābī al-Ḥalabī wa-Awlādih.

al-Janadī, Abū 'Abd Allāh Bahā' al-Dīn Muḥammad (died 723/1323)
1403-9/1983–89 *al-Sulūk fī ṭabaqāt al-'ulamā' wa-al-mulūk.* 2 vols. Publication Project 1/12. Ṣan'ā': Y.A.R. Ministry of Information and Culture.

al-Jarrāfī, Ibrāhīm Ismā'īl
1983 *Amrāḍ al-'uyūn wa-'alājuhā fī al-Yaman wa-al-jazīra al-'Arabīya.* Damascus: Maṭba'at al-Kātib al-'Arabī.

al-Jarwān, Muḥammad Rāshid
1987 *Amīrat al-ṣaḥrā'.* Dubai: al-Maṭba'a al-Iqtiṣādīya.

Jastrow, O.
1983 *Glossar der arabischen Mundart von Jiblah (Nordjemen).* Erlangen.

al-Jawālīqī, Abū Manṣūr Mawhūb ibn Aḥmad (died 540/1145-46)
n.d. *Sharḥ adab al-kātib.* Edited by Muṣṭafā Ṣādiq al-Rāfi'ī. Beirut: Dār al-Kitāb al-'Arabī.

Jaycox, E. R., and J. Karpowicz
1990 A beekeeping project in the Yemen Arab Republic. *Arabian Studies* 9:1–10.

Jennings, M. G.
1991 *Atlas of the breeding birds of Arabia: Survey no 8. Results of an ornithological survey of South Yemen, 23 October to 9 November 1989.* Technical Report 25. Riyadh: National Commission for Wildlife Conservation and Development.

Johnson, F.
1852 *A dictionary of Persian, Arabic, and English.* London: W. H. Allen.

Johnstone, T. H.
1974 Folklore and folk literature in Oman and Socotra. *Arabian Studies* 1:7–23.
1981 *Jabbali lexicon.* Oxford: Oxford University Press.

Joly, A.
1905 Un calendrier agricole marocain. *Archives Marocaines* 3:301–19.

Karpowicz, J.
1983 Beekeeping in the Yemen Arab Republic. Unpublished ms.

al-Kawkabānī, Shihāb al-Dīn Aḥmad (died 1151/1738–39)
1985 *Ḥadā'iq al-nammām fī al-kalam 'alā mā yata'allaqu bi-al-ḥammām*. Edited by 'Abd Allāh al-Ḥibshī. Ṣan'ā': Y.A.R. Wizārat al-Awqāf wa-al-Irshād.

Kay, H. C.
1892 *Yaman: Its early medieval history*. London: Edward Arnold.

Kennedy, E. S.
1956 A survey of Islamic astronomical tables. *Transactions of the American Philosophical Society* 46:123–77.

Kessler, J. J., and A. W. al-Khuleidi
1987 *Common plant species of the Dhamar montane plains: Notes on colloquial names, distribution and local use*. RLIP Communication 12. Dhamār: Ministry of Agriculture and Fisheries.

al-Khatib, A.
1978 *A dictionary of agricultural and allied terminology: Arabic-English*. Beirut: Librairie du Liban.

al-Khawārizmī (al-Khuwārizmī), Muḥammad ibn Aḥmad (died 387/997)
1404/1984 *Mafātīḥ al-'ulūm*. Beirut: Dār al-Kitāb al-'Arabī.

al-Khazrajī, Abū al-Ḥasan 'Alī ibn al-Ḥasan (died 812/1410)
1906–18 *The pearl strings; A history of the Resuliyy dynasty of Yemen*. 5 vols. Edited and translated by J. W. Redhouse. London: Luzac and Co.
1981 *al-'Asjad al-masbūq fīman waliya al-Yaman min al-mulūk*. Publication Project 1/2. Y.A.R.: Ministry of Information and Culture.

al-Khulaidi, Abdul Wali Ahmed
1989 A comparative vegetation survey of four physiographic regions in the Yemen Arab Republic (YAR). M.A. thesis, International Institute for Aerospace Survey and Earth Science, Enschede, Netherlands.

Khūrī, Ibrāhīm
1970 *Arab nautical sciences: Sulaymān al-Mahri's works*. Damascus: Arab Academy.
1981 Arājīz milāḥīya. *al-Iklīl* 1/3–4:139–219.
1988 *Aḥmad ibn Mājid*. Silsilat al-Milāḥīya al-'Arabīya al-Falakīya 4. Ras El Kheima, United Arab Emirates: Markaz al-Dirāsāt wa-al-Wathā'iq fī al-Dīwān al-Amīrī bi-Ra's al-Khayma.

al-Kindī, Sālim ibn Muḥammad
1991 *Ta'rīkh Ḥaḍramawt al-musammā bi-al-'udda al-mufīda*. Ṣan'ā':

Maktabat al-Irshād.

King, D. A.

1975 On the astronomical tables of the Islamic Middle Ages. *Studia Copernica* 13:37–56. (Reprinted in King 1986.)

1977 Astronomical timekeeping in Ottoman Turkey. *Proceedings of the International Symposium on the Observatories in Islam*, 303–12. Istanbul. (Reprinted in King 1986.)

1982 Astronomical alignments in medieval Islamic religious architecture. *Annals of the New York Academy of Sciences* 385:303–12.

1983a *Mathematical astronomy in medieval Yemen: A biobibliographic survey*. Malibu: Undena.

1983b Mathematical astronomy in medieval Yemen. In R. B. Serjeant and R. Lewcock (editors), *Ṣan'ā', an Arabian Islamic city*, 34–35. London: World of Islam Festival Trust.

1985 The medieval Yemeni astrolabe in the Metropolitan Museum of Art in New York City. *Zeitschrift für Geschichte der arabisch-islamischen Wissenschaften* 2:99–122.

1986 *Islamic mathematical astronomy*. London: Variorum. (Reprints.)

1987 Astronomy in medieval Yemen. In W. Daum (editor), *Yemen: 3000 years of art and civilisation in Arabia Felix*, 300–8. Innsbruck: Pinguin.

1990 A survey of medieval Islamic shadow schemes for simple time-reckoning. *Oriens* 32:138–82.

Klein-Franke, A.

1989 The Jews of Yemen. In W. Daum (editor), *Yemen: 3000 years of art and civilisation in Arabia Felix*, 265–99. Innsbruck: Pinguin.

Klunzinger, C. B.

1878 *Upper Egypt: Its people and its products*. London: Blackie and Son. (Translated from the German.)

Knappert, J.

1993 AL-NUDJŪM, In East Africa. In *The encyclopaedia of Islam*, 2nd ed., 8:105.

Kopp, H.

1981 *Die Agrargeographie der arabischen Republik Jemen*. Erlanger Geographische Arbeiten, Sonderband 11. Erlangen.

Koukoulez, P.

1952 *Vyzantinon vios kai politismos*. Vol. 5. Athens.

Kratschkovsky, I.

1926 Ibn Khālawaih's Kitāb al-Rīḥ. *Islamica* 2:331–43.

Kraus, F. R.
1968 Sesam im alten Mesopotamien. In W. W. Hallo (editor), *Essays in memory of E. A. Speiser,* 112–19. American Oriental Series 53. New Haven: American Oriental Society.

Kummer, H., et al.
1981 A survey of hamadryas baboons in Saudi Arabia. *Fauna of Saudi Arabia* 3:441–71.

Kunitzsch, P.
1961 *Untersuchungen zur Sternnomenklatur der Araber.* Wiesbaden: Harrassowitz.
1967 Zur Stellung den Nautikertexte innerhalb der Sternnomenklatur der Araber. *Der Islam* 43:53–74.
1974 *Der Almagest: Die Syntaxis Mathematica des Claudius Ptolemäus in arabisch-lateinischer Überlieferung.* Wiesbaden: Harrassowitz.
1977 On the medieval Arabic knowledge of the star Alpha Eridani. *Journal for the History of Arabic Science* 1:263–67.
1983 *Über eine* anwā'*-Tradition mit bischer unbekannten Sternnamen.* Beiträge zur Lexikographie des Klassischen Arabisch 4. Munich: Bayerischen Akademie der Wissenschaften.
1993 AL-NUDJŪM. In *The encyclopaedia of Islam, 2nd ed.,* 8:97–105.

Kunitzsch, P., and W. Hartner
1990 MINṬAḲAT AL-BURŪDJ. In *The encyclopaedia of Islam,* 2nd ed., 7:81–87.

Labib, S. Y.
1975 KĀRIMĪ. In *The encyclopaedia of Islam*, 2nd ed., 4:640–43.

Landberg, C.
1901–13 *Études sur les dialectes de l'Arabie méridionale.* 2 vols. Leiden: Brill.
1920–42 *Glossaire Daṭînois.* 3 vols. Leiden: Brill.

Lane, E.
[1860] 1973 *The manners and customs of the modern Egyptians.* Reprint. New York: Dover Publications.
[1863-88] 1984 *Arabic-English Lexicon.* Cambridge: Islamic Texts Society.

Langner, B.
1983 *Untersuchungen zur historischen Volkskunde Ägyptens nach mamlukischen Quellen.* Berlin: Klaus Schwartz.

Larsen, T. B.
1983 Insects of Saudi Arabia. Lepidoptera, Rhopolocera (a monograph of the butterflies of the Arabian Peninsula). *Fauna of Saudi*

Arabia 5:333–478.
1984 *Butterflies of Saudi Arabia and its neighbors*. London: Stacey.

Leslau, W.
1938 *Lexique soqoṭri*. Paris.

Lewcock, R.
1983 The painted dome of the Ashrafiyyah in Ta'izz. In R. Bidwell and G. R. Smith (editors), *Arabian and Islamic studies*, 100–17. London: Longman.

Lewis, A.
1973 Maritime skills in the Indian Ocean, 1368–1500. *Journal of the Economic and Social History of the Orient* 16:238–64.

Levey, M.
1973 *Early Arabic pharmacology*. Leiden: Brill.

Lockhart, L.
1971 HURMUZ. In *The encyclopaedia of Islam*, 2nd ed., 3:584–86.

Löfgren, O. (editor)
1936–50 *Arabische Texte zur Kenntnis der Stadt Aden im Mittelalter*. Uppsala: Almqvist and Wiksells.

Löw, I.
1926–34 *Die Flora der Juden*. 4 vols. Vienna: Löwit.

Luqmān, Ḥamza 'Alī
1978 *Ma'ārik ḥāsima min ta'rīkh al-Yaman*. Ṣan'ā': Markaz al-Dirāsāt al-Yamanī.
ca. 1980 *Asāṭīr min ta'rīkh al-Yaman*. Ṣan'ā': Markaz al-Dirāsāt wa-al-Buḥūth al-Yamanī.
1985 *Ta'rīkh al-qabā'il al-Yamanīya*. Ṣan'ā': Dār al-Kalima.

Ma Huan (fl. A.D. 1433)
1970 *Ying-Yai Sheng-Lan: "The overall survey of the ocean's shores."* Translated by J. Mills. Cambridge: Cambridge University Press.

Madden, R. R.
1829 *Travels in Turkey, Egypt, Nubia and Palestine*. London: Henry Colburn.

Mahler, E., and F. Wüstenfeld
1961 *Wüstenfeld-Mahler'sche Vergleichungs-Tabellen*. Wiesbaden: Deutsche Morgenlandische Gesellschaft.

Maimonides, Moses
1979 *Glossary of drug names*. Translated by F. Rosner. Memoirs of the American Philosophical Society 135. Philadelphia: American Philosophical Society.

Maktari, A.
1971 *Water rights and irrigation practices in Laḥj*. Cambridge:

Cambridge University Press.

von Maltzan, H.
1873 *Reise nach Südarabien.* Brunswick: Viewig.

al-Ma'lūf, A.
1932 *Mu'jam al-ḥayawān.* Damascus. Reprint, Beirut.

Manniche, L.
1989 *An ancient Egyptian herbal.* Austin: University of Texas Press.

Manzoni, R.
1884 *El Yèmen: Tre anni nell'Arabia Felice.* Rome: Botta.

al-Maqḥafī, Ibrāhīm Aḥmad
1985 *Mu'jam al-mudun wa-al-qabā'il al-Yamanīya.* Ṣan'ā': Dār al-Kalima.

al-Maqrīzī, Taqī al-Dīn Aḥmad (died 845/1442)
1926 *al-Mawā'iẓ wa-al-i'tibār fī dhikr al-khiṭāṭ wa-al-athār.* Memoires de l'Institut d'Archéologie Orientale du Caire 49/4. Cairo. (See Griveau 1914.)

Marín, M., and D. Waines
1989 The balanced way: Food for pleasure and health in medieval Islam. *Manuscripts of the Middle East* (Leiden) 4:123–32.

Markwart, J.
1937 The navrôz: Its history and its significance. *Journal of the K. R. Cama Oriental Institute* (Bombay) 31:1–51. (Translated from the German)

Marsh, G. P.
1856 *The camel: His organization, habits and uses.* Boston: Gould and Lincoln.

al-Marzūqī, Abū 'Alī (died 453/1061)
1332/1914 *Kitāb al-Azmina wa-al-amkina.* 2 vols. Hyderabad: Maṭba'at Majlis Dā'irat al-Ma'ārif al-'Uthmānīya.
1388/1968 *Kitāb al-Azmina wa-al-amkina.* 2 vols. Doha, Qatar.

al-Marzūqī, al-Mu'ataz
1981 Al-Kamāt min al-mann wa-mā'hā shifā' li-al-'ayn. In 'Abd al-Raḥman al-'Awaḍī (editor), *al-Ṭibb al-Islāmi,* 412–17. Kuwait: Ministry of Health.

Masse, H.
1954 *Persian beliefs and customs.* New Haven: Human Relations Area Files.

al-Mas'ūdī, Abū al-Ḥasan 'Alī (died 335/956)
1861–77 *Murūj al-dhahab wa-ma'ādin al-jawhar.* 9 vols. Edited and translated by C. de Meynard and P. de Courteille. Paris.

1894 *al-Tanbīḥ*. Leiden: Brill.

1982 *Murūj al-dhahab wa-ma'ādin al-jawhar*. 4 vols. Beirut: Dār al-Kutub al- Lubnānī.

Meinertzhagen, R.

1954 *Birds of Arabia*. Edinburgh: Oliver and Boyd.

Messick, B.

1978 Transactions in Ibb: Economy and society in a Yemeni highland town. Ph.D. dissertation, Princeton University.

Meyerhoff, M.

1944 Sur un traité d'agriculture composé par un sultan yéménite du XIVe siècle. *Bulletin de l'Institut d'Égypte* 25:55–63; 26:51–65.

Millás Vallicrosa, J. M.

1948 La traduccion castellana del "Tratado de Agricultura" de Ibn Baṣṣāl. *al-Andalus* 13:347–430.

Miller, A. G., et al.

1982 Studies in the flora of Arabia. I. A botanical bibliography of the Arabian Peninsula. *Notes of the Royal Botanical Garden of Edinburgh* 40:43–61.

Minorsky, V.

1937 *Ḥudūd al-'ālam. "The Regions of the world": A Persian geography, 372 A.H.-982 A.D.* Gibb Memorial Series 11. London: Luzac.

Miquel, A.

1967 *Géographie et géographie humaine dans le littérature arabe des origines à 1050*. Paris: La Haye.

1975 *La géographie humaine du monde musulmane jusqu'au milieu du 11e siècle. Géographie arabe et représentation du monde: La terre et l'etranger*. Paris: La Haye.

1980 *Géographie arabe et représentation du monde: Le milieu natural*. Paris: La Haye.

Mitchell, B., et al.

1978 Yemen *Arab Republic. A baseline socio-economic survey of the Wadi Mawr region*. Washington, D.C.: World Bank.

Mitchell (Michell), R.

1877 *Egyptian calendar for the year 1295 AH (1878 AD)*. Alexandria: French Printing Office.

1900 *An Egyptian calendar for the Koptic year 1617 (1900–1901 AD)*. London: Luzac.

Moreland, W. H.

1939 The ships of the Arabian Sea about A.D. 1500. *Journal of the Royal Asiatic Society* 63–74, 173–92.

Mortel, R. T.
1990 Weights and measures in Mecca during the late Ayyūbid and Mamlūk periods. *Arabian Studies* 9:177–85.

Moyer, G.
1982 The Gregorian calendar. *Scientific American* 246/5:144–52.

al-Mujāhid, ʻAbd Allāh Muḥammad
1980 *Uss zirā'a wa-intāj al-maḥāṣīl al-ḥaqalīya fī al-arāḍī al-Yamanīya.* Cairo: ʻĀlam al-Kutub.

Müller-Wodarg, D.
1957 Die Landwirtschaft Ägyptens in der frühen ʻAbbāsidenzeit 750–969 n. Chr. (132–358 d.H.) (1. Forsetzung). *Der Islam* 32/3:14–78.

Muñoz, R.
1977 Un calendario egipcio del siglo xviii (1.a parte). *Awrāq* 1:67–81.

al-Muqaddasī, Abū ʻAbd Allāh Shams al-Dīn Muḥammad (died 381/991)
1906 *Aḥsan al-taqāsīm fī ma'rifat al-aqālīm.* Edited by M. J. de Goeje. Leiden: Brill.
1989 *Aḥsanu-T-Taqāsīm Fī Ma'rifat al-Aqālīm.* Translated by G. S. A. Ranking and R. F. Azoo. Frankfurt: Institut für Geschichte der arabisch-islamischen Wissenschaften. (Original in *Bibliotheca Indica* 1897–1910.)

Musallam, B. F.
1983 *Sex and society in Islam.* Cambridge Studies in Islamic Civilization. Cambridge University Press.

Musil, A.
1928 *The manners and customs of the Rwala Bedouins.* New York: American Geographical Society.

al-Musṭawfī al-Qazwīnī, Ḥamd Allāh ibn Abū Bakr (fl. eighth/fourteenth century)
1928 The *zoological section of the Nuzhatu-L-Qulub of Ḥamdullah al-Mustawfī al-Qazwīnī.* Translated by J. Stephenson. Oriental Translation Fund 30. London: Royal Asiatic Society.

al-Muṭayrī, Shāhir Muḥsin Fallāj al-Aḥīqī
1404/1984 *al-Dīwān al-atharī. 'Ādāt wa-turāth al-bādīya al-a'rāf wa-al-muṣṭalaḥāt al-qabīlīya.* Kuwait: Dār al-Siyāsa.

Myntti, C.
1983 Medicine in its social context: Observations from rural North Yemen. Ph.D. dissertation, London School of Economics.
1988 Hegemony and healing in rural North Yemen. *Social Science and Medicine* 27/5:515–20.
1990 Notes on mystical healers in the Ḥugariyyah. *Arabian Studies* 8:171–76.

Nāmī, Khalīl
1948 Mufradāt min Ta'izz wa-Turbat Dhubḥān. *Majallat Kullīyat al-Adâb* (Cairo) 10/1:2–10.

al-Nāshirī, Taqī al-Dīn Abū al-'Abbās Ḥamza (died 926/1520)
1985 *Intihāz al-furaṣ fī al-ṣayd wa-al-qanaṣ*. Edited by 'Abd Allāh Muḥammad al-Ḥibshī. Ṣan'ā': al-Dār al-Yamanīya li-al-Nashr wa-al-Tawzī'.

Nashwān ibn Sa'īd al-Ḥimyarī (died 573/1177)
1916 *Shams al-'ulūm*. Leiden: Brill.
1951–53 *Shams al-'ulūm*. 2 vols. Edited by K. V. Zettersteen. Leiden: Brill.

Nasr, S. H.
1978 *An introduction to Islamic cosmological doctrines*. Rev. ed. Boulder: Shambhala.

Navarro, M. Á.
1990 *Risāla fī awqāt al-sana*. Granada: Consejo Superior de Investigaciones Científicas, Escuela de Estudios Árabes.

Naẓīr, Wilyam
1969 *al-Zirā'a fī Miṣr al-islāmīya*. Cairo: Murāqaba al-Taḥrīr wa-al-Nashr wa-al-Maktabāt.

Niebuhr, C.
1792 *Travels through Arabia*. 2 vols. Edinburgh: Morison and Son. (Translated from the German.)

al-Nuwayrī, Aḥmad ibn 'Abd al-Wahhāb (died 732/1332)
1342–85/1923–65 *Nihāyat al-'Arab fī funūn al-adab*. 18 vols. Cairo.

Osgood, J. B. F.
1854 *Notes of travel or recollections of Majunga, Zanzibar, Muscat, Aden, Mocha, and other eastern ports*. Salem: George Creamer.

Padwick, C. E.
1924 Notes on the jinn and the ghoul in the peasant mind of Lower Egypt. *Bulletin of the School of Oriental and African Studies* 3:421–46.

Parr, D. (editor)
1987 *Sandgrouse* (Journal of the Ornithological Society of the Middle East) 9.

Pellat, C.
1955 Dictons rimes, *anwā'* et mansions lunaires chez les Arabes. *Arabica* 2:17–41.
1979 Le "calendrier agricole" de Qalqašandī. *Annales Islamologiques* 15:165–85.
1986 *Cinq calendriers égyptiens*. Textes Arabes et Études Islamiques

26. Cairo: Institut Française d'Archéologie Orientale.

Pellat, C., et al.
1971 ḤAYAWĀN. In *The encyclopaedia of Islam,* 2nd ed., 3:304–15.

Philby, H. St. John
1928 *Arabia of the Wahhabis.* London: Constable and Company.
1981 *The Queen of Sheba.* London: Quartet Books.

Phillott, D. C. (translator)
1908 *The Bāz-Nāma-Yi Nāṣirī: A Persian treatise on falconry.* London: Bernard Quariteh.

Piamenta, M.
1990–91 *Dictionary of post-classical Yemeni Arabic.* 2 vols. Leiden: Brill. (See Varisco 1994.)

Pingree, D.
1990 Astrology. In M. J. L. Young et al., *Religion, learning, and science in the 'Abbasid period,* 290–300. Cambridge: Cambridge University Press.

Pirenne, J.
1978 *La maîtrise de l'eau en Arabie du Sud antique.* Memoirs de l'Académie des Inscriptions et Belles-Lettres, 2. Paris.

Polo, Marco (died 1324)
1958 *The travels of Marco Polo.* Translated by R. Latham. Middlesex, England: Penguin.

Popenoe, P.
1922 The pollenation of the date palm. *Journal of the American Oriental Society* 42:343–54.
1973 *The date palm.* Edited by H. Field. Miami: Field Research Projects.

Porter, R. F., and S. Christensen
1987 The autumn migration of raptors and other soaring birds in North Yemen. *Sandgrouse* (England) 9:121–24.

Pseudo-Apollonios von Tyana (fl. first century B.C.)
1979 *Buch über das Geheimnis der Schöpfung und die Darstellung der Natur.* Edited by Ursula Weisser. Aleppo: Institute for the History of Arab Sciences.

Pseudo-Aristotle (Ikhwān al-Ṣafā')
1983 *Sirr al-asrār li-ta'sīs al-siyāsa wa-tartīb al-riyāsa.* Edited by Aḥmad al-Turaykī. Beirut: Dār al-Kalima.

Ptolemy, Claudius (fl. second century A.D.)
[1822] 1976 *Ptolemy's Tetrabiblos.* Translated by J. M. Ashmond. Reprint. North Hollywood, Calif.: Symbols and Signs.

al-Qalqashandī, Abū al-ʻAbbās Aḥmad (died 821/1418)
1913–19 *Ṣubḥ al-aʻshā fī ṣināʻat al-inshā'*. 14 vols. Cairo. (See Pellat 1979.)

Qāsim, Qāsim ʻAbduh
1978 *al-Nīl wa-al-mujtamaʻ al-Maṣrī fī ʻaṣr salāṭīn al-mamālik*. Cairo: Dār al-Maʻārif.

al-Qazwīnī, Zakarīyā ibn Muḥammad (died 682/1283)
1849 *'Ajā'ib al-makhlūqāt wa-gharā'ib al-mawjūdāt*. Edited by F. Wüstenfeld. Leiden: Brill.
1859 *Calendarium Syriacum*. Edited and translated by G. Volck. Lipsae: E. Bredt.
1981 *'Ajā'ib al-makhlūqāt wa-gharā'ib al-mawjūdāt*. 4th ed. Edited by Fārūq Saʻd. Beirut: Dār al-Afāq.

Quṭrub, Abū ʻAlī Muḥammad (died ca. 206/821)
1922 Kitāb al-Azmina. *Majallat al-Majmaʻ al-ʻIlmī al-ʻArabī* (Damascus) 2:33–46.
1985 *Kitāb al-Azmina wa-talbīyat al-jāhilīya*. Edited by Ḥannā Jamīl Ḥaddād. al-Zarqā', Jordan: Maktabat al-Manār.

al-Quwayʻī, Muḥammad ʻAbd al-ʻAzīz
1405/1984 *Turāth al-ajdād*. Vol. 2. Saudi Arabia: Maṭbaʻat al-Majd al-Tijārīya.

Rabie, H.
1981 Some technical aspects of agriculture in medieval Egypt. In A. L. Udovitch (editor), *The Islamic Middle East, 700–1900: Studies in economic and social history*, 59–90. Princeton: Darwin Press.

Rabin, C.
1951 *Ancient West-Arabian*. London: Taylor's Foreign Press.

Rachie, K.
1970 Sorghum in Asia. In J. S. Wall and W. M. Ross (editors), *Sorghum production and utilization*, 328–81. Westport, Conn.: AVI Publishing Company.

Rands, M., et al.
1987 *Birds in the Yemen Arab Republic: Report of the Ornithological Society of the Middle East Expedition, October–December, 1985*. England: Ornithological Society of the Middle East.

Rathjens, C., et al.
1956 *Beiträge zur Klimakunde Südwestarabiens*. Deutscher Wetterdienst Seewetteramt 11. Hamburg.

Rathjens, C., and H. von Wissmann
1934 *Landeskundliche Ergebnisse*. Abhandlungen aus dem Gebiet der Auslandskunde, Hamburg Universität. 38/B/20:3.

al-Rāzī, Muḥammad ibn Abī Bakr (died ca. 660/1262)
1979 *Mukhtār al-ṣiḥāḥ*. Beirut: Dār al-Qalam.

al-Rāzī al-Ṣan'ānī, Aḥmad ibn 'Abd Allāh (died 460/1068)
1974 *Ta'rīkh madīnat Ṣan'ā'*. Edited by Ḥusayn al-'Amrī and 'Abd al-Jabbār Zakkār. Damascus.

Reinaud, J.
1845 *Relation des voyages faits par les Arabes et les Persans dans l'Inde et le Chine*. 2 vols. Paris.

Renaud, H. P. J. (editor)
1948 *Le calendrier d'Ibn al-Bannā' de Marrakech*. Paris: Larose.

Rhodokanakis, N.
1911 *Die vulgararabische Dialekt im Ḍofâr (Ẓafâr)*. 2 vols. Vienna: Holder.

Riddle, J. M.
1985 *Dioscorides on pharmacy and medicine*. Austin: University of Texas Press.

Robin, C.
1981 Le calendrier himyarite: Nouvelles suggestions. *Proceedings of the Seminar for Arabian Studies* 11:43–52.

Rodinson, M.
1977 Esquisse d'une monographie du *qāt*. *Journal Asiatique* 265:71–96.

Rossi, E.
1939 *L'Arabo Parlato a Ṣan'â'*. Rome: Instituto per l'Orient.
1940 Vocaboli sud-arabici nelle odierne parlate arabe del Yemen. *Rivista degli Studi Orientali* 18:299–314.
1953 Note sull' irrigazione, l'agricoltura e le stagioni nel Yemen. *Oriente Moderno* 33:349–61.

Rowand, A.
1915 Sailing craft of the Persian Gulf. In J. G. Lorimer, *Gazetteer of the Persian Gulf, 'Oman, and Central Arabia*, 1/2:2319–32. Calcutta: Superintendent Govt. Printing Office.

Ruffer, A.
1919 Food in Egypt. *Memoires de l'Institut d'Egypte* 1. Cairo.

Ryckmans, J.
1975–76 Une expression astrologique méconnue dans des inscriptions sabéenes. *Orientalia Lovaniensia Periodica* 6-7:521–29.

al-Sa'īdān, Ḥamad Muḥammad
1981 *al-Mawsū'a al-Kuwaytīya al-mukhtaṣara*. 2nd ed. 2 vols. Kuwait: Wakalat al-Maṭbū'āt.

Saliba, G.
1985 A medieval note on the Himyarite dialect. *Journal of the American Oriental Society* 105:717–19.

Ṣāliḥīya, Muḥammad ʿĪsā
1985 *al-Ṣaqr wa-al-ṣayd ʿinda al-ʿArab: Risālat nādira li-Kushājim.* Kuwait: Maktabat Sharakat Kāẓimat.

Ṣāliḥīya, Muḥammad ʿĪsā, and Iḥsān al-ʿAmd (editors)
1984 *Miftāḥ al-rāḥa li-ahl al-filāḥa.* al-Silsila al-Turāthīya 9. Kuwait: al-Majlis al-Waṭanī li-al-Thaqāfa wa-al-Funūn wa-al-Adāb.

Samso, J.
1978 Un calendrier tunisien – d'origine andalouse? – du XIXe siècle. *Cahiers de Tunisie* 26:67–84.

Samuel, J.
1844 *Journey of a missionary tour through the desert of Arabia to Baghdad.* Edinburgh: MacLachlan, Stewart and Co.

Sauvaget, J.
1948 Sur d'anciennes instructions nautiques arabes pour les mers de l'Inde. *Journal Asiatique* pp. 11–20.

al-Sayāghī, Ḥusayn ibn Aḥmad (editor)
1404/1984 *Ṣafaḥāt majhūla min taʾrīkh al-Yaman.* Ṣanʿāʾ: Markaz al-Dirāsāt wa-al-Buḥūth al-Yamanī.

Sayyid, Ayman Fuʿād
1974 *Sources de l'histoire du Yémen à l'époque Musulmane.* Cairo: Institut Française d'Archéologie Orientale.

al-Sayyid-Marsot, A. L. (editor)
1979 *Society and the sexes in medieval Islam.* Malibu: Undena Publications.

Sbath, P.
1932–33 Le livre des temps d'Ibn Massawaih, médecin chrétien célèbre décédé en 857. *Bulletin de l'Institut d'Egypte* 15:235–57.

Schimmel, A.
1980 *The triumphal sun.* London: East-West Publications.

Schjellerup, H. C. F. C.
1874 *Description des étoiles fixes.* Saint Petersburg: Commissionaíres de l'Académie Impériale des Sciences. (Translation of al-Ṣūfī's *Ṣuwar al-kawākib.*)

Schmidt, K. P.
1954 *Amphibians and reptiles of Yemen.* Fieldiana, Zoology, 34/24. Chicago: Field Museum.

Scholte, P. T., and A. W. al-Khuleidi

1989 *The herbarium collection of the RLIP, Dhamār, YAR.* RLIP Communication No. 37. Dhamār: Ministry of Agriculture and Fisheries.

Scholte, P. T., et al.

1991 *The vegetation of the Yemen Arab Republic (western part).* Ṣan'ā': Environmental Protection Council and Agricultural Research Authority.

Schopen, A.

1983 *Traditionelle Heilmittel in Jemen.* Wiesbaden: Franz Steiner.

Schopen, A., and O. Kahl

1993 *Die Natā'iğ al-fikar des Šha'bān ibn Sālim aṣ-Ṣan'ānī: Eine jemenitische Gesundheitsfibel aus dem frühen 18. Jahrhundert.* Wiesbaden: Harrassowitz.

Schram, R.

1908 *Kalendariographische und chronologische Tafeln.* Leipzig: J. C. Hinrich's.

Schweinfurth, G.

1912 *Arabische Pflanzenamen aus Aegypten, Algerien, und Jemen.* Berlin: Reimer.

Sclater, W. L.

1917 The birds of Yemen, southwestern Arabia, with an account of his journey thither by the collector, G. Wyman Bury. *Ibis*, Series 10, 5:129–86.

Scott, H.

1942 *In the high Yemen.* London: Murray.

Serjeant, R. B.

1954 Star calendars and an almanac from south-west Arabia. *Anthropos* 49:433–59.

1958 Professor A. Guillaume's translation of the Sīrah. *Bulletin of the School of Oriental and African Studies* 21/1:1–14.

1962a Recent marriage legislation from al-Mukallā, with notes on marriage customs. *Bulletin of the School of Oriental and African Studies* 25:472–98. (Reprinted in Serjeant 1991.)

1962b Sex, birth, circumcision: Some notes from south-west Arabia. In A. Leidlmair (editor), *Hermann von Wissmann–Festschrift*, 193–208. Tübingen. (Reprinted in Serjeant 1991.)

1965 Notices on the "Frankish chancre" (syphilis) in Yemen, Egypt, and Persia. *Journal of Semitic Studies* 10:241–52. (Reprinted in Serjeant 1991.)

1970 Maritime customary law off the Arabian coast. In M. Mollat (editor), *Sociétés et compagnies de commerce en Orient et dans l'océan Indien.* Actes du VIIIième Colloque International Maritime (Beyrouth, 5–10 septembre 1966). Paris. (Reprinted in Serjeant 1991.)

1974a The cultivation of cereals in medieval Yemen. *Arabian Studies* 1:25–74.

1974b The ports of Aden and Shihr (medieval period). In *Les grandes escales I. Recueils de la Sociéte Jean Bodin* 32 (10e Colloque d'Histoire Maritime), 207–24. Brussels. (Reprinted in Serjeant 1981b.).

1974c *The Portuguese off the South Arabian coast.* Beirut: Librairie du Liban.

1976 *South Arabian hunt.* London: Luzac.

1981a A *maqāmah* on palm protection (*shirāḥah*). *Journal of Near Eastern Studies* 40/4:307–22.

1981b *Studies in Arabian history and civilization.* London: Variorum.

1982 Ḥaḍramawt to Zanzibar: The pilot-poem of the nākhudhā Sa'īd Bā Ṭāyi' of al-Ḥāmī. *Paideuma* 28:109–27.

1989 A Socotran star calendar. In A. K. Irvine et al. (editors), *Miscellany of Middle Eastern articles: Memorial Thomas Muir Johnstone, 1924–1983,* 94–100. London: Longman.

1991 *Customary and* shari'ah *law in Arabian society.* London: Variorum.

Serjeant, R. B., and Ḥusayn al-'Amrī

1981 A Yemeni agricultural poem. In W. al-Qāḍī (editor), *Studia Arabica et Islamica,* 407–27. Beirut: American University of Beirut.

Serjeant, R. B., and R. Lewcock (editors)

1983 *Ṣan'ā': An Arabian Islamic city.* London: World of Islam Festival Trust.

Serradj, Mohamed Ben Hadji

1953 L'automne et l'hiver chez les fellahs Azailis. *Institut des Belles-Lettres Arabes* 16:297–316.

Sezgin, F.

1979 *Geschichte des arabischen Schrifttums.* Vol. 7. Leiden: Brill.

Sharaf al-Dīn, Aḥmad Ḥusayn

1405/1985 *Al-Ṭarā'if al-mukhtāra min shi'r al-Khanfanjī wa-al-Qāra.* Ṣan'ā': Dār al-Kalima.

al-Shawkānī, Muḥammad ibn 'Alī (died 1173/1760)

1348/1929 *al-Badr al-ṭāli'.* 2 vols. Cairo: Maṭba'at al-Sa'āda.

n.d. *Tuḥfat al-dhākirīn.* Beirut: Dār al-Fikr.

Shihāb, Ḥasan Ṣāliḥ

1981 *Aḍwā' 'alā ta'rīkh al-Yaman al-baḥrīya.* Beirut: Dār al-'Awda.

1982 *Fann al-milāḥa 'inda al-'Arab.* Beirut: Dār al-'Awda.

1983 *al-Dalīl al-baḥrī 'inda al-'Arab.* Kuwait: Kuwait University, Department of Geography.

1987 *Qawā'id 'ilm al-baḥr.* Kuwait: Kuwait University, Department of Geography.

al-Sijistānī, Abū al-Ḥātim Sahl (died ca. 250/864)

1985 *Kitāb al-Nakhl.* Beirut: Mu'assasat al-Risāla.

al-Sirāfī, Abū Zayd al-Ḥasan (fl. third/ninth century)

1948 *Akhbār as-Sīn wa L-Hind: Relations de la Chine et de l'Inde.* Edited and translated by J. Sauvaget. Paris: Société d'Edition "Les Belles Lettres."

al-Sirājī, Muḥammad Ṣāliḥ

1379/1959 *Hādhihi dā'irat ma'ālim al-zirā'a al-Yamanīya.* Ṣan'ā'. (Circular chart; see Varisco 1982a:554-76.)

Smith, G. R.

1969 The Ayyubids and Rasulids – the transfer of power in 7th/13th century Yemen. *Islamic Culture* 43:175–88.

1974 The Yemenite settlement of Tha'bāt: Historical, numismatic and epigraphic notes. *Arabian Studies* 1:119–31.

1978 *The Ayyubids and early Rasulids in the Yemen (567–694/1173–1295).* 2 vols. Gibb Memorial Series 16. London: Luzac.

1983 The early and medieval history of Ṣan'ā', ca. 622–953/1515. In R. B. Serjeant and R. Lewcock (editors), *Ṣan'ā': An Arabian Islamic city,* 49–67. London: World of Islam Festival Trust.

1985 Ibn al-Mujāwir on Dhofar and Socotra. *Proceedings of the Seminar for Arabian Studies* 15:79–92.

1988 The Rasulids in Dhofar in the VIIth–VIIIth/XIII–XIVth centuries. *Journal of the Royal Asiatic Society*, pp. 26–32.

1989 Ibn al-Mujāwir's 7th/13th century Arabia – the wondrous and the humorous. In A. K. Irvine et al. (editors), *Miscellany of Middle Eastern articles: Memorial Thomas Muir Johnstone, 1924–1983,* 105–18. London: Longman.

1990 Yemenite history–problems and misconceptions. *Proceedings of the Seminar for Arabian Studies* 20:131–39.

Somogyi, J.

1957 Medicine in Ad-Damiri's Hayat al-Hayawan. *Journal of Semitic Studies* 2:62–91.

Spate, O. H. K.

1963 *India and Pakistan.* 2nd ed. London: Methuen.

Stark, F.
1940 *A winter in Arabia*. London: Murray.

Steffen, H., et al.
1978 *Final report on the Airphoto Interpretation Project of the Swiss Technical Co-operation Service*. Berne.

Stein, B.
1965 Coromandel trade in medieval India. In J. Parker (editor), *Merchants and scholars: Essays in the history of exploration and trade*, 47–62. Minneapolis: University of Minnesota Press.

Steinglass, F.
1930 *A comprehensive Persian-English dictionary*. London.

Stone, F. (editor)
1985 *Studies on the Tihāmah*. London: Longman.

Stookey, R.
1978 *Yemen: The politics of the Yemen Arab Republic*. Boulder: Westview Press.

al-Ṣūfī, Abū al-Ḥusayn ʻAbd al-Raḥmān (died 376/986)
1373/1954 *Ṣuwar al-Kawākib al-thamānīya wa-al-arbaʻīn*. Hyderabad: Maṭbaʻat Majlis Dā'irat al-Maʻārif al-ʻUthmānīya.

Sulaymān al-Mahrī
1925 al-ʻUmda al-Mahrīya. In G. Ferrand (editor), *Instructions nautiques et routiers arabes et portugais des XVe et XVIe siècles* 2. Paris: Paul Geunther.

Sultanate of Oman
1979 *Oman: A seafaring nation*. Muscat: Ministry of Information and Culture.

al-Suwaydā', ʻAbd al-Raḥman ibn Zayd
1983 *Najd fī al-ams al-qarīb*. Riyadh: Dār al-ʻUlūm.

al-Suyūṭī, Jalāl al-Dīn ʻAbd al-Raḥmān (died 911/1505)
n.d. *al-Raḥma fī al-ṭibb wa-al-ḥikma*. Beirut: al-Maktaba al-Shaʻbīya.
1986 *al-Manhaj al-sawī wa-al-manhal al-rawī fī al-ṭibb al-nabawī*. Edited by Ḥasan Muḥammad Maqbūlī al-Ahdal. Ṣanʻā': Maktabat al-Jīl al-Jadīd.

Swagman, C.
1988 *Development and change in highland Yemen*. Salt Lake City: University of Utah Press.

Tāj al-Dīn ʻAbd al-Baqī ibn ʻAbd al-Majīd (died 733/1333)
1965 *Ta'rīkh al-Yaman al-musammā bi-ḥajat al-zaman fī ta'rīkh al-Yaman*. Edited by Muṣṭafā Ḥijāzī. Cairo: Maṭbaʻat Mukhaymir.
1985 *Ta'rīkh al-Yaman al-musammā bi-ḥajat al-zaman fī ta'rīkh al-Yaman*. 2nd ed. Ṣanʻā': Dār al-Kalima.

BIBLIOGRAPHY

Talmon, S.
1986 *King, cult and calendar in ancient Israel.* Leiden: Brill.

Teixeira da Mota, A.
1963 Méthodes de navigation et cartographie nautique dans l'ocean Indien avant le XVIe siecle. *Studia* (Lisbon) 11:49–90.

al-Tha'ālibī, Abū Manṣūr (died 430/1038–39)
n.d. *Fiqh al-lugha wa-asrār al-'Arabīya.* Beirut: Manshūrāt Dār Maktabat al-Ḥayāt.

al-Thawr, 'Abd Allāh Aḥmad
1972 *Hādhihī hīya al-Yaman.* Cairo: al-Maṭba'a al-Salifīya.

Theophrastus (died ca. 287 B.C.)
1916 *Enquiry into plants.* 2 vols. Translated by Sir Arthur Holt. Loeb Classical Library. Cambridge: Harvard University Press.

Thomas, B.
1932 *Arabia Felix: Across the Empty Quarter of Arabia.* New York: Scribner's Sons.

Tibbetts, G. R.
1965 The star nomenclature of the Arab navigators. *Der Islam* 40:188–97.
1971 *Arab navigation in the Indian Ocean before the coming of the Portuguese.* London: Royal Asiatic Society of Great Britain and Ireland.
1974 Arabia in the fifteenth-century navigational texts. *Arabian Studies* 1:86–101.

al-Tīfāshī, Abū al-'Abbās Aḥmad
1980 *Surūr al-nafs bi-madārik al-ḥawās al-khams.* Edited by Iḥsān 'Abbās. Beirut: al-Mu'assasa al-'Arabīya li-al-Dirāsāt wa-al-Nashr.

al-Timimi, F. A.
1987 *Falcons and falconry in Qatar.* Doha: Ali Bin Ali Publishers.

Tisserant, E.
1915 Le calendrier d'Abou'l-Barakât. In *Patrologia Orientalis* 10/13:245–86.

Tolmacheva, M.
1980 On the Arab system of nautical orientation. *Arabica* 27/2:180–92.

Trachtenberg, J.
1982 *Jewish magic and superstition: A study in folk religion.* New York: Atheneum.

Trimingham, J. S.
1975 The Arab geographers and the East African coast. In H. N.

Chittick and R. I. Rotberg (editors), *East Africa and the Orient*, 115–46. New York: Africana Publishing Company.

Troupeau, G.
1968 Le livre des temps de Jean ibn Māsawayh, traduit et annoté. *Arabica* 15:113–42.

'Ubādī, Nabīl 'Abd al-Laṭīf
1989 *Al-Ṭuyūr al-Yamanīya*. Singapore: Kerjaya Printing Industries.

Ullmann, M.
1972 *Die Natur- und Geheimwissenschaften im Islam*. Leiden: Brill.
1978 *Islamic medicine*. Edinburgh: Edinburgh University Press.

'Umar, al-Fāḍil
1990 *Al-Ḥabba al-sawdā' fī al-ṭibb al-sha'bī*. Mekka: Dār al-Maṭbū'āt al-Ḥadītha.

'Umar ibn Yūsuf, al-Malik al-Ashraf (died 696/1296)
1949 *Turfat al-aṣḥāb fī ma'rifat al-ansāb*. Edited by K. V. Zettersteen. Damascus.
1985a Mulaḥ al-malāḥa fī ma'rifat al-filāḥa. Edited by Muḥammad 'Abd al-Raḥīm Jāzm. *al-Iklīl* (Ṣan'ā') 3/1:165–207.
1985b *Turfat al-aṣḥāb fī ma'rifat al-ansāb*. 2nd ed. Ṣan'ā': Dār al-Kalima.
1987 *Milḥ al-malāḥa fī ma'rifat al-filāḥa*. Edited by 'Abd Allāh Muḥammad al-Mujāhid. Damascus: Dār al-Fikr.

('Umāra) Najm al-Dīn 'Umāra ibn 'Alī al-Yamanī (died 569/1173–74)
1396/1976 *Ta'rīkh al-Yaman*. 2nd ed. Edited by Muḥammad ibn 'Alī al-Akwa'. Cairo: Maṭba'at al-Sa'āda. (See Kay 1892.)

al-'Umarī, Ibn Faḍl Allāh (died 749/1349)
1974 *Masālik al-abṣār fī mamālik al-amṣār*. Cairo: Dār al-'Itiṣār.
1985 *Masālik al-abṣār fī mamālik al-amṣār*. Edited by Ayman Fu'ad Sayyid. Cairo: Institut Français d'Archéologie Orientale.

Van der Meulen, D. and H. von Wissmann
1932 *Ḥaḍramaut*. Leiden: Brill.

Van Enk, D. C. and J. van der Gun
1984 *Hydrology and hydrogeology of the Yemen Arab Republic*. Ṣan'ā': YOMINCO, Department of Hydrology.

Van Lennep, H.
1875 *Bible lands: Their modern customs and manners illustrative of scripture*. New York: Harpers.

Varisco, D. M.
1982a The adaptive dynamics of water allocation in al-Ahjur, Yemen Arab Republic. Ph.D. dissertation, University of Pennsylvania, Philadelphia.

1982b The ard in highland Yemeni agriculture. *Tools and Tillage* 4/3:158–72.

1983 Arab classical writings and agriculture: The agricultural almanac. Paper presented at the Third International Symposium on the History of Arab Sciences, December. Kuwait.

1985a The production of sorghum (*dhurah*) in highland Yemen. *Arabian Studies* 7:53–88.

1985b al-Tawqīʻāt al-zirāʻīya wa-al-ʻilmīya bi-al-taqwīm al-majhūl min ʻaṣr Banī Rasūl. *Dirāsāt Yamanīya* (Ṣanʻā') 20:192–222.

1987 The rain periods in pre-Islamic Arabia. *Arabica* 34:251–66.

1988 Table salt and other folktales from Yemen. *The World & I* 3/7:503–9.

1989a The *anwā'* stars according to Abū Isḥāq al-Zajjāj. *Zeitschrift für Geschichte der arabisch-islamischen Wissenschaften* 5:145–66.

1989b al-Ḥiṣāb al-zirāʻī fī urjūzat Ḥasan al-ʻAffārī. Dirāsāt fī al-taqwīm al-zirāʻī al-Yamanī. *al-Ma'thūrāt al-Shaʻbīya* (Doha) 16:7–29.

1989c Medieval agricultural texts from Rasulid Yemen. *Manuscripts of the Middle East* (Leiden) 4:150–54.

1990 Folk astronomy and the seasons in the Arabian Gulf. *al-Ma'thūrāt al-Shaʻbīya* 19:7–27.

1991a The origin of the *anwā'* in Arab tradition. *Studia Islamica* 74:5–28.

1991b A royal crop register from Rasulid Yemen. *Journal of the Economic and Social History of the Orient* 34:1–22.

1993a The agricultural marker stars in Yemeni folklore. *Asian Folklore Studies* 52/1:119–42.

1993b Texts and pretexts: The unity of the Rasulid state under al-Malik al-Muẓaffar. *Revue du Monde Musulman et de la Méditerranée* 67:13-23.

1993c A Rasulid agricultural almanac for 808/1405–6. *New Arabian Studies* 1:108–23.

1994 Yemen Reviews: Dictionary of post-classical Yemeni Arabic. *Yemen Update* 34:34–36, 44.

Varisco, D. M., et al.

1984 *Social and institutional profile of Yemen.* Ṣanʻā': American Institute for Yemeni Studies. (Report submitted to the United States Agency for International Development.)

1990 *Biological diversity assessment of North Yemen.* Cambridge: International Council for Bird Preservation. (Report submitted to the United States Agency for International Development.)

1992 *Indigenous plant protection practices in Yemen.* Ṣan'ā'. (Report submittedto Yemeni German Plant Protection Project, Ministry of Agriculture and Water Resources, Republic of Yemen.)

Varisco, D. M., and D. A. King

forthcoming A unique zodiacal almanac from Rasulid Yemen.

Varro, Marcus Terentius (died 27 B.C.)

1935 *On agriculture.* Translated by W. D. Hooper. Loeb Classical Library 283. Cambridge: Harvard University Press.

di Varthema, L.

1928 *The travels of Ludivico di Varthema in Egypt, Syria, Arabian Deserta, and Arabia Felix.* Edited by G. P. Badger. Translated by J. W. Jones. London: Hakluyt Society.

de Vaux, R.

1965 *Ancient Israel: Its life and institutions.* London: Darton, Longman, and Todd.

Villiers, A.

1940 *Sons of Sindbad.* London: Hodder and Stoughton.

Viré, F.

1967 *Le traité de l'art de volerie (Kitāb al-Bayzara).* Leiden: Brill.

1977 Essai de détermination des oiseaux-de-vol mentionnés dans les principaux manuscrits Arabes médiévaux sur la fauconneries. *Arabica* 24:138–49.

1978 KHAYL. In *The encyclopaedia of Islam*, 2nd ed., 4/1143–46.

Wall, W. M.

1978 al-ISKANDAR. In *The encyclopaedia of Islam*, 2nd ed., 4:127.

Wallin, G. A.

1854 Narrative on a journey from Cairo to Medina and Mecca, by Suez, Arabá, Tawilá, al-Jawf, Jubbé, Haîl, and Nejd, in 1854. *Journal of the Royal Geographical Society* 24:115–207.

Walther, W.

1993 *Women in Islam.* Princeton: Markus Wiener Publishing.

al-Wāsi'ī, 'Abd al-Wāsi' ibn Yaḥyā

1367/1947 *Kanz al-thiqāt fī 'ilm al-awqāt.* Cairo: Maṭba'at al-Ḥijāzī.

1402/1982 *Ta'rīkh al-Yaman.* 2nd ed. Ṣan'ā': al-Dār al-Yamanīya li-al-Nashr wa-al-Tawzī'.

Wassef, C. W.

1971 *Pratiques rituelles et alimentaires des Coptes.* Bibliotheque d'Études Coptes 9. Cairo: Institut Français de l'Archéologie Orientale.

1991 Calendar and agriculture. In A. S. Atiya (editor), *The Coptic encyclopedia,* 440–43. New York: Macmillan.

Watson, A. M.
1983 *Agricultural innovation in the early Islamic world.* Cambridge: Cambridge University Press.

Watt, W. M.
1974 The Queen of Sheba in Islamic tradition. In J. B. Pritchard (editor), *Solomon & Sheba,* 85–103. London: Phaidon.

al-Waṭwāṭ, Jamāl al-Dīn Muḥammad (died 718/1318)
1990 *Mabāhij al-fikr wa-manāhij al-'ibar.* 2 vols. Frankfurt: Institut für Geschichte der arabisch-islamischen Wissenschaften. (Facsimile edition of ms. 4116 Süleymaniye, Istanbul)

al-Waysī, Ḥusayn ibn 'Alī
1382/1962 *al-Yaman al-kubrā.* Cairo: Maṭba'at al-Nahḍa al-'Arabīya.

al-Wazīr, 'Abd Allāh ibn 'Alī (died 1147/1735)
1405/1985 *Ta'rīkh al-Yaman.* Edited by Muḥammad'Abd al-Raḥīm Jāzm. Ṣan'ā': Markaz al-Dirāsāt wa-al-Buḥūth al-Yamanī.

Wehr, H.
1961 *A dictionary of modern written Arabic.* Edited by J. M. Cowan. Wiesbaden: Harrassowitz.

Weiser, F. X.
1958 *Handbook of Christian feasts and customs.* New York: Harcourt, Brace and Company.

Wensinck, A. J.
1971 HUDHUD. In *The encyclopaedia of Islam,* 2nd ed., 3:541–42.

Westermarck, E.
1926 *Ritual and belief in Morocco.* 2 vols. London: Macmillan.

Whitcomb, D. S.
1988 Islamic archaeology in Aden and the Hadhramaut. In D. T. Potts (editor), *Araby the Blest: Studies in Arabian archaeology,* 176–262. Copenhagen: Carsten Niebuhr Institute.

Wigboldus, J. S.
1991a Early presence of African millets near the Indian Ocean. In J. E. Reade (editor), *The Indian Ocean in antiquity.* London: Kegan Paul International.

1991b Pearl millet outside northeast Africa, particularly in northern West Africa: Continuously cultivated from c. 1350 A.D. only? In R. E. Leakey and L. Y. Sikkerveer (editors), *Origins and development of agriculture in East Africa: The ethnosystems approach to the study of early food production in Kenya.* Studies in Technology and Change 20. Ames: Iowa State University.

Wilson, R.
1980 The investigation, collection and evaluation of geographic material in Yemeni texts for the mapping of historical North-West

Yemen. Ph.D. dissertation, Cambridge University.

Wood, D.

1979 Index to local names of maize, sorghum, wheat and barley collected in Yemen by D. Wood, 1978-79. Unpublished typescript.

Wood, J. R. I.

1985 Flora. In F. Stone (editor), *Studies on the Tihāmah*, 14–17. London: Longman.

in press *A handbook of the Yemen flora*. London: Routledge and Kegan Paul.

Yaḥyā ibn al-Ḥusayn ibn al-Qāsim (died 1100/1689)

1388/1968 *Ghāyat al-amānī fī akhbār al-quṭr al-Yamanī*. 2 vols. Edited by Sa'īd 'Abd al-Fattāḥ 'Āshūr. Cairo: Dār al-Kutub al-'Arabī. (This is an unreliable edition; see Smith 1990.)

Yajima, H.

1974 *A chronicle of the Rasulid dynasty of Yemen*. Tokyo. (See al-Ḥibshī 1984.)

Yāqūt, Shihāb al-Dīn Abū 'Abd Allāh (died 626/1229)

1399/1979 *Mu'jam al-buldān*. 5 vols. Beirut: Dār Ṣādir.

Yemen Arab Republic

1983 *Khulāṣat al-natā'ij al-nahā'iya li-al-ta'dād al-zirā'ī fī muḥāfaẓāt al-jumhūriya*. Ṣan'ā': Yemen Arab Republic, Ministry of Agriculture and Fisheries, Department of Planning and Statistics.

1984a *Nashra irshādīya 'an zirā'at ba'ḍ al-maḥāṣīl: al-Fawākih*. Ta'izz: Yemen Arab Republic, Ministry of Agriculture and Fisheries, Agricultural Research Authority.

1984b *Nashra irshādīya 'an zirā'at ba'ḍ al-maḥāṣīl: al-Ḥubūb*. Ta'izz: Yemen Arab Republic, Ministry of Agriculture and Fisheries, Agricultural Research Authority.

Yūsuf ibn 'Umar, al-Malik al-Muẓaffar (died 694/1295)

1402/1982 *al-Mu'tamad fī al-adwīya al-mufrada*. Reprint. Beirut: Dār al-Ma'ārif.

Zabāra, Muḥammad ibn Muḥammad

1952 *A'immat al-Yaman*. Ta'izz: Maṭba'at al-Naṣr al-Naṣirīya.

n.d. *Nashr al-'arf*. Ṣan'ā': Markaz al-Dirāsāt wa-al-Buḥūth al-Yamanī.

al-Zabīdī, Muḥammad ibn Muḥammad al-Murtaḍā (died 1205/1790)

1306/1888 *Tāj al-'arūs min jawāhir al-qāmūs*. 10 vols. Cairo: al-Maṭba'a al-Khayrīya al-Munsha'at bi-Jamālīya.

al-Zamakhsharī, Abū al-Qāsim Maḥmūd (died 538/1143-4)

1402/1982 *Asās al-balāgha*. Edited by 'Abd al-Raḥīm Maḥmūd. Beirut: Dār al-Ma'rifa.

al-Zawzanī, Abū 'Abd Allāh al-Ḥusayn ibn Aḥmad

1398/1978 *Sharḥ al-mu'allaqāt al-sab'*. Beirut: Dār al-Kutub al-'Ilmīya.

Index and Gazetteer of Place Names in the Almanac

'Abadān VIII:19

This is an area east of Ta'izz. Al-Ḥajrī (1984:3:573) cites a village by this name at Jabal Ṣabir and a wadi near Banī Sarḥa in the Ibb area. Al-Hamdānī (1983:144) noted that it was famous for its grapes and fruits. Yāqūt mentioned it without defining the location.

Abyan XII:1

This is an area about forty-five miles east of Aden. The name is said to be derived from a Himyarite king, either Dhū Abyan ibn Dhī Yaqdum ibn al-Sawwar ibn 'Abd al-Shams (Nashwān ibn Sa'īd 1916:11) or Abyan ibn Zuhayr ibn Ayman ibn al-Hamaysa' ibn Ḥimyar ibn Saba' (Yāqūt). For more details on this area, see al-Ḥajrī (1984:1:55–56), Smith (1978:2:130), al-Tamīmī (in 'Afīf et al. 1992:1:42–42), and 'Umāra (1976:49, note 4).

'Adan (Aden) I:9; III:8,23,26; IV:15,17; V:6,16,26; VI:4,5,6,30; VIII:14,20,21,24; IX:3,6,13,28; X:13,16,21; XI:1,6,20,21,22; XII:11,16,21

Aden was the main southern port for medieval Yemen and the most important link in the trade route between India and Africa. Aden is frequently mentioned in the Rasulid chronicles. The name is said to come from a descendant of the legendary 'Adnān called 'Adan or from the verb *'adana,* meaning "to settle down in a place" (Yāqūt). For further information, see al-Ḥajrī (1984:3:582–90), Löfgren (1960), Muḥayriz (in 'Afīf et al. 1992:2:641–44), and Serjeant (1974b). Among the Arab travelers who described Aden were Ibn Baṭṭūṭa (1980:251–52) and Ibn al-Mujāwir (1954). Early Western travelers included Marco Polo (1958) and di Varthema (1928:26–37).

al-'Amākir VII:23

Yāqūt identified this as a village in the area of Sanḥān, between Ṣan'ā' and Bilād al-Rūs in the central highlands.

al-'Āra X:21

This was at the southernmost point of the Arabian Peninsula, near Bāb al-Mandab and the entrance to the Red Sea. There is a large lagoon just east of the medieval town. From here to Aden was a journey by ship of two days (al-'Aqīlī 1958:112). This name is usually corrupted in later Yemeni almanac copies. For more information on the location of al-'Āra, see Ibn al-Mujāwir (1954:100–2, 269).

'Arār VII:23

This is an unidentified place name near Ta'izz. It is not the town of 'Arār in the al-Bawn region near 'Amrān. The term *'arār* can refer to a plant with a pleasant smell (*Tāj al-'arūs, '-r-r*).

Ba'dān XI:11

This refers to an area west of Ibb in the Saḥūl district. The most famous towns in this area were Raymān and Ḥabb. It is said to be named for Ba'dān ibn Jashm ibn 'Abd al-Shams ibn Wā'il (al-Hamdānī 1983:197, note 1). For more information, see al-Ḥajrī (1984:1:43–46).

al-Baḥr al-Māliḥ V:19

Mediterranean Sea.

Barbara IX:13; X:21

There is some confusion over this name, since it referred to several areas along the Africa coast. The general reference in the medieval sources is to the site of Bandar 'Abbās (Lewis 1960:1172) on the coast of modern Somalia. Barbara was also used for the area along the Somali coast extending to the port of Marka, south of which the term "Zanj" was generally used. At times Barbara is associated with the island of Socotra (al-Hamdānī 1983:93–94), which was noted for the medicinal plants of aloe and dragon's blood. Socotra was an important stopping point on the trade route between Aden and the southeastern African coast. Marco Polo (1958:297) stated, "You must know that all the merchant ships bound for Aden call in at this island." There was a Christian population on the island with links to the patriarchy in Baghdad during the Rasulid period. The Gulf of Aden was sometimes called Baḥr Barbarā or Khalīj Barbarā (Becker and Beckingham 1960:93).

al-Dathīna XII:3,29

This is a well-known area between Aden and Ḥaḍramawt. Yāqūt claimed that it was called Dafīna in the pre-Islamic period. A lexicon of the Dathīna dialect has been provided by Landberg (1920–42).

al-Dhanbatayn VII:23

This village was located northwest of al-Janad; it was mentioned by Ibn al-Dayba' (1983:76).

Dhubḥān VIII:1

This is an area in modern al-Ḥujarīya about seventy kilometers south of Ta'izz near the start of the Sarāt mountain chain (al-Ḥajrī 1984:2:234). Al-Khazrajī (1908:3:55) claimed that the first legal scholar in Aden to drink coffee was a certain Jamāl al-Dīn Abū 'Abd Allāh Muḥammad from this area. For more information, see Smith (1978:2:148).

Dijla VII:24
Tigris River.

al-Dumluwa IV:25; XI:7
This was one of the main treasure cities of the Rasulids, who maintained a fortress here. It was located about forty kilometers east of Ta'izz south of Wādī al-Jannāt (al-Ḥajrī 1984:2:236–37). Al-Malik al-Muẓaffar captured this citadel from Ayyubid control in 650/1252. For more information, see al-'Amrī (in 'Afīf et al. 1992:1:444), Ibn al-Mujāwir (1954:153–54), Smith (1978:2:150), and al-Waysī (1962:39).

al-Furāt IV:24; V:31; VII:22,24
Euphrates River.

al-Ḥawāzz I:3
This term refers to the area of coastal foothills, especially in the southern part of the Tihāma ('Abd Allāh al-Ḥibshī, personal communication). The singular is Ḥāzza, with alternative plurals of Ḥāzzāt (al-Wazīr 1985:242) and Aḥwāzz (al-Ḥajrī 1984:2: 803). In *Tāj al-'arūs* (*ḥ-z-z*), "Ḥazz" is used for the area adjacent to the Sarāt range. *Mulakhkhaṣ* (fol. 17r) notes that there was an official for the two Ḥāzza between Zabīd and Ḥaraḍ during the Rasulid era. According to al-Sayāghī (1984:27) the villages surrounding Ṣan'ā' at the edge of the mountains were also called Ḥawāzz.

al-Ḥijāz VIII:9; IX:26
The Hejaz is the part of Arabia where Mecca and Medina are located. This term is said to be derived from the fact that the area served as a barrier (*ḥijāz*) between the low coastal area and desert plain (Yāqūt). The medieval travelers Ibn al-Mujāwir (1954), Ibn Baṭṭūṭa (1980), and Ibn Jubayr (1984) all described the Hejaz, including the sacred *ka'ba* and the pilgrimage ritual.

Hind I:8,10; III:8,16,26; IV:15; VI:5; VIII:21,23; IX:6,13; X:16; XI:1,6; XII:21
India. For more information on India in the medieval period, see Ahmad et al. (1971). Valuable details on the coastal geography are provided by Tibbetts (1971:449-70). See also al-Ṣūliyān.

Hurmuz (Hormuz) V:16; VI:5; IX:3; XII:11
Hormuz was the most important port on the Persian side of the Persian Gulf and a major

transfer point for the overland trade route to Aleppo. It was the main seaport for the Persian areas of Kirmān, Sīstān, and Khūzistān. In 669/1300 the capital was moved from the mainland to the nearby island of Jārūn, due to raiding from the Tartars. For more information, see Ibn Baṭṭūṭa (1980:273–76), Lockhardt (1971), and Polo (1958:312).

'Irāq VII:22; VIII:8
Iraq.

al-Janad IV:5; XI:25
This major Yemeni town is located about twenty kilometers northeast of Ta'izz. It was the site of an important pre-Islamic market (al-Hamdānī 1983:296) and an early mosque (Costa 1983; Finster in 'Afīf et al. 1992:1:310–11). Yāqūt said that this term applied to the general area between Ṣan'ā' and Ḥaḍramawt at the beginning of the Islamic period. It is said to be named for Janad ibn Shahrān, a tribal division (*baṭn*) of Ma'āfir. For more information, see al-Ḥajrī (1984:1:146–50), Ibn al-Mujāwir (1954:161–64), and Smith (1978:2:165).

al-Jannāt VI:12,22; VII:3,5
This is a wadi near the town of Juwwa in the area near al-Ḥujarīya below Ta'izz (Ibn al-Mujāwir 1954:154). Al-Hamdānī (1983:143) described it as a lush garden area, with grapes, *wars*, bananas, sugarcane, citron, cucumber, sorghum, snake cucumber, coriander, etc., similar to Wādī Ḍahr near Ṣan'ā'. The pre-Islamic Warazān dam was built to water the fields in this wadi (al-Waysī 1962:39). For more information, see al-Ḥajrī (1984:1:192).

Jibla (Dhū Jibla) V:23
This important town near Ibb was the capital of the Sulayhid dynasty in Yemen. It was in the area known as Mikhlāf Ja'far. Yāqūt said it was one of the best towns in Yemen. 'Umāra (1976) claimed it was named for a Jew of this name who sold pottery here. For more information, see al-Ḥajrī (1984:1:34), Ibn al-Mujāwir (1954:168, 171–72), and Smith (1978:2:149).

Laḥj VIII:2
This is the rich agricultural area to the north of Aden. Yāqūt said it was named for Laḥj ibn Wā'il ibn al-Ghawth ibn Qaṭn ibn 'Arīb ibn Zuhayr ibn Ayman ibn al-Hamaysa' ibn Ḥimyar. For more information, see al-Ḥajrī (1984:4:677–79), al-Hamdānī (1983:191–92), and Smith (1978:2:173).

al-Ma'āfir VIII:1
Area in the region now called al-Ḥujarīya. Al-Hamdānī (1983:240) said it was the

southernmost extent of the Sarāt mountain chain. It was named for Ma'āfir ibn Ya'fur ibn Mālik ibn al-Ḥārith ibn Murra, who was a descendant of Saba', according to Yāqūt. The treasure city of al-Dumluwa is located here, as is the important site of Jaba' (al-Hamdānī 1983:118–19). This area was famous for a breed of donkey (al-Hamdānī 1983:320) and a type of clothing (Nashwān ibn Sa'īd 1916:73; Yāqūt).

Madāra (?) XI:15

According to the almanac this was an area in Wādī Surdud from which honey was exported. Al-Malik al-Afḍal (*Bughya*, fol. 108r) said that *al-ḥabba al-sawdā'* (*Nigella sativa*) was exported from here to al-Mahjam, which indicates that al-Mahjam would have been the nearest large town. Perhaps the term is derived from *madar*, in reference to mudbrick construction, which is mentioned by Yāqūt as the name of a village near Ṣan'ā'.

al-Maghrib I:17

The Maghrib or Maghreb refers to the North African coast of Morocco and extending east toward Libya. The reference in the almanac is to a location for the observation of Canopus. The almanac also refers to the Mediterranean Sea as al-Baḥr al-Maghrib.

al-Maḥālib IX:18

Important Rasulid town on Wādī Mawr in the coastal region. Al-Malik al-Muẓaffar built a mosque here (Ibn al-Dayba' 1983:91). It should not be confused with the market of Maḥālib near Ta'izz (see Ibn Baṭṭūṭa 1980:249).

al-Mahjam III:3; V:29; XII:20

This was an important Rasulid town and royal mint along Wādī Surdud, where the sultans had extensive holdings of agricultural land. Al-Idrīsī (1970:1:55) said it was the border between the Tihāma and the Yemeni highlands. Al-Khazrajī (1908:3:50) noted that it was located three days' journey from Zabīd, as was also recorded by Yāqūt. Ibn al-Mujāwir (1954:58) claimed the name is derived from the fact that descendants (*ashrāf*) of the Prophet Muḥammad attacked (*hajama*) this area. According to al-Hamdānī (1983:97) the upper part of this area was settled by Khawlān and the lower part by 'Akk. Al-Malik al-Muẓaffar built a mosque here, and al-Malik al-Ashraf was appointed governor here. After the Rasulid period, the city was in ruins (Yaḥyā ibn al-Ḥusayn 1968:1:475).

Maqdashū VI:4,6; X:13; XI:22; XII:16

Mogadishu, the important port on the African coast in modern Kenya. A description of the medieval town was provided by Ibn Baṭṭūṭa (1980:253–55). This has long been one of the major trading ports for the dhow trade from Yemen.

Mashāriq Ṣan'ā' VIII:19
Agricultural region east of Ṣan'ā'. This was especially known for its grapes.

Mawr (Wādī Mawr) I:5; III:28,29; V:1; VIII:10; IX:18
Largest of the coastal wadis. This has been called the largest drainage (*mīzāb*) of the Tihāma (al-Hamdānī 1983:134). Yāqūt said the term means "turning" or "rotation" (*dawrān*). The tribe of 'Akk settled here (al-Hamdānī 1983:97). The main medieval town along the wadi was al-Maḥālib. For more information, see al-Ḥajrī (1984:4:723–24) and al-Hamdānī (1983:134).

Mikhlāf VIII:19; IX:1; XI:11; XII:5
This is an ancient Yemeni term for a district, defined as equivalent to *kūra* (Nashwān ibn Sa'īd 1916:34), *quṭr* ('Umāra 1976:48), *sawād* in Iraq, and *rustāq* in Khorasan (al-Tha'ālibī n.d.:20). Ibn al-Mujāwir (1954:169) defined it as the environs of a fortified center (*ḥuṣn*) in the mountains, including the villages and agricultural lands. The various districts (*makhālīf*) of medieval Yemen are listed by Ibn Khurradādhbih (1899:136–45), al-Khazrajī (1908:3:50), al-Muqaddasī (1989:139–42), and Yāqūt. In the Rasulid texts Mikhlāf generally refers to the area of Mikhlāf Ja'far near Ibb. This includes the areas of Ba'dān, Banī Ḥubaysh, Banī Ṣayf, Ibb, Jibla, Ma'shar, al-Shawāfī, Saḥūl, and Ta'kar (al-Burayhī 1984:17). The district was named for Ja'far ibn Ibrāhīm ibn Muḥammad, a descendant of Ḥimyar ('Umāra 1976:48, note 4; Kay 1892:4–5).

Miṣr/Maṣr I:22; IV:15,17,23; V:6,9,16,20; VI:8,30; VII:15,25; VIII:14,20; X:2,9,12,16,19; XI:1,6,21,30; XII:27
Egypt.

Nbṭī (?) IX:13
The reference to this sailing period is unclear in the text but appears to be based on a place name on the African coast near Barbara. Perhaps this is a miscopying of Baṭa or Baqaṭī on the African coast? Could the reference be to Madagascar (Qumr), which is not mentioned in the Rasulid texts but was an important stop south of Mogadishu on the coastal trade route?

Najrān VIII:19
Famous oasis in northeast Yemen, where an important pre-Islamic market and a religious shrine rivaling that of Mecca were located. Yāqūt said the name is derived from Najrān ibn Zaydān ibn Saba' or from the piece of wood used as a doorsill. Most of the tribespeople here were from Yām (al-Hamdānī 1983:162-64). For more information, see al-Ḥajrī (1984:4:734–38) and Smith (1978:2:186–87).

al-Nīl I:20; VI:8,23; X:2
Nile River.

Qā' al-Ajnād VII:23; X:30
This is an obscure reference in the almanac that must refer to 'Udayna in Ta'izz, where the soldiers (*ajnād*) of the sultan lived (see Ibn Baṭṭūṭa 1980:248). The reference does not appear to be related to the town of al-Janad north of Ta'izz, although Ibn al-Mujāwir (1954:164) recorded the usage of Qā'/Qārī' al-Ajnād for al-Janad.

Qalhāt I:9; II:27; V:16,26: VI:5; IX:3
Important port in Oman with commanding view of entrance to the Persian Gulf. This was the seat of the chief governor of the king of Hormuz. Descriptions of this port are provided by Ibn Baṭṭūṭa (1980:270–71) and Marco Polo (1958:311). For more information, see Ibn al-Mujāwir (1954:272ff.) and Smith (1978:2:189).

Qays V:16,24; VI:5; IX:3; XI:6; XII:11
This island off the coast of Oman was the important port of Sirāf. In 626/1229 it came under the control of the king of Hormuz. This port was visited by Ibn Baṭṭūṭa (1980:278). This was a famous pearling area. For more information, see Ibn al-Mujāwir (1954:287–300).

al-Quṣayba I:26; II:5; III:24; X:1,10,25; XI:18
Lush agricultural area north of Ta'izz (*Ma'rifa*). The reference in the almanac is to a variety of wheat sown here.

al-Rūm I:6
The reference in the almanac is to Byzantium.

Ṣabir (Jabal Ṣabir) IX:7; X:4
Large mountain (ca. 3,000 meters elevation) overlooking Ta'izz. The original inhabitants were said to be al-Rakab and al-Ḥawāshib from Ḥimyar and Saksak (Yāqūt). Al-Hamdānī (1983:195) called it the barrier between the regions of Jaba' and al-Janad. This mountain was known for its springs and gardens. Yāqūt said the name was derived from the term for aloe (*ṣabr*). For more information, see al-Ḥajrī (1984:1:153), Ibn al-Mujāwir (1954:156–59), and Smith (1978:2:196).

Ṣan'ā' V:18; VIII:19; IX:10,13,29; X:23
This is the traditional capital of the Zaydī imams in the highlands. According to legend, Ṣan'ā' was built by Shem and is one of the oldest cities in the world. A complete and authoritative study of the city has been edited by Serjeant and Lewcock (1983). For the legendary and early history, see al-Rāzī al-Ṣan'ānī (1974); for the

Rasulid period, see Smith (1983).

Sayalān/Sīlān VIII:20

Ceylon, or modern Sri Lanka. It was also known as Sarandīb/Sirandīb and was an important stop on the sea route between India and China. For more information, see Ferrand (1913–14), al-Nuwayrī (1923:1:241), and Tibbetts (1971:462–65).

al-Sha'bānīya I:27; IV:11: V:7; VII:26; IX:25; X:17

Area north of Ta'izz bordering Wādī Warazān and Birkat al-Ḥawbān (Ibn al-Mujāwir 1954:161). Al-Hamdānī (1983:138) noted that it was near Ṣabir. Ibn al-Mujāwir recorded the plural variant al-Sha'bānīyāt. Today there is a distinction between al-Sha'bānīya al-'Ulyā' and al-Sha'bānīya al-Suflā'. It was named for a tribe of Ḥimyar called Dhū Sha'bān (Nashwān ibn Sa'īd 1916:56). A pre-Islamic fortress and dam were built here. For more information, see al-Ḥajrī (1984:3:452).

al-Shām/al-Sha'm II:10; VIII:13; XI:1

Syria.

al-Shiḥr IX:28

This term refers to the coastal strip between Yemen and Oman (Nashwān ibn Sa'īd 1916:53), although Yāqūt said it could refer to any narrow coastal strip. Al-Hamdānī (1983:90) defined it as the term for a salt pan. The Yemeni port of al-Shiḥr is located about forty miles east of al-Mukallā on the southern coast. For more information, see al-'Amrī (in Afīf et al. 1992:2:548–49), al-Ḥajrī (1984:3:447–48), Serjeant (1974b, 1974c:25–27), and 'Umāra (1976:49, note 3).

Sihām/Sahām IX:18

This is one of the major wadis in the coastal region. The main town here in the Rasulid period was al-Kadrā', which was a day and a half north of Zabīd. Yāqūt said the name means *mukhāṭ al-shayṭān* (i.e., a gossamer), but another meaning of *sahām* is hot wind (Ibn Sīda 1965:9:87). Yāqūt claimed that the name derives from a certain Sihām ibn Summān ibn al-Ghawth ibn Ḥimyar. For more information, see al-Ḥajrī (1984:3:435–36) and al-Hamdānī (1983:133).

Ṣihla V:14; VII:5

Area near Ta'izz (al-Khazrajī 1906:1:288; 1918:4:379,382). This was one of the prime garden areas of Yemen (*Bughya*; *Kifāya*). It was famous for a variety of fig (*balas*).

al-Ṣūliyān VIII:20

The Coromandel coast, or Cholas, on the eastern part of the Indian subcontinent was called Barr al-Ṣūliyān/al-Shūliyān. The main medieval port was Ballin. Marco Polo (1958:260) claimed it was the best part of India. For more information, see Ferrand (1913:2:496, note 5) and Tibbetts (1971:466).

Surdud I:8,27; III:29; IV:4; VIII:10; XI:15

Major coastal wadi between Wādī Sihām and Wādī Mawr. The main Rasulid town was al-Mahjam. For more information, see 'Afīf et al. (1992:2:517), al-Hamdānī (1983:133–34), Smith (1978:2:208), and Yāqūt.

Ta'izz IV:11; VIII:9; IX:25

This was the Rasulid capital located in the southern highlands. Towering over the city is Jabal Ṣabir. The Rasulid sultans built palaces and gardens at nearby Tha'bāt (Smith 1974). Ibn Bā Makhrama (in al-Ḥajrī 1984:1:145) called Ta'izz the "Damascus of Yemen." For more information, see 'Abd Allāh (in 'Afīf et al. 1992:1:240–42), Ibn Baṭṭūṭa (1980:249–50), Smith (1978:2:208), and al-Waysī (1961:33–34).

Tihāma (Tahā'im, plural) I:9,16; II:1; III:9; IV:4,19; V:4,10,15,20; VII:10,31; VIII:4; IX:5,13,19,26,30; X:23; XI:8,16,23,25; XII: 9,19,28

Coastal region bordering the Red Sea. This was the lowland (*ghawr*) of Yemen (Nashwān ibn Sa'īd 1916:81). Ibn Sīda (1965:9:72) said it was so called because of the intensely hot and still air (*taham*). Ibn Mājid (Tibbetts 1971:217) said it was called this because it drops down. For more information, see al-Ḥajrī (1984:1:156–62), al-Hamdānī (1983:231–32), Stone (1985), and al-Wasi'ī (1982:113–18).

al- 'Udayn IX:10

Area in Mikhlāf Ja'far west of Ibb. A major market and hot springs were located here. For more information, see al-'Amrī (in 'Afīf et al. 1992:2:644) and al-Ḥajrī (1984:4:590–95).

'Udayna X:17

Wadi on the western outskirts of Ta'izz, where the sultan's soldiers were based. Al-Malik al-Muẓaffar built a mosque here (Ibn al-Dayba' 1983:91). For more information, see al-Ḥajrī (1984:1:146), Ibn al-Mujāwir (1954:233), Smith (1978:2:212), and Yāqūt.

al-Yaman I:21; II:10; IV:22; V:8; VII:29-30; VIII:6,9; XI:1; XII:13

Yemen. For the various theories on the origin of the name, see the discussion in Yāqūt.

Zabīd VIII:14; IX:2

This was the most famous town in the coastal region and an important medieval center of learning. The Rasulids made this their coastal capital and established a mint here. The town was also known as Ḥuṣayb, with Zabīd being applied to the whole wadi as well. The Prophet Muḥammad mentioned the *baraka* (divine blessing) of Zabīd (Ibn al-Mujāwir 1954:82 and al-Janadī 1984:1:220). It was an important commercial center, especially for trade with East Africa (al-Idrīsī 1970:1:52). For the medieval history of Zabīd, see Chelhod (1978) and especially Ibn al-Dayba' (1983). Ibn al-Mujāwir (1954) and Ibn Baṭṭūṭa (1980:247) visited here. See also al-Ḥajrī (1984:2:381–91), al-Hamdānī (1983:132), Smith (1978:2:216), and Yāqūt. Edward Keall of the Royal Ontario Museum has conducted archaeological fieldwork in Zabīd over the last decade.

Ẓafār III:23; VI:16; VIII:24; IX:4,6; XI:2,20
Dhofar on the southwestern coast of the peninsula. It was known as Ẓafār al-Ḥabūḍī in the medieval period (al-Khazrajī 1908:3:60) and was a major port known for incense and excellent horses. For more information, see Costa (1979), Ibn al-Mujāwir (1954:260–62), Serjeant (1974b), Smith (1978:2:219; 1988), and Yāqūt.

al-Ẓāhir IX:10
This is a general term for the highland area east of Ṣan'ā' (al-Khazrajī 1908:3:88). It was so named because it was high and thus the opposite of a low plateau (*bāṭin*), according to al-Ḥajrī (1984:3:563). There was an upper and lower Ẓāhir (*'Aqd*, fol. 198r). The fortresses here were listed by al-Hamdānī (1938:64).

Zayla' (Ziyāli', plural) X:21
Coastal part of the medieval kingdom of Ifat in Ethiopia. Ibn Baṭṭūṭa (1980:252) said the coastal area below Zayla' was called Sūdān. The port here is located only sixty-nine miles from Bāb al-Mandab. Al-Hamdānī (1983:93) said this port was on an island. For more information, see 'Abd Allāh (in 'Afīf et al. 1992:1:499–500), al-Ḥajrī (1984:2:400), and Yāqūt.

Index of Major Arabic Terms in the Almanac Text

INDEX OF MAJOR ARABIC TERMS

INDEX OF MAJOR ARABIC TERMS

INDEX OF MAJOR ARABIC TERMS

General Index

bābūnaj (camomile), 198
Babylonian, 195
Babylonian calendar, 63
bad', 234
Ba'dān, 25, 177
bādhān/bādhām, 198
badhanjā' sorghum, 170
bādhinjān. See eggplant
badr (full moon), 140
badrī hawk, 24, 27, 39, 140
Baghdad, 6, 75, 79
bahā'im (large domestic animals), 28, 151–52
bahīma (donkey or domestic animal)
bahma (female calf), 151
bahr (sea), 120
Bahr al-Barbarā (Gulf of Aden), 222
Bahr al-Fāris (Persian Gulf), 222, 224
Bahr al-Hind (Indian Ocean), 222
al-Bahr al-Maghrib (western Mediterranean Sea), 220
al-Bahr al-Mālih (Mediterranean Sea), 33, 220
al-Bahr al-Na'āmī, 10
Bahr al-Qulzum (Red Sea), 222
Bahr al-Rūm (Mediterranean Sea), 220
Bahr al-Yaman (Red Sea), 222
bāhūr. See *ayyām al-bāhūr*
bajānīs, 221
bājis, 102, 168, 241. See Sirius
bājisī sorghum, 35, 102, 168
bajrī (pearl millet), 250
bakhānis, 221
bakhnas, 221
bakhnīṭas, 31–32, 221, 236
Bakil, 6
baknīs, 221
baknīṭas, 221
bakūr (first fruits), 69
bakūr wheat and barley, 168, 251
baladī banana, 190
baladī rose, 201
baladī sesame, 196
balaḥ dates, 158, 193
balas. See fig and sycamore fig
balas ṣihla fig, 35, 183
balasa (fig tree), 183
balasān. See balsam of Mecca
balda, 35, 101, 110, 202
balgham (phlegm), 204
Ballin, 230
balm of Gilead. See balsam of Mecca
balsam, 31, 199
balsam of kataf (*qaṭaf*), 182
balsam of Mecca, 198–99
bamboo, 219
bāmīya. See okra
bān (*Moringa peregrina*), 34, 135, 182, 246
banafsaj (violet), 198
banana (*mawz*), 25, 32, 182, 190, 199, 210–11, 229, 231, 252
banāt na'sh al-kubrā. See Ursa Major
banāt wardān (cockroaches), 147
Bandar 'Abbās, 225
Banī Mājid, 227
Banī Sayf, 172
Banī Sum'ay, 67
Bāniyān, 219
baptism of Christ, 77
baqar (cattle), 151
baqar banana, 190
Baqāṭi, 229
bāqillā'. See broad bean
al-bāqillā' al-maṣrī, 252
baqlat al-malik (fumitory), 200
baqq (bedbug or mosquito), 145, 147, 247
barāghīth. See fleas
baraḥ (breeze), 114
barā'iṭ (sand grouse), 143
baraka (blessing), 245
al-Barbara. See Berbera
barbarī (ram), 151
Barbarī ships, 39, 225, 229

eggplant (*bādhinjān*), 182
eggs: chicken, 24, 141; hatching, 31, 33, 139; laying, 142–43; silkworm, 147
Egypt, 10, 17–18, 23–27, 32–35, 38, 63, 72, 77, 101, 103, 114–16, 121, 126, 129–31, 135–36, 140–46, 154–55, 159, 165, 175, 179–81, 185–86, 189, 194, 198–202, 206, 216, 219–22, 227–28, 239, 243–44, 248–54
Egyptian clover (*birsīm* and *qurṭ*), 23, 28, 154, 194
Egyptian (Maṣrī) ships, 32–33, 36–37, 228–29
elements, 86
elephant, 130, 152, 226, 230, 248. See also ivory
Elizabeth, 78
emeralds, 230
emmer wheat (*'alas* and *nusūl*), 36, 163, 176–78, 251
Empty Quarter, 152
endive (*hindibā'*), 181–82, 210
Epiphany (*'īd al-ghiṭās*), 27, 76–77, 118, 235, 239
Era of the Martyrs, 72
Ethiopia, 106, 248, 250. See Abyssinians
Euphorbia inarticulata. See *ṣuyyāb*
Euphrates (al-Furāt), 32, 34, 36, 131, 245
Europe, 216, 221, 255
exercise, 208
Exodus, 239
eye diseases (*awjā' al-'ayn*), 31, 35, 206, 254
eyes, 136

faḍah dates, 193
faḍīkh (date wine), 158
Falco columbarius aesalon. See merlin
falcon, 138–39, 142, 247. See also *bazāt*, merlin, and *ṣaqr*
faq' (truffles), 246
faqqūs/*faqqūz* (watermelon or snake cucumber), 184, 251. See also melon
faqqūsa (unripe melon), 251
far, 175
farārīj (chicks), 141
farḍ dates, 28, 191
al-fargh al-mu'akhkhar, 31, 35, 39, 111, 121, 148, 185, 194. See also Pegasus
al-fargh al-muqaddam, 30, 35, 39, 109, 174, 237. See also Pegasus
farī (quail), 144
farīk. See parching
al-Fārisī. See Abū 'Abd Allāh Muḥammad al-Fārisī
fārisī peach, 189
farqadān (β γ Ursae Minoris), 217
farqūs/*farqūṣ* (watermelon), 184. See also melon
farts, 220
faṣd (bleeding or bloodletting), 207
Fashāl, 161, 175, 192–93
fasīl (palm shoot), 192
faṣīl (young camel), 153
fatḥ (surface flow), 161
faṭīr (unleavened bread), 80
al-faṭīr, 'īd (Passover), 80
fatwa, 253
fauna, 138–55, 246
fava bean. See broad bean
fawākih (fruits), 182
Fayoum, 198
fear, 204
Feast of Forty Martyrs, 75
Feast of Tabernacles (*'īd al-miẓalla*), 32, 80
fennel (*rāzayānaj* and *shamār*), 151, 182
fenugreek (*ḥilba*/*ḥulba*), 65, 181, 211
Festival of Balsam, 199
Festival of the Cross, 131, 143, 245
Festival of the Olive Branches, 78
Festival of the Rose, 33, 78
Festival of St. Michael, 130
Festival of Weeks, 157

fever, 207
Ficus carica. See fig
Ficus sycamorus. See sycamore fig
fig (*balas* and *tīn*), 33, 35–36, 65, 182–83, 196–97, 253
fijl. See radish
firewood, 126, 132–34
firṣād. See mulberry
First of the Season (*awwal al-zamān*), 23–24, 27, 31, 33, 224–26, 228–30
fish, 131, 209–10, 216, 229–31
fiṣḥ, *'īd* (Easter or Passover), 78, 80
fishing, 219
flax (*bizr al-kattān*, *kattān*, and *mūma*), 32, 182, 201–2, 253
fleas (*barāghīth* and *qummāl*), 23, 36, 145–46, 231
flies (*dhubāb*), 30, 145–47, 206
flora: natural, 131–38, 245. See also flowers
flowers, 198–201
fodder, 134–36, 165, 167, 171, 194
folk astronomy, 81, 84, 97, 111
Formica sp. See ants
Forskal/Forsskal, 245–46
Forty Days. See *arba'īniyāt*
fowl, 27, 39, 209–11, 213. See also chicken
frankincense. See incense
Frankish chancre (*al-ḥabb al-Ifranjī*). See syphilis
frost (*ḍarīb*), 25, 119, 122, 124, 162, 234–35, 243, 249
fruits (*fawākih*), 38, 181–98, 209, 211, 219, 231
f-ṣ-ḥ (?), 198
fṣy'a (?), 25
fūdanj. See pennyroyal
fūfal. See betel nut
fūl. See broad bean
fulful al-ṣūdān, 185
full/fill (jasmine), 201
al-full al-hindī (Indian jasmine), 198
Fumaria officinalis. See fumitory
fumitory (*baqlat al-malik*, *shāhtarraj*, and *sulṭān al-buqūl*), 31, 182, 200
al-Furāt (Euphrates), 236
furū' (branches), 132
furwat (quail), 144
fuṣlān (young camels or sheep and goats), 153
fustuq. See pistachio
fuwwa. See madder

gale (*naw'*), 220, 255
Galen, 203
gall bladder (*marāra*), 204
galleons, 216
game, 209–10
garlic (*thūm*), 182, 209–10
gazelle, 138, 142
Gemini (*jawzā'*), 33, 86, 124, 169
genealogical texts, 15–16
Geniza texts, 221–22, 224, 228
ghaḍīr tax, 161
ghafr, 24, 32, 92–93, 131, 139
ghalla (crop yield), 28, 161–62
ghalq (closed), 224
ghamām (winter mists and thick clouds), 29, 106
ghanam (sheep), 151
ghanam banana, 190
gharib (broomcorn millet), 250
ghayl (spring flow), 129, 245
ghaym (mist or rain clouds), 68, 106
ghee (*samn*), 26, 152, 209, 215, 219. See also butter
ghiṭās (Epiphany), 77
ghūl (evil spirit), 26, 155, 248
al-Ghulayfiqa, 222
ghurnūq (crane), 142
ghurūb (setting), 92
gilliflower (*khīrī*), 198
ginger (*zanjabīl*), 76, 182, 208–9
gnats, 147

al-ḥuṣūn al-maḥrūsa (fortified towns), 160
ḥūt (Pisces), 8
hyacinth bean (*hurṭumān*), 23, 25, 27, 181, 189
Hyphaene thebaica. See *dawm*
hyrax (*wabr*), 138

Ibb, 105, 140, 242
ibex, 138
ibl. See camel
Iblīs (Devil), 220
Ibn al-Ajdābī, 91
Ibn Baṣṣāl, xi
Ibn Baṭṭūṭa, 157–58, 215–16, 218–19, 222, 225–27, 229, 231
Ibn al-Bayṭār, 203, 253
Ibn Jaḥḥāf, 11
Ibn Kunāsa, 67, 70, 109, 125
Ibn Mājid, 18, 73–74, 215, 255
Ibn Māsawayh, 91
Ibn al-Mujāwir, 215
Ibn Qutayba, 91–92, 95
Ibn Waḥshīya, xi, 164
ice, 76, 198
Ifāt, 231
'ifrada (quail), 144
ijjāṣ. See plum
'ijl (male calf), 151
ikhtirāf (harvesting), 70
iklīl, 25, 33, 119, 217
iklīl al-mālik (crown imperial), 198
ilb. See *'ilb*
'ilb (*Ziziphus spina-christi*), 17, 28, 135–36, 149, 235
'ilb, 102. See Sirius
'ilm (scholarship), x
Ilumqah, ix
Imru' al-Qays, 68
imtizāj al-faṣlayn (mixing of the seasons), 204
'inab. See grapes
incense (*lubān*), 157, 219, 230–31, 255–56
India, 30, 32–33, 38, 79, 89, 91, 106, 108, 114–15, 134, 155, 159–60, 179, 181, 215–16, 219, 222, 224, 226, 230–31, 250
Indian jasmine (*al-full al-hindī*), 198
Indian labarnum (*khiyār shanbar*), 182
Indian New Year, 73–74, 168
Indian Ocean (Baḥr al-Hind), 73, 100, 102–3, 106, 117, 143, 215–17, 220, 222, 224
Indian ships, 24–25, 27, 30–32, 34, 38–39, 160, 219, 225–26
indigo (*nīla*), 157
Indigofera sp. See indigo
infisāḥ, 234
inflorescence (*ṭal'*), 27, 192
inḥidār (descending), 92
injāṣ. See plum
inqiḍā' (last), 236–37
inqishā', 234
insects, 145–50, 247
inṣirām ayyām al-nakhl, 252
Iran, 79
Iraq, 36–37, 79, 103, 131, 137, 140, 143, 185, 203, 219, 243, 247
al-'irḍīya al-jabalīya camel, 152
al-'irḍīya al-yamānīya camel, 152
'irj (*Ziziphus spina-christi*), 136
iron, 216, 219
iṣba' (finger), 217
isfānākh. See spinach
'ishā' (evening rising), 96, 169
Ishmael, 80
'ishwī sorghum, 23, 32, 96, 169
Isis, 130
Israelites, 75–77, 171, 254
istikhrāj (tax assessment), 160
istisqā' (dropsy), 143
istisqā' (rain invocation), 159
istitār (disappearance), 97, 104
ithab (*Ficus* sp.), 196
i'tirāḍ (disappearance), 37, 104
ivory, 219, 226, 229

179, 186–88, 190, 195, 197, 205, 213, 233, 237, 246, 248–49, 254
sand grouse (*qaṭā*), 26, 30, 139, 143–44, 210
sandalwood, 230
sanṭ 'asalī (*Acacia mellifera*), 138
sap: flowing of, 27, 29, 132–33
sapphires, 230
sāq (stalk), 132, 197
saqī' (ice or frost), 122
saqla barley, 251
ṣaqr (falcon), 144
ṣaraba, 66
ṣarām. See *ṣirām*
ṣarama, 66
ṣarāṣir, 123, 243
Sarāt, 4, 105, 135, 150, 232
saraṭān. See Cancer
sarb, 100
ṣarbay, 248
sardines, 155
ṣarfa, 26, 30, 39, 67, 123–25
ṣarṣār, 243
Sasanians, 89
Saturday, 32–33, 157–58
Saturn, 86
Saudi Arabia, 12, 76, 145, 154, 245–46
ṣawāb. See Pegasus
ṣawm (fast), 77, 79
al-ṣawm al-kabīr (Lent), 29, 77
ṣawm al-naṣāra (Lent), 77
ṣawmī sorghum, 23, 29, 36, 172, 178, 251
Sayalān (Ceylon), 229, 237
ṣayf season, 69, 83–84, 153, 162, 172, 202
ṣayf/ṣayfī sorghum, 32–33, 39, 162, 172–73
Sayf al-Dīn Ṣunqur ibn 'Abd Allāh al-Ātabik, 165
ṣayfī/ṣayfīya cotton, 34, 202
ṣayfīya camels, 26, 28, 31, 33, 36, 39, 153
sayl (flood), 104, 241
ṣayyif rain, 67, 69, 110
scarecrow, 139
scents, 207–8
scorpion (*'aqrab*), 119, 147, 150
Scorpions of Winter (*'aqārib al-shitā'*), 118–19
Scorpius (*'aqrab*), 23, 29, 86, 119, 163, 166, 217
screwpine (*kadar, kādhī, kiyūra,* and *'ūd al-dhi'b*), 26, 33, 198
seasons, 83–85
sesame (*juljul/jiljil, juljulān,* and *simsim*), 32, 40, 166, 181, 195–96
Sesamum indicum. See sesame
Seth, 244
Seville, xi. See also Spain
sex: animals, 29, 138; attitudes, 249, 254; and astrology, 212; birds, 139; camels, 26, 152; cure for madness, 212; dildo, 213; diseases, 214, 254; elephant, 248; and hot bath, 212; reasons for, 212; and *sabt al-subūt*, 158; and sesame, 196; silkworm, 147; and summer, 212; times for, 34, 120, 212; and *quṭrub*, 155. See also adultery and aphrodisiacs
al-sha'ānīn al-kabīr (Palm Sunday), 78
al-sha'ānīn al-ṣaghīr, 31, 78
sha'arā' (swarm of blue flies), 146
shāba (youth), 83
shabāb (youth), 83–84
shabaka (bundle of straw), 176
Sha'bān, 218
al-Sha'bānīya, 24, 28, 31, 33, 36, 39, 66, 152–53, 161–62
shabb (alum), 173
shabb sorghum, 23, 25, 37, 160, 170–71, 173
shabba, 173
shabk (honeycomb), 148
shadhāb. See rue
shadn, 134, 246
shadow lengths, 17, 81, 88–89, 240
al-Shāfi'ī, 252
Shahāra, ix

Vegetius, 220
Venice, 215
Venus, 86
Verbenacea, 201
vermin. See *hawāmm*
verruca, 137
Vicia faba. See broad bean
Vigna sinensis. See cowpeas
vinegar, 210
violet (*banafsaj*), 198
Virgo (*sunbula*), 37, 86, 224
Vitus vinifera. See grapes
vulture (*rakham*), 140, 142

wabā' (infectious disease), 205–6, 254
wabr, 125, 138
waghra period, 102, 119, 127, 244
wagtail (*abū fuṣāda, dhu'ara, hazār al-dhayl, ṭayr al-baqar*, and *ẓīṭa*), 23, 139, 140, 143
waḥsh al-zabad (wild cat), 230
wajh al-arḍ (ground surface), 234
wakhim sorghum, 167
walī rain, 26, 106, 111
walnut (*jawz*), 35–36, 182, 188, 208–9
waqda, 127
waqf, 160
waqt al-madhārī, 70
waram (swelling), 206
ward (rose), 182, 200, 208
al-ward, 'īd (Festival of the Rose), 78–79
wars (*Memecylon tinctorium*), 157, 219, 248
wasm rain, 110, 137
wasmī rain, 24, 28, 101, 106, 109–11, 177–78
wasmī sorghum, 36, 172
wasnī wheat, 36, 163, 177–79
water sources: decline, 23, 30, 92, 128; increase, 31, 128
watercress (*ḥilf* and *jirjīr*), 12, 170, 181
watermelon. See melon
wāthiba (white cowpeas), 190
wazn. See *muḥlifān*
weapons, 227. See also swords
wedding (*'urs*), 129, 254–55
weights. See measures
well (*bi'r*), 3, 122, 126
whale, 216
wheat (*burr*), 24, 36, 38–39, 70, 79, 121, 163, 170, 175–79, 183, 188, 211, 227–28, 238, 250–51
white ant. See termite
white mallow (*khaṭmīya*), 198
wild cat (*waḥsh al-zabad*), 230
wind, 18, 23, 25, 29–32, 34, 97, 111–18, 126, 155, 193, 206, 215, 220, 222, 224–26, 228, 230–31, 242–43
wine, 158
winter solstice, 77, 118
wolf's wood. See *'ūd al-dhi'b*
women: fidelity of, 137; looking too long at, 85. See also sex
wood cutting. See firewood
worms, 132–33, 147, 155
wounds, 134, 195
wuḥūsh (wild animals), 138

yabisu (dry up), 116
Ya'fūr, 78
yaman (south), 111–12
al-Yaman al-asfal, 241
al-Yaman al-khaḍrā', 3, 159
yamānīya camel, 152
Yanbu, 145
yanghaliqu (locked up), 220
yaqṭīn. See gourd
yāsamīn/*yāsimīn* (jasmine), 198, 201
ya'ṣaru (press), 236
yasimu (marks), 111
yaṣlūna (arrive), 234
Yazdagird calendar, 18, 73, 239
yellow bile (*al-mirra al-ṣafrā'*), 204
Yemen: geography, 3–4, 232
yubyub/*yudyud*/*yumyum* (hoopoe), 141

Bill Tucker – Santa Monica
c96